Fifth Edition / ALL NEW

The No. 1 Price Guide to
M.I.HUMMEL®

Figurines, Plates, More

- accurate prices
- easy-to-use
- pocket size

by renowned expert
ROBERT L. MILLER

special consultant
DEAN A. GENTH
appraiser - collector - specialist of
Goebel "M.I. Hummel" Figurines

PORTFOLIO PRESS
Huntington, New York 11743

This book is dedicated to my wife Ruth,
the "Original" M.I. HUMMEL Figurine Collector.

We solicit your questions, suggestions, opinions and criticisms. If we can be of help in making your collecting more complete and enjoyable, or if you just want to say "hello" — call or write:

Robert L. Miller
112 Woodland Drive, Eaton, Ohio 45320
1-513-456-3735

The No. 1 Price Guide to
M.I. HUMMEL
Fifth Edition/First Printing

M.I. Hummel® and Hummel®, in signature and block forms, are registered trademarks of W. Goebel Porzellanfabrik, Germany.

M.I. Hummel figurines, plates and bells are copyrighted products of W. Porzellanfabrik, Germany.

Exclusively Distributed in the United States by Schmid.

Library of Congress Catalog Card Number
87-61697
ISBN 0-942620-15-1

Introduction

This price guide is designed to meet the growing needs of dealers and insurance underwriters, as well as the collector-enthusiast. It is primarily intended as an aid in identifying, dating and pricing both current and older "M.I. Hummel" figurines, along with plates, bells, lamps, and other related "M.I. Hummel" items produced through the years by W. Goebel Porzellanfabrik of Roedental, West Germany.

This new, revised edition contains over 400 photographs and over 3,000 prices, plus reliable, pertinent information on size and color variations, and restyling or structural changes that have evolved to the present date. The inclusion of *all known* data, along with photographs; makes this the only complete and accurate price guide ever to be published. Since the author has had free access to the Goebel factory archives and the total cooperation of the Goebel company officials, the authenticity of the material contained in this price guide cannot be questioned. In addition, the author has worked with and studied "M.I. Hummel" figurines and other items of Hummel art continuously for over 25 years. The publication of this book has been approved by W. Goebel Porzellanfabrik, the sole manufacturers of the "M.I. Hummel" figurines, plates, and bells.

The format of this guide provides a flexible bracket or price range, rather than one arbitrary price for each item. It is extremely difficult to assign an exact value for each figurine since many factors can affect this valuation. Prices do vary from one section of the country to another—and even sales within a given area may be at different figures. General economic conditions prevailing at the time of sale can affect valuations too. Exact values on older specimens of Hummel figurines are impossible to ascertain, because so many factors must be taken into consideration. In such instances, the rarity of the piece, its general condition (whether mint, restored, damaged), its color, its authenticity, and finally, its appeal to the collector, must be considered.

Certain figurines have always been more appreciated than others—hence they are more in demand and thus command higher prices proportionately. The same is true of ashtrays and holy water fonts, which have never been as popular as the figurines themselves. They, of course, usually sell at lower prices.

The price ranges quoted in this book reflect the current retail prices as opposed to wholesale or dealer prices. Thus a person selling a certain item cannot expect to receive the top bracket price in most instances. It is more likely he may receive a figure somewhere between the low and high quoted. Some dealers use the price ranges in this guide as a "bench mark," and offer the seller a percentage of either the high or the low figure. Again the rarity of the piece enters into the actual value determination. After reading the above, you may question the worth of any price guide in the first place. However, the author firmly believes the astronomical growth in Hummel collecting over the past few years dictates the necessity for such a yardstick of value. More and more collectors, novices and veterans alike, have been asking, "What should I expect to pay for this or that figurine?" "What should I sell my figurines for?" "What should I insure my collection for?" These questions are answered intelligently in this up-to-date list of values. The easy-to-read format provides simple and understandable information which reflects prices on today's market.

The author, having years of experience in buying and selling "M.I. Hummel" figurines and related items, would be the first to admit that there are wide fluctuations or variations in market prices today. It would be foolhardy and misleading to think that this or any other price guide could assign exact values for each and every Hummel piece. What has been provided in this guide is an accurate and reasonable range or "norm" so that the collector, dealer, or insurance agent can intelligently place a true valuation on each item. When it comes to a matter of worth, you must remember: it is "what the buyer is willing to pay, and the seller is willing to accept" that really sets the price. It takes *two* to strike a bargain!

Robert L. Miller

—Robert L. Miller

The Remarkable Story of Sister M.I. Hummel

Children are children the world over, impish or shy, saucy or quiet, mischievous or thoughtful ... language differences don't matter, nor do variances in national custom. The innocence of childhood produces a universality that is loved and understood everywhere. This is perhaps the key to the remarkable and enduring popularity of the wonderful creations of Sister Maria Innocentia Hummel.

Berta Hummel was born in the town of Massing in Lower Bavaria, Germany, on May 21, 1909, one of six children of Adolph and Viktoria Hummel. Although a closely knit family, the children were not carbon copies of one another. While her older sisters were industriously helping their mother with household chores, Berta was busy drawing, making costumes for her dolls, and putting on theatricals for family and friends.

War broke out when she was only six. Her father was drafted into the army and the family was left without his guiding influence. Berta, whose artistic talents he had always encouraged, began to show signs of willfulness and lack of discipline, often taxing the patience of her teachers. Fortunately, her creativity was to be recognized early; due to the efforts of one of her teachers, she was enrolled at a fine religious boarding school at Simbach, near Massing, the Institute of English Sisters.

It was here that she first received artistic direction. Her flair for scenic and costume design fostered just for fun in the family's backyard, now began to emerge as a genuine talent. Soon she was designing for school productions. In four years, she progressed from only sketching the friends of her childhood and illustrating folk tales to painting landscapes in watercolor.

The religious training at the school proved to be good discipline, and her de-

velopment into a young lady and a promising artist was a delight to behold.

In 1927, when she was 18, Berta's proud father went with her to Munich where she was enrolled in the Academy of Fine Arts, to be on some familiar ground in otherwise strange territory, she took up residence outside the Academy in a dormitory run by a religious order.

The Academy, a prestigious center of design and applied arts, provided her with still more extensive training. Soon she began to paint in oils, and her experience with costumes was now expanded to include weaving of fabrics and designing clothing.

She was soon under the wing of a leading artist and teacher, who hoped she would remain at the Academy after graduation as his assistant. But a conflict was developing within Berta. Although she was gaining a great knowledge of art, its history, its scope and an exciting awareness of what travel and study in other cities, perhaps even other lands, might offer a young student, she was still the simple Bavarian girl from a warm, loving family, and her ties to her background were strong. Her feelings of religion were profound, and through a warm friendship at the dormitory with two Franciscan nuns who were also studying at the Academy, became even more important.

Her wonderful sense of fun never left her, and to the delight of her fellow students (and often the chagrin of the Mother Superior) she would play pranks at the residence. But more than anything, she was a gentle, emotional person, deeply affected by people and events.

In 1929, Hitler's National Socialist Party was on the rise in Munich, making specific promises of employment within the party. It offered an economic stability in depression years for sympathizers among the students of the Academy. But the militarism and politics of the Nazis were counter to Berta's sensitivities, and she turned with even greater need to the quiet, withdrawn life of her two religious friends.

With graduation drawing near, the pressures were becoming stronger for her to make a decision. On the one hand were her professors, eager for her to remain with them and continue her promising development. But on the other hand, with the frightening political atmosphere growing, there was the draw of fulfillment to be found behind the cloistered walls of a convent where she could continue her art while serving humanity through her devotion to God.

By the time of graduation in March 1931, she had made her decision. On April 22, she entered the convent of Siessen at Saulgau, and two years later was ordained Sister Maria Innocentia of the Sisters of the Third Order of St. Francis.

While a novice, she had taught art to children in kindergarten, and by late 1933 had so developed that she exhibited her work in a nearby town. In March 1933, the convent at Siessen sent a letter with proof sheets of sketches of the artist Berta Hummel to the publishing company in Munich named "Ars Sacra Josef Mueller Verlag," who specialized in the printing of religious art and books. Ars Sacra was very appreciative of the first pictures and asked for more sketches. Thus started a prosperous relationship between Sister Maria Innocentia Hummel and the publishing house "Ars Sacra Josef Mueller." The

artwork of Sister Maria Innocentia was first known to the public in the two-dimensional form. The postcards with the Hummel motifs became very popular and found their way into the United States shortly before World War II. Franz Goebel, fourth-generation head of W. Goebel, first became aware of her in 1934, and sought permission from her and the convent to translate her sketches of sparkling children and serene religious figures into three-dimensional form. This marked the beginning of a relationship between Sister Maria Innocentia, the convent and W. Goebel that continues to endure, long years after her death.

But dark clouds were hovering everywhere, and soon the sisters began to live in dread, for the Nazi government was determined to close the convent. In late 1940, the convent became a repatriation center for German nationals from other countries, and a small group of nuns, Sister Maria Innocentia included, remained to care for them.

It was a time of great deprivation. No longer able to remain in her spacious studio because of the terribly overcrowded conditions, Sister Maria Innocentia lived in a small, damp, basement room. Food and fuel were scarce, and she became terribly weakened by a lung infection. True to her dominant spirit, however, she tried to continue to work.

By November 1944 she was so ill that she was admitted to a sanitarium for treatment where her illness was finally diagnosed as chronic tuberculosis. In April 1945, the war ended and, feeling somewhat strengthened, Sister Maria Innocentia returned to the convent to help with the enormous task of rebuilding. Her spirit as ever was strong, but her physical condition had deteriorated so that she was forced to enter another sanitarium the following September, leaving it in late September 1946 to return to her beloved convent.

On November 6, 1946, at the hour of noon, the chapel bells rang out in solemn proclamation of the death of Sister Maria Innocentia at the age of 37.

A young life, full of spirit and love, came to a tragic end. But the youthful, loving spirit lives on in the pert faces of the Hummel children and the gentle bearing of the madonnas that are with us in ceramic. If we look at them a certain way, we can almost hear them breathe!

HANDI - GUIDE TO
M.J.Hummel
DATES

MARK		FIRST USED
①	(CROWN)	1935
②	(FULL BEE)	1950
③	(STYLIZED)	1957
④	© by W. Goebel W. Germany (THREE LINE)	1964
⑤	Goebel (GOEBEL BEE)	1972
⑥	Goebel	1979
⑦	Goebel Germany (CURRENT)	1991

*SOME VARIATIONS AND COMBINATIONS
USED IN BETWEEN ABOVE DATES*

M.J.Hummel © ℳ

Between 1935 and 1955, the company occasionally used a © ℳ mark on the side or top of the base of some models, before or after the "M.I. Hummel" signature. This is *NOT* considered a (TM 1) or "crown" trademark! It only means "copyright by W. Goebel".

History and Explanation of Marks and Symbols

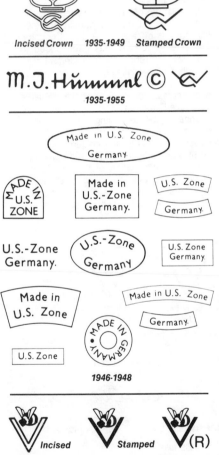

Incised Crown   **1935-1949**   **Stamped Crown**

M.I.Hummel © ℅

1935-1955

Made in U.S. Zone Germany.

MADE IN U.S. ZONE

Made in U.S.-Zone Germany.

U.S. Zone

Germany.

U.S.-Zone Germany.

U.S.-Zone Germany

U.S. Zone Germany.

Made in U.S. Zone

Made in U.S. Zone

Germany.

U.S. Zone

MADE IN GERMANY

1946-1948

Incised   **Stamped**   (R)

© W. Goebel   ©

Full Bee   **W. GOEBEL**

1950-1955

The "wide-crown-WG" trademark was used on the first "M.I. Hummel" figurines produced in 1935. On the earliest figurines it was incised on the bottom of the base along with the "M.I. Hummel" signature on the top or side of the base. Between 1935 and 1955, the company occasionally used a © ℅ mark on the side or top of the base of some models. It is seen occasionally to the right of the "M.I. Hummel" signature. The "crown" appears either incised or stamped. When both are used on the same piece it is known as a "double crown" mark.

From 1946 through 1948 it was necessary to add the stamped words "Made in the U.S. Zone Germany." This mark was used within various types of frames or without a frame, underglazed or stamped over the glaze in black ink.

In 1950, four years after Sister M.I. Hummel's death, Goebel wished in some way to pay tribute to her fine artistry. They radically changed the trademark, instituting the use of a bee flying high with a "V." (Hummel means "bumble bee" in German, and the "V" stands for "Verkaufs-gesellschaft" or distribution company.) This mark, known as the full bee trademark, was used until 1955 and appeared —sometimes both incised and underglazed—in black or blue and occasionally in green or magenta. In addition, the stamp "Germany" and later "West Germany" appeared. An (R) appearing beside the trademark stands for "Registered."

Sometimes the molds were produced with a lightly incised circle on the bottom of the base in which the trademark was centered. It has no significance other than as a target for the location of the decal. Some current production figurines still have this incised circle even though it is no longer used for that purpose.

Always searching for a mark that would blend esthetics with professionalism, the company continued to modify the trademark. In 1956, the company—still using the bee inside the "V"—made the bee smaller, with its wing tips parallel with the top of the "V". In 1957, the bee remained, although once again rising slightly above the "V". In 1958, the bee was smaller still and it flew deep within the "V", reflecting the changing trends of modern design. The year 1959 saw the beginning of stylization and the wings of the bee became sharply angular.

In 1960, the completely stylized bee with "V" mark came into use, appearing with "W. Germany." It was used in one form or another until 1979. In addition to its appearance with "W. Germany" to the right (1960–1963), it appeared above the "West Germany" (1960–1972), and to the left of the "three line mark" (mid-1960's to 1972). The three line mark was used intermittently and sometimes concurrently with the small, stylized 1960–1972 mark. It was the most prominent trademark in use prior to the "Goebel bee" trademark.

It became apparent that the public was equating the "V and Bee" mark only with "M.I. Hummel" items, not realizing that the mark included the full scope of Goebel products. It was decided to experiment further with marks. In 1972, satisfied that it now had a mark designating a quality

Goebel product, the company began using a printed "Goebel" with the stylized bee poised between the letters "b" and "e."

Since 1976, the Goebel trademark on Hummel figurines has been affixed by a decal on top of the glaze. It is possible for two figurines on the primary market to have differing decals.

In 1979, the stylized bee was dropped and only the name *Goebel* appears. The year of production will be on the base next to the initials of the chief decorator. These changes will be incorporated into production as existing stocks of figurines are exhausted.

In 1991, the W. (West) was deleted, with only the word Germany remaining, since Germany is once again a united country. The original "crown" has been added to the new current (TM7) trademark, although, I think, a little small!

The above information is a concise documentation of all W. Goebel trademarks authorized for use on "M.I. Hummel" figurines. In searching for accurate documentation on all W. Goebel trademarks used in conjunction with "M.I.Hummel" figurines, the author made a thorough investigation of the W. Goebel archives and queried the world's leading collectors. But it is always possible that a few rare and undocumented variations may exist.

| Small Bee 1956 | High Bee 1957 | Baby Bee 1958 | V Bee 1959 |

SHOULD BE CLASSIFIED AS "FULL BEE" (TM2)

Early Stylized (Incised Circle) 1957-1960

GERMANY

Germany

West Germany

Western Germany

Western Germany

© *W. Goebel*

Copr. *W. Goebel*

1935-1955

W. Germany

1960-1963

V
W. Germany
1960-1972

V © by
W. Goebel
W. Germany
1964-1972

W. Germany   W. Germany   W. Germany

Evolution of Goebel Bee
Trademark in use since 1972

Goebel®

W. Germany

Goebel trademark
(since 1979)

Goebel

Germany

Current trademark
(since 1991)

DOUBLE TRADEMARK FIGURINES

Occasionally an older "M.I. Hummel" figurine will be found with an incised "crown" trademark as well as a stamped "full bee" trademark on the same figurine. It is neither a crown nor a full bee; it is a *combination.* A figurine with this double mark would have been sold in the very early 1950's. The incised crown was in the mold, and the figurine itself was quite possibly produced in the late 1940's, but then actually painted and sold in the early 1950's during the change over from one trademark to the other.

When using the *No. 1 Price Guide* to determine the value of a figurine with both the crown and the full bee trademark, we recommend using the high side of the full bee price bracket and the low side of the crown bracket. For example, HUM 1

"Puppy Love" with full bee (TM 2) is listed at $450 to $550, and the same with a crown (TM 1) is valued at $650 to $900. The new bracket value would be $550 to $650.

This double marking makes it a distinctive piece and puts it in a class by itself. It is better (or earlier) than a double full bee or a plain full bee, but not quite as good (or as early) as the crown or double crown marking. This combination of two different trademarks normally occurred only during this brief change over period and has not happened since, to my knowledge. Not all models can be found with this combination marking, and it is good to have an example of this in your collection.

EXAMPLE: ❶ $650–900   } 550–650
              ❷ $450–550

The Collection

Here is the revised and fully-authorized documentation of the complete collection of "M.I. Hummel" figurines, plates, plaques and all other art objects. This is the most definitive listing and photographic collection ever assembled. This list, compiled from the W. Goebel production journal in Roedental, West Germany, constitutes a record of all "M.I. Hummel" figurines identification numbers run in ascending order from 1 to 968. English names of the figurines, as well as their sizes, notes, and most models, will be found in the special annotated listing.

All sizes are approximate and depend upon exact method of measurement. Minor variations occur frequently and therefore should not be considered significant.

"M.I. Hummel" figurine identification numbers and their corresponding figurines are divided into seven distinct categories:

Open Edition (OE): Pieces currently in W. Goebel's production program.

Closed Edition (CE): Pieces formerly in W. Goebel production program but no longer produced.

Open Number (ON): An identification number, which in W. Goebel's numerical identification system has not yet been used, but which may be used to identify new "M.I. Hummel" figurines as they are released in the future.

Closed Number (CN): An identification number in W. Goebel's numerical identification system that was used to identify a design or sample models for possible production, but then for various reasons never authorized for release.

Possible Future Edition (PFE): Pieces that have been designed and approved for production and possible release in future years.

Temporarily Withdrawn (TW): Pieces that have been suspended or withdrawn from Goebel's current production program, but may be reinstated and produced at some future date.

Exclusive Edition (EE): Pieces that are originally sold only to members of the M.I. Hummel Club.

Many collectors are interested in the trademarks that were used on "M.I. HUMMEL" figurines; therefore, we have used the numbering system of:

❶ =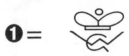

Crown

❷ =

Full Bee

❸ =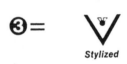

Stylized

❹ =

Three Line

❺ =

Goebel Bee

❻ = Goebel®

❼ = ©Goebel

Germany

Current

to identify each mark that a particular figure can be found with. There may be some exceptions to this rule. Some early figurines will be found with no trademark at all. This fact does not lessen their value to any great extent, but does make it more difficult to determine their age. When figurines vary greatly in size, we will use the "bracket" system, showing the smallest to the largest size, i.e. 5½" to 6". Your measurement may vary depending on what means you use to measure. To properly measure a figurine, you should place it on a flat surface, then stand a ruler beside it. Place another ruler or straight object horizontally touching the highest point of the figurine and the perpendicular ruler. You will then have an accurate measurement.

Decoration-designations for "M.I. Hummel" figurines

All "M.I. Hummel" figurines are hand-painted according to "M.I. Hummel's" original design. The decoration techniques had to be numbered because the factory uses so many.

The "M.I. Hummel" decor is done in painting method number eleven. A stroke-eleven (/11) is added to the model number following the size indicator in the factory's literature and some price lists. *It does not, however, appear incised on the base.* In this book we only refer to incised numbers.

Decor. No.	Marked	Description
11	/11	all matte-finish colors in rich variety of pastels inspired by rural surroundings
11 blue	/11 blue	madonna with dark blue cloak; rest of figurine in pastels
13	/13	ivory decoration in pastels
6 blue	/6 blue	madonna with pastel blue cloak; rest of figurine in matching pastels
6 red	/6 red	madonna with light red cloak; rest of figurine in matching pastels
83	/83	matte-finish shading on bisque body
H	/H	brown matte decor, very rare — not made after 1955
W	/W	white overglaze

SPECIAL NOTE: In previous price guides we listed trademark 1, 2, 3, 4, and 5 items as Open Editions (OE), which was not quite accurate. We wanted to indicate that a certain *model* was still being produced, even though the trademark had changed.

With this edition, we show each former trademark as a Closed Edition (CE).The only Open Editions (OE) will be items with trademark seven (TM 7) that are currently in W. Goebel's production program.

Alphabetical Listing

The following is a listing of all "M.I. Hummel" Figurines and other related items. A valuable cross-reference to use alone or in conjunction with The Collection.

Old   New

HUM 1
Puppy Love (CE)
First modeled by master sculptor Arthur Moeller in 1935. A very few early models were
made with the head tilted at a different angle and without tie. This old style is considered extremely rare and would command a premium of over $2,000. Always featured
with a black hat. In old catalog listed as the "Little Violinist." "Puppy Love" was permanently retired by Goebel in the fall of 1988 and will not be produced again. Old 1955
price list shows a price of $6.50 while 1988 price list shows a price of $125, the last
year it was sold on the primary market.

☐ 1 . . . . 5 to 5¼" . . . . . (CE) . . ❶ . . . $650–900
☐ 1 . . . . 5 to 5¼" . . . . . (CE) . . ❷ . . . $450–550
☐ 1 . . . . 5 to 5¼" . . . . . (CE) . . ❸ . . . $400–450
☐ 1 . . . . 5 to 5¼" . . . . . (CE) . . ❹ . . . $300–400
☐ 1 . . . . 5 to 5¼" . . . . . (CE) . . ❺ . . . $250–300
☐ 1 . . . . 5 to 5¼" . . . . . (CE) . . ❻ . . . $225–250

HUM 2
Little Fiddler

Also modeled by master sculptor Arthur Moeller in 1935, this figurine differs from the boy in "Puppy Love" in the fact that it always has a brown hat with an orange hat band. There are many size variations and all sizes have now been restyled with the new textured finish. Old name: "Violinist" or "The Wandering Fiddler." Same as HUM 4 except for the color of hat. Sometimes incised 2/3 instead of 2/III. A new miniature size figurine was issued in the fall of 1984 with a suggested retail price of $39 to match a new miniature plate series called the "Little Music Makers" — one each year for four years. This is the first in the series. This miniature size figurine has an incised 1984 copyright date. The large sizes (2/II and 2/III) were "temporarily withdrawn" from production on 31 December 1989, but may be reinstated at some future date.

□ 2 4/0	3″	(CE)	❻	$80–85
□ 2 4/0	3″	**(OE)**	❼	$80
□ 2/0	5¾ to 6½″	(CE)	❶	$600–750
□ 2/0	5¾ to 6½″	(CE)	❷	$335–475
□ 2/0	5¾ to 6½″	(CE)	❸	$285–335
□ 2/0	5¾ to 6½″	(CE)	❹	$240–285
□ 2/0	5¾ to 6½″	(CE)	❺	$200–220
□ 2/0	5¾ to 6½″	(CE)	❻	$190–200
□ 2/0	5¾ to 6½″	**(OE)**	❼	$190
□ 2/I	7½″	(CE)	❶	$1100–1500
□ 2/I	7½ to 8″	(CE)	❷	$650–925
□ 2/I	7½ to 8″	(CE)	❸	$560–650
□ 2/I	7½ to 8″	(CE)	❹	$460–555
□ 2/I	7½ to 8″	(CE)	❺	$390–400
□ 2/I	7½ to 8″	(CE)	❻	$370–390
□ 2/I	7½ to 8″	**(OE)**	❼	$370
□ 2/II	10¾″	(CE)	❶	$2500–3500
□ 2/II	10¾″	(CE)	❷	$1800–2300
□ 2/II	10¾″	(CE)	❸	$1500–1600
□ 2/II	10¾″	(CE)	❹	$1300–1500
□ 2/II	10¾″	(CE)	❺	$1200–1300
□ 2/II	10¾″	(TW)	❻	$1100–1200
□ 2/III	12¼″	(CE)	❶	$3500–4000
□ 2/III	12¼″	(CE)	❷	$2300–2800
□ 2/III	12¼″	(CE)	❸	$1600–1800
□ 2/III	12¼″	(CE)	❹	$1400–1600
□ 2/III	12¼″	(CE)	❺	$1300–1400
□ 2/III	12¼″	(TW)	❻	$1200–1300

3/I

HUM 3
Book Worm

This figurine was modeled by master sculptor Arthur Moeller in 1935. Old name: "Little Book Worm." Size 3/I has only one flower on page, while sizes 3/II and 3/III have two flowers on page. Sometimes incised 3/2 instead of 3/II and 3/3 instead of 3/III but does not affect the value as Arabic or Roman size indicators were used interchangeably for no basic reason. Same design was used for HUM 8. "Book Worm" was restyled by master sculptor Gerhard Skrobek in 1972 with the new textured finish. Size 3/II has an incised 1972 copyright date. Size 3/III has no incised copyright date at all. The large sizes (3/II and 3/III) were "temporarily withdrawn" (TW) from production on 31 December 1989, but may be reinstated at some future date.

☐ 3/I	5½"	(CE)	❶	$800–1000
☐ 3/I	5½"	(CE)	❷	$450–625
☐ 3/I	5½"	(CE)	❸	$375–450
☐ 3/I	5½"	(CE)	❹	$310–375
☐ 3/I	5½"	(CE)	❺	$260–275
☐ 3/I	5½"	(CE)	❻	$250–260
☐ 3/I	5½"	(OE)	❼	$250
☐ 3/II	8"	(CE)	❶	$2500–3500
☐ 3/II	8"	(CE)	❷	$1800–2300
☐ 3/II	8"	(CE)	❸	$1500–1600
☐ 3/II	8"	(CE)	❹	$1300–1500
☐ 3/II	8 to 9"	(CE)	❺	$1200–1300
☐ 3/II	8 to 9"	(TW)	❻	$1100–1200
☐ 3/III	9 to 9½"	(CE)	❶	$3500–4000
☐ 3/III	9 to 9½"	(CE)	❷	$2300–2800
☐ 3/III	9 to 9½"	(CE)	❸	$1600–1800
☐ 3/III	9 to 9½"	(CE)	❹	$1400–1600
☐ 3/III	9 to 10"	(CE)	❺	$1300–1400
☐ 3/III	9 to 10"	(TW)	❻	$1200–1300

Notice great variations in sizes

HUM 4
Little Fiddler

Same as HUM 2 except it has a charcoal black hat. Many size variations. Old name: "Violinist" or "The Wandering Fiddler." First modeled by master sculptor Arthur Moeller in 1935 but current production models have been restyled with the new textured finish. One of several figurines that make up the Hummel orchestra. A very few early models were made with the head tilted at a different angle and without tie. This old style is considered extremely rare and would command a premium of $2000–3000. See old style "Puppy Love" HUM 1.

☐ 4 . . . . 4¾ to 5¾″ . . . . (CE) . . ❶ . . . $500–675
☐ 4 . . . . 4¾ to 5¾″ . . . . (CE) . . ❷ . . . $300–425
☐ 4 . . . . 4¾ to 5¾″ . . . . (CE) . . ❸ . . . $260–300
☐ 4 . . . . 4¾ to 5¾″ . . . . (CE) . . ❹ . . . $215–260
☐ 4 . . . . 4¾ to 5¾″ . . . . (CE) . . ❺ . . . $175–185
☐ 4 . . . . 4¾ to 5¾″ . . . . (CE) . . ❻ . . . $170–175
☐ 4 . . . . 4¾ to 5¾″ . . . . (OE) . . ❼ . . . $170

Old style   *New style*

New style   *Old style*

HUM 5
Strolling Along (CE)
Originally modeled by master sculptor Arthur Moeller in 1935. Older models have eyes that glance off to one side. New models look straight ahead. Color of dog will vary. "Strolling Along" was permanently retired by Goebel in the fall of 1989 and will not be produced again. Old 1955 price list shows a price of $6.00 while 1989 price list shows a price of $120, the last year it was sold on the primary market.

☐ 5 . . . . 4¾ to 5¾" . . . . (CE) . . ❶ . . . $600–800
☐ 5 . . . . 4¾ to 5¾" . . . . (CE) . . ❷ . . . $400–500
☐ 5 . . . . 4¾ to 5¾" . . . . (CE) . . ❸ . . . $300–400
☐ 5 . . . . 4¾ to 5¾" . . . . (CE) . . ❹ . . . $250–300
☐ 5 . . . . 4¾ to 5¾" . . . . (CE) . . ❺ . . . $225–250
☐ 5 . . . . 4¾ to 5¾" . . . . (CE) . . ❻ . . . $200–225

TM 1   TM 3   TM 6

HUM 6
Sensitive Hunter

Modeled by master sculptor Arthur Moeller in 1935. Was originally called "The Timid Hunter." The lederhosen straps on older models of size 6 or 6/0 are parallel in back. Newer models have crossed-strap suspenders. All other sizes have crossed straps in all time periods. Sometimes incised 6/2 instead of 6/II. All sizes were restyled in 1981 and now have a more natural-looking *brown* rabbit instead of the original *orange*-colored rabbit. Some variations in the position of the ears of the rabbit in older models. A new small size "Sensitive Hunter" was issued in 1985 at a suggested retail price of $60. It has an incised 1984 copyright date. The large size (6/II) was listed as "Temporarily Withdrawn" (TW) from production on 31 December 1984 but could possibly be reinstated at some future date. The small size (6/0) "Sensitive Hunter" sold for $6.00 in 1955.

TM 1   TM 3   TM 6

TM 1   *TM 3*   *TM 6*

☐ 6 2/0	4″	(CE)	❻	$125–130
☐ 6 2/0	4″	**(OE)**	❼	$125
☐ 6/0	4¾″	(CE)	❶	$480–640
☐ 6/0	4¾″	(CE)	❷	$280–400
☐ 6/0	4¾″	(CE)	❸	$240–280
☐ 6/0	4¾″	(CE)	❹	$200–240
☐ 6/0	4¾″	(CE)	❺	$170–175
☐ 6/0	4¾″	(CE)	❻	$160–165
☐ 6/0	4¾″	**(OE)**	❼	$160
☐ 6/I	5½ to 6″	(CE)	❶	$625–840
☐ 6/I	5½ to 6″	(CE)	❷	$370–525
☐ 6/I	5½ to 6″	(CE)	❸	$315–370
☐ 6/I	5½″	(CE)	❹	$265–315
☐ 6/I	5½″	(CE)	❺	$220–230
☐ 6/I	5½″	(CE)	❻	$210–220
☐ 6/I	5½″	**(OE)**	❼	$210
☐ 6/II	7 to 7½″	(CE)	❶	$1500–2000
☐ 6/II	7 to 7½″	(CE)	❷	$950–1250
☐ 6/II	7 to 7½″	(CE)	❸	$520–635
☐ 6/II	7 to 7½″	(CE)	❹	$450–520
☐ 6/II	7 to 7½″	(CE)	❺	$400–450
☐ 6/II	7 to 7½″	(TW)	❻	$325–400
☐ 6	5″	(CE)	❶	$675–850

7/I "double base" variation

HUM 7
Merry Wanderer

Can be found in more size variations than any other figurine. A six-foot model was placed in front of the Goebel factory in Roedental in 1971 to commemorate Goebel's 100th anniversary and in 1987 an eight-foot model was unveiled in front of the former headquarters of the Goebel Collectors' Club (now The M.I. Hummel Club) in Tarrytown, New York. First modeled by master sculptor Arthur Moeller in 1935. Was restyled by master sculptor Gerhard Skrobek in size 7/II with the new textured finish in 1972, with an incised copyright date. Size 7/III was restyled in 1978 but without an incised copyright date. Older models of size 7/I have what collectors call a "double base" or "stair step" base. This accounts for the wide price variation of 7/I in trademark 3 since it was produced with either normal or "double base". All sizes and all time periods of HUM 7 usually have only five buttons on vest. Sometimes incised 7/2 instead of 7/II. The 32 inch model (HUM 7/X) was first sold in the U.S. market in 1976 and "temporarily withdrawn" (TW) from production as of 1 January 1991, but may be reinstated at some future date. The large size (7/III) was "temporarily withdrawn" (TW) from production on 31 December 1989, but may be reinstated at some future date. The small size "Merry Wanderer" (7/0) sold for $6.00 in 1955.

☐ 7/0	....	6 to 6¼″	.....	(CE)	..	❶	...	$660–880
☐ 7/0	....	6 to 6¼″	.....	(CE)	..	❷	...	$385–550
☐ 7/0	....	6 to 6¼″	.....	(CE)	..	❸	...	$330–385
☐ 7/0	....	6 to 6¼″	.....	(CE)	..	❹	...	$275–330
☐ 7/0	....	6 to 6¼″	.....	(CE)	..	❺	...	$230–240
☐ 7/0	....	6 to 6¼″	.....	(CE)	..	❻	...	$220–230
☐ 7/0	....	6 to 6¼″	.....	(OE)	..	❼	...	$220
☐ 7/I	......	7 to 8″	....	(CE)	..	❶	...	$1250–1500
☐ 7/I	......	7 to 8″	....	(CE)	..	❷	...	$1100–1250

(prices cont. on next page)

8

☐ 7/I	7 to 8″	(CE)	❸	$550–1000
☐ 7/I	7 to 8″	(CE)	❹	$450–540
☐ 7/I	7 to 8″	(CE)	❺	$375–400
☐ 7/I	7 to 8″	(CE)	❻	$360–375
☐ 7/I	7 to 8″	(OE)	❼	$360
☐ 7/II	9½ to 10¼″	(CE)	❶	$3000–3500
☐ 7/II	9½ to 10¼″	(CE)	❷	$1900–2750
☐ 7/II	9½ to 10¼″	(CE)	❸	$1650–1800
☐ 7/II	9½ to 10¼″	(CE)	❹	$1375–1650
☐ 7/II	9½ to 10¼″	(CE)	❺	$1150–1200
☐ 7/II	9½ to 10¼″	(CE)	❻	$1100–1150
☐ 7/II	9½ to 10¼″	(OE)	❼	$1100
☐ 7/III	11 to 12″	(CE)	❶	$3300–4000
☐ 7/III	11 to 12″	(CE)	❷	$2500–3000
☐ 7/III	11 to 12″	(CE)	❸	$1700–2000
☐ 7/III	11 to 12″	(CE)	❹	$1300–1500
☐ 7/III	11 to 12″	(CE)	❺	$1250–1300
☐ 7/III	11 to 12″	(TW)	❻	$1200–1250
☐ 7/X	32″	(CE)	❺	$10,000–17,000
☐ 7/X	32″	(TW)	❻	$10,000–17,000

HUM 8
Book Worm
Same as HUM 3 except smaller in size. Has only one flower on page. Old name: "Little Book Worm." Factory records indicate that this figurine was modeled by master sculptor Reinhold Unger in 1935. This figurine sold for $8.00 in 1955.

☐ 8	4 to 4½″	(CE)	❶	$550–700
☐ 8	4 to 4½″	(CE)	❷	$350–450
☐ 8	4 to 4½″	(CE)	❸	$270–315
☐ 8	4 to 4½″	(CE)	❹	$225–270
☐ 8	4 to 4½″	(CE)	❺	$190–200
☐ 8	4 to 4½″	(CE)	❻	$180–190
☐ 8	4 to 4½″	(OE)	❼	$180

New   Very old

New style   Old style

HUM 9
Begging His Share

There is much size variation in this figurine. Originally modeled by master sculptor Arthur Moeller in 1935 as a candleholder. Restyled in 1964, reduced slightly in size and made with a solid cake rather than with a hole for a candle. Can be found in trademark 3 with or without hole for candle. Called "Congratulatory Visit" in some old catalogues. Very early models have brightly colored striped socks. Has also been found in "crown" trademark without hole for candle.

☐ 9	5¼ to 6″	(CE)	❶	$650–800
☐ 9	5¼ to 6″	(CE)	❷	$400–500
☐ 9	5¼ to 6″	(CE)	❸	$300–350
☐ 9	5¼ to 6″	(CE)	❹	$250–300
☐ 9	5¼ to 6″	(CE)	❺	$210–220
☐ 9	5¼ to 6″	(CE)	❻	$200–210
☐ 9	5¼ to 6″	(OE)	❼	$200

Old 10/3   New 10/III   Old 10/1   New 10/I

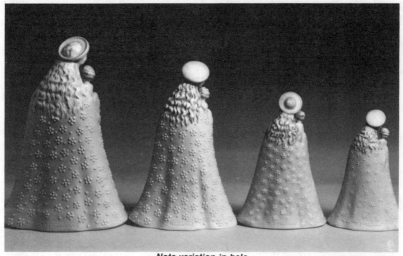

Note variation in halo

HUM 10
Flower Madonna

First created in 1935 by master sculptor Reinhold Unger according to the original drawing of Sister M.I. Hummel. In 1956 the mold was renewed (restyled) by Theo R. Menzenbach and made approximately 2 inches smaller. The halo was changed at that time from the open style to the flat style. It has been produced in white overglaze, pastel blue cloak, brown cloak, ivory cloak and pastel yellow. Also has been found in reddish brown terra cotta finish, signed "M. I. Hummel" with the "crown" trademark in the 10/I size, — now part of the Robert L. Miller collection. Only the pastel blue and the white overglaze are currently produced. The older color variations will usually range from $2,500 to $3,500 depending on color, condition and other variations. Old catalogues list it as large as 14 inches. Some earlier models appear with only the number 10 (no size designator). Also called "Sitting Madonna with Child" or "Virgin With Flowers" in old catalogues. Sometimes incised 10/3 instead of 10/III. In the spring of 1982 the large size (10/III), in both pastel blue and white overglaze, was listed as "temporarily withdrawn" by Goebel, possibly to be reinstated at a later date.

					Color	White
10/I	8¼ to 9½"	(CE)	❶		☐ $700–850	☐ $500–600
10/I	9 to 9½"	(CE)	❷		☐ $550–700	☐ $300–475
10/III	12 to 13"	(CE)	❶		☐ $800–1200	☐ $450–750
10/III	12 to 13"	(CE)	❷		☐ $700–800	☐ $450–650
10/I	7¾ to 8¼"	(CE)	❸		☐ $300–550	☐ $200–250
10/I	7¾ to 8¼"	(CE)	❹		☐ $400–500	☐ $180–200
10/I	7¾ to 8¼"	(CE)	❺		☐ $360–385	☐ $170–180
10/I	7¾ to 8¼"	(CE)	❻		☐ $350–360	☐ $165–170
10/I	7¾ to 8¼"	**(OE)**	❼		☐ $350	☐ $165
10/III	11 to 11½"	(CE)	❷		☐ $600–850	☐ $425–500
10/III	11 to 11½"	(CE)	❸		☐ $550–600	☐ $400–450
10/III	11 to 11½"	(CE)	❹		☐ $500–550	☐ $375–400
10/III	11 to 11½"	(CE)	❺		☐ $475–500	☐ $310–330
10/III	11 to 11½"	(TW)	❻		☐ $450–475	☐ $300–310

HUM 11
Merry Wanderer
Same style as Hum 7. Also modeled by master sculptor Arthur Moeller in 1935. Most models of "Merry Wanderer" have five buttons on vest. Some models in size 11 2/0 have six or seven buttons, and usually command a slight premium of 10%–15%.

☐ 11	4¾"	(CE)	❶	$550–700
☐ 11 2/0	4¼ to 4½"	(CE)	❶	$400–460
☐ 11 2/0	4¼ to 4½"	(CE)	❷	$200–285
☐ 11 2/0	4¼ to 4½"	(CE)	❸	$175–200
☐ 11 2/0	4¼ to 4½"	(CE)	❹	$145–175
☐ 11 2/0	4¼ to 4½"	(CE)	❺	$120–125
☐ 11 2/0	4¼ to 4½"	(CE)	❻	$115–120
☐ 11 2/0	4¼ to 4½"	(OE)	❼	$115
☐ 11/0	4¾ to 5"	(CE)	❶	$500–650
☐ 11/0	4¾ to 5"	(CE)	❷	$280–400
☐ 11/0	4¾ to 5"	(CE)	❸	$240–280
☐ 11/0	4¾ to 5"	(CE)	❹	$200–240
☐ 11/0	4¾ to 5"	(CE)	❺	$165–175
☐ 11/0	4¾ to 5"	(CE)	❻	$160–165
☐ 11/0	4¾ to 5"	(OE)	❼	$160

HUM 12
Chimney Sweep
Originally modeled by master sculptor Arthur Moeller in 1935, but has been restyled several times through the years. There is much size variation in both sizes. Old name: "Smoky" or "Good Luck". The small size 12 2/0 sold for $8.00 in 1955.

☐ 12 2/0	... 4 to 4¼″	..... (CE)	.. ❷ ...	$200−275
☐ 12 2/0	... 4 to 4¼″	..... (CE)	.. ❸ ...	$165−195
☐ 12 2/0	... 4 to 4¼″	..... (CE)	.. ❹ ...	$140−165
☐ 12 2/0	... 4 to 4¼″	..... (CE)	.. ❺ ...	$115−120
☐ 12 2/0	... 4 to 4¼″	..... (CE)	.. ❻ ...	$110−115
☐ 12 2/0	... 4 to 4¼″	..... (OE)	.. ❼ ...	$110
☐ 12/I	..... 5½ to 6½″	.... (CE)	.. ❶ ...	$540−700
☐ 12/I	..... 5½ to 6½″	.... (CE)	.. ❷ ...	$315−400
☐ 12/I	..... 5½ to 6½″	.... (CE)	.. ❸ ...	$270−315
☐ 12/I	..... 5½ to 6½″	.... (CE)	.. ❹ ...	$225−270
☐ 12/I	..... 5½ to 6½″	.... (CE)	.. ❺ ...	$190−200
☐ 12/I	..... 5½ to 6½″	.... (CE)	.. ❻ ...	$180−190
☐ 12/I	..... 5½ to 6½″	.... (OE)	.. ❼ ...	$180
☐ 12	...... 6 to 6¼″	..... (CE)	.. ❶ ...	$600−750
☐ 12	...... 6 to 6¼″	..... (CE)	.. ❷ ...	$350−450

13/II New   **13/2 Old**

HUM 13
Meditation

First modeled by master sculptor Reinhold Unger in 1935 in two sizes: 13/0 and 13/2. Size 13/2 was originally styled with flowers in the back half of basket, but in 1978 was restyled by master sculptor Gerhard Skrobek with no flowers in basket. Large size (13/V) was modeled by Theo R. Menzenbach in 1957 with full basket of flowers. The small size (13/2/0) was modeled by master sculptor Gerhard Skrobek in 1962. Three variations in hair ribbons were used through the years in 13/0 size: the early crown mark figurines usually had a very short pigtail with only a red painted band for the ribbon; the early full bee trademark examples were made with a longer pigtail but no ribbon or bows at all; the later models were made with the longer pigtails and a little red bow or ribbon on each pigtail. All "Meditations" made since the early 1950's would be of this last style. A 1962 copyright date appears on newer models of size 13/2/0. Also called "The Little Messenger." Sometimes 13/2 instead of 13/II and 13/5 instead of 13/V. The larger size (13/II) was listed as "temporarily withdrawn" (TW) from production on 31 December 1984 and (13/V) was listed as "temporarily withdrawn" (TW) on 31 December 1989, but may be reinstated at some future date.

☐ 13 2/0	... 4¼"	....	(CE)	.. ❷ ...	$200−300
☐ 13 2/0	... 4¼"	....	(CE)	.. ❸ ...	$180−200
☐ 13 2/0	... 4¼"	....	(CE)	.. ❹ ...	$150−180
☐ 13 2/0	... 4¼"	....	(CE)	.. ❺ ...	$125−130
☐ 13 2/0	... 4¼"	....	(CE)	.. ❻ ...	$120−125
☐ 13 2/0	... 4¼"	....	(OE)	.. ❼ ...	$120
☐ 13/0	..... 5 to 6"	....	(CE)	.. ❶ ...	$575−750
☐ 13/0	..... 5 to 6"	....	(CE)	.. ❷ ...	$330−450
☐ 13/0	..... 5 to 6"	....	(CE)	.. ❸ ...	$285−330
☐ 13/0	..... 5 to 6"	....	(CE)	.. ❹ ...	$240−285
☐ 13/0	..... 5 to 6"	....	(CE)	.. ❺ ...	$200−210
☐ 13/0	..... 5 to 6"	....	(CE)	.. ❻ ...	$190−200
☐ 13/0	..... 5 to 6"	....	(OE)	.. ❼ ...	$190
☐ 13	...... 7 to 7¼"	.....	(CE)	.. ❶ ...	$3500−4000
☐ 13/II	.... 7 to 7¼"	.....	(CE)	.. ❶ ...	$3500−4000
☐ 13/II	.... 7 to 7¼"	.....	(CE)	.. ❷ ...	$3000−3500
☐ 13/II	.... 7 to 7¼"	.....	(CE)	.. ❸ ...	$2500−3000
☐ 13/II	.... 7 to 7¼"	.....	(CE)	.. ❺ ...	$360−400
☐ 13/II	.... 7 to 7¼"	.....	(TW)	.. ❻ ...	$325−360
☐ 13/V	.... 13¼ to 14"	...	(CE)	.. ❶ ...	$4000−5000
☐ 13/V	.... 13¼ to 14"	...	(CE)	.. ❷ ...	$3000−3500
☐ 13/V	.... 13¼ to 14"	...	(CE)	.. ❸ ...	$1700−2200
☐ 13/V	.... 13¼ to 14"	...	(CE)	.. ❹ ...	$1300−1400
☐ 13/V	.... 13¼ to 14"	...	(CE)	.. ❺ ...	$1250−1300
☐ 13/V	.... 13¼ to 14"	...	(TW)	.. ❻ ...	$1150−1250

14/B   *14/A*

HUM 14
Book Worm, Bookends, Boy and Girl
These figurines are weighted with sand through a hole on the bottom and closed with a cork or plastic plug. Sometimes sealed with a paper sticker and inscription "75 Years Goebel." The girl is the same as HUM 3 and HUM 8 except that the pictures on book are black and white rather than in color. Modeled by master sculptor Reinhold Unger in 1935. The boy was made only as part of bookend set and not normally sold separately. This policy, however, was changed and the boy can now be purchased alone and unweighted. This was done mainly to satisfy collectors who desired a figurine to match the 1980 Annual Bell that had a motif similar to the bookend boy. Then in 1981 HUM 415 "Thoughtful" was released in the U.S. market to match the annual bell. Bookworm, bookends were "temporarily withdrawn" (TW) from production on 31 December 1989, but may be reinstated at some future date. "Bookworm," bookends listed at $15.00 a pair on 1955 price list.

☐ 14 A&B .. 5½" .... (CE) .. ❶ ... $1000–1500
☐ 14 A&B .. 5½" .... (CE) .. ❷ ... $550–700
☐ 14 A&B .. 5½" .... (CE) .. ❸ ... $500–550
☐ 14 A&B .. 5½" .... (CE) .. ❹ ... $425–500
☐ 14 A&B .. 5½" .... (CE) .. ❺ ... $400–425
☐ 14 A&B .. 5½" .... (TW) .. ❻ ... $375–400
☐ 14 A .... 5½" .... (CE) .. ❺ ... $200–220
☐ 14 A .... 5½" .... (TW) .. ❻ ... $190–200

Old model   *New model*

HUM 15
Hear Ye, Hear Ye

Old name: "Night Watchman." There are some variations in color of mittens. Right hand facing photo (left hand of figurine) shows fingers on older models. Originally modeled by master sculptor Arthur Moeller in 1935. Older models usually incised 15/2 instead of 15/II. A new small size (15 2/0) "Hear Ye, Hear Ye" was first issued in 1985 with a suggested retail price of $60. It has an incised 1984 copyright date.The 6 inch size 15/I sold for $7.50 on 1955 price list.

☐ 15 2/0	4″	(CE)	❻	$125–130
☐ 15 2/0	4″	(OE)	❼	$125
☐ 15/0	5 to 5¼″	(CE)	❶	$500–675
☐ 15/0	5 to 5¼″	(CE)	❷	$325–425
☐ 15/0	5 to 5¼″	(CE)	❸	$255–300
☐ 15/0	5 to 5¼″	(CE)	❹	$215–255
☐ 15/0	5 to 5¼″	(CE)	❺	$175–185
☐ 15/0	5 to 5¼″	(CE)	❻	$170–175
☐ 15/0	5 to 5¼″	(OE)	❼	$170
☐ 15/I	6 to 6¼″	(CE)	❶	$600–800
☐ 15/I	6 to 6¼″	(CE)	❷	$350–500
☐ 15/I	6 to 6¼″	(CE)	❸	$300–350
☐ 15/I	6 to 6¼″	(CE)	❹	$250–300
☐ 15/I	6 to 6¼″	(CE)	❺	$210–220
☐ 15/I	6 to 6¼″	(CE)	❻	$200–210
☐ 15/I	6 to 6¼″	(OE)	❼	$200
☐ 15/II	7 to 7½″	(CE)	❶	$1200–1500
☐ 15/II	7 to 7½″	(CE)	❷	$700–1000
☐ 15/II	7 to 7½″	(CE)	❸	$600–700
☐ 15/II	7 to 7½″	(CE)	❹	$500–600
☐ 15/II	7 to 7½″	(CE)	❺	$420–440
☐ 15/II	7 to 7½″	(CE)	❻	$400–420
☐ 15/II	7 to 7½″	(OE)	❼	$400
☐ 15	7¼″	(CE)	❶	$1400–1700

HUM 16
Little Hiker
This figurine was originally modeled by master sculptor Arthur Moeller in 1935. The old name of "Happy-Go-Lucky" was used in early catalogues. Slight changes can be noticed when comparing older models with new. Many old crown trademark pieces have a high gloss finish.

☐ 16 2/0	3¾ to 4¼"	(CE)	❶	$300–400
☐ 16 2/0	3¾ to 4¼"	(CE)	❷	$175–350
☐ 16 2/0	3¾ to 4¼"	(CE)	❸	$150–175
☐ 16 2/0	3¾ to 4¼"	(CE)	❹	$125–150
☐ 16 2/0	3¾ to 4¼"	(CE)	❺	$105–110
☐ 16 2/0	3¾ to 4¼"	(CE)	❻	$100–105
☐ 16 2/0	3¾ to 4¼"	(OE)	❼	$100
☐ 16	5½ to 5¾"	(CE)	❶	$600–700
☐ 16	5½ to 5¾"	(CE)	❷	$400–500
☐ 16/I	5½ to 6"	(CE)	❶	$525–600
☐ 16/I	5½ to 6"	(CE)	❷	$315–450
☐ 16/I	5½ to 6"	(CE)	❸	$275–315
☐ 16/I	5½ to 6"	(CE)	❹	$225–275
☐ 16/I	5½ to 6"	(CE)	❺	$190–200
☐ 16/I	5½ to 6"	(CE)	❻	$180–190
☐ 16/I	5½ to 6"	(OE)	❼	$180

Current production on left

Rare sample

HUM 17
Congratulations
First modeled by master sculptor Reinhold Unger in 1935. Called "I Congratulate" in old catalogues. Older models do not have socks. Restyled in 1971 by master sculptor Gerhard Skrobek, who added socks, new hair and textured finish. Larger size (17/2) is no longer produced and considered extremely rare. Early crown mark pieces are marked 17 with either a zero or a 2 directly underneath. Old catalogue dated 1955 lists size of 3¾" which is believed to be in error. Crown and some full bee pieces have the handle of the horn pointing to the back. Since the larger size is closed edition (CE) and will not be produced again in the future, the size designator on the remaining size will eventually be eliminated, according to factory information, and will be incised 17 only. Note rare sample piece with attached pot. This was not approved for production by Siessen Convent.

☐ 17/0	5½ to 6"	(CE)	❶	$475–650
☐ 17/0	5½ to 6"	(CE)	❷	$280–400
☐ 17/0	5½ to 6"	(CE)	❸	$240–280
☐ 17/0	5½ to 6"	(CE)	❹	$200–240
☐ 17/0	6"	(CE)	❺	$170–175
☐ 17/0	6"	(OE)	❻	$160–170
☐ 17/0	6"	**(OE)**	❼	$160
☐ 17/2	7¾ to 8¼"	(CE)	❶	$6500–8000
☐ 17/2	7¾ to 8¼"	(CE)	❷	$5500–6500
☐ 17/2	7¾ to 8¼"	(CE)	❸	$4500–5500

Early models larger than newer models

HUM 18
Christ Child

Early models measure 3¾″ x 6½″. Old name: "Christmas Night." At one time this piece was sold in Belgium in the white overglaze finish and would now be considered extremely rare. These white pieces usually bring about double the price of a colored piece. Originally modeled by master sculptor Reinhold Unger in 1935. Christ Child in white overglaze finish listed at $4.00 on 1955 price list. Christ Child was "temporarily withdrawn" (TW) from production on 31 December 1990, but may be reinstated at some future date.

☐ 18	......	3¾ x 6½″	....	(CE)	..	❶	...	$325−475
☐ 18	......	3¾ x 6½″	....	(CE)	..	❷	...	$200−275
☐ 18	......	3¾ x 6½″	....	(CE)	..	❸	...	$170−200
☐ 18	......	3¼ x 6	....	(CE)	..	❹	...	$140−170
☐ 18	......	3¼ x 6	....	(CE)	..	❺	...	$120−125
☐ 18	......	3¼ x 6	....	(TW)	..	❻	...	$115−120

```
─────────── HUM TERM ───────────

  OVERSIZE: This description refers to a
  piece that has experienced "mold growth"
  size expansion. A figurine that measures
  larger than the standard size is said to be
  "oversized."
```

HUM 19
Prayer Before Battle, Ashtray (CN)
Factory book of models indicates: "Big round tray with praying child (with flag and trumpet) standing at wooden (toy) horse. Prayer Before Battle, modeled by A. Moeller—June 20, 1935." An additional note states that this item was not accepted by the Convent at Siessen. An example of this rare piece was recently located on the East Coast of the U.S. This is the best photograph we could obtain. The piece is actually an ashtray and does have the "M. I. Hummel" signature, scratched in by hand. It is different material than the normal "M.I. Hummel" figurines. The owner washed it in an automatic dishwasher and much of the paint washed off. It is likely that this piece had not been fired after the painting process, thus the paint washed off. The final firing locks on the paint in a normally completed figurine, thus enabling the collector to wash them without fear of damage.

☐ 19 . . . . 5½" . . . . (CN) . . ❶ . . . $5,000–10,000

HUM 20
Prayer Before Battle
Created in 1935 by master sculptor Arthur Moeller. Only slight variations between old and new models. Some color variations, but most noticeable difference is in size. Newer models are smaller. Some older pieces of HUM 20 will have a little paint or highlight inside the handle of the horn; most newer ones do not have. Also, another interesting variation appears on the front of the horn. Sometimes this area is recessed on older examples; most newer figurines will be almost flat and will have a little paint for highlight in this area. These are interesting variations, but they will not affect the value. Prayer before battle listed for $7.50 on old 1955 price list.

☐ 20	4 to 4½″	(CE)	❶	$450–575
☐ 20	4 to 4½″	(CE)	❷	$300–375
☐ 20	4 to 4½″	(CE)	❸	$220–250
☐ 20	4 to 4½″	(CE)	❹	$180–220
☐ 20	4 to 4½″	(CE)	❺	$150–160
☐ 20	4 to 4½″	(CE)	❻	$145–150
☐ 20	4 to 4½″	(OE)	❼	$145

HUM 21
Heavenly Angel
First figurine to have "½" size designator. Much variation in size. Old name: "Little Guardian" or "Celestial Messenger." First modeled by master sculptor Reinhold Unger in 1935. Sometimes incised 21/2 instead of 21/II. According to factory information, this figurine was also sold in white overglaze at one time. "Heavenly Angel" motif was used for the first annual plate in 1971 (HUM 264).

☐ 21/0	4 to 4¾"	(CE)	❶	$300–400
☐ 21/0	4 to 4¾"	(CE)	❷	$175–250
☐ 21/0	4 to 4¾"	(CE)	❸	$150–175
☐ 21/0	4 to 4¾"	(CE)	❹	$125–150
☐ 21/0	4 to 4¾"	(CE)	❺	$105–110
☐ 21/0	4 to 4¾"	(CE)	❻	$100–105
☐ 21/0	4 to 4¾"	(OE)	❼	$100
☐ 21/0½	5¾ to 6½"	(CE)	❶	$500–650
☐ 21/0½	5¾ to 6½"	(CE)	❷	$300–425
☐ 21/0½	5¾ to 6½"	(CE)	❸	$255–300
☐ 21/0½	5¾ to 6½"	(CE)	❹	$215–255
☐ 21/0½	5¾ to 6½"	(CE)	❺	$180–190
☐ 21/0½	5¾ to 6½"	(CE)	❻	$170–180
☐ 21/0½	5¾ to 6½"	(OE)	❼	$170
☐ 21/I	6¾ to 7¼"	(CE)	❶	$600–850
☐ 21/I	6¾ to 7¼"	(CE)	❷	$370–500
☐ 21/I	6¾ to 7¼"	(CE)	❸	$315–370
☐ 21/I	6¾ to 7¼"	(CE)	❹	$260–315
☐ 21/I	6¾ to 7¼"	(CE)	❺	$220–230
☐ 21/I	6¾ to 7¼"	(CE)	❻	$210–220
☐ 21/I	6¾ to 7¼"	(OE)	❼	$210
☐ 21/II	8½ to 8¾"	(CE)	❶	$1150–1500
☐ 21/II	8½ to 8¾"	(CE)	❷	$675–975
☐ 21/II	8½ to 8¾"	(CE)	❸	$575–675
☐ 21/II	8½ to 8¾"	(CE)	❹	$475–575
☐ 21/II	8½ to 8¾"	(CE)	❺	$410–430
☐ 21/II	8½ to 8¾"	(CE)	❻	$390–410
☐ 21/II	8½ to 8¾"	(OE)	❼	$390

22/I   22

HUM 22
Holy Water Font, Angel With Bird
First modeled by master sculptor Reinhold Unger in 1935. Old name: "Sitting Angel."
Variations in size, color and design of bowl are found on other models. This small size
font sold for $1.35 on 1955 price list.

☐ 22	3⅛ to 4½"	(CE)	. . ❶ . . .	$250–275
☐ 22/0	3 x 4"	(CE)	. . ❶ . . .	$200–250
☐ 22/0	3 x 4"	(CE)	. . ❷ . . .	$100–125
☐ 22/0	3 x 4"	(CE)	. . ❸ . . .	$50–60
☐ 22/0	3 x 4"	(CE)	. . ❹ . . .	$45–50
☐ 22/0	3 x 4"	(CE)	. . ❺ . . .	$37–40
☐ 22/0	3 x 4"	(CE)	. . ❻ . . .	$35–37
☐ 22/0	3 x 4"	(OE)	. . ❼ . . .	$35
☐ 22/I	3½ to 4⅞"	(CE)	. . ❶ . . .	$350–550
☐ 22/I	3½ to 4⅞"	(CE)	. . ❷ . . .	$300–350
☐ 22/I	3½ to 4⅞"	(CE)	. . ❸ . . .	$250–300

HUM 23
Adoration

This ever popular design was modeled by master sculptor Reinhold Unger in 1935. Size 23/I was restyled in 1978, with new textured finish, by master modeler Gerhard Skrobek. Older models can be found with either Arabic (23/3) or Roman (23/III) three. Both sizes were sold in white overglaze at one time in Belgium and would be considered extremely rare today. Old name: "Ave Maria." Most older models have rounded corners on the base of the large size while newer models are more square. Early double crown-marked, large size found without size designator — 23 only. Early crown-marked, small size usually found without flowers on base. The small size adoration (23/I) sold for $12.00 on 1955 price list.

☐ 23/I	6¼ to 7"	(CE)	❶	$900–1200
☐ 23/I	6¼ to 7"	(CE)	❷	$525–750
☐ 23/I	6¼ to 7"	(CE)	❸	$450–525
☐ 23/I	6¼ to 7"	(CE)	❹	$375–450
☐ 23/I	6¼ to 7"	(CE)	❺	$315–330
☐ 23/I	6¼ to 7"	(CE)	❻	$300–315
☐ 23/I	6¼ to 7"	(OE)	❼	$300
☐ 23	8¾ to 9"	(CE)	❶	$1500–2000
☐ 23/III	8¾ to 9"	(CE)	❶	$1400–1900
☐ 23/III	8¾ to 9"	(CE)	❷	$825–1200
☐ 23/III	8¾ to 9"	(CE)	❸	$700–825
☐ 23/III	8¾ to 9"	(CE)	❹	$580–700
☐ 23/III	8¾ to 9"	(CE)	❺	$490–510
☐ 23/III	8¾ to 9"	(CE)	❻	$470–490
☐ 23/III	8¾ to 9"	(OE)	❼	$470

24/III   24/I

HUM 24
Lullaby, Candleholder

Records show that this figurine was first modeled in 1935. Both Arthur Moeller and Reinhold Unger are given credit — possibly one created the small size while the other the larger size. Variations are found in size and construction of socket for candle on size 24/I. Old name: "Cradle Song." Also made without hole for candle — see HUM 262. Size 24/III had been considered rare but is once again in current production. Sometimes incised 24/3 instead of 24/III. In the spring of 1982 the large size (24/III) was listed by Goebel as "temporarily withdrawn," to be possibly reinstated at a future date. The small size (24/I) also was "temporarily withdrawn " from production on 31 December 1989, but may be reinstated at some future date.

☐ 24/I	3½ x 5 to 5½"	(CE)	❶	$450–600
☐ 24/I	3½ x 5 to 5½"	(CE)	❷	$300–375
☐ 24/I	3½ x 5 to 5½"	(CE)	❸	$225–250
☐ 24/I	3½ x 5 to 5½"	(CE)	❹	$185–225
☐ 24/I	3½ x 5 to 5½"	(CE)	❺	$160–170
☐ 24/I	3½ x 5 to 5½"	(TW)	❻	$150–160
☐ 24/III	6¼ x 8¾"	(CE)	❶	$1250–1750
☐ 24/III	6¼ x 8¾"	(CE)	❷	$850–1150
☐ 24/III	6¼ x 8¾"	(CE)	❸	$550–650
☐ 24/III	6¼ x 8¾"	(CE)	❹	$475–550
☐ 24/III	6¼ x 8¾"	(CE)	❺	$450–475
☐ 24/III	6¼ x 8¾"	(TW)	❻	$425–450

Crown *Full bee*

HUM 25
Angelic Sleep, Candleholder
Records indicate that this figurine was first modeled in 1935 and that both Arthur Moeller and Reinhold Unger were involved with the design. At one time this figurine was sold in Belgium in the white overglaze finish and would now be considered extremely rare. Listed as "Angel's Joy" in some old catalogues. In some old, as well as new catalogues and price lists shown as 25/I in error. Made only one size and incised 25 only. (Candleholder figures are not always photographed with candles with this guide.) This is figurine was "temporarily withdrawn" (TW) from production on 31 December 1989, but may be reinstated at some future date.

☐ 25	. . . . . .	3½ x 5 to 5½″ .	(CE)	. . . ❶ . . .	$450–600
☐ 25	. . . .	3½ x 5 to 5½″ .	(CE)	. . . ❷ . . .	$300–375
☐ 25	. . . .	3½ x 5 to 5½″ .	(CE)	. . . ❸ . . .	$225–250
☐ 25	. . . .	3½ x 5 to 5½″ .	(CE)	. . . ❹ . . .	$185–225
☐ 25	. . . .	3½ x 5 to 5½″ .	(CE)	. . . ❺ . . .	$160–170
☐ 25	. . . .	3½ x 5 to 5½″ .	(TW)	. . . ❻ . . .	$150–160

———— HUM TERM ————

TEMPORARILY WITHDRAWN: A designation assigned by the W. Goebel Porzellanfabrik to indicate that a particular item is being withdrawn from production for some time, but may be reinstated at a future date.

26/0   26/I

HUM 26
Holy Water Font, Child Jesus
Originally modeled by master sculptor Reinhold Unger in 1935. The normal color for the gown is a dark red but is occasionally found in a light blue color. All that I have ever seen with the blue gown were in the small (26/0) size and with the small stylized (TM 3) trademark. Old crown mark and full bee pieces in both sizes usually have scalloped edge on bowl of font. This "Christ Child" font listed for $1.35 on 1955 price list.

☐ 26/0	. . . . .	2¾ x 5¼"	. . . .	(CE)	. . ❶ . . .	$200–250
☐ 26/0	. . . . .	2¾ x 5¼"	. . . .	(CE)	. . ❷ . . .	$100–125
☐ 26/0	. . . . .	2¾ x 5¼"	. . . .	(CE)	. . ❸ . . .	$50–60
☐ 26/0	. . . . .	2¾ x 5¼"	. . . .	(CE)	. . ❹ . . .	$45–50
☐ 26/0	. . . . .	2¾ x 5¼"	. . . .	(CE)	. . ❺ . . .	$37–40
☐ 26/0	. . . . .	2¾ x 5¼"	. . . .	(CE)	. . ❻ . . .	$35–37
☐ 26/0	. . . . .	2¾ x 5¼"	. . . .	(OE)	. . ❼ . . .	$35
☐ 26	. . . . . .	3 x 5¾"	. . . . . .	(CE)	. . ❶ . . .	$300–500
☐ 26/I	. . . . .	3¼ x 6"	. . . . . .	(CE)	. . ❶ . . .	$300–500
☐ 26/I	. . . . .	3¼ x 6"	. . . . . .	(CE)	. . ❷ . . .	$250–300
☐ 26/I	. . . . .	3¼ x 6"	. . . . . .	(CE)	. . ❸ . . .	$200–250

27/I   27/3

HUM 27
Joyous News

This figurine was made in two sizes. The small size is a candleholder while the larger size is a figurine. Both were modeled by master sculptor Reinhold Unger in 1935. 27/I is so similar to III/40/I that it is extremely difficult to tell the difference unless they are clearly marked. The small size "Joyous News" candleholder (27/I) is no longer produced and is considered rare. Usually found only in crown trademark. Can be found with the candleholder on the front side or on the back side. 27/I is also sometimes found with light purple shoes. Some models designed to hold .6 cm size candles while others designed to hold 1 cm size candles. The small size also found with incised number III/27/1 which indicates made for larger 1 cm size candles. The larger size "Joyous News" is rare in the older trademarks: TM 1, TM 2 and TM 3 but was reinstated in 1978 using the original molds, and the original number 27/3 (Arabic 3). In 1979 when it was restyled with the new textured finish the number was changed to 27/III (Roman III). Both 27/3 (old mold) and 27/III (new mold) can be found in TM 5.

☐ 27/I ..... 2¾" .... (CE) .. ❶ ... $300–500
☐ 27/I ..... 2¾" .... (CE) .. ❷ ... $250–400
☐ 27/3 ..... 4¼ x 4¾" .... (CE) .. ❶ ... $1500–2000
☐ 27/3 ..... 4¼ x 4¾" .... (CE) .. ❷ ... $1000–1500
☐ 27/3 ..... 4¼ x 4¾" .... (CE) .. ❸ ... $750–1000
☐ 27/3 ..... 4¼ x 4¾" .... (CE) .. ❺ ... $190–200
☐ 27/III .... 4¼ x 4¾" .... (CE) .. ❻ ... $180–190
☐ 27/III .... 4¼ x 4¾" .... (OE) .. ❼ ... $180

HUM TERM

PAINT FLAKE: The term used to designate a flaw in a ceramic figurine whereby the paint has been chipped. This type flaw does not go beyond the glazed surface.

28/III (TM 3)   *28/II (Double crown)*

HUM 28
Wayside Devotion

First modeled by master sculptor Reinhold Unger in 1935. Old name: "The Little Shepherd" or "Evensong." According to factory information, this figurine was also sold in white overglaze finish at one time. Sometimes incised 28/2 instead of 28/II or 28/3 instead of 28/III. Also found without a size designator on the large size — incised 28 only. The small size 28/II was restyled by Gerhard Skrobek in the early 1970's. Made without the shrine (see HUM 99) and was named "Eventide." The small size "Wayside Devotion" listed for $16.50 on 1955 price list.

☐ 28/II	.... 7 to 7½"	..... (CE)	.. ❶	...	$1000–1300
☐ 28/II	.... 7 to 7½"	..... (CE)	.. ❷	...	$600–700
☐ 28/II	.... 7 to 7½"	..... (CE)	.. ❸	...	$550–625
☐ 28/II	.... 7 to 7½"	..... (CE)	.. ❹	...	$450–550
☐ 28/II	.... 7 to 7½"	..... (CE)	.. ❺	...	$380–400
☐ 28/II	.... 7 to 7½"	..... (CE)	.. ❻	...	$370–380
☐ 28/II	.... 7 to 7½"	..... (OE)	.. ❼	...	$370
☐ 28	...... 8¾"	.... (CE)	.. ❶	...	$1500–1750
☐ 28/III	.... 8¾"	.... (CE)	.. ❶	...	$1200–1500
☐ 28/III	.... 8¾"	.... (CE)	.. ❷	...	$850–1100
☐ 28/III	.... 8¾"	.... (CE)	.. ❸	...	$700–850
☐ 28/III	.... 8¾"	.... (CE)	.. ❹	...	$600–700
☐ 28/III	.... 8¾"	.... (CE)	.. ❺	...	$500–550
☐ 28/III	.... 8¾"	.... (CE)	.. ❻	...	$480–500
☐ 28/III	.... 8¾"	.... (OE)	.. ❼	...	$480

29 Crown   29/0 Full bee   248/0

HUM 29
Holy Water Font, Guardian Angel

(CE) Closed Edition. Modeled by master sculptor Reinhold Unger in 1935 in two sizes. Because of the fragile wing design, it was discontinued in 1958 and replaced with a new design by Gerhard Skrobek and given the new model number HUM 248.

- ☐ 29 . . . . . . 2½ x 5¾" . . . . . (CE) . . ❶ . . . $1300–1500
- ☐ 29/0 . . . . . 2⅞ x 6" . . . . . . (CE) . . ❶ . . . $1300–1500
- ☐ 29/0 . . . . . 2⅞ x 6" . . . . . . (CE) . . ❷ . . . $1000–1250
- ☐ 29/0 . . . . . 2⅞ x 6" . . . . . . (CE) . . ❸ . . . $950–1000
- ☐ 29/I . . . . . 3 x 6⅜" . . . . . . (CE) . . ❶ . . . $1500–2000
- ☐ 29/I . . . . . 3 x 6⅜" . . . . . . (CE) . . ❷ . . . $1500–1750

HUM TERM

MUSTERZIMMER: The German word meaning sample model designating that this piece is to be held at the W. Goebel Porzellanfabrik in the "sample room" to be used for future reference by production artists.

30/0 A   30/0 B

30/0 A   30/I A

30/0 B   30/I B

HUM 30
Ba-Bee-Ring

Old name: "Hummel Rings." Originally modeled in 1935 by master sculptor Reinhold Unger. There is some size variation between old and new pieces. Early red color rings are extremely rare. Now produced in tan color only. The girl, 30 B always has orange color hair ribbon, except on red color rings, then it is blue. Although now made in only one size, current production models still have incised "O" size designator. Factory representatives state that this "will possibly disappear sometime in the future." Priced by the set of two. Also found unpainted in white overglaze finish. "Ba-Bee-Rings" sold for $4.00 a pair on 1955 price list.

☐ 30/0 A&B	. 4¾ x 5″	. . . . . .	(CE)	. . ❶ . . .	$400–650
☐ 30/0 A&B	. 4¾ x 5″	. . . . . .	(CE)	. . ❷ . . .	$280–350
☐ 30/0 A&B	. 4¾ x 5″	. . . . . .	(CE)	. . ❸ . . .	$250–280
☐ 30/0 A&B	. 4¾ x 5″	. . . . . .	(CE)	. . ❹ . . .	$200–250
☐ 30/0 A&B	. 4¾ x 5″	. . . . . .	(CE)	. . ❺ . . .	$170–180
☐ 30/0 A&B	. 4¾ x 5″	. . . . . .	(CE)	. . ❻ . . .	$160–170
☐ 30/0 A&B	. 4¾ x 5″	. . . . . .	(OE)	. . ❼ . . .	$160
☐ 30/I A&B	.. 5¼ x 6″	. . . . . .	(CE)	. . ❶ . . .	$2000–3500
☐ 30/0 A&B	. Red Rings	. . . .	(CE)	. . ❶ . . .	$6000–7000
☐ 30/I A&B	.. Red Rings	. . . .	(CE)	. . ❶ . . .	$8000–9000

Note black child on left

HUM 31
Silent Night with Black Child/Advent Group with Candle (CE)
Similar to HUM 54 except embossed earring and bare feet of black child. Modeled in 1935 by master sculptor Arthur Moeller but not produced in quantity. HUM 31 was also produced and sold with all white children and also considered extremely rare. HUM 31 was still listed in old German price lists as late as 1956. That does not necessarily mean that it was produced and sold at that time. It could possibly have been listed in error since so very, very few have been located. According to factory representatives, a few HUM 54 were produced with a black child, but wearing shoes instead of bare feet or without shoes with white marks to indicate toes. The figurine photographed here is particularly unique since it was originally purchased from Mrs. Victoria Hummel, the mother of Sister Hummel. Her mother died on 24 October 1983 at the age of 98. This figurine is part of the Robert L. Miller collection.

☐ 31 . . . . . . 3½ x 5″ . . . . . . (CE) . . ❶ . . . $10,000–15,000 (White children)
☐ 31 . . . . . . 3½ x 5″ . . . . . . (CE) . . ❶ . . . $20,000–25,000 (Black child)

32

32/0   32/0   32/I

HUM 32
Little Gabriel
There are many size variations in this figurine that was first modeled by master sculptor Reinhold Unger in 1935. Called "Joyous News" in some old catalogues. Newer models have no size designator since it is now produced in only the small size. The large size is found incised 32/I or 32 only and is considered extremely rare. "Little Gabriel" was restyled in 1982 with several changes — arms are now apart, angle of the wings is longer and the incised "M.I. Hummel" signature is on the top of the base rather than on the side, as in the past.

☐ 32/0	5 to 5½"	(CE)	❶	$400–500
☐ 32/0	5 to 5½"	(CE)	❷	$250–350
☐ 32/0	5 to 5½"	(CE)	❸	$175–200
☐ 32/0	5 to 5½"	(CE)	❹	$150–175
☐ 32/0	5"	(CE)	❺	$125–150
☐ 32	5"	(CE)	❺	$125–150
☐ 32	5"	(CE)	❻	$115–120
☐ 32	5"	(OE)	❼	$115
☐ 32/I	5¾ to 6"	(CE)	❶	$1500–1800
☐ 32/I	5¾ to 6"	(CE)	❷	$1200–1500
☐ 32/I	5¾ to 6"	(CE)	❸	$900–1200
☐ 32	5¾ to 6"	(CE)	❶	$1500–1800
☐ 32	5¾ to 6"	(CE)	❷	$1200–1500

New   Old

HUM 33
Ashtray, Joyful

First modeled by master sculptor Reinhold Unger in 1935. Older models have slightly different construction of ashtray. HUM 33 "Joyful Ashtray" was listed as "temporarily withdrawn" (TW) from production on 31 December 1984, but may be reinstated at some future date. It is very unlikely, in our opinion, that this item will ever be made again.

☐ 33 ...... 3½ x 6" ...... (CE) .. ❶ ... $350–600
☐ 33 ...... 3½ x 6" ...... (CE) .. ❷ ... $250–300
☐ 33 ...... 3½ x 6" ...... (CE) .. ❸ ... $180–200
☐ 33 ...... 3½ x 6" ...... (CE) .. ❹ ... $150–180
☐ 33 ...... 3½ x 6" ...... (CE) .. ❺ ... $140–150
☐ 33 ...... 3½ x 6" ...... (TW) .. ❻ ... $130–140

─── HUM TERM ───

PAINT RUB: A general wearing away of the paint surface of a figurine in a particular spot. This condition is usually caused by excessive handling of a figurine, thin paint in a given area of the figurine, or the excessive use of abrasive cleaners.

HUM 34
Ashtray, Singing Lesson

First modeled by master sculptor Arthur Moeller in 1935. Slight variation in colors of older models. Several variations in construction on bottom of ashtray. The "M.I. Hummel" signature is usually found under the lip of the ashtray on most older models, and on top of rim on newer models. "Singing Lesson" ashtray was "temporarily withdrawn" (TW) from production on 31 December 1989, but may be reinstated at some future date.

☐ 34	3½ x 6¼"	(CE)	❶	$400–600
☐ 34	3½ x 6¼"	(CE)	❷	$250–300
☐ 34	3½ x 6¼"	(CE)	❸	$180–200
☐ 34	3½ x 6¼"	(CE)	❹	$150–180
☐ 34	3½ x 6¼"	(CE)	❺	$140–150
☐ 34	3½ x 6¼"	(TW)	❻	$130–140

HUM TERM

STYLIZED TRADEMARK: The symbol used by the Goebel Company from 1957 until 1964. It is recognized by the V with a bumblebee that has triangular or "stylized" wings.

35/I   35/0

HUM 35
Holy Water Font, Good Shepherd
First modeled by master sculptor Reinhold Unger in 1935. There are slight variations in size as well as variations in the construction of the bowl of font. Also found in the large size without a size designator — incised 35 only.

☐ 35/0 . . . . . 2½ x 4¾" . . . . (CE) . . ❶ . . . $200–250
☐ 35/0 . . . . . 2½ x 4¾" . . . . (CE) . . ❷ . . . $100–125
☐ 35/0 . . . . . 2½ x 4¾" . . . . (CE) . . ❸ . . . $50–60
☐ 35/0 . . . . . 2½ x 4¾" . . . . (CE) . . ❹ . . . $45–50
☐ 35/0 . . . . . 2½ x 4¾" . . . . (CE) . . ❺ . . . $37–40
☐ 35/0 . . . . . 2½ x 4¾" . . . . (CE) . . ❻ . . . $35–37
☐ 35/0 . . . . . 2½ x 4¾" . . . . (**OE**) . . ❼ . . . $35
☐ 35/I . . . . . 2¾ x 5¾" . . . . (CE) . . ❶ . . . $250–400
☐ 35/I . . . . . 2¾ x 5¾" . . . . (CE) . . ❷ . . . $250–350
☐ 35/I . . . . . 2¾ x 5¾" . . . . (CE) . . ❸ . . . $150–200
☐ 35 . . . . . . 2¾ x 5¾" . . . . (CE) . . ❶ . . . $275–425

36/I   36/0

HUM 36
Holy Water Font, Child with Flowers
First modeled by master sculptor Reinhold Unger in 1935. There are slight variations in size, color and in the construction of the bowl of the font. Also called "Flower Angel" or "Angel with Flowers".

☐ 36/0 . . . . . 3¼ × 4¼" . . . (CE) . . ❶ . . . $200–250
☐ 36/0 . . . . . 3¼ × 4¼" . . . (CE) . . ❷ . . . $100–125
☐ 36/0 . . . . . 3¼ × 4¼" . . . (CE) . . ❸ . . . $50–60
☐ 36/0 . . . . . 3¼ × 4¼" . . . (CE) . . ❹ . . . $45–50
☐ 36/0 . . . . . 3¼ × 4¼" . . . (CE) . . ❺ . . . $37–40
☐ 36/0 . . . . . 3¼ × 4¼" . . . (CE) . . ❻ . . . $35–37
☐ 36/0 . . . . . 3¼ × 4¼" . . . (OE) . . ❼ . . . $35
☐ 36/I . . . . . 3½ × 4½" . . . (CE) . . ❶ . . . $250–400
☐ 36/I . . . . . 3½ × 4½" . . . (CE) . . ❷ . . . $250–350
☐ 36/I . . . . . 3½ × 5" . . . . . (CE) . . ❸ . . . $150–200
☐ 36 . . . . . . 3½ × 4½" . . . (CE) . . ❶ . . . $275–425

HUM TERM

GOEBEL BEE: A name used to describe the trademark used by the Goebel Company from 1972 until 1979. This trademark incorporates the GOEBEL name with the V and bee.

New model　　　　　*Old model*

HUM 37
Herald Angels, Candleholder

Many variations through the years. On older models the candleholder is much taller than on the newer ones. The order of placement of the angels may vary on the older models. Current production pieces have a half-inch wider base. Originally modeled in 1935 by master sculptor Reinhold Unger. Early "crown" mark examples are sometimes found with light purple shoes rather than the dark brown shoes found on newer models. "Herald Angels" candleholder was "temporarily withdrawn" (TW) from production on 31 December 1989, but may be reinstated at some future date.

☐ 37 . . . . . . 2¾ × 4" . . . . . (CE) . . ❶ . . . $500–700
☐ 37 . . . . . . 2¾ × 4" . . . . . (CE) . . ❷ . . . $350–400
☐ 37 . . . . . . 2¾ × 4 to 4½" . (CE) . . ❸ . . . $240–270
☐ 37 . . . . . . 2¾ × 4 to 4½" . (CE) . . ❹ . . . $210–240
☐ 37 . . . . . . 2¾ × 4 to 4½" . (CE) . . ❺ . . . $180–190
☐ 37 . . . . . . 2¾ × 4 to 4½" . (TW) . . ❻ . . . $175–180

─── HUM TERM ───

OUT OF PRODUCTION: A term used by the Goebel Company to designate items that are not currently in production, yet have not been given an official classification as to their eventual fate. Some items listed as out of production may become closed editions, remain temporarily withdrawn, or ultimately return to current production status.

38/0   39/0   40/0

HUM 38
Angel, Joyous News with Lute,
Candleholder

HUM 39
Angel, Joyous News with Accordion,
Candleholder

HUM 40
Angel, Joyous News with Trumpet,
Candleholder
Roman numerals to the left of the HUM number indicate the size of the candle that fits into the figurine. Size I is .6 cm, size III is 1 cm. (Note: Not all figurines which hold candles are photographed with candles in this book, but they are usually sold with candles.) Also called "Little Heavenly Angel" in old catalogues. Also known as "Angel Trio" candleholders. Candleholders are always on right side of angel. These three figurines were originally modeled in 1935 by master sculptor Reinhold Unger. Very early pieces do not have a size designator — incised 38. 39. 40. only. Since these figurines are relatively small in size, the signature may be only "Hum" on the back or on the leg of the angel. HUM 38/0 sometimes found with green shoes. HUM 38, HUM 39 and HUM 40 are not currently available in the United States.

☐ 1/38/0	2 to 2½"	(CE)	❶	$125–175
☐ 1/38/0	2 to 2½"	(CE)	❷	$80–100
☐ 1/38/0	2 to 2½"	(CE)	❸	$60–75
☐ 1/38/0	2 to 2½"	(CE)	❹	$50–60
☐ 1/38/0	2 to 2½"	(CE)	❺	$45–50
☐ 1/38/0	2 to 2½"	(TW)	❻	$40–45
☐ III/38/0	2 to 2½"	(CE)	❶	$125–175
☐ III/38/0	2 to 2½"	(CE)	❷	$80–100
☐ III/38/0	2 to 2½"	(CE)	❸	$60–75
☐ III/38/0	2 to 2½"	(CE)	❹	$50–60
☐ III/38/0	2 to 2½"	(CE)	❺	$45–50
☐ III/38/0	2 to 2½"	(TW)	❻	$40–45
☐ III/38/I	2½ to 2¾"	(CE)	❶	$250–300
☐ III/38/I	2½ to 2¾"	(CE)	❷	$200–250
☐ III/38/I	2½ to 2¾"	(CE)	❸	$150–200

(Continued on next page)

☐ 1/39/0	2 to 2½"	(CE)	❶	$125–175
☐ 1/39/0	2 to 2½"	(CE)	❷	$80–100
☐ 1/39/0	2 to 2½"	(CE)	❸	$60–75
☐ 1/39/0	2 to 2½"	(CE)	❹	$50–60
☐ 1/39/0	2 to 2½"	(CE)	❺	$45–50
☐ 1/39/0	2 to 2½"	(TW)	❻	$40–45
☐ III/39/0	2 to 2½"	(CE)	❶	$125–175
☐ III/39/0	2 to 2½"	(CE)	❷	$80–100
☐ III/39/0	2 to 2½"	(CE)	❸	$60–75
☐ III/39/0	2 to 2½"	(CE)	❹	$50–60
☐ III/39/0	2 to 2½"	(CE)	❺	$45–50
☐ III/39/0	2 to 2½"	(TW)	❻	$40–45
☐ III/39/I	2½ to 2¾"	(CE)	❶	$250–300
☐ III/39/I	2½ to 2¾"	(CE)	❷	$200–250
☐ III/39/I	2½ to 2¾"	(CE)	❸	$150–200
☐ 1/40/0	2 to 2½"	(CE)	❶	$125–175
☐ 1/40/0	2 to 2½"	(CE)	❷	$80–100
☐ 1/40/0	2 to 2½"	(CE)	❸	$60–75
☐ 1/40/0	2 to 2½"	(CE)	❹	$50–60
☐ 1/40/0	2 to 2½"	(CE)	❺	$45–50
☐ 1/40/0	2 to 2½"	(TW)	❻	$40–45
☐ III/40/0	2 to 2½"	(CE)	❶	$125–175
☐ III/40/0	2 to 2½"	(CE)	❷	$80–100
☐ III/40/0	2 to 2½"	(CE)	❸	$60–75
☐ III/40/0	2 to 2½"	(CE)	❹	$50–60
☐ III/40/0	2 to 2½"	(CE)	❺	$45–50
☐ III/40/0	2 to 2½"	(TW)	❻	$40–45
☐ III/40/I	2½ to 2¾"	(CE)	❶	$250–300
☐ III/40/I	2½ to 2¾"	(CE)	❷	$200–250
☐ III/40/I	2½ to 2¾"	(CE)	❸	$150–200

HUM 41
Singing Lesson (without base) (CN)
Factory book of models indicates this piece is similar to HUM 34 (Singing Lesson, Ashtray). Closed 31 October 1935. No known examples.

☐ 41 . . . . (CN) $5,000–10,000

42/0   42/I

HUM 42
Good Shepherd

First modeled by master sculptor Reinhold Unger in 1935. Normally has a rust-colored gown. Factory sample of small size 42/0 has light blue gown but is doubtful that it was ever sold in blue color. Size 42/I is considered extremely rare and no longer produced in large size. Factory information states that (0) size designator will eventually be dropped from number. Current production still incised 42/0.

☐ 42/0 . . . . . 6¼ to 6½" . . . . (CE) . . ❶ . . . $600–750
☐ 42/0 . . . . . 6¼ to 6½" . . . . (CE) . . ❷ . . . $350–500
☐ 42/0 . . . . . 6¼ to 6½" . . . . (CE) . . ❸ . . . $300–350
☐ 42/0 . . . . . 6¼ to 6½" . . . . (CE) . . ❹ . . . $250–300
☐ 42/0 . . . . . 6¼" . . . . (CE) . . ❺ . . . $210–220
☐ 42/0 . . . . . 6¼" . . . . (CE) . . ❻ . . . $200–210
☐ 42/0 . . . . . 6¼" . . . . (OE) . . ❼ . . . $200
☐ 42/I . . . . . 7¼ to 7¾" . . . . (CE) . . ❶ . . . $7000–8000
☐ 42/I . . . . . 7¼ to 8" . . . . . (CE) . . ❷ . . . $6000–7000

TM 2   TM 1   TM 3

HUM 43
March Winds
Many size variations with older pieces slightly larger. First modeled by master sculptor Reinhold Unger in 1935. Called "Urchin" in some old catalogues. There is some variation in the front "flap" of boys trousers; sometimes this is in the mold, other times made with white paint — not attributed to any certain time period.

☐ 43	4¾ to 5½"	(CE)	❶	$400–550
☐ 43	4¾ to 5½"	(CE)	❷	$240–340
☐ 43	4¾ to 5½"	(CE)	❸	$200–240
☐ 43	4¾ to 5½"	(CE)	❹	$170–200
☐ 43	4¾ to 5½"	(CE)	❺	$140–150
☐ 43	4¾ to 5½"	(CE)	❻	$135–140
☐ 43	4¾ to 5½"	(OE)	❼	$135

HUM TERM

HOLLOW MOLD: The term used by "M.I. Hummel" collectors to describe a figurine that is open on the underside of the base. With these particular bases the collector can visually see into the cavity of the figurine.

44 A   44 B

HUM 44 A
Culprits, Table Lamp

Originally modeled by master sculptor Arthur Moeller in 1935. Older models have a half-inch larger base, and hole for electrical switch on top of base. They usually have a 1935 copyright date incised. "Culprits" table lamp was "temporarily withdrawn" (TW) from production on 31 December 1989, but may be reinstated at some future date.

☐ 44	8½ to 9½"	(CE)	❶	$600–750
☐ 44A	8½ to 9½"	(CE)	❶	$450–600
☐ 44A	8½ to 9½"	(CE)	❷	$400–450
☐ 44A	8½ to 9½"	(CE)	❸	$375–400
☐ 44A	8½"	(CE)	❹	$350–375
☐ 44A	8½"	(CE)	❺	$325–350
☐ 44A	8½"	(TW)	❻	$300–325

Hum 44 B
Out of Danger, Table Lamp

Originally modeled by master sculptor Arthur Moeller in 1935. Older models have a half-inch larger base, and hole for electrical switch on top of base. They usually have a 1936 copyright date incised. Variation in color of the girl's dress. Old "crown" trademark (TM 1) examples are found with girl in black dress while the normal blue dress is found on all others. "Out of Danger" table lamp was "temporarily withdrawn" (TW) from production on 31 December 1989, but may be reinstated at some future date.

☐ 44B	8½ to 9½"	(CE)	❶	$450–600
☐ 44B	8½ to 9½"	(CE)	❷	$400–450
☐ 44B	8½ to 9½"	(CE)	❸	$375–400
☐ 44B	8½"	(CE)	❹	$350–375
☐ 44B	8½"	(CE)	❺	$325–350
☐ 44B	8½"	(TW)	❻	$300–325

Many size and color variations

HUM 45
Madonna With Halo

HUM 46
Madonna Without Halo

These beautiful Madonnas were first modeled by master sculptor Reinhold Unger in 1935. Sometimes called "The Holy Virgin" in old catalogues. There are many size variations as well as color variations. Produced in white overglaze, pastel blue, pastel pink, heavy blue and ivory finish. Also has been found in reddish brown terra cotta finish signed "M.I. Hummel" but without incised number — height 11 inches. Some pieces have been mismarked 45 instead of 46, etc. Some pieces have been found with both 45 and 46 on the same piece. In the spring of 1982 the large sizes (45/III and 46/III) (both white overglaze finish as well as color) were listed by Goebel as "temporarily withdrawn," to be possibly reinstated at a future date. Sometimes an Arabic size designator is used on older models. The small sizes (45/0 and 46/0), both in white overglaze finish as well as color, were "temporarily withdrawn" (TW) from production on 31 December 1984, but may be reinstated at some future date. The medium size (46/I), both in white overglaze finish and in color, were "temporarily withdrawn" (TW) from production on 31 December 1989, but may be reinstated at some future date. This leaves only the 45/I "Madonna With Halo" as an "open edition" in this series at this time.

(continued on next page)

				Color	White
45/0	10½"	(CE)	❶	☐ $200–275	☐ $125–175
45/0	10½"	(CE)	❷	☐ $95–175	☐ $85–125
45/0	10½"	(CE)	❸	☐ $85–95	☐ $55–70
45/0	10½"	(CE)	❹	☐ $70–85	☐ $50–55
45/0	10½"	(CE)	❺	☐ $65–70	☐ $45–50
45/0	10½"	(TW)	❻	☐ $60–65	☐ $40–45

				Color	White
45/I	11½ to 13¼"	(CE)	❶	☐ $250–350	☐ $150–200
45/I	11½ to 13¼"	(CE)	❷	☐ $150–200	☐ $100–150
45/I	11½ to 13¼"	(CE)	❸	☐ $120–130	☐ $90–100
45/I	11½ to 13¼"	(CE)	❹	☐ $115–120	☐ $80–90
45/I	11½ to 13¼"	(CE)	❺	☐ $110–115	☐ $73–77
45/I	11½ to 13¼"	(CE)	❻	☐ $105–110	☐ $70–73
45/I	11½ to 13¼"	(OE)	❼	☐ $105	☐ $70
45/III	15½ to 16¾"	(CE)	❶	☐ $400–600	☐ $250–350
45/III	15½ to 16¾"	(CE)	❷	☐ $275–375	☐ $175–225
45/III	15½ to 16¾"	(CE)	❸	☐ $175–220	☐ $140–165
45/III	15½ to 16¾"	(CE)	❹	☐ $165–175	☐ $115–140
45/III	15½ to 16¾"	(CE)	❺	☐ $155–165	☐ $110–115
45/III	15½ to 16¾"	(TW)	❻	☐ $150–155	☐ $105–110

				Color	White
46/0	10¼"	(CE)	❶	☐ $200–275	☐ $125–175
46/0	10¼"	(CE)	❷	☐ $95–175	☐ $85–125
46/0	10¼"	(CE)	❸	☐ $85–95	☐ $55–70
46/0	10¼"	(CE)	❹	☐ $70–85	☐ $50–55
46/0	10¼"	(CE)	❺	☐ $65–70	☐ $45–50
46/0	10¼"	(TW)	❻	☐ $60–65	☐ $40–45
46/I	11¼ to 13"	(CE)	❶	☐ $250–350	☐ $150–200
46/I	11¼ to 13"	(CE)	❷	☐ $150–200	☐ $100–150
46/I	11¼ to 13"	(CE)	❸	☐ $120–130	☐ $90–100
46/I	11¼ to 13"	(CE)	❹	☐ $115–120	☐ $80–90
46/I	11¼ to 13"	(CE)	❺	☐ $110–115	☐ $75–80
46/I	11¼ to 13"	(TW)	❻	☐ $105–110	☐ $70–75
46/III	15¼ to 16¼"	(CE)	❶	☐ $400–600	☐ $250–350
46/III	15¼ to 16¼"	(CE)	❷	☐ $275–375	☐ $175–225
46/III	15¼ to 16¼"	(CE)	❸	☐ $175–220	☐ $140–165
46/III	15¼ to 16¼"	(CE)	❹	☐ $165–175	☐ $115–140
46/III	15¼ to 16¼"	(CE)	❺	☐ $155–165	☐ $110–115
46/III	15¼ to 16¼"	(TW)	❻	☐ $150–155	☐ $105–110

NOTE: HUM 1 through HUM 46 were all put
on the market in 1935.

HUM TERM

WHITE OVERGLAZE: The term used to designate an item that has not been painted, but has been glazed and fired. These pieces are completely white. All "M.I. Hummel" items are produced in this finish before being individually hand painted.

| 47/II (TM 5) | 47/0 (TM 2) | 47/0 (TM 5) | 47 3/0 (TM 1) |

HUM 47
Goose Girl
First modeled by master sculptor Arthur Moeller in 1936. There are many size variations between the older and newer models. Sometimes called "Little Gooseherd" in old catalogues. Older models have a blade of grass between the geese. This has been eliminated completely or reduced in size on newer models. The large size 47/II was restyled with the new textured finish in the early 1970's. Sometimes incised 47/2 or 47.2. instead of 47/II.

☐ 47 3/0	... 4 to 4¼"	..... (CE)	.. ❶	...	$425–575
☐ 47 3/0	... 4 to 4¼"	..... (CE)	.. ❷	...	$250–350
☐ 47 3/0	... 4 to 4¼"	..... (CE)	.. ❸	...	$215–250
☐ 47 3/0	... 4 to 4¼"	..... (CE)	.. ❹	...	$180–215
☐ 47 3/0	... 4 to 4¼"	..... (CE)	.. ❺	...	$150–160
☐ 47 3/0	... 4 to 4¼"	..... (CE)	.. ❻	...	$145–150
☐ 47 3/0	... 4 to 4¼"	..... (OE)	.. ❼	...	$145
☐ 47/0	..... 4¾ to 5¼"	.... (CE)	.. ❶	...	$600–750
☐ 47/0	..... 4¾ to 5¼"	.... (CE)	.. ❷	...	$325–600
☐ 47/0	..... 4¾ to 5¼"	.... (CE)	.. ❸	...	$275–325
☐ 47/0	..... 4¾ to 5¼"	.... (CE)	.. ❹	...	$230–275
☐ 47/0	..... 4¾ to 5¼"	.... (CE)	.. ❺	...	$190–200
☐ 47/0	..... 4¾ to 5¼"	.... (CE)	.. ❻	...	$185–190
☐ 47/0	..... 4¾ to 5¼"	.... (OE)	.. ❼	...	$185
☐ 47/II	.... 7 to 7½"	..... (CE)	.. ❶	...	$1000–1300
☐ 47/II	.... 7 to 7½"	..... (CE)	.. ❷	...	$650–850
☐ 47/II	.... 7 to 7½"	..... (CE)	.. ❸	...	$570–650
☐ 47/II	.... 7 to 7½"	..... (CE)	.. ❹	...	$475–570
☐ 47/II	.... 7 to 7½"	..... (CE)	.. ❺	...	$400–420
☐ 47/II	.... 7 to 7½"	..... (CE)	.. ❻	...	$380–400
☐ 47/II	.... 7 to 7½"	..... (OE)	.. ❼	...	$380
☐ 47	...... 5"	.... (CE)	.. ❶	...	$800–900

Current model

HUM 48
Madonna Plaque

This bas-relief plaque was first modeled by master sculptor Reinhold Unger in 1936. Old crown mark pieces are slightly smaller in size. Newer models have hole on back for hanging while older models have two small holes to use for hanging on wall with cord. Sometimes incised 48/2 instead of 48/II and 48/5 instead of 48/V. Also sold in white overglaze finish at one time in Belgium but are now considered extremely rare. Very early models have a flat back while all others have a recessed back. Large size 48/II was listed as "temporarily withdrawn" (TW) from production on 31 December 1984, and the small size 48/0 was "temporarily withdrawn" (TW) from production on 31 December 1989, but may be reinstated at some future date.

☐ 48/0	3¼ × 4¼"	(CE)	❶	$300–350
☐ 48/0	3¼ × 4¼"	(CE)	❷	$150–200
☐ 48/0	3¼ × 4¼"	(CE)	❸	$100–125
☐ 48/0	3¼ × 4¼"	(CE)	❹	$85–100
☐ 48/0	3⅓ × 4¼"	(CE)	❺	$80–85
☐ 48/0	3¼ × 4¼"	(TW)	❻	$75–80
☐ 48	4¾ × 5¾"	(CE)	❶	$600–800
☐ 48/II	4¾ × 5¾"	(CE)	❶	$500–750
☐ 48/II	4¾ × 5¾"	(CE)	❷	$350–500
☐ 48/II	4¾ × 5¾"	(CE)	❸	$175–225
☐ 48/II	4¾ × 5¾"	(CE)	❹	$150–175
☐ 48/II	4¾ × 5¾"	(CE)	❺	$125–135
☐ 48/II	4¾ × 5¾"	(TW)	❻	$120–125
☐ 48/V	8¾ × 10¾"	(CE)	❶	$1500–2000
☐ 48/V	8¾ × 10¾"	(CE)	❷	$1250–1500
☐ 48/V	8¾ × 10¾"	(CE)	❸	$1000–1250

White variation of 48/0

49/I	*49/0*	*49 3/0*

HUM 49
To Market

First modeled by master sculptor Arthur Moeller in 1936. Sometimes called "Brother and Sister" in old catalogues. Small size 49 3/0 never has bottle in basket. Some newly produced figurines in 6¼" size have appeared without a size designator. Only the number 49 is incised on the bottom along with the 5 trademark. This was corrected on later production. Girl is same as HUM 98 "Sister." The large size (49/I) was listed as "temporarily withdrawn" (TW) on 31 December 1984, but may be reinstated at some future date.

☐ 49 3/0 . . . 4" . . . . (CE) . . ❶ . . . $400–550
☐ 49 3/0 . . . 4" . . . . (CE) . . ❷ . . . $250–350
☐ 49 3/0 . . . 4" . . . . (CE) . . ❸ . . . $210–240
☐ 49 3/0 . . . 4" . . . . (CE) . . ❹ . . . $175–210
☐ 49 3/0 . . . 4" . . . . (CE) . . ❺ . . . $145–155
☐ 49 3/0 . . . 4" . . . . (CE) . . ❻ . . . $140–145
☐ 49 3/0 . . . 4" . . . . (OE) . . ❼ . . . $140
☐ 49/0 . . . . . 5 to 5½" . . . . . (CE) . . ❶ . . . $675–900
☐ 49/0 . . . . . 5 to 5½" . . . . . (CE) . . ❷ . . . $400–550
☐ 49/0 . . . . . 5 to 5½" . . . . . (CE) . . ❸ . . . $340–390
☐ 49/0 . . . . . 5 to 5½" . . . . . (CE) . . ❹ . . . $280–340
☐ 49/0 . . . . . 5 to 5½" . . . . . (CE) . . ❺ . . . $235–245
☐ 49/0 . . . . . 5 to 5½" . . . . . (CE) . . ❻ . . . $225–235
☐ 49/0 . . . . . 5 to 5½" . . . . . (OE) . . ❼ . . . $225
☐ 49/I . . . . . 6¼ to 6½" . . . . (CE) . . ❶ . . . $1400–1700
☐ 49/I . . . . . 6¼ to 6½" . . . . (CE) . . ❷ . . . $1200–1400
☐ 49/I . . . . . 6¼ to 6½" . . . . (CE) . . ❸ . . . $500–700
☐ 49/I . . . . . 6¼ to 6¼" . . . . (CE) . . ❹ . . . $450–500
☐ 49/I . . . . . 6¼ to 6¼" . . . . (CE) . . ❺ . . . $425–450
☐ 49/I . . . . . 6¼ to 6¼" . . . . (TW) . . ❻ . . . $400–425
☐ 49 . . . . . . 6¼ to 6½" . . . . (CE) . . ❶ . . . $1400–1700
☐ 49 . . . . . . 6¼ to 6½" . . . . (CE) . . ❷ . . . $1200–1400
☐ 49 . . . . . . 6¼ to 6½" . . . . (CE) . . ❺ . . . $550–650

| 50/I (TM 5) | 50/0 (TM 5) | 50 2/0 (TM 3) |

HUM 50
Volunteers

Originally modeled by master sculptor Reinhold Unger in 1936. Listed as "Playing Soldiers" in old catalogues. Sizes 50/0 and 50/I are difficult to find in older trademarks but were reinstated in 1979 with 5 trademark. The original drawing for this figurine was used by Ars Sacra Herbert Dubler on small note paper bearing a 1943 copyright date. The large size (50/I) was listed as "temporarily withdrawn" (TW) from production on 31 December 1984, but may be reinstated at some future date. The small size (50 2/0) was produced with special commemorative backstamp in limited quantity and was available only through U.S. Military Exchanges; retail price was $150–175.

☐ 50 2/0	4¾ to 5"	(CE)	❷	$390–450
☐ 50 2/0	4¾ to 5"	(CE)	❸	$285–325
☐ 50 2/0	4¾ to 5"	(CE)	❹	$240–285
☐ 50 2/0	4¾ to 5"	(CE)	❺	$200–210
☐ 50 2/0	4¾ to 5"	(CE)	❻	$190–200
☐ 50 2/0	4¾ to 5"	(OE)	❼	$190
☐ 50/0	5½ to 6"	(CE)	❶	$750–1000
☐ 50/0	5½ to 6"	(CE)	❷	$425–600
☐ 50/0	5½ to 6"	(CE)	❸	$375–425
☐ 50/0	5½ to 6"	(CE)	❹	$315–375
☐ 50/0	5½ to 6"	(CE)	❺	$260–275
☐ 50/0	5½ to 6"	(CE)	❻	$250–260
☐ 50/0	5½ to 6"	(OE)	❼	$250
☐ 50/I	6½ to 7"	(CE)	❶	$1000–1300
☐ 50/I	6½ to 7"	(CE)	❷	$650–850
☐ 50/I	6½ to 7"	(CE)	❸	$500–650
☐ 50/I	6½ to 7"	(CE)	❹	$450–500
☐ 50/I	6½ to 7"	(CE)	❺	$425–450
☐ 50/I	6½ to 7"	(TW)	❻	$400–425
☐ 50	7"	(CE)	❶	$1100–1500

51/I (TM 1) *51/0 (TM 1)* *51 2/0 (TM 5)* *50 3/0 (TM 1)*

HUM 51
Village Boy

First modeled by master sculptor Arthur Moeller in 1936. Has been slightly restyled several times through the years. Size 51/0 was restyled by Theo R. Menzenbach in 1960. Some newer models have a 1961 incised copyright date. Called "Country Boy" in old catalogues. Many size variations in the older pieces. Occasionally found in the small size 51 3/0 in crown trademark with yellow tie and blue jacket—value: $750–1000. The large size (51/I) was listed as "temporarily withdrawn" (TW) from production on 31 December 1984, but could possibly be reinstated at some future date.

☐ 51 3/0	4″	(CE)	❶	$300–400
☐ 51 3/0	4″	(CE)	❷	$175–250
☐ 51 3/0	4″	(CE)	❸	$150–175
☐ 51 3/0	4″	(CE)	❹	$125–150
☐ 51 3/0	4″	(CE)	❺	$105–110
☐ 51 3/0	4″	(CE)	❻	$100–105
☐ 51 3/0	4″	(OE)	❼	$100
☐ 51 2/0	5″	(CE)	❶	$325–450
☐ 51 2/0	5″	(CE)	❷	$200–275
☐ 51 2/0	5″	(CE)	❸	$175–200
☐ 51 2/0	5″	(CE)	❹	$145–175
☐ 51 2/0	5″	(CE)	❺	$120–125
☐ 51 2/0	5″	(CE)	❻	$115–120
☐ 51 2/0	5″	(OE)	❼	$115
☐ 51/0	6 to 6¾″	(CE)	❶	$575–750
☐ 51/0	6 to 6¾″	(CE)	❷	$350–450
☐ 51/0	6 to 6¾″	(CE)	❸	$300–340
☐ 51/0	6 to 6¾″	(CE)	❹	$250–300
☐ 51/0	6 to 6¾″	(CE)	❺	$205–215
☐ 51/0	6 to 6¾″	(CE)	❻	$195–205
☐ 51/0	6 to 6¾″	(OE)	❼	$195
☐ 51/I	7¼ to 8″	(CE)	❶	$750–1000
☐ 51/I	7¼ to 8″	(CE)	❷	$400–500
☐ 51/I	7¼ to 8″	(CE)	❸	$300–350
☐ 51/I	7¼ to 8″	(CE)	❹	$275–300
☐ 51/I	7¼ to 8″	(CE)	❺	$250–275
☐ 51/I	7¼ to 8″	(TW)	❻	$225–250
☐ 51	8″	(CE)	❶	$850–1100

Old   52/I   New   Old   52/0   New

HUM 52
Going to Grandma's
Originally modeled in 1936 by master sculptor Reinhold Unger. Called "Little Mothers of the Family" in old catalogues. All large size and older small size figurines were produced with rectangular base. Small size was restyled in the early 1960's and changed to an oval base. The objects protruding from the cone represent candy and sweets rather than flowers. The cone appears empty on the large size models. In 1979 size 52/I was restyled with a new textured finish, an oval base and sweets in the cone. Both the old and new styles are found with 5 trademark. The large size (52/I) was listed as "temporarily withdrawn" (TW) from production on 31 December 1984, but could possibly be reinstated at some future date.

☐ 52/0 . . . . . 4½ to 5" . . . . . (CE) . . ❶ . . . $650–900
☐ 52/0 . . . . . 4½ to 5" . . . . . (CE) . . ❷ . . . $400–550
☐ 52/0 . . . . . 4½ to 5" . . . . . (CE) . . ❸ . . . $350–400
☐ 52/0 . . . . . 4½ to 5" . . . . . (CE) . . ❹ . . . $290–350
☐ 52/0 . . . . . 4½ to 5" . . . . . (CE) . . ❺ . . . $240–250
☐ 52/0 . . . . . 4½ to 5" . . . . . (CE) . . ❻ . . . $230–240
☐ 52/0 . . . . . 4½ to 5" . . . . . (OE) . . ❼ . . . $230
☐ 52/I . . . . . 6 to 6¼" . . . . . (CE) . . ❶ . . . $1200–1500
☐ 52/I . . . . . 6 to 6¼" . . . . . (CE) . . ❷ . . . $700–850
☐ 52/I . . . . . 6 to 6¼" . . . . . (CE) . . ❸ . . . $600–700
☐ 52/I . . . . . 6 to 6¼" . . . . . (CE) . . ❺ . . . $390–725
☐ 52/I . . . . . 6 to 6¼" . . . . . (TW) . . ❻ . . . $360–390
☐ 52 . . . . . . 6¼" . . . . (CE) . . ❶ . . . $1300–1600
☐ 52 . . . . . . 6¼" . . . . (CE) . . ❷ . . . $850–1000

┌─────────── HUM TERM ───────────┐

CURRENT TRADEMARK: Designates the symbol presently being used by the W. Goebel Porzellanfabrik to represent the company's trademark.

└─────────────────────────────────┘

HUM 53
Joyful

First modeled by master sculptor Reinhold Unger in 1936. Many size variations—older pieces usually much larger. Some early crown mark examples have orange dress and blue shoes—value: $750–1000. Listed as "Singing Lesson" in some catalogues. Current models have a brown-colored mandolin. Also called "Banjo Betty" in old 1950 catalogue.

☐ 53	3½ to 4¼"	(CE)	❶	$300–400
☐ 53	3½ to 4¼"	(CE)	❷	$175–250
☐ 53	3½ to 4¼"	(CE)	❸	$150–175
☐ 53	3½ to 4¼"	(CE)	❹	$125–150
☐ 53	3½ to 4¼"	(CE)	❺	$105–110
☐ 53	3½ to 4¼"	(CE)	❻	$100–105
☐ 53	3½ to 4¼"	(OE)	❼	$100

Old bowl style

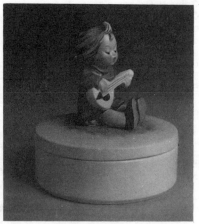

New jar style

HUM III/53
Joyful, Box

Bowl style box first produced in 1936. Jar style first produced and sold in 1964. Model number is found on underside of lid. "M.I. Hummel" signature is found on topside of lid directly behind figure. "Joyful" candy box was "temporarily withdrawn" (TW) from production on 31 December 1989, but may be reinstated at some future date.

☐ III/53	6½"	(CE)	❶	$650–750	
☐ III/53	6½"	(CE)	❷	$525–600	
☐ III/53	6½"	(CE)	❸	$425–500	OLD STYLE
☐ III/53	5¾"	(CE)	❸	$180–200	NEW STYLE
☐ III/53	5¾"	(CE)	❹	$170–180	
☐ III/53	5¾"	(CE)	❺	$160–170	
☐ III/53	5¾"	(TW)	❻	$150–160	

HUM 54
Silent Night, Candleholder
This candleholder was first modeled by master sculptor Reinhold Unger in 1936. There are some color variations in the wings of angel. Early crown mark figurines are usually very light in color. Older pieces have smaller socket for candle. Almost identical to the model used for HUM 31 with the exception of the embossed earring and bare feet. Factory representatives state that a small quantity of HUM 54 were painted with a black child in the standing position — usually wearing shoes and a painted rather than an embossed earring. Silent Night, Candleholder HUM 54 is not currently available in the United States.

☐ 54	3½ × 4¾"	(CE)	**❶**	$750–1000
☐ 54	3½ × 4¾"	(CE)	**❷**	$500–625
☐ 54	3½ × 4¾"	(CE)	**❸**	$375–425
☐ 54	3½ × 4¾"	(CE)	**❹**	$300–375
☐ 54	3½ × 4¾"	(CE)	**❺**	$260–275
☐ 54	3½ × 4¾"	(TW)	**❻**	$250–260
☐ 54	3½ × 4¾"	(CE)	**❷**	$7,500–10,000 (with Black Child)

HUM 55
Saint George
First modeled by master sculptor Reinhold Unger in 1936. Early crown mark models are sometimes found with bright orange-red saddle on horse. Old name: "Knight St. George" or "St. George and Dragon." The original drawing by Sister Hummel for this figurine was reproduced in the 1934 German edition of "Das Hummel Buch," published by Emil Fink of Stuttgart, Germany.

☐ 55	6¾"	(CE)	❶	$2500–3000 (with Red saddle)
☐ 55	6¾"	(CE)	❶	$900–1200
☐ 55	6¾"	(CE)	❷	$500–650
☐ 55	6¾"	(CE)	❸	$400–475
☐ 55	6¾"	(CE)	❹	$350–400
☐ 55	6¾"	(CE)	❺	$290–300
☐ 55	6¾"	(CE)	❻	$280–290
☐ 55	6¾"	(OE)	❼	$280

HUM TERM

DOUBLE CROWN: This term is used to describe the Goebel Company trademark found on some "M.I. Hummel" figurines. On "double crown" pieces the crown trademark is usually found incised and stamped.

56 A   *56 B*

HUM 56 A
Culprits
Originally modeled in 1936 by master sculptor Arthur Moeller but has been restyled in later years. Restyled figurines have an extra branch by boy's feet. Variations in height and size of base. Old name "Apple Thief." Crown mark and early full bee trademarked pieces incised 56 only. Older models have the boy's eyes open while newer version eyes are looking down at dog.

☐ 56	6¼ to 6¾"	(CE) ..	❶ ...	$700−900
☐ 56/A	6¼ to 6¾"	(CE) ..	❷ ...	$425−600
☐ 56/A	6¼ to 6¾"	(CE) ..	❸ ...	$375−425
☐ 56/A	6¼ to 6¾"	(CE) ..	❹ ...	$300−375
☐ 56/A	6¼ to 6¾"	(CE) ..	❺ ...	$255−270
☐ 56/A	6¼ to 6¾"	(CE) ..	❻ ...	$245−255
☐ 56/A	6¼ to 6¾"	(OE) ..	❼ ...	$245

HUM 56 B
Out of Danger
This companion figurine was first modeled by master sculptor Arthur Moeller in March of 1952, therefore will not be found with the crown trademark. Variation in height, and size of base. On older models the girl's eyes are open; on the newer version her eyes are looking down at dog. Full bee models have an extra flower on base.

☐ 56/B	6¼ to 6¾"	(CE) ..	❷ ...	$425−600
☐ 56/B	6¼ to 6¾"	(CE) ..	❸ ...	$375−425
☐ 56/B	6¼ to 6¾"	(CE) ..	❹ ...	$300−375
☐ 56/B	6¼ to 6¾"	(CE) ..	❺ ...	$255−270
☐ 56/B	6¼ to 6¾"	(CE) ..	❻ ...	$245−255
☐ 56/B	6¼ to 6¾"	(OE) ..	❼ ...	$245

57/I   57/0

HUM 57
Chick Girl
First modeled by master sculptor Reinhold Unger in 1936 and later remodeled by master sculptor Gerhard Skrobek in 1964. Small size has two chicks in basket while large size has three chicks. Old name: "Little Chicken Mother" or "The Little Chick Girl." There are three different styles of construction that have been used on bottom of base: quartered, doughnut and plain. A new small size (57 2/0) was issued in 1985 with a suggested retail price of $60. Has an incised 1984 copyright date.

☐ 57 2/0 ... 3″ .... (CE) .. ❻ ... $125–130
☐ 57 2/0 ... 3″ .... (**OE**) .. ❼ ... $125
☐ 57/0 ..... 3½″ .... (CE) .. ❶ ... $425–550
☐ 57/0 ..... 3½″ .... (CE) .. ❷ ... $250–325
☐ 57/0 ..... 3½″ .... (CE) .. ❸ ... $220–250
☐ 57/0 ..... 3½″ .... (CE) .. ❹ ... $180–220
☐ 57/0 ..... 3½″ .... (CE) .. ❺ ... $150–160
☐ 57/0 ..... 3½″ .... (CE) .. ❻ ... $145–150
☐ 57/0 ..... 3½″ .... (**OE**) .. ❼ ... $145
☐ 57/I ..... 4¼″ .... (CE) .. ❶ ... $600–800
☐ 57/I ..... 4¼″ .... (CE) .. ❷ ... $375–500
☐ 57/I ..... 4¼″ .... (CE) .. ❸ ... $330–375
☐ 57/I ..... 4¼″ .... (CE) .. ❹ ... $275–330
☐ 57/I ..... 4¼″ .... (CE) .. ❺ ... $230–240
☐ 57/I ..... 4¼″ .... (CE) .. ❻ ... $220–230
☐ 57/I ..... 4¼″ .... (**OE**) .. ❼ ... $220
☐ 57 ...... 4 to 4⅜″ ..... (CE) .. ❶ ... $650–850
☐ 57 ...... 4 to 4⅜″ ..... (CE) .. ❷ ... $400–550

Old bowl style   *New jar style*

HUM III/57 Chick Girl, Box
Bowl style first produced in 1936. Jar style first produced and sold in 1964. Sometimes found with the incised number III 57/0 on the bowl style pieces. Model number is found on underside of lid. "M.I.Hummel" signature is found on topside of lid directly behind figure. "Chick Girl" candy box was "temporarily withdrawn" (TW) from production on 31 December 1989, but may be reinstated at some future date.

☐ III/57 .... 6 to 6¼″ ..... (CE) .. ❶ ... $650–750
☐ III/57 .... 6 to 6¼″ ..... (CE) .. ❷ ... $525–600
☐ III/57 .... 6 to 6¼″ ..... (CE) .. ❸ ... $425–500 OLD STYLE
☐ III/57 .... 5″ .... (CE) .. ❸ ... $180–200 NEW STYLE
☐ III/57 .... 5″ .... (CE) .. ❹ ... $170–180
☐ III/57 .... 5″ .... (CE) .. ❺ ... $160–170
☐ III/57 .... 5″ .... (TW) .. ❻ ... $150–160

HUM 58
Playmates

Originally modeled by master sculptor Reinhold Unger in 1936 and later restyled by master sculptor Gerhard Skrobek in 1964. Some size and color variations between old and new figurines. Both ears of rabbit pointing up on large size 58/I. Ears are separated on small size 58/0. Old name: "Just Friends." Three different styles of construction on bottom of base: quartered, doughnut and plain. A new small size (58 2/0) "Playmates" was issued in 1986 with a suggested retail price of $68. Has an incised 1984 copyright date.

58/I   58/0

☐ 58 2/0	. . . 3½"	. . . .	(CE)	. . ❻	. . $125–130
☐ 58 2/0	. . . 3½"	. . . .	**(OE)**	. . ❼	. . $125
☐ 58/0	. . . . 4"	. . . .	(CE)	. . ❶	. . $425–550
☐ 58/0	. . . . 4"	. . . .	(CE)	. . ❷	. . $250–325
☐ 58/0	. . . . 4"	. . . .	(CE)	. . ❸	. . $220–250
☐ 58/0	. . . . 4"	. . . .	(CE)	. . ❹	. . $180–220
☐ 58/0	. . . . 4"	. . . .	(CE)	. . ❺	. . $150–160
☐ 58/0	. . . . 4"	. . . .	(CE)	. . ❻	. . $145–150
☐ 58/0	. . . . 4"	. . . .	**(OE)**	. . ❼	. . $145
☐ 58/I	. . . . 4¼"	. . . .	(CE)	. . ❶	. . $600–800
☐ 58/I	. . . . 4¼"	. . . .	(CE)	. . ❷	. . $375–500
☐ 58/I	. . . . 4¼"	. . . .	(CE)	. . ❸	. . $330–375
☐ 58/I	. . . . 4¼"	. . . .	(CE)	. . ❹	. . $275–330
☐ 58/I	. . . . 4¼"	. . . .	(CE)	. . ❺	. . $230–240
☐ 58/I	. . . . 4¼"	. . . .	(CE)	. . ❻	. . $220–230
☐ 58/I	. . . . 4¼"	. . . .	**(OE)**	. . ❼	. . $220
☐ 58	. . . . . . 4 to 4½"	. . . . .	(CE)	. . ❶	. . $650–850
☐ 58	. . . . . . 4 to 4½"	. . . . .	(CE)	. . ❷	. . $400–550

Old bowl style   *New jar style*

HUM III/58 Playmates, Box

Bowl style first produced in 1936. Jar style first produced and sold in 1964. Sometimes found with the incised number III 58/0 on the old bowl style pieces. Model number is found on underside of lid. "M.I.Hummel" signature is found on topside of lid directly behind figure. "Playmates" candy box was "temporarily withdrawn" (TW) from production on 31 December 1989, but may be reinstated at some future date.

☐ III/58	. . . . 6¾"	. . . .	(CE)	. . ❶	. . $650–750
☐ III/58	. . . . 6¾"	. . . .	(CE)	. . ❷	. . $525–600
☐ III/58	. . . . 6¾"	. . . .	(CE)	. . ❸	. . $425–500 OLD STYLE
☐ III/58	. . . . 5½"	. . . .	(CE)	. . ❸	. . $180–200 NEW STYLE
☐ III/58	. . . . 5½"	. . . .	(CE)	. . ❹	. . $170–180
☐ III/58	. . . . 5½"	. . . .	(CE)	. . ❺	. . $160–170
☐ III/58	. . . . 5½"	. . . .	(TW)	. . ❻	. . $150–160

| Wooden poles | Plastic poles | Metal poles |

HUM 59
Skier

First modeled by master sculptor Reinhold Unger in 1936. Older models were sold with wooden poles and fiber disks; newer models with plastic poles for a short period of time. The metal poles have been used since 1970. Many size variations; the full bee pieces usually the largest. Original wooden poles are reflected in the prices of the older models. Original plastic poles are the most difficult to locate and some avid collectors would probably pay a premium for them.

☐ 59 . . . . . . 5 to 6″ . . . . (CE) . . ❶ . . . $550–750
☐ 59 . . . . . . 5 to 6″ . . . . (CE) . . ❷ . . . $325–450
☐ 59 . . . . . . 5 to 6″ . . . . (CE) . . ❸ . . . $280–325
☐ 59 . . . . . . 5 to 6″ . . . . (CE) . . ❹ . . . $230–280
☐ 59 . . . . . . 5 to 6″ . . . . (CE) . . ❺ . . . $195–200
☐ 59 . . . . . . 5 to 6″ . . . . (CE) . . ❻ . . . $185–195
☐ 59 . . . . . . 5 to 6″ . . . . (OE) . . ❼ . . . $185

```
────────── HUM TERM ──────────

MODEL: This term most often refers to a
particular "M.I. Hummel" figurine, plate,
bell, or other item in the line. When not
used in reference to a specific motif, the
word model also can refer to the sculptor's
working model from which the figurines are
made.
```

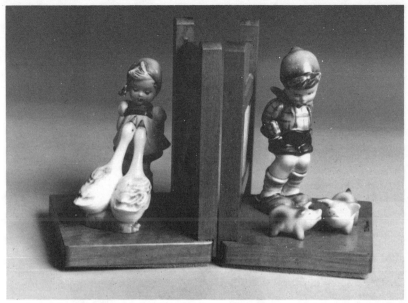

60/B   60/A

HUM 60 A Farm Boy
HUM 60 B Goose Girl, Bookends

First produced in September 1936. Trademarks usually stamped on wood base rather than on figurine. The number 60 A is found incised on bottom of feet of "Farm Boy" in crown and full bee trademarks. Have been unable to find a similar number on any "Goose Girls" that have been separated from wooden base. See HUM 148 and HUM 149 for additional information. This pair of bookends was listed as "temporarily withdrawn" (TW) from production on 31 December 1984, but may be reinstated at some future date. Note: 60/A and 60/B have "Hummel" incised on back of slippers on some TM 1 and TM 2 examples.

☐ 60 A&B . . 4¾" . . . . (CE) . . ❶ . . . $900–1200
☐ 60 A&B . . 4¾" . . . . (CE) . . ❷ . . . $600–900
☐ 60 A&B . . 4¾" . . . . (CE) . . ❸ . . . $375–450
☐ 60 A&B . . 4¾" . . . . (CE) . . ❹ . . . $375–450
☐ 60 A&B . . 4¾" . . . . (CE) . . ❺ . . . $350–375
☐ 60 A&B . . 4¾" . . . . (TW) . . ❻ . . . $350–375

HUM 61 A Playmates
HUM 61 B Chick Girl, Bookends
First produced in November 1936. Trademarks stamped on wood base rather than on figurine. This pair of bookends was listed as "temporarily withdrawn" (TW) on 31 December 1984, but may be reinstated at some future date.

☐ 61 A&B . .	4"	. . . .	(CE)	. . ❶ . . .	$900–1200
☐ 61 A&B . .	4"	. . . .	(CE)	. . ❷ . . .	$600–900
☐ 61 A&B . .	4"	. . . .	(CE)	. . ❸ . . .	$375–450
☐ 61 A&B . .	4"	. . . .	(CE)	. . ❹ . . .	$375–450
☐ 61 A&B . .	4"	. . . .	(CE)	. . ❺ . . .	$350–375
☐ 61 A&B . .	4"	. . . .	(TW)	. . ❻ . . .	$350–375

HUM 62
Happy Pastime, Ashtray
Slight difference in construction of ashtray on older models. Crown mark piece has "M.I. Hummel" signature on back of ashtray while newer models have signature on back of girl. First modeled by master sculptor Arthur Moeller in 1936. "Happy Pastime" ashtray was "temporarily withdrawn" (TW) from production on 31 December 1989, but may be reinstated at some future date.

☐ 62	. . . . . .	3½ × 6¼"	. . . . .	(CE)	. . ❶ . . . $400–600
☐ 62	. . . . . .	3½ × 6¼"	. . . . .	(CE)	. . ❷ . . . $250–300
☐ 62	. . . . . .	3½ × 6¼"	. . . . .	(CE)	. . ❸ . . . $180–200
☐ 62	. . . . . .	3½ × 6¼"	. . . . .	(CE)	. . ❹ . . . $150–180
☐ 62	. . . . . .	3½ × 6¼"	. . . . .	(CE)	. . ❺ . . . $140–150
☐ 62	. . . . . .	3½ × 6¼"	. . . . .	(TW)	. . ❻ . . . $130–140

HUM 63
Singing Lesson

First modeled by master sculptor Arthur Moeller in 1937. Some variations in size between old and new models. Sometimes a slight variation in tilt of boy's head and position of hand. Old name: "Duet" or "Critic." "Singing Lesson" is the motif used on the 1979 Annual Plate, HUM 272.

☐ 63	2¾ to 3″	(CE)	❶	$300–400
☐ 63	2¾ to 3″	(CE)	❷	$175–250
☐ 63	2¾ to 3″	(CE)	❸	$150–175
☐ 63	2¾ to 3″	(CE)	❹	$125–150
☐ 63	2¾ to 3″	(CE)	❺	$105–110
☐ 63	2¾ to 3″	(CE)	❻	$100–105
☐ 63	2¾ to 3″	(OE)	❼	$100

Old bowl style

New jar style

HUM III/63
Singing Lesson, Box

Bowl style first produced in 1937. Jar style first produced and sold in 1964. Old name: "Duet" box. Model number is found on underside of lid. "M.I. Hummel" signature is found on topside of lid directly behind figure. "Singing Lesson" candy box was "temporarily withdrawn" (TW) from production on 31 December 1989, but may be reinstated at some future date.

☐ III/63	5¾″	(CE)	❶	$650–750	
☐ III/63	5¾″	(CE)	❷	$525–600	
☐ III/63	5¾″	(CE)	❸	$425–500	OLD STYLE
☐ III/63	4¾″	(CE)	❸	$180–200	NEW STYLE
☐ III/63	4¾″	(CE)	❹	$170–180	
☐ III/63	4¾″	(CE)	❺	$160–170	
☐ III/63	4¾″	(TW)	❻	$150–160	

Old *New*

HUM 64
Shepherd's Boy

First modeled by master sculptor Arthur Moeller in 1937. Restyled with the new textured finish in the late 1970's by master sculptor Gerhard Skrobek. Many size variations—note photo. Old name: "The Good Shepherd." "Shepherd's Boy" sold for $9.00 on old 1955 price list.

☐ 64 ...... 5½ to 6¼" .... (CE) .. ❶ ... $600–750
☐ 64 ...... 5½ to 6¼" .... (CE) .. ❷ ... $325–450
☐ 64 ...... 5½ to 6¼" .... (CE) .. ❸ ... $275–300
☐ 64 ...... 5½ to 6¼" .... (CE) .. ❹ ... $230–275
☐ 64 ...... 5½ to 6¼" .... (CE) .. ❺ ... $190–200
☐ 64 ...... 5½ to 6¼" .... (CE) .. ❻ ... $185–190
☐ 64 ...... 5½ to 6¼" .... (OE) .. ❼ ... $185

HUM TERM

DOUGHNUT BASE: A term used to describe the raised circular support on the underside of a figurine. Many figurine bases with a circle inside the regular circular base gave rise to the term, but has now been used to describe many bases with the circular support on the underside.

| 65 | 65/I | 65/0 |

HUM 65
Farewell

First modeled by master sculptor Arthur Moeller in 1937. Restyled in 1964 by master sculptor Gerhard Skrobek. The small size (65/0) was modeled in 1955 by Gerhard Skrobek. 65/0 is extremely rare since only a few sample pieces were produced. Called "So Long" in some old catalogues. Many size variations. Currently produced in only one size with incised number 65 only. A new variation of "Farewell" was created by error in the early 1980's. During the assembly process, the basket was improperly placed, giving the appearance that part of the handle was missing. This "missing handle" variation now commands a premium of $50 to $100.

☐ 65	4¾″	(CE)	❺	$230–240
☐ 65	4¾″	(CE)	❻	$220–230
☐ 65	4¾″	(OE)	❼	$220
☐ 65/0	4″	(CE)	❷	$6000–7000
☐ 65/0	3¾″	(CE)	❸	$5000–6000
☐ 65/I	4½ to 4⅞″	(CE)	❶	$650–900
☐ 65/I	4½ to 4⅞″	(CE)	❷	$385–500
☐ 65/I	4½ to 4⅞″	(CE)	❸	$330–385
☐ 65/I	4½ to 4⅞″	(CE)	❹	$275–330
☐ 65/I	4½ to 4⅞″	(CE)	❺	$230–240
☐ 65	4¾ to 5″	(CE)	❶	$650–900
☐ 65	4¾ to 5″	(CE)	❷	$385–500

HUM TERM

OPEN EDITION: Pieces currently in W. Goebel's production program.

Double crown   *Full bee*

HUM 66
Farm Boy
Many size variations. Old name: "Three Pals " or "Happy-Go-Lucky Fellow." Originally modeled in 1937 by master sculptor Arthur Moeller. Also called "Little Pig-Driver" in some old catalogues. "Farm Boy" sold for $9.00 on old 1955 price list.

☐ 66	5 to 5¾"	(CE)	❶	$575–750
☐ 66	5 to 5¾"	(CE)	❷	$350–475
☐ 66	5 to 5¾"	(CE)	❸	$290–330
☐ 66	5 to 5¾"	(CE)	❹	$240–290
☐ 66	5 to 5¾"	(CE)	❺	$200–210
☐ 66	5 to 5¾"	(CE)	❻	$190–200
☐ 66	5 to 5¾"	(OE)	❼	$190

```
                        HUM TERM

    DECIMAL POINT: This incised "period" or
    dot was used in a somewhat random fash-
    ion by the W. Goebel Porzellanfabrik over
    the years. The decimal point is and was
    primarily used to reduce confusion in read-
    ing the incised numbers on the underside
    of the figurines. Example: 66. helps one
    realize that the designation is sixty-six and
    not ninety-nine.
```

Old   *New*

HUM 67
Doll Mother

First modeled by master sculptor Arthur Moeller in 1937 but has been restyled in recent years. Slight difference in hair ribbon on girl. Old name: "Little Doll Mother" or "Little Mother of Dolls" in some catalogues. "Doll Mother" sold for $8.00 on old 1955 price list.

☐ 67 ...... 4¼ to 4¾" .... (CE) .. ❶ ... $575–750
☐ 67 ...... 4¼ to 4¾" .... (CE) .. ❷ ... $350–475
☐ 67 ...... 4¼ to 4¾" .... (CE) .. ❸ ... $290–330
☐ 67 ...... 4¼ to 4¾" .... (CE) .. ❹ ... $240–290
☐ 67 ...... 4¼ to 4¾" .... (CE) .. ❺ ... $200–210
☐ 67 ...... 4¼ to 4¾" .... (CE) .. ❻ ... $190–200
☐ 67 ...... 4¼ to 4¾" .... (OE) .. ❼ ... $190

HUM TERM

MOLD GROWTH: In the earlier days of figurine production the working molds were made of plaster of paris. As these molds were used, the various molded parts became larger due to the repeated usage. With modern technology at the Goebel factory and the use of acrylic resin molds, this problem has been eliminated and today the collector finds very few size differences within a given size designation.

68 2/0   68/0   68 Crown   68 Full bee   68 Double crown

HUM 68
Lost Sheep

Originally modeled by master sculptor Arthur Moeller in 1937 and later restyled by a combination of several modelers. Many size and color variations. Older models have dark brown trousers. Similar to HUM 64 "Shepherd's Boy" except for single lamb and different colors. "Lost Sheep" sold for $7.50 on old 1955 price list. Both sizes of "Lost Sheep" will be permanently retired by Goebel in the fall of 1992 and will not be produced again.

☐ 68 2/0	4¼ to 4½"	(CE)	❷	$225–300
☐ 68 2/0	4¼ to 4½"	(CE)	❸	$190–210
☐ 68 2/0	4¼ to 4½"	(CE)	❹	$160–190
☐ 68 2/0	4¼ to 4½"	(CE)	❺	$130–135
☐ 68 2/0	4¼ to 4½"	(CE)	❻	$125–130
☐ 68 2/0	4¼ to 4½"	(OE)	❼	$125
☐ 68/0	5½"	(CE)	❷	$325–425
☐ 68/0	5½"	(CE)	❸	$270–320
☐ 68/0	5½"	(CE)	❹	$225–270
☐ 68/0	5½"	(CE)	❺	$190–200
☐ 68/0	5½"	(CE)	❻	$180–190
☐ 68/0	5½"	(OE)	❼	$180
☐ 68	5½ to 6½"	(CE)	❶	$550–700
☐ 68	5½ to 6½"	(CE)	❷	$350–450
☐ 68	5½ to 6½"	(CE)	❸	$300–350

HUM 69
Happy Pastime

First modeled by master sculptor Arthur Moeller in 1937. Very little difference between old and new models. Older models slightly larger. Called "Knitter" in old catalogues. The "M.I. Hummel" signature is very faint or difficult to see on some old models. Occasionally found with a stamped "M. I. Hummel" signature on the bottom. Sometimes found without dots on the head scarf. "Happy Pastime" is the motif used on the 1978 Annual Plate, Hum 271.

☐ 69	3½"	(CE)	❶	$400–550
☐ 69	3½"	(CE)	❷	$250–325
☐ 69	3½"	(CE)	❸	$200–230
☐ 69	3½"	(CE)	❹	$170–200
☐ 69	3½"	(CE)	❺	$140–150
☐ 69	3½"	(CE)	❻	$135–140
☐ 69	3½"	(OE)	❼	$135

Old bowl style

New jar style

HUM III/69
Happy Pastime, Box

Bowl style first produced in 1937. Jar style first produced and sold in 1964. Model number is found on underside of lid. "M.I.Hummel" signature is found on topside of lid directly behind figure. "Happy Pastime" candy box was "temporarily withdrawn"(TW) from production on 31 December 1989, but may be reinstated at some future date.

☐ III/69	6½"	(CE)	❶	$650–750
☐ III/69	6½"	(CE)	❷	$525–600
☐ III/69	6½"	(CE)	❸	$425–500 OLD STYLE
☐ III/69	5¼"	(CE)	❸	$180–200 NEW STYLE
☐ III/69	5¼"	(CE)	❹	$170–180
☐ III/69	5¼"	(CE)	❺	$160–170
☐ III/69	5¼"	(TW)	❻	$150–160

HUM 70
Holy Child

Factory records indicate this was originally modeled in 1937 by a combination of modelers. Has been restyled in later years with newer models having the textured finish on gown and robe. Many size variations. Also listed as "Child Jesus" in some old catalogues. "Holy Child" was "temporarily withdrawn" (TW) from production on 31 December 1990, but may be reinstated at some future date.

☐ 70	6¾ to 7½"	(CE)	❶	$600–700
☐ 70	6¾ to 7½"	(CE)	❷	$275–375
☐ 70	6¾ to 7½"	(CE)	❸	$225–270
☐ 70	6¾ to 7½"	(CE)	❹	$190–225
☐ 70	6¾ to 7½"	(CE)	❺	$160–170
☐ 70	6¾ to 7½"	(TW)	❻	$150–160

HUM TERM

U.S. ZONE: The words "U.S. ZONE—GERMANY" were used on figurines produced by the W. Goebel Porzellanfabrik after W.W. II when the country of Germany was yet undivided and the Goebel Factory was part of the U.S. Zone. The U.S. ZONE marking was used either alone or with the Crown trademark from 1946 until 1948. Once the country was divided into East and West, the W. Goebel Porzellanfabrik used the Western or West designation.

| 71 (TM 2) | 71/I (TM 6) | 71 2/0 (TM 6) |

HUM 71
Stormy Weather
Originally modeled by master sculptor Reinhold Unger in 1937. Has been restyled several times through the years. Many size variations. Full bee models are usually the largest size. Old name "Under One Roof." Slight difference between old and new models other than size. Several variations in structure of bottom of base design. This motif was used for the first Anniversary Plate, HUM 280 in 1975. A new small size (71 2/0) was issued in the spring of 1985 at a suggested retail price of $120. The large size has now been renumbered 71/1. There are two variations of the new small size. The first production appeared with the inside of the umbrella hand painted with obvious brush strokes while later production has the inside painted by air brush. These early pieces usually sell for $500–750. "Stormy Weather" sold for $16.50 on old 1955 price list.

☐ 71 2/0	. . . 4½" to 5"	. . . . . (CE)	. . ❻ . . .	$250–260
☐ 71 2/0	. . . 4½" to 5"	. . . . . (OE)	. . ❼ . . .	$250
☐ 71	. . . . . . 6 to 7"	. . . . (CE)	. . ❶ . . .	$1000–1200
☐ 71	. . . . . . 6 to 7"	. . . . (CE)	. . ❷ . . .	$700–850
☐ 71	. . . . . . 6 to 7"	. . . . (CE)	. . ❸ . . .	$450–600
☐ 71	. . . . . . 6 to 6¼"	. . . . . (CE)	. . ❹ . . .	$425–450
☐ 71	. . . . . . 6 to 6¼"	. . . . . (CE)	. . ❺ . . .	$400–425
☐ 71	. . . . . . 6 to 6¼"	. . . . . (CE)	. . ❻ . . .	$390–400
☐ 71/I	. . . . . 6 to 6¼"	. . . . . (CE)	. . ❻ . . .	$380–390
☐ 71/I	. . . . . 6 to 6¼"	. . . . . (OE)	. . ❼ . . .	$380

NOTE: See RARE VARIATIONS in back of book for an unusual variation of this figurine.

(TM 1)	*(TM 3)*	*(TM 6)*

HUM 72
Spring Cheer

First modeled in 1937 by master sculptor Reinhold Unger. Older models have yellow dress and no flowers in right hand. Restyled in 1965 by master sculptor Gerhard Skrobek who added flowers to right hand and changed color of dress to dark green. Both mold variations can be found with (TM3) stylized trademark. Older style can also be found with dark green dress. This variation would be considered rare and would bring a premium usually anywhere from $1,500 to $2,000. Old name:"Spring Flowers". Crown mark pieces have a flower on reverse side. Later production pieces omitted this flower. "Spring Cheer" was listed as "temporarily withdrawn" (TW) from production on 31 December 1984, but may be reinstated at some future date. The suggested retail price for "Spring Cheer" on the 1984 price list was $55.

☐ 72 ...... 5 to 5½" ..... (CE) .. ❶ ... $450–600
☐ 72 ...... 5 to 5½" ..... (CE) .. ❷ ... $300–350
☐ 72 ...... 5 to 5½" ..... (CE) .. ❸ ... $275–300
☐ 72 ...... 5 to 5½" ..... (CE) .. ❹ ... $225–275
☐ 72 ...... 5 to 5½" ..... (CE) .. ❺ ... $200–225
☐ 72 ...... 5 to 5½" ..... (TW) .. ❻ ... $150–200

HUM TERM

CURRENT PRODUCTION: The term used to describe those items currently being produced by the W. Goebel Porzellanfabrik of Roedental, West Germany.

HUM 73
Little Helper
Very little variation between old and new pieces. Older figurines are usually slightly larger. Old name: "Diligent Betsy" or "The Little Sister." Originally modeled in 1937 by master sculptor Reinhold Unger. "Little Helper" sold for $4.00 on old 1955 price list.

☐ 73 . . . . . . 4¼ to 4½" . . . . (CE) . . ❶ . . . $300–400
☐ 73 . . . . . . 4¼ to 4½" . . . . (CE) . . ❷ . . . $175–250
☐ 73 . . . . . . 4¼ to 4½" . . . . (CE) . . ❸ . . . $150–175
☐ 73 . . . . . . 4¼ to 4½" . . . . (CE) . . ❹ . . . $125–150
☐ 73 . . . . . . 4¼ to 4½" . . . . (CE) . . ❺ . . . $105–110
☐ 73 . . . . . . 4¼ to 4½" . . . . (CE) . . ❻ . . . $100–105
☐ 73 . . . . . . 4¼ to 4½" . . . . (OE) . . ❼ . . . $100

HUM TERM

REINSTATED: The term used to indicate that a figurine has been placed back into production by the W. Goebel Porzellanfabrik after some prior classification of non-production.

| Crown | Crown | Full Bee | Stylized |

HUM 74
Little Gardener

Originally modeled by master sculptor Reinhold Unger in 1937 but has undergone many changes through the years. Older models have an oval base. Restyled in the early 1960's and changed to a round base and smaller flower. Many color variations on girl's apron. "Little Gardener" sold for $4.00 on old 1955 price list. Used as a *demonstration promotion* piece for 1992 — sold only at stores having a Goebel "M. I. Hummel" promotion in 1992. Not sold at other stores for two years.

☐ 74 ...... 4 to 4½" ..... (CE) .. ❶ ... $300–400
☐ 74 ...... 4 to 4½" ..... (CE) .. ❷ ... $175–250
☐ 74 ...... 4 to 4½" ..... (CE) .. ❸ ... $150–175
☐ 74 ...... 4 to 4½" ..... (CE) .. ❹ ... $125–150
☐ 74 ...... 4 to 4½" ..... (CE) .. ❺ ... $105–110
☐ 74 ...... 4 to 4½" ..... (CE) .. ❻ ... $100–105
☐ 74 ...... 4 to 4½" ..... (OE) .. ❼ ... $100

HUM TERM

THREE LINE TRADEMARK: The symbol used by the W. Goebel Porzellanfabrik from 1964 until 1972 as their factory trademark. The name for this trademark was adopted to recognize that the V and bee was accompanied by three lines of print to the right of the V. Also known as TM 4.

HUM 75
Holy Water Font, White Angel

First modeled by master sculptor Reinhold Unger in 1937. Newer models have hole for hanging font. Older models provide a hole only on back. Variation in construction of bowl. Also called "Angelic Prayer" in some catalogues.

☐ 75	3¼ to 4½"	(CE)	❶	$200–250
☐ 75	3¼ to 4½"	(CE)	❷	$100–125
☐ 75	3¼ to 4½"	(CE)	❸	$50–60
☐ 75	3¼ to 4½"	(CE)	❹	$45–50
☐ 75	3¼ to 4½"	(CE)	❺	$37–40
☐ 75	3¼ to 4½"	(CE)	❻	$35–37
☐ 75	3¼ to 4½"	(OE)	❼	$35

HUM 76 A
Doll Mother

HUM 76 B
Prayer Before Battle, Bookends
No known examples other than this half of set which was located in Goebel factory. Originally modeled by master sculptor Arthur Moeller. Factory note indicates: "Not produced after 28 February 1938."

☐ 76	A & B	(CE)	❶	$10,000–15,000

HUM 77
Holy Water Font, Cross With Doves
First modeled by master sculptor Reinhold Unger in 1937 but according to factory information was made as samples only and never in production. Listed as a closed edition on 21 October 1937. As of this date, eight examples are known to exist. One is now in the Robert L. Miller Collection, thanks to a collector from California.

☐ 77 . . . . . . 1¾ × 6¼" . . . (CN) $5,000–10,000

Old style   *New style*

HUM 78
Blessed Child (Infant of Krumbad)
In 1984 the official name was changed from "Infant of Krumbad" to the "Blessed Child." It was also listed as "In the Crib" in an old 1950 catalogue. This figurine has been produced in three different finishes. Produced in brownish bisque finish (U.S. Market); full color and white overglaze (various other countries), sometimes found in Belgium. Note variations in older models. First modeled by master sculptor Erich Lautensack in 1937. (Lautensack died during the Second World War.) Restyled by master sculptor Gerhard Skrobek in 1965. The two small holes on the back are designed to hold a wire halo. Full color and white overglaze pieces command varied premiums. Also found with the incised number 78/6 (arabic) in "full bee" (TM 2) trademark.

Factory records for Blessed Child indicate the following:

Originally modeled by:			Restyled:	
78/0	Lautensack . .	1937 . .	Skrobek . . .	1962 (discontinued 1983)
78/I	Skrobek	1964 . .	Skrobek . . .	1965
78/II	Skrobek	1964 . .	Skrobek . . .	1965
78/III	Lautensack . .	1937 . .	Skrobek . . .	1965
78/V	Skrobek	1963 . .	Skrobek . . .	1965
78/VI or 78/6 .	Lautensack . .	1937 . .	Skrobek . . .	1965
78/VIII	Lautensack . .	1937 . .	Skrobek . . .	1965

B.C.W . . . .

☐☐☐	78/0	.. 2¼″	.... (CE)	.. ❷	... $200–300
☐☐☐	78/0	.. 2¼″	.... (CE)	.. ❸	... $150–200
☐☐☐	78/I	... 2½″	.... (CE)	.. ❸	... $40–50
☐☐☐	78/I	... 2½″	.... (CE)	.. ❹	... $35–40
☐☐☐	78/I	... 2½″	.... (CE)	.. ❺	... $30–35
☐☐☐	78/I	... 2½″	.... (TW)	.. ❻	... $30–35
☐☐☐	78/II	... 3½″	.... (CE)	.. ❸	... $50–60
☐☐☐	78/II	... 3½″	.... (CE)	.. ❹	... $45–50
☐☐☐	78/II	... 3½″	.... (CE)	.. ❺	... $40–45
☐☐☐	78/II	... 3½″	.... (TW)	.. ❻	... $35–40
☐☐☐	78/III	.. 4½ to 5¼″	.... (CE)	.. ❶	... $350–400
☐☐☐	78/III	.. 4½ to 5¼″	.... (CE)	.. ❷	... $250–350
☐☐☐	78/III	.. 4½ to 5¼″	.... (CE)	.. ❸	... $60–70
☐☐☐	78/III	.. 4½ to 5¼″	.... (CE)	.. ❹	... $55–60
☐☐☐	78/III	.. 4½ to 5¼″	.... (CE)	.. ❺	... $50–55
☐☐☐	78/III	.. 4½ to 5¼″	.... (TW)	.. ❻	... $45–50
☐☐☐	78/V	.. 7½ to 7¾″	.... (CE)	.. ❸	... $125–150
☐☐☐	78/V	.. 7½ to 7¾″	.... (CE)	.. ❹	... $100–125
☐☐☐	78/V	.. 7½ to 7¾″	.... (CE)	.. ❺	... $90–100
☐☐☐	78/V	.. 7½ to 7¾″	.... (TW)	.. ❻	... $80–90
☐☐☐	78/VI	. 10 to 11¼″	.... (CE)	.. ❶	... $600–850
☐☐☐	78/VI	. 10 to 11¼″	.... (CE)	.. ❷	... $400–600
☐☐☐	78/VI	. 10 to 11¼″	.... (CE)	.. ❸	... $200–250
☐☐☐	78/VI	. 10 to 11¼″	.... (CE)	.. ❹	... $200–250
☐☐☐	78/VI	. 10 to 11¼″	.... (CE)	.. ❺	... $150–175
☐☐☐	78/VI	. 10 to 11¼″	.... (TW)	.. ❻	... $150–175
☐☐☐	78/VIII	. 13¼ to 14¼″	.. (CE)	.. ❶	... $750–1000
☐☐☐	78/VIII	. 13¼ to 14¼″	.. (CE)	.. ❷	... $500–750
☐☐☐	78/VIII	. 13¼ to 14¼″	.. (CE)	.. ❸	... $350–400
☐☐☐	78/VIII	. 13¼ to 14¼″	.. (CE)	.. ❹	... $350–400
☐☐☐	78/VIII	. 13¼ to 14¼″	.. (CE)	.. ❺	... $300–325
☐☐☐	78/VIII	. 13¼ to 14¼″	.. (TW)	.. ❻	... $300–325
☐☐☐	78/II½	. 4¼″	.... (CE)	.. ❻	... $50–100
☐☐☐	78/II½	. 4¼″	.... (OE)	.. ❼	... $35–50

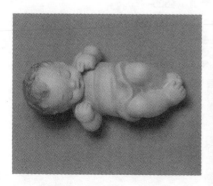 

A new small size "Blessed Child" is now being produced for the exclusive sale of the Siessen Convent in Germany. It has an incised 78/II½ model number, incised 1987 copyright date and the current (TM 6) trademark. This is only the second time a "Hummel" figurine has been produced using the "½" size designator. (The other figurine is "Heavenly Angel" HUM 21/0½.) This new "Blessed Child" reverts back to the old original style modeled by Lautensack rather than the newer Skrobek design. The price at the Siessen Convent was DM 48 or approximately $31 in U.S. currency in 1991.

New   Old

HUM 79
Globe Trotter
Originally modeled by master sculptor Arthur Moeller in 1937. Remodeled in 1955 at which time the basket weave was changed from a double weave to a single weave. Crown mark pieces usually have a tan-colored handle on umbrella while others are black. Some variation of color on the inside of basket. Some old catalogues list name as "Happy Traveller." Some older models have dark green hat. This motif is used on the 1973 Annual Plate, HUM 266. "Globe Trotter" was permanently retired by Goebel in the fall of 1991 and will not be produced again. The 1991 price list shows a price of $170, the last year it was sold on the primary market.

☐ 79	5 to 5¼"	(CE)	❶	$550–725
☐ 79	5 to 5½"	(CE)	❷	$325–450
☐ 79	5 to 5¼"	(CE)	❸	$275–325
☐ 79	5 to 5¼"	(CE)	❹	$225–275
☐ 79	5 to 5¼"	(CE)	❺	$190–200
☐ 79	5 to 5¼"	(CE)	❻	$180–190
☐ 79	5 to 5¼"	(CE)	❼	$170–180

New   Old

HUM 80
Little Scholar

Original model made by master sculptor Arthur Moeller in 1937. Some color variations. Old models have brown shoes. The cone in boy's right arm is called Schultute or Zuckertute, a paper cone containing school supplies and other goodies, which German parents traditionally give their children on the first day of school. "Little Scholar" sold for $7.00 on old 1955 price list.

☐ 80	5¼ to 5¾	(CE)	❶	$550–700
☐ 80	5¼ to 5¾	(CE)	❷	$325–450
☐ 80	5¼ to 5¾	(CE)	❸	$275–315
☐ 80	5¼ to 5¾	(CE)	❹	$225–275
☐ 80	5¼ to 5¾	(CE)	❺	$190–200
☐ 80	5¼ to 5¾	(CE)	❻	$180–190
☐ 80	5¼ to 5¾	(OE)	❼	$180

HUM TERM

SAMPLE MODEL: Generally a figurine that was made as a sample only and not approved by the Siessen Convent for production. Sample models (in the true sense of the term) are extremely rare items and command a premium price on the secondary market.

| 81 | 81/0 | 81 2/0 | 81 2/0 |

HUM 81
School Girl

Old name: "Primer Girl." Original model made by master sculptor Arthur Moeller in 1937. Many size variations as well as color variations. Size 81 2/0 basket filled; all others, baskets empty. Old catalogue listing of 7¾″ is in error. This motif is used on the 1980 Annual Plate, HUM 273. Early "crown" trademark examples are sometimes found with orange color skirt and blouse rather than the normal dark colored blouse.

☐ 81 2/0	4¼ to 4¾″	(CE)	❶	$375–500
☐ 81 2/0	4¼ to 4¾″	(CE)	❷	$210–300
☐ 81 2/0	4¼ to 4¾″	(CE)	❸	$180–210
☐ 81 2/0	4¼ to 4¾″	(CE)	❹	$150–180
☐ 81 2/0	4¼ to 4¾″	(CE)	❺	$125–130
☐ 81 2/0	4¼ to 4¾″	(CE)	❻	$120–125
☐ 81 2/0	4¼ to 4¾″	(OE)	❼	$120
☐ 81/0	4¾ to 5¼″	(CE)	❶	$500–650
☐ 81/0	4¾ to 5¼″	(CE)	❷	$280–400
☐ 81/0	4¾ to 5¼″	(CE)	❸	$250–280
☐ 81/0	4¾ to 5¼″	(CE)	❹	$200–250
☐ 81/0	4¾ to 5¼″	(CE)	❺	$170–180
☐ 81/0	4¾ to 5¼″	(CE)	❻	$160–170
☐ 81/0	4¾ to 5¼″	(OE)	❼	$160
☐ 81	5⅛ to 5½″	(CE)	❶	$550–700
☐ 81	5⅛ to 5½″	(CE)	❷	$325–450

| 82/2 | 82/0 | 82/0 | 82 2/0 | 82 2/0 |

HUM 82
School Boy

First modeled by master sculptor Arthur Moeller in 1938. Many size variations. Old name: "Little Scholar," "School Days" or "Primer Boy." The larger size 82/II (82/2) has been considered rare but is once again back in current production. See HUM 329. To my knowledge, the large size (82/II) was not produced in (TM 4) "three line" trademark.

☐ 82 2/0 . . . 4 to 4½″ . . . . . (CE) . . ❶ . . . $375–500
☐ 82 2/0 . . . 4 to 4½″ . . . . . (CE) . . ❷ . . . $210–300
☐ 82 2/0 . . . 4 to 4½″ . . . . . (CE) . . ❸ . . . $180–210
☐ 82 2/0 . . . 4 to 4½″ . . . . . (CE) . . ❹ . . . $150–180
☐ 82 2/0 . . . 4 to 4½″ . . . . . (CE) . . ❺ . . . $125–130
☐ 82 2/0 . . . 4 to 4½″ . . . . . (CE) . . ❻ . . . $120–125
☐ 82 2/0 . . . 4 to 4½″ . . . . . (OE) . . ❼ . . . $120
☐ 82 . . . . . . 5″ . . . . (CE) . . ❶ . . . $550–700
☐ 82/0 . . . . . 4¾ to 6″ . . . . . (CE) . . ❶ . . . $500–650
☐ 82/0 . . . . . 4¾ to 6″ . . . . . (CE) . . ❷ . . . $280–400
☐ 82/0 . . . . . 4¾ to 6″ . . . . . (CE) . . ❸ . . . $250–280
☐ 82/0 . . . . . 4¾ to 6″ . . . . . (CE) . . ❹ . . . $200–250
☐ 82/0 . . . . . 4¾ tc 6″ . . . . . (CE) . . ❺ . . . $170–180
☐ 82/0 . . . . . 4¾ to 6″ . . . . . (CE) . . ❻ . . . $160–170
☐ 82/0 . . . . . 4¾ to 6″ . . . . . (OE) . . ❼ . . . $160
☐ 82/II . . . . 7½″ . . . . (CE) . . ❶ . . . $1100–1500
☐ 82/II . . . . 7½″ . . . . (CE) . . ❷ . . . $800–1000
☐ 82/II . . . . 7½″ . . . . (CE) . . ❸ . . . $550–650
☐ 82/II . . . . 7½″ . . . . (CE) . . ❺ . . . $400–420
☐ 82/II . . . . 7½″ . . . . (CE) . . ❻ . . . $380–400
☐ 82/II . . . . 7½″ . . . . (OE) . . ❼ . . . $380

HUM 83
Angel Serenade (with Lamb)
Old name: "Psalmist" in some early Goebel catalogues. First modeled by master sculptor Reinhold Unger in 1938. Very little change in design through the years. This figurine had not been produced in quantity since the early 1960's and was considered rare. It is now back on the market with the current trademark. The "Angel Serenade" name is also used for HUM 214/D (part of small Nativity set) and HUM 260/E (part of large Nativity set).

☐ 83 ...... 5½ to 5¾" .... (CE) .. ❶ ... $550–700
☐ 83 ...... 5½ to 5¾" .... (CE) .. ❷ ... $450–500
☐ 83 ...... 5½ to 5¾" .... (CE) .. ❸ ... $350–450
☐ 83 ...... 5½ to 5¾" .... (CE) .. ❹ ... $250–350
☐ 83 ...... 5½ to 5¾" .... (CE) .. ❺ ... $190–200
☐ 83 ...... 5½ to 5¾" .... (CE) .. ❻ ... $180–190
☐ 83 ...... 5½ to 5¾" .... (OE) .. ❼ ... $180

HUM 84
Worship
Originally modeled by master sculptor Reinhold Unger in 1938. Old name: "At The Wayside" or "Devotion" in some catalogues. The small size 84/0 was also sold in white overglaze at one time in Belgium and would be considered extremely rare. Current models of the large size 84/V have "M.I. Hummel" signature on back of shrine while older models have signature on back of base. Sometimes incised 84/5 instead of 84/V. The large size (84/V) was "temporarily withdrawn" (TW) from production on 31 December 1989, but may be reinstated at some future date.

☐ 84	White 5¼"	(CE)	❶	$1000–1500
☐ 84	5¼"	(CE)	❶	$450–550
☐ 84/0	5 to 5½"	(CE)	❶	$400–500
☐ 84/0	5 to 5½"	(CE)	❷	$250–330
☐ 84/0	5 to 5½"	(CE)	❸	$200–230
☐ 84/0	5"	(CE)	❹	$170–200
☐ 84/0	5"	(CE)	❺	$140–150
☐ 84/0	5"	(CE)	❻	$135–140
☐ 84/0	5"	(OE)	❼	$135
☐ 84/V	12½ to 13¼"	(CE)	❶	$2000–3000
☐ 84/V	12½ to 13¼"	(CE)	❷	$1500–2000
☐ 84/V	12½ to 13¼"	(CE)	❸	$1200–1300
☐ 84/V	12½ to 13¼"	(CE)	❹	$1100–1200
☐ 84/V	12½ to 13¼"	(CE)	❺	$1050–1100
☐ 84/V	12½ to 13¼"	(TW)	❻	$1000–1050

Note fingers

HUM 85
Serenade
First modeled by master sculptor Arthur Moeller in 1938. Many size variations. Note variation of boy's fingers on flute — cannot be attributed to any one time period. Old model with 85/0 number has fingers up. Size 85/0 has recently been restyled with a new hair style and textured finish. Normal hat color is dark gray or black. Older models also found with light gray hat. Old large size figurine with crown trademark has 85 number. Also found with incised number 85.0. or 85. in crown trademark in the small size. Sometimes incised 85/2 instead of 85/II. One of several figurines that make up the Hummel orchestra. Old name: "The Flutist." A new miniature size figurine was issued in 1985 with a suggested retail price of $39 to match a new mini size plate series called the "Little Music Makers" — one each year for four years. This is the second in the series. 85 4/0 has an incised 1984 copyright date.

☐ 85 4/0	3½"	(CE)	❻	$80–84
☐ 85 4/0	3½"	(**OE**)	❼	$80
☐ 85/0	4¾ to 5¼"	(CE)	❶	$325–425
☐ 85/0	4¾ to 5¼"	(CE)	❷	$200–275
☐ 85/0	4¾ to 5¼"	(CE)	❸	$170–190
☐ 85/0	4¾ to 5¼"	(CE)	❹	$140–170
☐ 85/0	4¾ to 5¼"	(CE)	❺	$115–120
☐ 85/0	4¾ to 5¼"	(CE)	❻	$110–115
☐ 85/0	4¾ to 5¼"	(**OE**)	❼	$110
☐ 85	7 to 7½"	(CE)	❶	$1150–1500
☐ 85	7 to 7½"	(CE)	❷	$750–950
☐ 85/II	7 to 7½"	(CE)	❶	$1100–1400
☐ 85/II	7 to 7½"	(CE)	❷	$700–900
☐ 85/II	7 to 7½"	(CE)	❸	$575–650
☐ 85/II	7 to 7½"	(CE)	❹	$475–575
☐ 85/II	7 to 7½"	(CE)	❺	$400–420
☐ 85/II	7 to 7½"	(CE)	❻	$380–400
☐ 85/II	7 to 7½"	(**OE**)	❼	$380

HUM 86
Happiness
Many size variations. Made with either square or rectangular base. Old name: "Wandersong" or "Traveller's Song" in early Goebel catalogue. First modeled by master sculptor Reinhold Unger in 1938.

☐ 86	4½ to 5"	(CE)	❶	$325–425
☐ 86	4½ to 5"	(CE)	❷	$200–275
☐ 86	4½ to 5"	(CE)	❸	$170–190
☐ 86	4½ to 5"	(CE)	❹	$140–170
☐ 86	4½ to 5"	(CE)	❺	$115–120
☐ 86	4½ to 5"	(CE)	❻	$110–115
☐ 86	4½ to 5"	(OE)	❼	$110

HUM 87
For Father
First modeled in 1938 by master sculptor Arthur Moeller. Some size and color variations between old and new models. Boy is carrying white (with brownish-tan highlights) radishes and beer stein. Some models have orange-colored vegetables that would appear to be carrots — usually found only with "full bee" (TM 2) or early stylized (TM 3) trademarks. The orange carrot variation normally sells in the $2,500 to $3,500 price range. Old name: "Father's Joy."

☐ 87	5½"	(CE)	❶	$550–725
☐ 87	5½"	(CE)	❷	$325–450
☐ 87	5½"	(CE)	❸	$275–315
☐ 87	5½"	(CE)	❹	$225–275
☐ 87	5½"	(CE)	❺	$190–200
☐ 87	5½"	(CE)	❻	$180–190
☐ 87	5½"	(OE)	❼	$180

88/I   *88/2*

HUM 88
Heavenly Protection

Originally modeled by master sculptor Reinhold Unger in 1938. Some size and color variations between old and new models. Small size 88/I first put on the market in early 1960's. Some pieces have an incised 1961 copyright date on bottom. Older pieces sometimes incised 88/2 instead of 88/II. Some variation in the location of the "M.I. Hummel" signature on the back side of this figurine. Sometimes on the base, sometimes on the bottom of the robe or sometimes in a diagonal position on the robe.

☐ 88	9¼″	(CE)	❶	$1700–2300
☐ 88	9¼″	(CE)	❷	$1200–1500
☐ 88	8¾ to 9¼″	(CE)	❸	$850–1000
☐ 88/I	6¼ to 6¾″	(CE)	❸	$500–600
☐ 88/I	6¼ to 6¾″	(CE)	❹	$450–500
☐ 88/I	6¼ to 6¾″	(CE)	❺	$380–400
☐ 88/I	6¼ to 6¾″	(CE)	❻	$370–380
☐ 88/I	6¼ to 6¾″	(OE)	❼	$370
☐ 88/II	8¾ to 9″	(CE)	❷	$950–1200
☐ 88/II	8¾ to 9″	(CE)	❸	$875–950
☐ 88/II	8¾ to 9″	(CE)	❹	$725–875
☐ 88/II	8¾ to 9″	(CE)	❺	$600–625
☐ 88/II	8¾ to 9″	(CE)	❻	$590–600
☐ 88/II	8¾ to 9″	(OE)	❼	$590

84

New   *Old*

HUM 89
Little Cellist
Modeled by master sculptor Arthur Moeller in 1938. Restyled in the early 1960's. Many size variations through the years. Older examples of size 89/I have eyes open and looking straight ahead. Newer pieces have eyes looking down. Older pieces have rectangular base while newer pieces have rectangular base with corners squared off. Name listed as "Musician" in some old catalogues.

☐ 89/I	5¼ to 6¼"	(CE)	❶	$550–725
☐ 89/I	5¼ to 6¼"	(CE)	❷	$325–450
☐ 89/I	5¼ to 6¼"	(CE)	❸	$275–315
☐ 89/I	5¼ to 6¼"	(CE)	❹	$225–275
☐ 89/I	5¼ to 6¼"	(CE)	❺	$190–200
☐ 89/I	5¼ to 6¼"	(CE)	❻	$180–190
☐ 89/I	5¼ to 6¼"	(OE)	❼	$180
☐ 89/II	7½ to 7¾"	(CE)	❶	$1100–1400
☐ 89/II	7½ to 7¾"	(CE)	❷	$700–900
☐ 89/II	7½ to 7¾"	(CE)	❸	$575–650
☐ 89/II	7½ to 7¾"	(CE)	❹	$475–575
☐ 89/II	7½ to 7¾"	(CE)	❺	$400–420
☐ 89/II	7½ to 7¾"	(CE)	❻	$380–400
☐ 89/II	7½ to 7¾"	(OE)	❼	$380
☐ 89	7½"	(CE)	❶	$1150–1500

Factory sample

HUM 90
Eventide

HUM 90
Adoration (Without Shrine), Bookends
Records indicate that this set of bookends was made in 1938 by a team of artists, which possibly included Reinhold Unger. Factory sample only. Extremely rare. Not produced after 28 February 1938. Listed as a closed edition. One half of this rare bookend (minus the wood base) was recently located in Michigan. This piece does not have the "M.I. Hummel" signature nor any identifying numbers — only a little dried glue remaining, indicating it had originally been attached to another object. Keep looking! Maybe you can locate the half!

☐ 90 A & B . . . . (CE) $10,000–15,000
☐ 90 B . . . . 4" . . . . (CE) $5,000–7,500

Found in Michigan

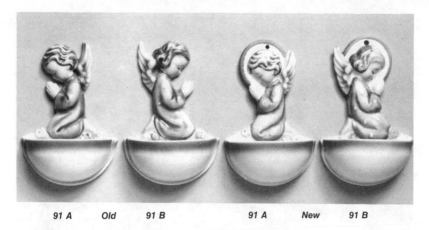

| 91 A | Old | 91 B | | 91 A | New | 91 B |

HUM 91 A & B
Holy Water Font, Angels at Prayer
Angel facing left was apparently made first since early crown mark pieces are incised 91 only (not part of set). Angel facing right (91 B) was probably introduced slightly later. Now listed as a pair—91 A & B. First modeled by master sculptor Reinhold Unger in 1938. Older models (left) do not have halos while more recent designs have halos and a redesigned water bowl. Trademarks 1, 2 and 3 are without halos, 3, 4, 5 and 6 with halos. Note: trademark 3 can be found either way.

Priced for pair.
- ☐ 91 .... 3¼ × 4½" .... (CE) ... ❶ ... $400–500
- ☐ 91 A & B . 3⅜ × 5" ...... (CE) ... ❶ ... $400–500
- ☐ 91 A & B . 3⅜ × 5" ...... (CE) ... ❷ ... $200–250
- ☐ 91 A & B . 3⅜ × 5" ...... (CE) ... ❸ ... $100–120
- ☐ 91 A & B . 3⅜ × 5" ...... (CE) ... ❹ ... $90–100
- ☐ 91 A & B . 3⅜ × 5" ...... (CE) ... ❺ ... $75–80
- ☐ 91 A & B . 3⅜ × 5" ...... (CE) ... ❻ ... $70–75
- ☐ 91 A & B . 3⅜ × 5" ...... (OE) ... ❼ ... $70

HUM TERM

UNDERGLAZE: The term used to describe especially the number 5 trademark that appears actually underneath the glaze as opposed to the later version of the number 5 trademark that appears on the top of the glaze.

Old   *New*

HUM 92
Merry Wanderer, Plaque

Many size variations. Crown mark pieces can be found in both sizes. Some have incised 1938 copyright date, others do not. Some pieces have "M.I. Hummel" signature on both front and back, while others have signature on back only. Some TM 2 plaques have copyright (©WG) on front lower right, signature on back. Originally modeled by master sculptor Arthur Moeller in 1938 but restyled several times in later years. The "Merry Wanderer" plaque was "temporarily withdrawn" (TW) from production on 31 December 1989, but may be reinstated at some future date.

☐ 92 ...... 4½ × 5 to 5 × 5½" . (CE) ... ❶ ... $400–525
☐ 92 ...... 4½ × 5 to 5 × 5½" . (CE) ... ❷ ... $250–325
☐ 92 ...... 4½ × 5" .... (CE) ... ❸ ... $200–225
☐ 92 ...... 4½ × 5" .... (CE) ... ❹ ... $160–200
☐ 92 ...... 4½ × 5" .... (CE) ... ❺ ... $140–150
☐ 92 ...... 4½ × 5" .... (TW) ... ❻ ... $130–140

Rare old style   New

HUM 93
Little Fiddler, Plaque

Originally modeled by master sculptor Arthur Moeller in 1938. Many size variations. Two different backgrounds as noted in photograph. Older model (left) extremely rare. Some models have 1938 copyright date. Some pieces have "M.I. Hummel" signature on both front and back, while others have signature on back only, or front only. Also sold in white overglaze at one time. The background on the left is similar to HUM 107. The "Little Fiddler" plaque was "temporarily withdrawn" (TW) from production on 31 December 1989, but may be reinstated at some future date.

☐ 93 ...... 4½ × 5 to 5 × 5½" ... (CE) ... ❶ ... $400–525
☐ 93 ...... 4½ × 5 to 5 × 5½" ... (CE) ... ❷ ... $250–325
☐ 93 ...... 4½ × 5" .... (CE) ... ❸ ... $200–225
☐ 93 ...... 4½ × 5" .... (CE) ... ❹ ... $160–200
☐ 93 ...... 4½ × 5" .... (CE) ... ❺ ... $140–150
☐ 93 ...... 4½ × 5" .... (TW) ... ❻ ... $130–140
☐ 93 ...... Rare old style .... (CE) ... ❶ ... $3000–5000

┌─────── HUM TERM ───────┐

RARE: (Webster) marked by unusual quality, merit, or appeal. Distinctive, superlative or extreme of its kind, seldom occuring or found, uncommon.

HUM 94
Surprise
Records indicate this model was produced by a team of sculptors in 1938. Old name: "The Duet" or "Hansel and Gretel." Also found listed with name of: "What's Up?" Older pieces marked "94" or "94/I" have rectangular base. All newer models have oval base. Slight variation in suspender straps on older models. Numbering errors occur occasionally—as an example, we have size 94/I that is marked 94/II in trademark 3. This trademark, however, has been "slashed" indicating that it was probably sold to a factory employee.

☐ 94 3/0 .... 4 to 4¼"	(CE)	.. ❶ ...	$400–500
☐ 94 3/0 .... 4 to 4¼"	(CE)	.. ❷ ...	$250–325
☐ 94 3/0 .... 4 to 4¼"	(CE)	.. ❸ ...	$200–225
☐ 94 3/0 .... 4 to 4¼"	(CE)	.. ❹ ...	$165–200
☐ 94 3/0 .... 4 to 4¼"	(CE)	.. ❺ ...	$135–140
☐ 94 3/0 .... 4 to 4¼"	(CE)	.. ❻ ...	$130–135
☐ 94 3/0 .... 4 to 4¼"	(OE)	.. ❼ ...	$130
☐ 94/I ...... 5¼ to 5½"	(CE)	.. ❶ ...	$700–900
☐ 94/I ...... 5¼ to 5½"	(CE)	.. ❷ ...	$425–575
☐ 94/I ...... 5¼ to 5½"	(CE)	.. ❸ ...	$350–400
☐ 94/I ...... 5¼ to 5½"	(CE)	.. ❹ ...	$295–350
☐ 94/I ...... 5¼ to 5½"	(CE)	.. ❺ ...	$245–260
☐ 94/I ...... 5¼ to 5½"	(CE)	.. ❻ ...	$235–245
☐ 94/I ...... 5¼ to 5½"	(OE)	.. ❼ ...	$235
☐ 94 .... 5¾"	(CE)	.. ❶ ...	$750–950
☐ 94 .... 5¾"	(CE)	.. ❷ ...	$450–600

HUM TERM

MEL: A Goebel-produced figurine with the letters "MEL" incised somewhere on the base of the piece. These pieces were designed from original drawings by Sister M.I. Hummel, but for some undetermined reasons were not approved by the Siessen Convent for inclusion in the "M.I. Hummel" line of figurines.

HUM 95
Brother

Many size and color variations. Old name: "Our Hero" or "Hero of The Village." Same boy as used in HUM 94 "Surprise." Records indicate this figurine was first modeled in 1938 by a team of sculptors. "Brother" sold for $6.50 on old 1955 price list.

☐ 95	5¼ to 5¾"	(CE)	❶	$500–650
☐ 95	5¼ to 5¾"	(CE)	❷	$325–400
☐ 95	5¼ to 5¾"	(CE)	❸	$250–290
☐ 95	5¼ to 5¾"	(CE)	❹	$200–250
☐ 95	5¼ to 5¾"	(CE)	❺	$170–180
☐ 95	5¼ to 5¾"	(CE)	❻	$165–170
☐ 95	5¼ to 5¾"	(OE)	❼	$165

HUM TERM

ROEDENTAL: The town in West Germany where the W. Goebel Porzellanfabrik is situated. Roedental is located near Coburg and lies only a few miles from the East German border. In 1981 Roedental became the official Sister City of Eaton, Ohio due to the longtime "Hummel" relationship with Robert L. Miller.

HUM 96
Little Shopper
Many size variations. Old name: "Errand Girl," "Gretel" or "Meg" in some older catalogues. Some catalogues and price lists indicate size as 5½". This is believed, by this author, to be in error. I have *never* seen it over 5 inches in over twenty years of collecting. Records indicate this figurine was first modeled in 1938 by a team of sculptors possibly including master sculptor Reinhold Unger. Same girl as used in HUM 94 "Surprise." "Little Shopper" sold for $5.50 on old 1955 price list.

☐ 96	4½ to 5"	(CE)	❶	$350–475
☐ 96	4½ to 5"	(CE)	❷	$225–300
☐ 96	4½ to 5"	(CE)	❸	$180–200
☐ 96	4½ to 5"	(CE)	❹	$150–180
☐ 96	4½ to 5"	(CE)	❺	$125–135
☐ 96	4½ to 5"	(CE)	❻	$120–125
☐ 96	4½ to 5"	(OE)	❼	$120

HUM TERM

SECONDARY MARKET: The buying and selling of items after the initial retail purchase has been transacted. Often times this post-retail trading is also referred to as the "after market." This very publication is intended to serve as a guide for the secondary market values of "M.I. Hummel" items.

HUM 97
Trumpet Boy
Originally modeled by master sculptor Arthur Moeller in 1938. Many size variations. Boy's coat is normally green. Old "U.S. Zone" specimen has blue coat shaded with green. Old name: "The Little Musician." There are a few rare pieces with the inscription "Design Patent No. 116,404" stamped on the bottom. This variation valued from $1000–1500. "Trumpet Boy" sold for $5.50 on old 1955 price list.

☐ 97	4½ to 4¾"	(CE)	❶	$325–450
☐ 97	4½ to 5¼"	(CE)	❷	$200–275
☐ 97	4½ to 5¼"	(CE)	❸	$170–190
☐ 97	4½ to 4¾"	(CE)	❹	$140–170
☐ 97	4½ to 4¾"	(CE)	❺	$115–120
☐ 97	4½ to 4¾"	(CE)	❻	$110–115
☐ 97	4½ to 4¾"	(OE)	❼	$110

98/0 (TM 3)   98 (TM 1)   98 2/0 (TM 4)

HUM 98
Sister

Originally modeled by master sculptor Arthur Moeller in 1938. Many size variations; otherwise very little change between old and new models. Old name: "The Shopper" or "The First Shopping" in some catalogues. Some pieces have an incised 1962 copyright date. A collector recently found this piece made with a purse instead of a basket. The purse, however, appears to be handmade rather than molded. Factory representatives believe that it *could* have been an experimental model, proposed by a sculptor but rejected even before a mold for the purse was produced. "Sister" is same girl as used on HUM 49 "To Market." "Sister" sold for $6.50 on old 1955 price list.

☐ 98	5¾"	(CE)	❶	$500–650
☐ 98	5¾"	(CE)	❷	$300–400
☐ 98	5¾"	(CE)	❸	$275–300
☐ 98 2/0	4½ to 4¾"	(CE)	❸	$180–200
☐ 98 2/0	4½ to 4¾"	(CE)	❹	$150–180
☐ 98 2/0	4½ to 4¾"	(CE)	❺	$125–135
☐ 98 2/0	4½ to 4¾"	(CE)	❻	$120–125
☐ 98 2/0	4½ to 4¾"	(OE)	❼	$120
☐ 98/0	5¼ to 5½"	(CE)	❸	$250–290
☐ 98/0	5¼ to 5½"	(CE)	❹	$200–250
☐ 98/0	5¼ to 5½"	(CE)	❺	$170–180
☐ 98/0	5¼ to 5½"	(CE)	❻	$165–170
☐ 98/0	5¼ to 5½"	(OE)	❼	$165

HUM 99
Eventide
Records indicate this model was produced in 1938 by a combination of modelers. Almost identical with "Wayside Devotion" HUM 28 but without the shrine. Many size variations. Note photo of rare crown mark piece with lambs in different position directly in front of children. At one time this figurine was sold in Belgium in the white overglaze finish and would now be considered extremely rare.

	Normal		Rare version

☐ 99	4¼ × 5″	(CE)	❶	$850−1100
☐ 99	4¼ × 5″	(CE)	❷	$550−700
☐ 99	4¼ × 5″	(CE)	❸	$450−500
☐ 99	4¼ × 5″	(CE)	❹	$375−450
☐ 99	4¼ × 5″	(CE)	❺	$300−320
☐ 99	4¼ × 5″	(CE)	❻	$290−300
☐ 99	4¼ × 5″	(OE)	❼	$290
☐ 99	Rare version	(CE)	❶	$2500−3000

HUM 100
Shrine, Table Lamp (CE)
This extremely rare lamp is similar to the figurine "Adoration" HUM 23. First modeled by Erich Lautensack in 1938 and produced in very limited quantities. Only a few examples known to exist. The example in our collection has a light beige-colored post, an incised crown trademark plus the stamped "U.S. Zone". Another example had a dark brown post, an incised crown trademark plus stamped "full bee." Also had 6/50 date.

☐ 100 ..... 7½ .... (CE) .. ❶ ... $8,000–10,000

Rare plain post

HUM 101
To market, Table Lamp (CE)

Originally modeled by master sculptor Arthur Moeller in 1937. Listed as a closed edition on factory records 20 April 1937. Redesigned and limited quantity produced in early 1950's with "tree trunk" post. Some incised with number II/101, III/101 and others with 101 only. Lamp was adapted from figurine "To Market" HUM 49. Master sculptor Arthur Moeller redesigned this lamp in 1952 into the 9½ inch size HUM 223.

☐ 101 ..... 7½" .... (CE) .. ❶ ... $8,000–10,000 Plain Post
☐ 101 ..... 7½" .... (CE) .. ❶ ... $1,500–2,000 Tree trunk post
☐ 101 ..... 7½" .... (CE) .. ❷ ... $750–1000
☐ 101 ..... 7½" .... (CE) .. ❸ ... $500–750

Plain post   **Tree trunk post**

HUM 102
Volunteers, Table Lamp (CE)
Originally modeled by Erich Lautensack in 1937. Listed as a closed edition in factory records 20 April 1937. In 1979 a rare specimen was found in Seattle, Washington, and is now in the Robert L. Miller collection. This piece has a double crown (incised and stamped) trademark. Since 1979 several other specimens have been found and the Goebel factory now has one in their archives.

☐ 102 ..... 7½" .... (CE) .. ❶ ... $8,000–10,000

HUM 103
Farewell, Table Lamp (CE)
Originally modeled by Erich Lautensack in 1937. Lised as a closed edition on factory records 20 April 1937. Several examples of this extremely rare lamp have recently been found and one is now in the Robert L. Miller collection. A second specimen was recently presented to the Goebel factory for their archives in Roedental, West Germany. Since 1983 several other specimens have been found, but is still considered extremely rare.

☐ 103 ..... 7½" .... (CE) .. ❶ ... $8,000–10,000

HUM 104
Eventide, Table Lamp(CE)
Originally modeled by Reinhold Unger in 1938. Listed as a closed edition on factory records 3 March 1938. This lamp was originally called "Wayside Devotion" in our earlier books but is now correctly named "Eventide." The first known example of this extremely rare lamp base was recently purchased from its original owner in northern Indiana and is now in the Robert L. Miller collection. The lamp was located through the help of Ralph and Terry Kovel and their syndicated newspaper column on antiques. Notice the position of lambs in this photo and then compare with photo of "Eventide" HUM 99.

☐ 104 ..... 7½" .... (CE) .. ❶ ... $8,000–10,000

HUM 105
Adoration With Bird (CE)
Very limited production. Listed as a closed edition on factory records 24 May 1938. All known examples have double crown (incised and stamped) trademark. Notice difference in pigtail of little girl in this comparative photograph. Unable to locate information on original sculptor or date of original model; probably master sculptor Reinhold Unger who created model for "Adoration" HUM 23 which is similar in design. This figurine is considered extremely rare.

☐ 105 ..... 4¾″ .... (CE) .. ❶ ... $7,000–8,000

HUM TERM

U.S. ZONE: The words "U.S. ZONE— GERMANY" were used on figurines produced by the W. Goebel Porzellanfabrik after W.W.II when the country of Germany was yet undivided and the Goebel factory was part of the U.S. Zone. The U.S. ZONE marking was used either alone or with the Crown trademark from 1946 until 1948. Once the country was divided into East and West, the W. Goebel Porzellanfabrik used the Western or West designation.

106 (TM 1)   107 (TM 1)

HUM 106
Merry Wanderer,
Plaque with wood frame (CE)
Very limited production. Listed as a closed edition on factory records 1 August 1938. First modeled by master sculptor Arthur Moeller in 1938. Similar to all-ceramic plaque of "Merry Wanderer" HUM 92 except for wood frame. Some variation in frames. Considered extremely rare.

☐ 106 . . . . . . 6 × 6″ . . . . (CE) . . ❶ . . . $5,000-6,000

HUM 107
Little Fiddler,
Plaque with wood frame (CE)
Very limited production. Listed as a closed on factory records 1 August 1938. First modeled by master sculptor Arthur Moeller in 1938. Similar to the all-ceramic plaque of "Little Fiddler" HUM 93 (rare old style background) except for the wood frame. Some variation in frames. Considered extremely rare.

☐ 107 . . . . . 6 × 6″ . . . . (CE) . . ❶ . . . $5,000–6,000

HS 01 (not 108)

HUM 108
Angel With Two Children At Feet (CN)
Originally modeled by master sculptor Reinhold Unger in 1938. No known examples. Listed on factory records of 14 October 1938 as a wall decoration. Pictured here is Goebel item HS 01 listed in 1950 Goebel catalogue. Factory representatives state that is possibly a Hummel design — probably rejected by Siessen Convent and then later marketed as a Goebel item. The "MM" painted on gown indicates this is a "muster" (the German word for sample). When and if found with the "M.I. Hummel" signature and incised 108 would have a value of $10,000–15,000.

☐ 108 . . . . (CN) . . ❶ . . $10,000–15,000

```
┌─────────── HUM TERM ───────────┐
│                                 │
│  SAMPLE MODEL: Generally a fig- │
│  urine that was made as a sam-  │
│  ple only and not approved by   │
│  the Siessen Convent for pro-   │
│  duction. Sample models (in the │
│  true sense of the term) are    │
│  extremely rare items and com-  │
│  mand a premium price on the    │
│  secondary market.              │
│                                 │
└─────────────────────────────────┘
```

109/II (TM 3)   *109 (TM 1 + 1)*   *109/0 (TM 2)*

HUM 109
Happy Traveller
First modeled by master sculptor Arthur Moeller in 1938 and has been produced in all trademark periods. The large size was permanently retired by Goebel in the spring of 1982. Early pieces were usually incised 109/2 instead of 109/II. Small size only is still in current production. Sometimes the small size is found without the size designator in trademarks 3,4 and 5. Listed as "Wanderer" in old catalogues. Small size was restyled in 1980 with the new textured finish.

☐ 109/0	4¾ to 5″	(CE)	❷	$250–300
☐ 109/0	4¾ to 5″	(CE)	❸	$180–200
☐ 109	4¾ to 5″	(CE)	❸	$180–200
☐ 109/0	4¾ to 5″	(CE)	❹	$150–180
☐ 109	4¾ to 5″	(CE)	❹	$150–180
☐ 109/0	4¾ to 5″	(CE)	❺	$125–130
☐ 109	4¾ to 5″	(CE)	❺	$125–130
☐ 109/0	4¾ to 5″	(CE)	❻	$120–125
☐ 109/0	4¾ to 5″	(OE)	❼	$120
☐ 109/II	7½″	(CE)	❷	$750–850
☐ 109/II	7½″	(CE)	❸	$450–500
☐ 109/II	7½″	(CE)	❹	$400–450
☐ 109/II	7½″	(CE)	❺	$350–375
☐ 109/II	7½″	(CE)	❻	$325–350
☐ 109	7¾″	(CE)	❶	$1000–1250

110 (TM 1) *110/0 (TM 3)*

HUM 110
Let's Sing

Originally modeled by master sculptor Reinhold Unger in 1938. There are many size variations. Some have an incised 1938 copyright date. Some incised model numbers are difficult to read because of the extremely small bases. "Let's Sing" sold for $6.00 on old 1955 price list.

☐ 110	4"	(CE)	❶	$425–550
☐ 110	4"	(CE)	❷	$300–375
☐ 110/0	3 to 3¼"	(CE)	❶	$300–425
☐ 110/0	3 to 3¼"	(CE)	❷	$200–260
☐ 110/0	3 to 3¼"	(CE)	❸	$160–185
☐ 110/0	3 to 3¼"	(CE)	❹	$130–160
☐ 110/0	3 to 3¼"	(CE)	❺	$110–115
☐ 110/0	3 to 3¼"	(CE)	❻	$105–110
☐ 110/0	3 to 3¼"	(OE)	❼	$105
☐ 110/I	3½ to 4"	(CE)	❷	$275–350
☐ 110/I	3½ to 4"	(CE)	❸	$200–240
☐ 110/I	3½ to 4"	(CE)	❹	$175–200
☐ 110/I	3½ to 4"	(CE)	❺	$145–150
☐ 110/I	3½ to 4"	(CE)	❻	$140–145
☐ 110/I	3½ to 4"	(OE)	❼	$140

HUM TERM

OVERSIZE: This description refers to a piece that has experienced "mold growth" size expansion. A figurine that measures larger than the standard size is said to be "oversized."

Old bowl style   *New jar style*

HUM III/110
Let's Sing, Box

Bowl style first produced in 1938. Jar style first produced and sold in 1964. Model number is found on underside of lid. The "M.I. Hummel" signature is found on topside of lid directly behind figure. "Let's Sing" candy box was "temporarily withdrawn" (TW) from production on 31 December 1989, but may be reinstated at some future date.

- ☐ III/110 ... 6¼" .... (CE) .. ❶ ... $650–750
- ☐ III/110 ... 6¼" .... (CE) .. ❷ ... $525–600
- ☐ III/110 ... 6¼" .... (CE) .. ❸ ... $425–500 OLD STYLE
- ☐ III/110 ... 5¼" .... (CE) .. ❸ ... $180–200 NEW STYLE
- ☐ III/110 ... 5¼" .... (CE) .. ❹ ... $170–180
- ☐ III/110 ... 5¼" .... (CE) .. ❺ ... $160–170
- ☐ III/110 ... 5¼" .... (TW) .. ❻ ... $150–160

HUM TERM

PAINT RUB: A general wearing away of the paint surface of a figurine in a particular spot. This condition is usually caused by excessive handling of a figurine, thin paint in a given area of the figurine, or the excessive use of abrasive cleaners.

111/I (TM 1)   *111 3/0 (TM 4)*

HUM 111
Wayside Harmony
First modeled in 1938 by master sculptor Reinhold Unger. There are many size variations. Normally has green-colored socks, but some crown and full bee trademark
pieces have yellow socks in the small (111 3/0) size. Old name: "Just Sittin-Boy."
Some models have a 1938 incised copyright date. The small size "Wayside Harmony"
listed for $5.00 while the large size listed for $10.00 on 1955 price list.

☐ 111 3/0	.. 3¾ to 4″	......	(CE)	... ❶ ...	$375–500
☐ 111 3/0	.. 3¾ to 4″	......	(CE)	... ❷ ...	$250–325
☐ 111 3/0	.. 3¾ to 4″	......	(CE)	... ❸ ...	$190–225
☐ 111 3/0	.. 3¾ to 4″	......	(CE)	... ❹ ...	$160–190
☐ 111 3/0	.. 3¾ to 4″	......	(CE)	... ❺ ...	$130–135
☐ 111 3/0	.. 3¾ to 4″	......	(CE)	... ❻ ...	$125–130
☐ 111 3/0	.. 3¾ to 4″	......	(OE)	... ❼ ...	$125
☐ 111/I	..... 5 to 5½″	......	(CE)	... ❶ ...	$600–750
☐ 111/I	..... 5 to 5½″	......	(CE)	... ❷ ...	$400–500
☐ 111/I	..... 5 to 5½″	......	(CE)	... ❸ ...	$325–375
☐ 111/I	..... 5 to 5½″	......	(CE)	... ❹ ...	$275–325
☐ 111/I	..... 5 to 5½″	......	(CE)	... ❺ ...	$230–240
☐ 111/I	..... 5 to 5½″	......	(CE)	... ❻ ...	$220–230
☐ 111/I	..... 5 to 5½″	......	(OE)	... ❼ ...	$220
☐ 111	...... 5½″	....	(CE)	... ❶ ...	$650–800

II/111   *224/I*

HUM II/111
Wayside Harmony, Table Lamp (CE)
This number was used briefly in the early 1950's. Later changed to 224/I. The only difference is that the boy is slightly larger. Some models have been found with number III/111/I.

☐ II/111 .... 7½" .... (CE) .. ❶ ... $500–750
☐ II/111 .... 7½" .... (CE) .. ❷ ... $400–500
☐ II/111 .... 7½" .... (CE) .. ❸ ... $350–500

--------- HUM TERM ---------

PAINT FLAKE: The term used to designate a flaw in a ceramic figurine whereby the paint has been chipped. This type flaw does not go beyond the glazed surface.

112/I (TM 2)   112 3/0 (TM 4)

HUM 112
Just Resting

First modeled in 1938 by master sculptor Reinhold Unger. Many size variations. Old name: "Just Sittin-Girl." Some models have a 1938 incised copyright date. There is an unusual example of size 112/I without a basket in front of the girl (not shown). The direction of the basket handle varies on old "crown" trademark examples.

☐ 112 3/0	3¾ to 4"	(CE)	❶	$375–500
☐ 112 3/0	3¾ to 4"	(CE)	❷	$250–325
☐ 112 3/0	3¾ to 4"	(CE)	❸	$190–225
☐ 112 3/0	3¾ to 4"	(CE)	❹	$160–190
☐ 112 3/0	3¾ to 4"	(CE)	❺	$130–135
☐ 112 3/0	3¾ to 4"	(CE)	❻	$125–130
☐ 112 3/0	3¾ to 4"	(OE)	❼	$125
☐ 112/I	4¾ to 5½"	(CE)	❶	$600–750
☐ 112/I	4¾ to 5½"	(CE)	❷	$400–500
☐ 112/I	4¾ to 5½"	(CE)	❸	$325–375
☐ 112/I	4¾ to 5½"	(CE)	❹	$275–325
☐ 112/I	4¾ to 5½"	(CE)	❺	$230–240
☐ 112/I	4¾ to 5½"	(CE)	❻	$225–230
☐ 112/I	4¾ to 5½"	(OE)	❼	$225
☐ 112	5½"	(CE)	❶	$650–800

II/112   225/I

HUM II/112
Just Resting, Table Lamp (CE)
This number was used briefly in the early 1950's. Later changed to 225/I. The only difference is that the girl is slightly larger. Some models have a 1938 incised copyright date. Some models have been found with numbers III/112/I and 2/112/I. Extremely rare with these numbers.

☐ II/112 .... 7½" .... (CE) .. ❶ ... $500–700
☐ II/112 .... 7½" .... (CE) .. ❷ ... $400–500
☐ II/112 .... 7½" .... (CE) .. ❸ ... $350–500

HUM 113
Heavenly Song, Candleholder (CE)

Originally modeled by master sculptor Arthur Moeller in 1938 but was produced in very limited quantities. Sometimes mistaken for HUM 54 "Silent Night;" which is similar. Was scheduled for production again in 1978 and listed in some catalogues and price lists. Because of its similarity to HUM 54 "Silent Night" the factory decided it should not be produced again so in 1980 it was listed as a closed edition. At least one piece is known to exist with the 5 trademark. All specimens would now be considered extremely rare.

☐ 113 ..... 3½ × 4¾" ... (CE) .. ❶ ... $6,000–10,000
☐ 113 ..... 3½ × 4¾" ... (CE) .. ❷ ... $4,500–5,500
☐ 113 ..... 3½ × 4¾" ... (CE) .. ❸ ... $3,500–4,500
☐ 113 ..... 3½ × 4¾" ... (CE) .. ❺ ... $3,000–3,500

Old style　　　　　*New style*

HUM 114
Let's Sing, Ashtray

First modeled in 1938 by master sculptor Reinhold Unger with the ashtray on the left (boy's right). Restyled in 1959 by master sculptor Theo R. Menzenbach with the ashtray on the right (boy's left). Old style would be considered rare. Both styles can be found with full bee trademark. "Let's Sing" ashtray was "temporarily withdrawn" (TW) from production on 31 December 1989, but may be reinstated at some future date.

☐ 114 ..... 3½ × 6¼" ... (CE) .. ❶ ... $850–1000
☐ 114 ..... 3½ × 6¼" ... (CE) .. ❷ ... $300–850
☐ 114 ..... 3½ × 6¼" ... (CE) .. ❸ ... $200–225
☐ 114 ..... 3½ × 6¼" ... (CE) .. ❹ ... $150–200
☐ 114 ..... 3½ × 6¼" ... (CE) .. ❺ ... $140–150
☐ 114 ..... 3½ × 6¼" ... (TW) .. ❻ ... $130–140

HUM TERM

REINSTATED: The term used to indicate that a figurine had been placed back into production by the W. Goebel Porzellanfabrik after some prior classification of non-production.

115 116 117

HUM 115
Advent Candlestick, Girl With Nosegay
HUM 116
Advent Candlestick, Girl With Fir Tree
HUM 117
Advent Candlestick, Boy with Horse
These three figurines were first modeled by master sculptor Reinhold Unger in 1939. They are similar to HUM 239 A, B & C (without candleholders). Very early models were incised with "Mel" instead of "M. I. Hummel." Reportedly sold only in Germany. Note: "Mel" is the last three letters of Hum**mel**. Some "Mel" pieces have been found with the early stylized trademark indicating that both "Hummel" and "Mel" pieces were being produced and marketed at the same time. Mel 1, Mel 2, and Mel 3 usually sell for *$300* to *$350* each depending on the condition.

☐ 115	3½"	(CE)	❶	$175–225
☐ 115	3½"	(CE)	❷	$100–125
☐ 115	3½"	(CE)	❸	$75–85
☐ 115	3½"	(CE)	❹	$65–75
☐ 115	3½"	(CE)	❺	$55–60
☐ 115	3½"	(CE)	❻	$50–55
☐ 115	3½"	(OE)	❼	$50
☐ 116	3½"	(CE)	❶	$175–225
☐ 116	3½"	(CE)	❷	$100–125
☐ 116	3½"	(CE)	❸	$75–85
☐ 116	3½"	(CE)	❹	$65–75
☐ 116	3½"	(CE)	❺	$55–60
☐ 116	3½"	(CE)	❻	$50–55
☐ 116	3½"	(OE)	❼	$50
☐ 117	3½"	(CE)	❶	$175–225
☐ 117	3½"	(CE)	❷	$100–125
☐ 117	3½"	(CE)	❸	$75–85
☐ 117	3½"	(CE)	❹	$65–75
☐ 117	3½"	(CE)	❺	$55–60
☐ 117	3½"	(CE)	❻	$50–55
☐ 117	3½"	(OE)	❼	$50

New style   *Old style*

HUM 118
Little Thrifty, Bank

This figurine is actually a bank. Made with a metal lock & key on bottom. Originally modeled by master sculptor Arthur Moeller in 1939. Restyled by Rudolf Wittman in 1963. Older models have a slightly different base design as noted in photograph. The object into which "Little Thrifty" is putting her coin is a medieval form of a poor box, something which can still be found in old European churches. To my knowledge, not produced with TM 4. "Little Thrifty" sold for $6.00 on old 1955 price list.

☐ 118 ..... 5 to 5½" ..... (CE) .. ❶ ... $450–650
☐ 118 ..... 5 to 5½" ..... (CE) .. ❷ ... $350–400
☐ 118 ..... 5 to 5½" ..... (CE) .. ❸ ... $200–250
☐ 118 ..... 5 to 5½" ..... (CE) .. ❺ ... $135-145
☐ 118 ..... 5 to 5½" ..... (CE) .. ❻ ... $130-135
☐ 118 ..... 5 to 5½" ..... (OE) .. ❼ ... $130

Current　　　　**Stylized**　　　　**Full bee**

HUM 119
Postman

Many size variations although officially made in one size only. First modeled by master sculptor Arthur Moeller in 1939. Later restyled by master sculptor Gerhard Skrobek in 1970 giving it the new textured finish. Newer models have four letters in the mail bag while older models have five letters. A new small size "Postman" (119 2/0) was released in 1989 with a suggested retail price of $90. It was modeled by master sculptor Gerhard Skrobek in 1985. It has an incised 1985 copyright date. The large size has been renumbered 119/0 and the old 119 is now classified as a closed edition (CE) because of this change.

☐ 119 2/0 ..	4½"	(CE) ..	➏ ...	$115-120
☐ 119 2/0 ..	4½"	**(OE)** ..	➐ ...	$115
☐ 119	5 to 5½"	(CE) ..	➊ ...	$550–700
☐ 119	5 to 5½"	(CE) ..	➋ ...	$325–425
☐ 119	5 to 5½"	(CE) ..	➌ ...	$250–275
☐ 119	5 to 5½"	(CE) ..	➍ ...	$215–250
☐ 119	5 to 5½"	(CE) ..	➎ ...	$180–190
☐ 119	5 to 5½"	(CE) ..	➏ ...	$175–180
☐ 119/0	5 to 5½"	(CE) ..	➏ ...	$170–175
☐ 119/0	5½"	**(OE)** ..	➐ ...	$170

HUM 120
Joyful and Let's Sing (on wooden base), Bookends (CE)
No known examples. Listed as a closed edition on factory records 16 June 1939. Records indicate this was made in 1939 by a combination of sculptors. Probably similar in design to Hum 122.

☐ 120 . . . . (CE) . . ❶ . . $10,000–20,000

HUM 121
Wayside Harmony and Just Resting (on wooden base), Bookends (CE)
Listed as a closed edition on factory records 16 June 1939. Records indicate this was made in 1939 by a combination of sculptors. This bookend (half only) was recently located in central Europe and is now part of the Robert L. Miller collection.

☐ 121 A . . . . (CE) . . ❶ . . $5,000–10,000
☐ 121 B . . . . (CE) . . ❶ . . $5,000–10,000

Factory prototype

HUM 122
Puppy Love and Serenade With Dog (on wooden base), Bookends (CE)
Factory sample only. Listed as a closed edition on factory records 16 June 1939. Records indicate this was made in 1939 by a combination of sculptors.

☐ 122 . . . . (CE) . . ❶ . . $10,000–20,000

Old style (TM 2)   *New style (TM 5)*

HUM 123
Max and Moritz
First modeled by master sculptor Arthur Moeller in 1939. Restyled in the early 1970's with the new textured finish. Old name: "Good Friends" in some catalogues. "Max and Moritz" sold for $8.00 on old 1955 price list.

☐ 123 . . . . . 5 to 5½" . . . . . (CE) . . ❶ . . . $600–750
☐ 123 . . . . . 5 to 5½" . . . . . (CE) . . ❷ . . . $375–475
☐ 123 . . . . . 5 to 5½" . . . . . (CE) . . ❸ . . . $290–325
☐ 123 . . . . . 5 to 5½" . . . . . (CE) . . ❹ . . . $240–290
☐ 123 . . . . . 5 to 5½" . . . . . (CE) . . ❺ . . . $200–210
☐ 123 . . . . . 5 to 5½" . . . . . (CE) . . ❻ . . . $190–200
☐ 123 . . . . . 5 to 5½" . . . . . (**OE**) . . ❼ . . . $190

HUM TERM

STYLIZED TRADEMARK: The symbol used by the Goebel Company from 1957 until 1964. It is recognized by the V with a bumblebee that has triangular or "stylized" wings.

| Current | Full Bee | Crown |

HUM 124
Hello

Many size variations. Earliest models produced had gray coat, grey trousers and pink vest. Changed to brown coat, green trousers and pink vest in early 1950's. Changed to dark brown coat, light brown trousers and blue-white vest in mid-1960's. Originally modeled by master sculptor Arthur Moeller in 1939. Has been restyled several times through the years. Old name: "The Boss" or "Der Chef." The large size 124/I had been difficult to find but was put back on the market in 1978, then in the spring of 1982 was listed as "temporarily withdrawn" by Goebel, to be reinstated at a later date. The small size only is still in current production. Some models have been painted with open eyes while most models have eyes looking down.

☐ 124	6½"	(CE)	❶	$750–1000
☐ 124	6½"	(CE)	❷	$400–550
☐ 124/0	5¾ to 6¼"	(CE)	❷	$350–400
☐ 124/0	5¾ to 6¼"	(CE)	❸	$275–315
☐ 124/0	5¾ to 6¼"	(CE)	❹	$225–275
☐ 124/0	5¾ to 6¼"	(CE)	❺	$190–200
☐ 124/0	5¾ to 6¼"	(CE)	❻	$180–190
☐ 124/0	5¾ to 6¼"	(OE)	❼	$180
☐ 124/I	6¾ to 7"	(CE)	❶	$750–1000
☐ 124/I	6¾ to 7"	(CE)	❷	$400–550
☐ 124/I	6¾ to 7"	(CE)	❸	$325–375
☐ 124/I	6¾ to 7"	(CE)	❹	$275–325
☐ 124/I	6¾ to 7"	(CE)	❺	$230–240
☐ 124/I	6¾ to 7"	(TW)	❻	$220–230

New style   **Old style**

HUM 125
Vacation Time, Plaque

First modeled in 1939 by master sculptor Arthur Moeller. Restyled in 1960 by master sculptor Theo R. Menzenbach. The newer model has five fence posts while the older one has six. Old name: "Happy Holidays" or "On Holiday." Newer models produced without string for hanging, only a hole on back for hanging. Both old style and new style can be found with the stylized (TM3) trademark. "Vacation Time" plaque was "temporarily withdrawn" (TW) from production on 31 December 1989, but may be reinstated at some future date.

☐ 125 ..... 4⅜ × 5¼″ ... (CE) .. ❶ ... $525–700
☐ 125 ..... 4⅜ × 5¼″ ... (CE) .. ❷ ... $350–450
☐ 125 ..... 4 × 4¾″ ..... (CE) .. ❸ ... $250–325
☐ 125 ..... 4 × 4¾″ ..... (CE) .. ❹ ... $200–250
☐ 125 ..... 4 × 4¾″ ..... (CE) .. ❺ ... $180–190
☐ 125 ..... 4 × 4¾″ ..... (TW) .. ❻ ... $175–180

HUM TERM

TEMPORARILY WITHDRAWN: A designation assigned by the W. Goebel Porzellanfabrik to indicate that a particular item is being withdrawn from production for some time, but may be reinstated at a future date.

HUM 126
Retreat to Safety, Plaque
First modeled by master sculptor Arthur Moeller in 1939. Older plaques are slightly larger. Slight color variations on older models. This same motif is also produced as a figurine by the same name although the colors are different. See "Retreat to Safety" HUM 201. "Retreat to Safety" plaque was "temporarily withdrawn" (TW) from production on 31 December 1989, but may be reinstated at some future date.

☐ 126 ... 4¾ × 4¾" to 5 × 5" ... (CE) .. ❶ ... $500–600
☐ 126 ... 4¾ × 4¾" to 5 × 5" ... (CE) .. ❷ ... $350–450
☐ 126 ... 4¾ × 4¾" .... (CE) .. ❸ ... $250–325
☐ 126 ... 4¾ × 4¾" .... (CE) .. ❹ ... $200–250
☐ 126 ... 4¾ × 4¾" .... (CE) .. ❺ ... $180–190
☐ 126 ... 4¾ × 4¾" .... (TW) . ❻ ... $175–180

Note size variation

HUM 127
Doctor
Originally modeled by master sculptor Arthur Moeller in 1939. Has been restyled with the new textured finish. Many variations in size through the years with older examples slightly larger. Old name: "The Doll Doctor." Legs of doll sometimes protrude over edge of base.

☐ 127 ..... 4¾ to 5¼" .... (CE) .. ❶ ... $400–550
☐ 127 ..... 4¾ to 5¼" .... (CE) .. ❷ ... $275–325
☐ 127 ..... 4¾ to 5¼" .... (CE) .. ❸ ... $200–225
☐ 127 ..... 4¾ to 5¼" .... (CE) .. ❹ ... $170–200
☐ 127 ..... 4¾ to 5¼" .... (CE) .. ❺ ... $140–150
☐ 127 ..... 4¾ to 5¼" .... (CE) .. ❻ ... $135–140
☐ 127 ..... 4¾ to 5¼" .... (**OE**) .. ❼ ... $135

TM 2   TM 3

HUM 128
Baker

This figurine was first modeled in 1939 by master sculptor Arthur Moeller. Has been restyled several times during the years — most recently in the mid-1970's with the new textured finish. Slight color variations can be noticed. The little baker is holding a "Gugelhupf" round pound cake, a popular Bavarian treat.

☐ 128 ..... 4¾ to 5″ ..... (CE) .. ❶ ... $500−650
☐ 128 ..... 4¾ to 5″ ..... (CE) .. ❷ ... $300−375
☐ 128 ..... 4¾ to 5″ ..... (CE) .. ❸ ... $250−275
☐ 128 ..... 4¾ to 5″ ..... (CE) .. ❹ ... $200−250
☐ 128 ..... 4¾ to 5″ ..... (CE) .. ❺ ... $165−175
☐ 128 ..... 4¾ to 5″ ..... (CE) .. ❻ ... $160−165
☐ 128 ..... 4¾ to 5″ ..... (OE) .. ❼ ... $160

129 4/0 (TM 6)

HUM 129
Band Leader

First modeled by master sculptor Arthur Moeller in 1939. Many size and color variations. Old name: "Leader." One of several figurines that make up the Hummel orchestra. A new miniature size was issued in 1987 with a suggested retail price of $50 to match a new mini plate series called the "Little Music Makers" — one each year for four years. This is the fourth and last in the series. This miniature figurine has an incised 1985 copyright date. The miniature "Band Leader" is made without a music stand.

☐ 129 4/0	3¼"	(CE)	❻	$80-85
☐ 129 4/0	3¼"	(OE)	❼	$80
☐ 129	5 to 5⅞"	(CE)	❶	$525–700
☐ 129	5 to 5⅞"	(CE)	❷	$325–425
☐ 129	5 to 5⅞"	(CE)	❸	$250–300
☐ 129	5 to 5⅞"	(CE)	❹	$215–250
☐ 129	5 to 5⅞"	(CE)	❺	$175–185
☐ 129	5 to 5⅞"	(CE)	❻	$170–175
☐ 129	5 to 5⅞"	(OE)	❼	$170

Old base variation

Normal model	TM 2	TM 3

HUM 130
Duet

Many size variations—from 5 to 5½". Originally modeled in 1939 by master sculptor Arthur Moeller. Early crown mark pieces have incised notes as well as painted notes on sheet music. Some early crown mark examples have a small "lip" on top edge of base. This variation should be valued from *$1,000 to $1,500*. Old name: "The Songsters." One of several figurines that make up the Hummel orchestra. "Duet" is similar to a combination of "Street Singer" HUM 131 and "Soloist" HUM 135. Occasionally found *no* tie on either boy. This variation would command a premium of over $2,000.

☐ 130 ..... 5 to 5½" ..... (CE) .. ❶ ... $700–900
☐ 130 ..... 5 to 5½" ..... (CE) .. ❷ ... $450–550
☐ 130 ..... 5 to 5½" ..... (CE) .. ❸ ... $350–400
☐ 130 ..... 5 to 5½" ..... (CE) .. ❹ ... $275–350
☐ 130 ..... 5 to 5½" ..... (CE) .. ❺ ... $235–245
☐ 130 ..... 5 to 5½" ..... (CE) .. ❻ ... $225–235
☐ 130 ..... 5 to 5½" ..... (OE) .. ❼ ... $225
☐ 130 ..... without ties ... (CE) .. ❷❸ . $2,000–2,500
☐ 130 ..... with "lip" base . (CE) .. ❶ ... $1,000–1,500

HUM TERM

UNDERGLAZE: The term used to describe especially the number 5 trademark that appears actually underneath the glaze as opposed to the later version of the number 5 trademark that appears on the top of the glaze.

| TM 2 | TM 3 | TM 1 |

HUM 131
Street Singer

Many size variations as well as some slight variations of this popular figurine. Originally modeled by master sculptor Arthur Moeller in 1939. Old name: "Soloist." One of several figurines that make up the Hummel orchestra.

☐ 131 ..... 5 to 5½" ..... (CE) .. ❶ ... $475–625
☐ 131 ..... 5 to 5½" ..... (CE) .. ❷ ... $300–375
☐ 131 ..... 5 to 5½" ..... (CE) .. ❸ ... $225–275
☐ 131 ..... 5 to 5½" ..... (CE) .. ❹ ... $200–225
☐ 131 ..... 5 to 5½" ..... (CE) .. ❺ ... $160–170
☐ 131 ..... 5 to 5½" ..... (CE) .. ❻ ... $155–160
☐ 131 ..... 5 to 5½" ..... (OE) .. ❼ ... $155

```
─────────── HUM TERM ───────────

  WAFFLE BASE: Another term to describe
  the quartered or divided bases.
```

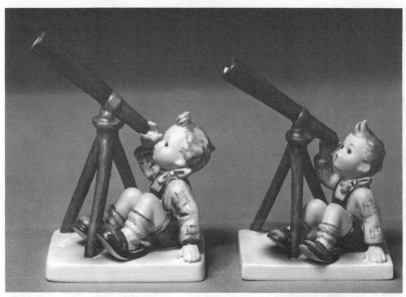

New model   Old model

HUM 132
Star Gazer

A very few older models have blue shirt. Most models in all trademark periods have purple shirts. Also some color variations on telescope. No cross-strap on boy's lederhosen on older models. "M. I. Hummel" signature is straight on early models; curved on later models. First modeled by master sculptor Arthur Moeller in 1939. Re-styled by current master sculptor Gerhard Skrobek in 1980 with the new textured finish and slightly rounded corners on the base.

☐ 132 ..... 4¾" .... (CE) .. ❶ ... $550–725
☐ 132 ..... 4¾" .... (CE) .. ❷ ... $350–450
☐ 132 ..... 4¾" .... (CE) .. ❸ ... $275–325
☐ 132 ..... 4¾" .... (CE) .. ❹ ... $225–275
☐ 132 ..... 4¾" .... (CE) .. ❺ ... $190–200
☐ 132 ..... 4¾" .... (CE) .. ❻ ... $180–190
☐ 132 ..... 4¾ to 5" ..... (OE) .. ❼ ... $180

HUM TERM

OUT OF PRODUCTION: A term used by the Goebel Company to designate items that are not currently in production, yet have not been given an official classification as to their eventual fate. Some items listed as out of production may become closed editions, remain temporarily withdrawn, or ultimately return to current production status.

TM 1 *TM 2* *TM 6*

HUM 133
Mother's Helper

This is the only figurine (in current production) produced with a cat. A similar figurine with a cat is named "Helping Mother" HUM 325 which is classified as a (PFE) possible future edition, and may be released at a later date. Older figurines are slightly larger in size. Originally modeled in 1939 by master sculptor Arthur Moeller. Note variations in photo.

☐ 133	4¾ to 5"	(CE)	❶	$475–625
☐ 133	4¾ to 5"	(CE)	❷	$325–400
☐ 133	4¾ to 5"	(CE)	❸	$250–275
☐ 133	4¾ to 5"	(CE)	❹	$200–250
☐ 133	4¾ to 5"	(CE)	❺	$165–175
☐ 133	4¾ to 5"	(CE)	❻	$160–165
☐ 133	4¾ to 5"	(OE)	❼	$160

```
──────────── HUM TERM ────────────

  OPEN EDITION: Pieces currently in W.
  Goebel's production program.
```

126

HUM 134
Quartet, Plaque
First modeled by master sculptor Arthur Moeller in 1939. Older models have "M.I. Hummel" signature on back while newer models have signature incised on front. Older models provided with two holes for cord to hang on wall while newer models have a centered hole on back for hanging. Quartet, Plaque was "temporarily withdrawn" (TW) from production on 31 December 1990, but may be reinstated at some future date.

☐ 134	..... 5½ × 6¼"	... (CE)	.. ❶	... $750–950
☐ 134	..... 5½ × 6¼"	... (CE)	.. ❷	... $500–600
☐ 134	..... 5½ × 6¼"	... (CE)	.. ❸	... $350–400
☐ 134	..... 5½ × 6¼"	... (CE)	.. ❹	... $300–350
☐ 134	..... 5½ × 6¼"	... (CE)	.. ❺	... $250–260
☐ 134	..... 5½ × 6¼"	... (TW)	.. ❻	... $240–250

———— HUM TERM ————

THREE LINE TRADEMARK: The symbol used by the W. Goebel Porzellanfabrik from 1964 until 1972 as their factory trademark. The name for this trademark was adopted to recognize that the V and bee was accompanied by three lines of print to the right of the V. Also known as TM 4.

135 (TM 1)   135 (TM 3)   135 4/0 (TM 6)

HUM 135
Soloist
Many size variations between old and new figurines. Originally modeled in 1940 by master sculptor Arthur Moeller. Old name "High Tenor." Similar to singer in figurine "Duet" HUM 130. One of several figurines that can be used to make up the Hummel orchestra. A new miniature size figurine was issued in 1986 with the suggested retail price of $45. Designed to match a new mini plate series called the "Little Music Makers"—one each year for four years. This is the third in the series. This miniature figurine has an incised 1985 copyright date. The large size has been renumbered 135/0 and the old 135 is now classified as a closed edition (CE) because of this change.

☐ 135 4/0	3″	(CE)	❻	$80-85
☐ 135 4/0	3″	(OE)	❼	$80
☐ 135	4½ to 5″	(CE)	❶	$350−450
☐ 135	4½ to 5″	(CE)	❷	$225−275
☐ 135	4½ to 5″	(CE)	❸	$170−190
☐ 135	4½ to 5″	(CE)	❹	$140−170
☐ 135	4½ to 5″	(CE)	❺	$120−125
☐ 135	4½ to 5″	(CE)	❻	$115−120
☐ 135/0	4¾″	(CE)	❻	$110−115
☐ 135/0	4¾″	(OE)	❼	$110

136/I (TM 5)   *136 Terra cotta (TM 1)*

HUM 136
Friends

Originally modeled by master sculptor Reinhold Unger in 1940. Spots on deer will vary slightly — sometimes three rows rather than two rows. Old name: "Good Friends" or "Friendship." The small size 136/I usually has an incised 1947 copyright date. Sold at one time in reddish-brown terra cotta finish in size 136 (10") with incised crown trademark. Very limited production in this finish; would be considered extremely rare. Value: *$15,000–20,000.* Also old crown trademark example (large size) found in white overglaze finish, but probably not sold that way. Sometimes incised 136/5 instead of 136/V.

☐ 136/I	....	5 to 5⅜"	.....	(CE)	.. ❶	... $700–850
☐ 136/I	....	5 to 5⅜"	.....	(CE)	.. ❷	... $350–450
☐ 136/I	....	5 to 5⅜"	.....	(CE)	.. ❸	... $275–315
☐ 136/I	....	5 to 5⅜"	.....	(CE)	.. ❹	... $225–275
☐ 136/I	....	5 to 5⅜"	.....	(CE)	.. ❺	... $190–200
☐ 136/I	....	5 to 5⅜"	.....	(CE)	.. ❻	... $180–190
☐ 136/I	....	5 to 5⅜"	.....	(OE)	.. ❼	... $180
☐ 136/V	...	10¾ to 11"	...	(CE)	.. ❶	... $3000–4000
☐ 136/V	...	10¾ to 11"	...	(CE)	.. ❷	... $1750–2500
☐ 136/V	...	10¾ to 11"	...	(CE)	.. ❸	... $1500–1750
☐ 136/V	...	10¾ to 11"	...	(CE)	.. ❹	... $1250–1500
☐ 136/V	...	10¾ to 11"	...	(CE)	.. ❺	... $1050–1100
☐ 136/V	...	10¾ to 11"	...	(CE)	.. ❻	... $1000–1050
☐ 136/V	...	10¾ to 11"	...	(OE)	.. ❼	... $1000
☐ 136	.....	10½"	....	(CE)	.. ❶	... $3000–4000
☐ 136	.....	10½"	....	(CE)	.. ❷	... $2000–3000
☐ 136	.....	10"	....	(CE)	.. ❶	... $15,000–20,000 (terra cotta)

137 A (TM 1)   *137 B (TM 2)*

HUM 137
Child in Bed, Wall Plaque
HUM 137 A (Child looking left) (CE)
HUM 137 B (Child looking right) (CE)

Originally modeled by master sculptor Arthur Moeller in 1940 as a set of two small wall plaques—one child looking left and one child looking right. Pictured here is the first known example of 137 A which was found hanging on a kitchen wall somewhere in Hungary in 1986. Since that time several other examples have been found in Europe.The child looking right (HUM 137 B) has been on the market for years and can be found in all trademark periods. Current production models are numbered 137 only, incised on the back along with the "M.I. Hummmel" signature. Also called "Baby Ring with Ladybug" or "Ladybug Plaque" in old catalogues.

☐ 137 A	... 3 × 3"	.... (CE)	.. ❶ ...	$5000–7000
☐ 137 B	... 3 × 3"	.... (CE)	.. ❶ ...	$300–500
☐ 137 B	... 3 × 3"	.... (CE)	.. ❷ ...	$175–200
☐ 137 B	... 3 × 3"	.... (CE)	.. ❸ ...	$100–125
☐ 137 B	... 3 × 3"	.... (CE)	.. ❹ ...	$75–100
☐ 137 B	... 3 × 3"	.... (CE)	.. ❺ ...	$60–65
☐ 137	... 3 × 3"	.... (CE)	.. ❺ ...	$57–60
☐ 137	... 3 × 3"	.... (CE)	.. ❻ ...	$55–57
☐ 137	... 3 × 3"	.... (OE)	.. ❼ ...	$55

137A Rear view

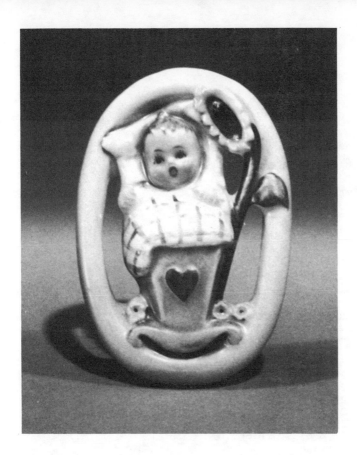

HUM 138 (CN)
Tiny Baby In Crib, Wall Plaque
According to factory information this small plaque was never produced for sale. The original model was made by master sculptor Arthur Moeller in 1940. Now listed on factory records as a Closed Number (CN) meaning that this design was produced as a sample model, but then for various reasons never authorized for release. Apparently, a very few examples left the factory and have been found in Germany. This plaque would be considered extremely rare.

☐ 138 . . . . . 2¼ × 3″ . . . . . (CN) . . ❷ . . . $3000–4000

ROEDENTAL: The town in West Germany where the W. Goebel Porzellanfabrik is situated. Roedental is located near Coburg and lies only a few miles from the East German border. In 1981 Roedental became the official Sister City of Eaton, Ohio due to the longtime "Hummel" relationship with Robert L. Miller.

Crown   Stylized   Full Bee

HUM 139
Flitting Butterfly, Wall Plaque

First modeled by master sculptor Arthur Moeller in 1940, this plaque is also known as
"Butterfly Plaque." Early crown mark pieces have no dots on girl's dress. The "M.I.
Hummel" signature has been on the back during all time periods. Redesigned in the
1960's with no air space behind girl's head. Some design and color variations have
evolved through the years of production. To my knowledge, not produced in
trademark 4.

☐ 139 ..... 2½ x2½" ..... (CE) .. ❶ ... $300–500
☐ 139 ..... 2½ x2½" ..... (CE) .. ❷ ... $200–250
☐ 139 ..... 2½ x2½" ..... (CE) .. ❸ ... $100–150
☐ 139 ..... 2½ x2½" ..... (CE) .. ❺ ... $60–65
☐ 139 ..... 2½ x2½" ..... (CE) .. ❻ ... $55–60
☐ 139 ..... 2½ x2½" ..... (OE) .. ❼ ... $55

--- HUM TERM ---

PAINTER'S SAMPLE: A figurine used by
the painters at the Goebel factory which
serves as a reference figurine for the painting of subsequent pieces. The painters of
"M.I. Hummel" figurines attempt to paint
their individual pieces to match the
painter's sample as precisely as possible.
Painter's Samples are sometimes marked
with a red line around the side of the base.

HUM 140
The Mail is Here, Plaque
Originally modeled by master sculptor Arthur Moeller in 1940, this plaque can be found in all trademark periods. At one time it was sold in Belgium in the white over-glaze finish and would now be considered extremely rare. Old name: "Post Carriage." Also known to collectors as "Mail Coach" plaque. In 1952 this same motif was made into a figurine by the same name (HUM226) by master sculptor Arthur Moeller. "The Mail is Here" plaque was "temporarily withdrawn" (TW) from production on 31 December 1989, but may be reinstated at some future date.

☐ 140 ..... 4¼ × 6¾" ... (CE) .. ❶ ... $600–900
☐ 140 ..... 4¼ × 6¾" ... (CE) .. ❷ ... $400–500
☐ 140 ..... 4¼ × 6¾" ... (CE) .. ❸ ... $300–325
☐ 140 ..... 4¼ × 6¾" ... (CE) .. ❹ ... $275–300
☐ 140 ..... 4¼ × 6¾" ... (CE) .. ❺ ... $235–250
☐ 140 ..... 4¼ × 6¾" ... (TW) .. ❻ ... $225–235

───── **HUM TERM** ─────
SCARCE: (Webster) Infrequently seen or found. Not plentiful or abundant.

141/V   **Old**   141/I   **New**   **Old** 141 3/0 **New**

HUM 141
Apple Tree Girl

First modeled by master sculptor Arthur Moeller in 1940 and has been restyled many times during the years that it has been produced. There are many size variations and early models have a tapered brown base. The smaller models have always been made without the bird in the tree. Size 141/V was first produced in the early 1970's and is found in 4, 5 and 6 trademarks only. Size 141/X was first produced in 1975. Old name: "Spring" or "Springtime." This same motif is used on the 1976 Annual Plate, HUM 269; Table Lamp, HUM 229; and Bookends, HUM 252 A. Size 141/X was "temporarily withdrawn" (TW), from production on 31 December 1990, but may be reinstated at some future date.

☐ 141 3/0	4 to 4¼″	(CE)	❶	$350–450
☐ 141 3/0	4 to 4¼″	(CE)	❷	$250–300
☐ 141 3/0	4 to 4¼″	(CE)	❸	$175–200
☐ 141 3/0	4 to 4¼″	(CE)	❹	$150–175
☐ 141 3/0	4 to 4¼″	(CE)	❺	$125–130
☐ 141 3/0	4 to 4¼″	(CE)	❻	$120–125
☐ 141 3/0	4 to 4¼″	(OE)	❼	$120
☐ 141	6 to 6¾″	(CE)	❶	$700–800
☐ 141	6 to 6¾″	(CE)	❷	$500–600
☐ 141/I	6 to 6¾″	(CE)	❶	$600–700
☐ 141/I	6 to 6¾″	(CE)	❷	$450–550
☐ 141/I	6 to 6¾″	(CE)	❸	$350–450
☐ 141/I	6 to 6¾″	(CE)	❹	$275–350
☐ 141/I	6 to 6¾″	(CE)	❺	$230–240
☐ 141/I	6 to 6¾″	(CE)	❻	$225–230
☐ 141/I	6 to 6¾″	(OE)	❼	$225
☐ 141/V	10¼″	(CE)	❹	$1250–1500
☐ 141/V	10¼″	(CE)	❺	$1050–1100
☐ 141/V	10¼″	(CE)	❻	$1000–1050
☐ 141/V	10¼″	(OE)	❼	$1000
☐ 141/X	32″	(CE)	❺	$10,000–17,000
☐ 141/X	32″	(TW)	❻	$10,000–17,000

142/V   Old   142/I   New   Old   142 3/0   New

HUM 142
Apple Tree Boy

This companion figurine to "Apple Tree Girl" was also modeled by master sculptor Arthur Moeller in 1940, and has been restyled many times during the years. There are many size variations and early models have a tapered brown base. The small size 142 3/0 with trademark 2 usually has a red feather in the boy's hat. Size 142/V was first produced in the early 1970's and is found in 4, 5 and 6 trademarks only. Old name: "Autumn" or "Fall." Smaller models have always been made without the bird in the tree. The same motif is used on the 1977 Annual Plate, HUM 270; Table Lamp, HUM 230; and Bookends, HUM 252 B.

continued on next page

☐ 142 3/0 . .	4 to 4¼″	. . . . . (CE) . .	❶ . . .	$350–450
☐ 142 3/0 . .	4 to 4¼″	. . . . . (CE) . .	❷ . . .	$250–300
☐ 142 3/0 . .	4 to 4¼″	. . . . . (CE) . .	❸ . . .	$175–200
☐ 142 3/0 . .	4 to 4¼″	. . . . . (CE) . .	❹ . . .	$150–175
☐ 142 3/0 . .	4 to 4¼″	. . . . . (CE) . .	❺ . . .	$125–130
☐ 142 3/0 . .	4 to 4¼″	. . . . . (CE) . .	❻ . . .	$120–125
☐ 142 3/0 . .	4 to 4¼″	. . . . . (OE) . .	❼ . . .	$120
☐ 142	6 to 6⅞″	. . . . . (CE) . .	❶ . . .	$700–800
☐ 142	6 to 6⅞″	. . . . . (CE) . .	❷ . . .	$500–600
☐ 142/I	6 to 6⅞″	. . . . . (CE) . .	❶ . . .	$600–700
☐ 142/I	6 to 6⅞″	. . . . . (CE) . .	❷ . . .	$450–550
☐ 142/I	6 to 6⅞″	. . . . . (CE) . .	❸ . . .	$350–375
☐ 142/I	6 to 6⅞″	. . . . . (CE) . .	❹ . . .	$275–350
☐ 142/I	6 to 6⅞″	. . . . . (CE) . .	❺ . . .	$230–240
☐ 142/I	6 to 6⅞″	. . . . . (CE) . .	❻ . . .	$225–230
☐ 142/I	6 to 6⅞″	. . . . . (OE) . .	❼ . . .	$225
☐ 142/V . . .	10¼″	. . . . (CE) . .	❹ . . .	$1250–1500
☐ 142/V . . .	10¼″	. . . . (CE) . .	❺ . . .	$1050–1100
☐ 142/V . . .	10¼″	. . . . (CE) . .	❻ . . .	$1000–1050
☐ 142/V . . .	10¼″	. . . . (OE) . .	❼ . . .	$1000

HUM 142
Apple Tree Boy *continued from previous page*

According to factory information, size 142/X (also known as "Jumbo" size) was first produced in the early 1960's with number 142/10 incised and the stylized trademark incised rather than stamped. A Canadian collector has a very early "Jumbo" Apple Tree Boy with the "full bee" (TM 2) trademark but no model number incised on it. The "Jumbo" size 142/X was restyled in the mid 1970's by master sculptor Gerhard Skrobek. Notice that the older model has two apples while the restlyed version has four apples. The newer version is slightly larger because of the extended branch on the boy's right. Size 142/X was "temporarily withdrawn" (TW) from production on 31 December 1990, but may be reinstated at some future date.

- ☐ 142/X . . . 30″ . . . . (CE) . . ❷ . . . $20,000–25,000
- ☐ 142/X . . . 30″ . . . . (CE) . . ❸ . . . $12,000–20,000
- ☐ 142/X . . . 30″ . . . . (CE) . . ❹ . . . $11,000–18,000
- ☐ 142/X . . . 30 to 32″ . . . . . (CE) . . ❺ . . . $10,000–17,000
- ☐ 142/X . . . 30 to 32″ . . . . . (TW) . . ❻ . . . $10,000–17,000

143/I (TM 2)   143/0 (TM 5)

HUM 143
Boots
First modeled by master sculptor Arthur Moeller in 1940. There are many size variations—from 5 to 5½" on the small; from 6 to 6¾" on the large. Old name: "Shoemaker." Both sizes were restyled with the new textured finish by current master modeler Gerhard Skrobek in the late 1970's.

☐ 143/0	5 to 5½"	(CE)	❶	$500–650
☐ 143/0	5 to 5½"	(CE)	❷	$325–400
☐ 143/0	5 to 5½"	(CE)	❸	$240–280
☐ 143/0	5 to 5½"	(CE)	❹	$200–240
☐ 143/0	5 to 5½"	(CE)	❺	$165–175
☐ 143/0	5 to 5½"	(CE)	❻	$160–165
☐ 143/0	5 to 5½"	(OE)	❼	$160
☐ 143/I	6½ to 6¾"	(CE)	❶	$750–900
☐ 143/I	6½ to 6¾"	(CE)	❷	$500–600
☐ 143/I	6½ to 6¾"	(CE)	❸	$400–475
☐ 143/I	6½ to 6¾"	(CE)	❹	$325–400
☐ 143/I	6½ to 6¾"	(CE)	❺	$280–290
☐ 143/I	6½ to 6¾"	(CE)	❻	$270–280
☐ 143/I	6½ to 6¾"	(OE)	❼	$270
☐ 143	6¾"	(CE)	❶	$800–950
☐ 143	6¾"	(CE)	❷	$550–650

HUM 144
Angelic Song
Originally modeled in 1941 by master sculptor Reinhold Unger. Little variation between old and new models. Old names: "Angels" or "Holy Communion."

☐ 144	..... 4″	....	(CE)	.. ❶	... $375–500
☐ 144	..... 4″	....	(CE)	.. ❷	... $250–300
☐ 144	..... 4″	....	(CE)	.. ❸	... $175–200
☐ 144	..... 4″	....	(CE)	.. ❹	... $150–175
☐ 144	..... 4″	....	(CE)	.. ❺	... $130–135
☐ 144	..... 4″	....	(CE)	.. ❻	... $125–130
☐ 144	..... 4″	....	**(OE)**	.. ❼	... $125

HUM 145
Little Guardian
This figurine was first modeled by master sculptor Reinhold Unger in 1941. The only noticeable difference would be in size, with the older pieces slightly larger.

☐ 145 ..... 3¾ to 4″ ..... (CE) .. ❶ ... $375–500
☐ 145 ..... 3¾ to 4″ ..... (CE) .. ❷ ... $250–300
☐ 145 ..... 3¾ to 4″ ..... (CE) .. ❸ ... $175–200
☐ 145 ..... 3¾ to 4″ ..... (CE) .. ❹ ... $150–175
☐ 145 ..... 3¾ to 4″ ..... (CE) .. ❺ ... $130–135
☐ 145 ..... 3¾ to 4″ ..... (CE) .. ❻ ... $125–130
☐ 145 ..... 3¾ to 4″ ..... (OE) .. ❼ ... $125

Old   *New*

HUM 146
Holy Water Font, Angel Duet
First modeled by master sculptor Reinhold Unger in 1941. This font has been restyled several times through the years with noticeable variations in the shape of angels' wings, construction of the back, holes between angels' heads and wings. Newer examples are completely solid and have the new textured finish.

☐ 146 ..... 3½ × 4¾" ... (CE) .. ❶ ... $150–200
☐ 146 ..... 3½ × 4¾" ... (CE) .. ❷ ... $100–125
☐ 146 ..... 3½ × 4¾" ... (CE) .. ❸ ... $70–90
☐ 146 ..... 3½ × 4¾" ... (CE) .. ❹ ... $60–70
☐ 146 ..... 3½ × 4¾" ... (CE) .. ❺ ... $47–50
☐ 146 ..... 3½ × 4¾" ... (CE) .. ❻ ... $45–47
☐ 146 ..... 3½ × 4¾" ... (**OE**) .. ❼ ... $45

Old   *New*

HUM 147
Holy Water Font, Angel Shrine
Originally modeled in 1941 by master sculptor Reinhold Unger and has been produced in all trademark periods. Older models are usually larger. Some variation in construction of back of font and water bowl. Old name: "Angel Devotion."

☐ 147 ... 3 × 5 to 3⅛ × 5¼" ... (CE) .. ❶ ... $200–250
☐ 147 ... 3 × 5 to 3⅛ × 5¼" ... (CE) .. ❷ ... $100–150
☐ 147 ... 3 × 5" .... (CE) .. ❸ ... $80–100
☐ 147 ... 3 × 5" .... (CE) .. ❹ ... $60–80
☐ 147 ... 3 × 5" .... (CE) .. ❺ ... $47–50
☐ 147 ... 3 × 5" .... (CE) .. ❻ ... $45–47
☐ 147 ... 3 × 5" .... **(OE)** .. ❼ ... $45

HUM 148 (CN)
Factory records indicate this was the same as the boy from HUM 60/A (Farm Boy, Bookend). Modeled in 1941 by a combination of the modelers. Listed as a Closed Number on 28 February 1941. No known examples or photographs.

☐ 148 .... (CN) ....

HUM 149 (CN)
Factory records indicate this was the same as the girl from HUM 60/B (Goose Girl, Bookend). Modeled in 1941 by a combination of modelers. Listed as a Closed Number on 28 February 1941. No known examples or photographs. A Closed Number (CN): an identification number in W. Goebel's numerical identification system, used to identify a design or sample model intended for possible production but then for various reasons never authorized for release.

☐ 149 .... (CN) ....

HUM 150
Happy Days
"Happy Days" was the very first "M.I. Hummel" figurine my wife, Ruth, acquired to start her collection. It reminded her of our daughter and son. We no longer have this first piece, as one of the children broke it; has since been replaced by an intact piece! "Happy Days" was first modeled in 1942 by a combination of modelers. All large size and older pieces have an extra flower on the base. The large size in the crown trademark usually does not have a size designator; incised 150 only. Sizes 150/0 and 150/I had been in very limited production, but are once again back on the market.

☐ 150 2/0	4¼"		(CE)	❷	$300–375
☐ 150 2/0	4¼"		(CE)	❸	$225–250
☐ 150 2/0	4¼"		(CE)	❹	$200–225
☐ 150 2/0	4¼"		(CE)	❺	$155–165
☐ 150 2/0	4¼"		(CE)	❻	$150–155
☐ 150 2/0	4¼"		(OE)	❼	$150
☐ 150/0	5 to 5¼"		(CE)	❷	$500–600
☐ 150/0	5 to 5¼"		(CE)	❸	$400–450
☐ 150/0	5 to 5¼"		(CE)	❹	$300–375
☐ 150/0	5 to 5¼"		(CE)	❺	$260–275
☐ 150/0	5 to 5¼"		(CE)	❻	$250–260
☐ 150/0	5 to 5¼"		(OE)	❼	$250
☐ 150/I	6¼ to 6½"		(CE)	❶	$1200–1500
☐ 150/I	6¼ to 6½"		(CE)	❷	$800–900
☐ 150/I	6¼ to 6½"		(CE)	❸	$600–700
☐ 150/I	6¼ to 6½"		(CE)	❹	$500–600
☐ 150/I	6¼ to 6½"		(CE)	❺	$420–440
☐ 150/I	6¼ to 6½"		(CE)	❻	$400–420
☐ 150/I	6¼ to 6½"		(OE)	❼	$400
☐ 150	6¼"		(CE)	❶	$1300–1600
☐ 150	6¼"		(CE)	❷	$900–1000

HUM 151
Madonna Holding Child
Known as the "Madonna with the Blue Cloak." Modeled by master sculptor Reinhold Unger in 1942. Was produced in five color variations: white overglaze, pastel blue cloak, dark blue cloak, brown cloak, and ivory finish. This figurine had not been produced for many years but was put back into production in 1977 and was produced in white overglaze and pastel blue only. Can now be found in 5 and 6 trademarks. This figurine sold for $44.00 on old 1955 price list. "Madonna Holding Child" in both color and white overglaze finish were "temporarily withdrawn" (TW) from production on 31 December 1989, but may be reinstated at some future date.

☐ 151 . . . . . . 12½" Blue . . . (CE) . . . ❶ . . . $2000–3000
☐ 151 . . . . . . 12½" Blue . . . (CE) . . . ❷ . . . $2000–2500
☐ 151 . . . . . . 12½" Blue . . . (CE) . . . ❺ . . . $825–850
☐ 151 . . . . . . 12½" Blue . . . (TW) . . . ❻ . . . $800–825
☐ 151 . . . . . . 12½" White . . (CE) . . . ❶ . . . $1500–2500
☐ 151 . . . . . . 12½" White . . (CE) . . . ❷ . . . $1000–2000
☐ 151 . . . . . . 12½" White . . (CE) . . . ❺ . . . $325–350
☐ 151 . . . . . . 12½" White . . (TW) . . ❻ . . . $320–325
☐ 151 . . . . . . 12½" Brown . (CE) . . . ❶ . . . $8000–10,000
☐ 151 . . . . . . 12½" Ivory . . . (CE) . . . ❶ . . . $8000–10,000
☐ 151 . . . . . . 12½" Dk. Blue (CE) . . . ❶ . . . $8000–10,000

152 (TM 1)   152/0 A (TM 2)

HUM 152 A
Umbrella Boy

Originally modeled by master sculptor Arthur Moeller in 1942. The crown mark piece in our collection is incised 152 only and is considered rare with that trademark. The large size was restyled in 1972 with a thin umbrella and new textured finish. Older models have the umbrella handle fastened on boy's right shoe while in newer models the handle is fastened to his left shoe. The small size was first produced in 1954 and can be found in all trademarks except the crown. Some small size examples have a *stamped* 1951 or 1956 copyright date while others have an *incised* 1957 date. Old name: "In Safety" or "Boy Under Umbrella."

☐ 152/0 A	4¾"	(CE)	❷	$1000–1500
☐ 152/0 A	4¾"	(CE)	❸	$725–850
☐ 152/0 A	4¾"	(CE)	❹	$600–725
☐ 152/0 A	4¾"	(CE)	❺	$500–525
☐ 152/0 A	4¾"	(CE)	❻	$490–500
☐ 152/0 A	4¾"	(OE)	❼	$490
☐ 152	8"	(CE)	❶	$3500–6000
☐ 152 A	8"	(CE)	❷	$2000–2500
☐ 152 A	8"	(CE)	❸	$1500–1800
☐ 152 A	8"	(CE)	❹	$1400–1500
☐ 152/II A	8"	(CE)	❹	$1400–1500
☐ 152/II A	8"	(CE)	❺	$1225–1300
☐ 152/II A	8"	(CE)	❻	$1200–1225
☐ 152/II A	8"	(OE)	❼	$1200

152/II B (TM 4)   *152/0 B (TM 3)*

HUM 152 B
Umbrella Girl
Originally modeled by master sculptor Arthur Moeller in 1949. We have never been able to locate "Umbrella Girl" with the crown trademark for our collection. It would be considered extremely rare, if it actually does exist. The large size was restyled in 1972 with a thin umbrella and new textured finish. The small size was first produced in 1954 and can be found in all trademarks except the crown. Some small size examples have an incised 1951 copyright date while others have an incised 1957 date. Old name: "In Safety" or "Girl Under Umbrella."

☐ 152/0 B	4¾"	(CE)	❷	$1000–1500
☐ 152/0 B	4¾"	(CE)	❸	$725–850
☐ 152/0 B	4¾"	(CE)	❹	$600–725
☐ 152/0 B	4¾"	(CE)	❺	$500–525
☐ 152/0 B	4¾"	(CE)	❻	$490–500
☐ 152/0 B	4¾"	**(OE)**	❼	$490
☐ 152 B	8"	(CE)	❶	$3500–6000
☐ 152 B	8"	(CE)	❷	$2000–2500
☐ 152 B	8"	(CE)	❸	$1500–1800
☐ 152 B	8"	(CE)	❹	$1400–1500
☐ 152/II B	8"	(CE)	❹	$1400–1500
☐ 152/II B	8"	(CE)	❺	$1225–1300
☐ 152/II B	8"	(CE)	❻	$1200–1225
☐ 152/II B	8"	**(OE)**	❼	$1200

153/0   153/I   153/0 Boy with hat (CE)

HUM 153
Auf Wiedersehen

Originally modeled by master sculptor Arthur Moeller in 1943. First produced in the large size only with plain 153 incised number. The small size was introduced in the early 1950's with the boy wearing a hat and waving his hand—always with full bee trademark and "0" size designator directly under the number "153"—considered rare. This style was made in the small size only. Both sizes have been restyled in recent years. Both styles of the small size can be found in full bee trademark. Also called "Good Bye" in old catalogues.

☐ 153/0 .... 5½ to 6" ..... (CE) .. ❷ ... $400–500
☐ 153/0 .... 5½ to 6" ..... (CE) .. ❸ ... $300–350
☐ 153/0 .... 5½ to 6" ..... (CE) .. ❹ ... $250–300
☐ 153/0 .... 5½ to 6" ..... (CE) .. ❺ ... $210–220
☐ 153/0 .... 5½ to 6" ..... (CE) .. ❻ ... $200–210
☐ 153/0 .... 5½ to 6" ..... (OE) .. ❼ ... $200
☐ 153/0 .... 5¼" .... (CE) .. ❷ ... $3000–4000 (with hat)
☐ 153 ..... 6¾ to 7" ..... (CE) .. ❶ ... $800–1100
☐ 153 ..... 6¾ to 7" ..... (CE) .. ❷ ... $600–700
☐ 153/I .... 6¾ to 7" ..... (CE) .. ❶ ... $700–1000
☐ 153/I .... 6¾ to 7" ..... (CE) .. ❷ ... $550–650
☐ 153/I .... 6¾ to 7" ..... (CE) .. ❸ ... $450–500
☐ 153/I .... 6¾ to 7" ..... (CE) .. ❹ ... $400–450
☐ 153/I .... 6¾ to 7" ..... (CE) .. ❺ ... $260–275
☐ 153/I .... 6¾ to 7" ..... (CE) .. ❻ ... $250–260
☐ 153/I .... 6¾ to 7" ..... (OE) .. ❼ ... $250

| 154/0 | 154/0 | 154/I | 154 (CE) |

HUM 154
Walter

Originally modeled by master sculptor Arthur Moeller in 1943. Was first produced in the 6½″ size and incised number 154 only, with gray coat and gray striped trousers. In the early 1950's the colors were changed to blue coat and tan striped trousers, and "Waiter" was produced in two sizes: 154/0 and 154/I. Has been produced with various names on bottle. "Rhein-wine" or "Rhein Wine" are the most common. "Whisky," "Hiher Mchie" and other illegible names have been used. Old name: "Chef of Service" in some old catalogues. Both sizes have recently been restyled with the new textured finish.

☐ 154/0	. . . .	6 to 6¼″	. . . . .	(CE)	. . ❶	. . .	$550–725
☐ 154/0	. . . .	6 to 6¼″	. . . . .	(CE)	. . ❷	. . .	$350–450
☐ 154/0	. . . .	6 to 6¼″	. . . . .	(CE)	. . ❸	. . .	$275–300
☐ 154/0	. . . .	6 to 6¼″	. . . . .	(CE)	. . ❹	. . .	$225–275
☐ 154/0	. . . .	6 to 6¼″	. . . . .	(CE)	. . ❺	. . .	$190–200
☐ 154/0	. . . .	6 to 6¼″	. . . . .	(CE)	. . ❻	. . .	$180–190
☐ 154/0	. . . .	6 to 6¼″	. . . .	(OE)	. . ❼	. . .	$180
☐ 154/I	. . . .	6½ to 7″	. . . . .	(CE)	. . ❶	. . .	$700–950
☐ 154/I	. . . .	6½ to 7″	. . . . .	(CE)	. . ❷	. . .	$450–550
☐ 154/I	. . . .	6½ to 7″	. . . . .	(CE)	. . ❸	. . .	$350–425
☐ 154/I	. . . .	6½ to 7″	. . . . .	(CE)	. . ❹	. . .	$300–350
☐ 154/I	. . . .	6½ to 7″	. . . . .	(CE)	. . ❺	. . .	$250–260
☐ 154/I	. . . .	6½ to 7″	. . . . .	(CE)	. . ❻	. . .	$240–250
☐ 154/I	. . . .	6½ to 7″	. . . .	(OE)	. . ❼	. . .	$240
☐ 154	. . . . .	6½″	. . . .	(CE)	. . ❶	. . .	$800–1100
☐ 154	. . . . .	6½″	. . . .	(CE)	. . ❷	. . .	$550–700
☐ 154/0	. . . .	6¼″	. . . .	(CE)	. . ❷	. . .	$1500–2000 (with whiskey)

HUM 155 (CN)

Factory records indicate: Madonna with cloak, sitting with child on her lap, Reinhold Unger in 1943. Listed as Closed Number on 18 May 1943. No known examples or photographs.

☐ 155 .... (CN) ....

HUM 156 (CN)

Factory records indicate: Wall picture with sitting woman and child, Arthur Moeller in 1943. Listed as Closed Number on 18 May 1943. No known examples or photographs.

☐ 156 .... (CN) ....

HUM 157 (CN)

Factory records indicate: Boy standing with flower basket. Sample model sculpted by Arthur Moeller in 1943. Considered for production but was never made. This factory sample does not have "M.I. Hummel" signature. Listed as Closed Number on 17 September 1943.

☐ 157 .... (CN) ....

HUM 158 (CN)
Factory records indicate: Girl standing with dog in her arms. Sample model sculpted by Arthur Moeller in 1943. Considered for production but was never made. This factory sample does not have "M.I. Hummel" signature. Listed as Closed Number on 17 September 1943.

☐ 158 . . . . (CN) . . . .

HUM 159 (CN)
Factory records indicate: Girl standing with flowers in her arms. Sample model sculpted by Arthur Moeller in 1943. Considered for production but was never made. This factory sample does not have "M.I. Hummel" signature. Listed as Closed Number on 17 September 1943.

☐ 159 . . . . (CN) . . . .

HUM 160 (CN)
Factory records indicate: Girl standing in
tiered dress and bouquet of flowers.
Sample model sculpted by Reinhold
Unger in 1943. Considered for production but was never made. This factory
sample does not have "M.I. Hummel" signature. Listed as Closed Number on 17
September 1943.

☐ 160 . . . . (CN) . . . .

HUM 161 (CN)
Factory records indicate: Girl standing
with hands in her pockets. Sample model
sculpted by Reinhold Unger in 1943.
Considered for production but was never
made. This factory sample does not have
"M.I. Hummel" signature. Listed as
Closed Number on 17 September 1943.

☐ 161 . . . . (CN) . . . .

Hum 162 (CN)
Factory records indicate: Girl standing with pocket-book (handbag). Sample model sculpted by Reinhold Unger in 1943. Listed as Closed Number on 11 October 1943. No known examples or photographs.

☐ 162 .... (CN) ....

Old   *New*

HUM 163
Whitsuntide
Originally modeled by master sculptor Arthur Moeller in 1946. Can be found in all trademarks except TM 4. Older models are larger than newer models. Old name: "Christmas". Sometimes referred to as "Happy New Year". Angel on base holds red or yellow candle on older models. Unusual variation has small hole in angel's cupped hands where candle should be. Had been considered rare at one time, but was put back into current production in 1978 and can be found with TM 5 and TM 6.

☐ 163 ..... 6½ to 7" ..... (CE) .. ❶ ... $1000–1200
☐ 163 ..... 6½ to 7" ..... (CE) .. ❷ ... $750–1000
☐ 163 ..... 6½ to 7" ..... (CE) .. ❸ ... $500–750
☐ 163 ..... 6½ to 7" ..... (CE) .. ❺ ... $280–300
☐ 163 ..... 6½ to 7" ..... (CE) .. ❻ ... $270–280
☐ 163 ..... 6½ to 7" ..... (OE) .. ❼ ... $270

Old   *New*

HUM 164
Holy Water Font, Worship

First modeled by master sculptor Reinhold Unger in 1946. There are variations in construction of this font in that older models do not have a rim on back side of bowl while newer models do. Also color variations on lip of water bowl — older ones were handpainted; newer ones are shaded with airbrush.

☐ 164	3¼ × 5"	(CE)	❶	$250–300
☐ 164	3¼ × 5"	(CE)	❷	$150–200
☐ 164	3¼ × 5"	(CE)	❸	$80–100
☐ 164	3¼ × 5"	(CE)	❹	$60–80
☐ 164	3¼ × 5"	(CE)	❺	$47–50
☐ 164	3¼ × 5"	(CE)	❻	$45–47
☐ 164	3¼ × 5"	(OE)	❼	$45

HUM 165
Swaying Lullaby, Wall Plaque

Originally modeled by master sculptor Arthur Moeller in 1946. Not pictured in older catalogues; most collectors were not aware of the existence of this plaque until the early 1970's. Our first purchase came through an American soldier who had been stationed in Panama. Put back into current production in 1978 and now available in TM 5 and TM 6. Older models have the "M.I. Hummel" signature on the back while newer models have signature on front lower right corner. Old name: "Child in a Hammock." Inscription reads: "Dreaming of better times." Considered rare in crown, full bee, and stylized trademarks. Restyled in 1979. Current production models are slightly thicker in depth, with signature on back. "Swaying Lullaby" wall plaque was "temporarily withdrawn" (TW) from production on 31 December 1989, but may be reinstated at some future date.

Stylized trademark

☐ 165	4½ × 5¼"	(CE)	❶	$750–1000
☐ 165	4½ × 5¼"	(CE)	❷	$500–750
☐ 165	4½ × 5¼"	(CE)	❸	$350–500
☐ 165	4½ × 5¼"	(CE)	❺	$160–170
☐ 165	4½ × 5¼"	(TW)	❻	$150–160

HUM 166
Boy With Bird, Ashtray
This ashtray was modeled by master sculptor Arthur Moeller in 1946. Only slight variations in color and construction through the years; no major differences between old and new models. "Boy with Bird" ashtray was "temporarily withdrawn" (TW) from production on 31 December 1989, but may be reinstated at some future date.

☐ 166	3¼ × 6"	(CE)	❶	$400–600
☐ 166	3¼ × 6"	(CE)	❷	$250–300
☐ 166	3¼ × 6"	(CE)	❸	$180–200
☐ 166	3¼ × 6"	(CE)	❹	$150–180
☐ 166	3¼ × 6"	(CE)	❺	$140–150
☐ 166	3¼ × 6"	(TW)	❻	$130–140

HUM 167
Holy Water Font, Angel Sitting
Also referred to as: "Angel-Bird" or "Angel with Bird" font. Newer models have a hole at top of font for hanging. Older models have hole on back of font for hanging. We recently found old crown (TM1) font that has both hole at top and on back, is smaller in size and has no rim on back edge of bowl. Variations in color on lip of water bowl — older ones were handpainted; newer ones are shaded with airbrush. First modeled by Reinhold Unger in 1945.

☐ 167	3¼ × 4⅛"	(CE)	❶	$250–300
☐ 167	3¼ × 4⅛"	(CE)	❷	$150–200
☐ 167	3¼ × 4⅛"	(CE)	❸	$80–100
☐ 167	3¼ × 4⅛"	(CE)	❹	$60–80
☐ 167	3¼ × 4⅛"	(CE)	❺	$47–50
☐ 167	3¼ × 4⅛"	(CE)	❻	$45–47
☐ 167	3¼ × 4⅛"	(OE)	❼	$45

Old-crown　　　　　*Old*　　　　　*New*

Stylized trademark

HUM 168
Standing Boy, Wall Plaque
Originally modeled by master sculptor Arthur Moeller in 1948. Not pictured in older catalogues; most collectors were not aware of the existence of this plaque until the early 1970's. Very limited early production, probably sold mostly in European market. Put back into current production in 1978 and now available in TM 5 and TM 6. Older models have only "Hummel" on front, lower left, along with " © WG" in lower right corner. Newer models have "M.I. Hummel" signature incised on back. This same motif was made into a figurine in 1979 by current master sculptor Gerhard Skrobek; see HUM 399 "Valentine Joy." "Standing Boy" wall plaque was "temporarily withdrawn" (TW) from production on 31 December 1989, but may be reinstated at some future date.

☐ 168 ..... 4⅛ × 5½" ... (CE) .. ❶ ... $750–1000
☐ 168 ..... 4⅛ × 5½" ... (CE) .. ❷ ... $500–750
☐ 168 ..... 4⅛ × 5½" ... (CE) .. ❸ ... $350–500
☐ 168 ..... 4⅛ × 5½" ... (CE) .. ❺ ... $160–170
☐ 168 ..... 4⅛ × 5½" ... (TW) .. ❻ ... $150–160

Old style　　　　　　　　**New style**

HUM 169
Bird Duet

Originally modeled in 1945 by master sculptor Arthur Moeller; later restyled in 1967 by current master sculptor Gerhard Skrobek. Many variations between old and new figurines. Variations are noted in angel's wings, gown and position of baton. Color variation in birds, angel's hair and gown, as well as music stand.

☐ 169	..... 3¾ to 4″	..... (CE)	.. ❶	...	$350–475
☐ 169	..... 3¾ to 4″	..... (CE)	.. ❷	...	$225–300
☐ 169	..... 3¾ to 4″	..... (CE)	.. ❸	...	$180–200
☐ 169	..... 3¾ to 4″	..... (CE)	.. ❹	...	$150–180
☐ 169	..... 3¾ to 4″	..... (CE)	.. ❺	...	$125–130
☐ 169	..... 3¾ to 4″	..... (CE)	.. ❻	...	$120–125
☐ 169	..... 3¾ to 4″	..... (OE)	.. ❼	...	$120

—————— HUM TERM ——————

SECONDARY MARKET: The buying and selling of items after the initial retail purchase has been transacted. Often times this post-retail trading is also referred to as the "after market." This very publication is intended to serve as a guide for the secondary market values of "M.I. Hummel" items.

170/III (TM 5)   170/I (TM 4)

HUM 170
School Boys
First modeled by master sculptor Reinhold Unger in 1943 and later remodeled by present master sculptor Gerhard Skrobek in 1961. Originally produced in one size with incised number 170 only. Small size first produced in the early 1960's and has an incised 1961 copyright date. Old name: "Difficult Problems." Some color variations on older models. Large size was again restyled in the eary 1970's with the new textured finish and 1972 copyright date. In the spring of 1982 the large size (170/III) was permanently retired by Goebel and will not be produced again. The small size 170/I is still in current production. The newly authorized retailer plaque (HUM 460) issued in 1986 utilizes the middle boy as part of the new plaque motif.

☐ 170/I	....	7¼ to 7½"	....	(CE)	..	❸	...	$1200–1500
☐ 170/I	....	7¼ to 7½"	....	(CE)	..	❹	...	$1100–1200
☐ 170/I	....	7¼ to 7½"	....	(CE)	..	❺	...	$1050–1100
☐ 170/I	....	7¼ to 7½"	....	(CE)	..	❻	...	$1000–1050
☐ 170/I	....	7¼ to 7½"	....	(OE)	..	❼	...	$1000
☐ 170	.....	10 to 10¼"	...	(CE)	..	❶	...	$4000–5000
☐ 170	.....	10 to 10¼"	...	(CE)	..	❷	...	$3000–4000
☐ 170	.....	10 to 10¼"	...	(CE)	..	❸	...	$2000–2200
☐ 170/III	...	10 to 10¼"	...	(CE)	..	❸	...	$2000–2200
☐ 170/III	...	10 to 10¼"	...	(CE)	..	❹	...	$1950–2000
☐ 170/III	...	10 to 10¼"	...	(CE)	..	❺	...	$1850–1950
☐ 170/III	...	10 to 10¼"	...	(CE)	..	❻	...	$1750–1850

Old style (TM 1)   *New style (TM 6)*

HUM 171
Little Sweeper
This figurine was first modeled by master sculptor Reinhold Unger in 1944. Very little change between older and newer models. Old name: "Mother's Helper." Restyled in 1981 by present master sculptor Gerhard Skrobek. The current production now has the new textured finish and is slightly larger. A new miniature size figurine was issued in 1988 with a suggested retail price of $45 to match a new miniature plate series called the "Little Homemakers" — one each year for four years. This is the first in the series. The miniature size figurine has an incised 1986 copyright date. The normal size will be renumbered 171/0 and the old number 171 is now classified as a closed edition (CE) because of this change.

☐ 171 4/0 .. 3" .... (CE) .. ❻ ... $80-85
☐ 171 4/0 .. 3" .... **(OE)** .. ❼ ... $80
☐ 171 ..... 4¼" .... (CE) .. ❶ ... $350–450
☐ 171 ..... 4¼" .... (CE) .. ❷ ... $225–275
☐ 171 ..... 4¼" .... (CE) .. ❸ ... $175–200
☐ 171 ..... 4¼" .... (CE) .. ❹ ... $140–175
☐ 171 ..... 4¼" .... (CE) .. ❺ ... $120–125
☐ 171 ..... 4¼" .... (CE) .. ❻ ... $115–120
☐ 171/0 .... 4¼" .... (CE) .. ❻ ... $110–115
☐ 171/0 .... 4¼ to 4½" .... **(OE)** .. ❼ ... $110

| Crown | Full Bee | Stylized |

HUM 172
Festival Harmony (Mandolin)

Originally modeled in 1947 by master sculptor Reinhold Unger in the large size only with incised number 172. Old crown mark and some full bee examples have the bird resting on flowers in front of angel (rare). Restyled in the early 1950's with bird resting on mandolin and one flower at hem of angel's gown. Restyled again in the late 1960's with the new textured finish and flowers placed at angel's feet. There are variations in color of gown and color of birds. The small size (172/0) was modeled by master sculptor Theo R. Menzenbach in 1961 and can be found in one style only. The large size (172/II) was "temporarily withdrawn" (TW) from production on 31 December 1984, but may be reinstated at some future date.

☐ 172/0	8″	(CE)	❸	$400–600	
☐ 172/0	8″	(CE)	❹	$325–400	
☐ 172/0	8″	(CE)	❺	$270–280	
☐ 172/0	8″	(CE)	❻	$260–270	
☐ 172/0	8″	(OE)	❼	$260	
☐ 172/II	10¼ to 10¾	(CE)	❸	$500–700	
☐ 172/II	10¼ to 10¾	(CE)	❹	$450–500	
☐ 172/II	10¼ to 10¾	(CE)	❺	$400–425	
☐ 172/II	10¼ to 10¾	(TW)	❻	$375–400	
☐ 172	10¾″	(CE)	❶	$2500–3000	(Bird in front)
☐ 172	10¾″	(CE)	❷	$2000–2500	(Bird in front)
☐ 172	10¾″	(CE)	❷	$1000–1250	(Flower at hem)
☐ 172	10¾″	(CE)	❸	$750–1000	(Flower at hem)

Crown   **Full Bee**   **Stylized**

HUM 173
Festival Harmony (Flute)
Originally modeled in 1947 by master sculptor Reinhold Unger in the large size only with incised number 173. Old crown mark and some full bee examples have a much larger bird and flower in front of angel (rare). Restyled in the early 1950's with smaller bird and one flower at hem of angel's gown. Restyled again in the late 1960's with the new textured finish and flowers placed at angel's feet. There are variations in color of gown and color of birds. The small size (173/0) was modeled by master sculptor Theo R. Menzenbach in 1961 and can be found in one style only. The large size (173/II) was "temporarily withdrawn" (TW) from production on 31 December 1984, but may be reinstated at some future date.

☐ 173/0	8″	(CE)	❸	$400–600	
☐ 173/0	8″	(CE)	❹	$325–400	
☐ 173/0	8″	(CE)	❺	$270–280	
☐ 173/0	8″	(CE)	❻	$260–270	
☐ 173/0	8″	(**OE**)	❼	$260	
☐ 173/II	10¼ to 11″	(CE)	❸	$500–700	
☐ 173/II	10¼ to 11″	(CE)	❹	$450–500	
☐ 173/II	10¼ to 11″	(CE)	❺	$400–425	
☐ 173/II	10¼ to 11″	(TW)	❻	$375–400	
☐ 173	11″	(CE)	❶	$2500–3000	(Flowers up front of dress)
☐ 173	11″	(CE)	❷	$2000–2500	(Flowers up front of dress)
☐ 173	11″	(CE)	❷	$1000–1250	(Flowers at hem)
☐ 173	11″	(CE)	❸	$750–1000	(Flower at hem)

TM 1   TM 2   TM 5

HUM 174
She Loves Me, She Loves Me Not!

Originally modeled by master sculptor Arthur Moeller in 1945. Has been restyled several times. Early crown mark pieces have smaller feather in boy's hat, no flower on left fence post and eyes are open. The 2, 3 and 4 trademark period pieces have a flower on left fence post and eyes are open. Current production pieces have no flower on left fence post (same as crown mark piece) but with eyes looking down. Newer models have an incised 1955 copyright date.

☐ 174 . . . . . 4¼" . . . . (CE) . . ❶ . . . $450–600
☐ 174 . . . . . 4¼" . . . . (CE) . . ❷ . . . $300–375
☐ 174 . . . . . 4¼" . . . . (CE) . . ❸ . . . $225–250
☐ 174 . . . . . 4¼" . . . . (CE) . . ❹ . . . $190–225
☐ 174 . . . . . 4¼" . . . . (CE) . . ❺ . . . $155–165
☐ 174 . . . . . 4¼" . . . . (CE) . . ❻ . . . $150–155
☐ 174 . . . . . 4¼" . . . . (OE) . . ❼ . . . $150

TM 1   TM 2

Old style (TM 1)   *New style (TM 3)*

HUM 175
Mother's Darling
Older models have pink and green-colored kerchiefs (bags) while models have blue ones. Older models do not have polka dots on head scarf. Old name: "Happy Harriet." First modeled by master sculptor Arthur Moeller in 1945, and has been restyled several times since then.

☐ 175	5½"	(CE)	❶	$525–700
☐ 175	5½"	(CE)	❷	$350–450
☐ 175	5½"	(CE)	❸	$275–325
☐ 175	5½"	(CE)	❹	$225–275
☐ 175	5½"	(CE)	❺	$190–200
☐ 175	5½"	(CE)	❻	$180–190
☐ 175	5½"	(OE)	❼	$180

---- HUM TERM ----

PAINTER'S SAMPLE: A figurine used by the painters at the Goebel factory which serves as a reference figurine for the painting of subsequent pieces. The painters of "M.I. Hummel" figurines attempt to paint their individual pieces to match the painter's sample as precisely as possible. Painter's Samples are sometimes marked with a red line around the side of the base.

176/I New   176/I Old

HUM 176
Happy Birthday
When first modeled in 1945 by master sculptor Arthur Moeller this figurine was produced in one size only with the incised number 176. A smaller size was issued in the
mid-1950's with the incised number 176/0 and an oval base. At the same time, the
large size was changed to 176/I. The large size figurine has always had a round base
until it was completely restyled in 1979 and now has an oval base, also.

☐ 176/0 . . . . 5 to 5¼″ . . . . . (CE) . . ❷ . . . $350–450
☐ 176/0 . . . . 5 to 5¼″ . . . . . (CE) . . ❸ . . . $275–325
☐ 176/0 . . . . 5 to 5¼″ . . . . . (CE) . . ❹ . . . $225–275
☐ 176/0 . . . . 5 to 5¼″ . . . . . (CE) . . ❺ . . . $190–200
☐ 176/0 . . . . 5 to 5¼″ . . . . . (CE) . . ❻ . . . $180–190
☐ 176/0 . . . . 5 to 5¼″ . . . . . (OE) . . ❼ . . . $180
☐ 176/I . . . . 5¾ to 6″ . . . . . (CE) . . ❶ . . . $750–1000
☐ 176/I . . . . 5¾ to 6″ . . . . . (CE) . . ❷ . . . $500–625
☐ 176/I . . . . 5¾ to 6″ . . . . . (CE) . . ❸ . . . $375–450
☐ 176/I . . . . 5¾ to 6″ . . . . . (CE) . . ❹ . . . $325–375
☐ 176/I . . . . 5¾ to 6″ . . . . . (CE) . . ❺ . . . $260–275
☐ 176/I . . . . 5¾ to 6″ . . . . . (CE) . . ❻ . . . $250–260
☐ 176/I . . . . 5¾ to 6″ . . . . . (OE) . . ❼ . . . $250
☐ 176 . . . . . 5½″ . . . . (CE) . . ❶ . . . $800–1000
☐ 176 . . . . . 5½″ . . . . (CE) . . ❷ . . . $550–675

177 (TM 2)   *177/I (TM 4)*

HUM 177
School Girls
First modeled by master sculptor Reinhold Unger in 1946 and later remodeled by master sculptor Theo R. Menzenbach in 1961. Originally produced in one size with incised number 177 only. Small size first produced in the early 1960's and has an incised 1961 copyright date. Old name: "Master Piece." Some slight color variations on older models, particularly the shoes. Large size again restyled in the early 1970's with the new textured finish and a 1972 incised copyright date. In the spring of 1982 the large size (177/III) was permanently retired by Goebel and will not be produced again. The small size (177/I) is still in current production. See HUM 255 "Stitch in Time" and HUM 256 "Knitting Lesson" for interesting comparison.

☐ 177/I	7½"	(CE)	❸	$1200–1500
☐ 177/I	7½"	(CE)	❹	$1100–1200
☐ 177/I	7½"	(CE)	❺	$1050–1100
☐ 177/I	7½"	(CE)	❻	$1000–1050
☐ 177/I	7½"	**(OE)**	❼	$1000
☐ 177	9½"	(CE)	❶	$4000–5000
☐ 177	9½"	(CE)	❷	$3000–4000
☐ 177	9½"	(CE)	❸	$2000–2200
☐ 177/III	9½"	(CE)	❸	$2000–2200
☐ 177/III	9½"	(CE)	❹	$1950–2000
☐ 177/III	9½"	(CE)	❺	$1850–1950
☐ 177/III	9½"	(CE)	❻	$1750–1850

Old style (TM 2)   *New style (TM 4)*

HUM 178
Photographer
Originally modeled by master sculptor Reinhold Unger in 1948 and has been restyled
several times through the years. There are many size variations with the older models
being larger. Some color variations on dog and camera. Newer models have a 1948
copyright date.

☐ 178 ..... 4¾ to 5¼" .... (CE) .. ❶ ... $650–900
☐ 178 ..... 4¾ to 5¼" .... (CE) .. ❷ ... $400–550
☐ 178 ..... 4¾ to 5¼" .... (CE) .. ❸ ... $350–400
☐ 178 ..... 4¾ to 5¼" .... (CE) .. ❹ ... $290–350
☐ 178 ..... 4¾ to 5¼" .... (CE) .. ❺ ... $240–250
☐ 178 ..... 4¾ to 5¼" .... (CE) .. ❻ ... $230–240
☐ 178 ..... 4¾ to 5¼" .... (**OE**) .. ❼ ... $230

HUM TERM

TERRA COTTA: A reddish clay used in an
experimental fashion by artisans at the W.
Goebel Porzellanfabrik. There are a few
sample pieces of "M.I. Hummel" figurines
that were produced with the terra cotta material. These terra cotta pieces have the
look of the reddish-brown clay and were
not painted.

Old style (TM 1)   *New style (TM 3)*

HUM 179
Coquettes
Modeled originally by master sculptor Arthur Moeller in 1948 and has been restyled in recent years. Older examples are usually slightly larger in size. Minor color variations can be found in older models.

☐ 179 ..... 5 to 5½″ ..... (CE) .. ❶ ... $650–900
☐ 179 ..... 5 to 5¼″ ..... (CE) .. ❷ ... $400–550
☐ 179 ..... 5 to 5¼″ ..... (CE) .. ❸ ... $350–400
☐ 179 ..... 5 to 5¼″ ..... (CE) .. ❹ ... $290–350
☐ 179 ..... 5 to 5¼″ ..... (CE) .. ❺ ... $240–250
☐ 179 ..... 5 to 5¼″ ..... (CE) .. ❻ ... $230–240
☐ 179 ..... 5 to 5¼″ ..... (OE) .. ❼ ... $230

HUM TERM

WHITE OVERGLAZE: The term used to designate an item that has not been painted, but has been glazed and fired. These pieces are completely white. All "M.I. Hummel" items are produced in this finish before being individually hand painted.

New style   *Old style*

HUM 180
Tuneful Good Night, Wall Plaque
Modeled by master sculptor Arthur Moeller in 1946. Recently restyled in 1981 by master sculptor Rudolf Wittman, a twenty-five-year veteran of the Goebel factory. In the restyled version, the position of the girl's head and hairstyle have been changed, as well as the position of the horn which is no longer attached to the heart-shaped back. Old name: "Happy Bugler" plaque. Had been considered rare and was difficult to find, but is readily available with 5 and 6 trademarks. "Tuneful Good Night" wall plaque was "temporarily withdrawn" (TW) from production on 31 December 1989, but may be reinstated at some future date.

☐ 180 ..... 5 × 4¾" ..... (CE) .. ❶ ... $500–750
☐ 180 ..... 5 × 4¾" ..... (CE) .. ❷ ... $350–500
☐ 180 ..... 5 × 4¾" ..... (CE) .. ❸ ... $300–350
☐ 180 ..... 5 × 4¾" ..... (CE) .. ❹ ... $250–300
☐ 180 ..... 5 × 4¾" ..... (CE) .. ❺ ... $160–170
☐ 180 ..... 5 × 4¾" ..... (TW) .. ❻ ... $150–160

HUM TERM

THREE LINE TRADEMARK: The symbol used by the W. Goebel Porzellanfabrik from 1964 until 1972 as their factory trademark. The name for this trademark was adopted to recognize that the V and bee was accompanied by three lines of print to the right of the V. Also known as TM 4.

Postcard drawing

HUM 181
Old Man Reading Newspaper (CN)

This unusual piece was made as a sample only in 1948 by master sculptor Arthur Moeller and was not approved by the Siessen Convent for production. It was not considered typical of Sister M.I. Hummel's work, although it is an exact reproduction of one of her early sketches. This early sample *does* have the familiar "M.I. Hummel" signature and is part of the Robert L. Miller collection. Listed as a Closed Number on 18 February 1948 and will not be produced again. Often referred to as one of the "Mamas" and the "Papas." Also produced as a lamp base; see HUM 202. Several other examples have been found in recent years. The original drawing shown here appeared on an old German post card.

☐ 181 ..... 6¾" .... (CN) $15,000–20,000

New style   Old style

HUM 182
Good Friends
Originally modeled by master sculptor Arthur Moeller in 1946 and later restyled by master sculptor Gerhard Skrobek in 1976. The current model is slightly larger and has the new textured finish. Called "Friends" in old catalogues.

☐ 182	4 to 4¼"	(CE)	❶	$475–650
☐ 182	4 to 4¼"	(CE)	❷	$300–400
☐ 182	4 to 4¼"	(CE)	❸	$240–280
☐ 182	4 to 4¼"	(CE)	❹	$200–240
☐ 182	4 to 4¼"	(CE)	❺	$165–175
☐ 182	4 to 4¼"	(CE)	❻	$160–165
☐ 182	4 to 4¼"	(OE)	❼	$160

HUM TERM

MOLD GROWTH: In the earlier days of figurine production the working molds were made of plaster of paris. As these molds were used, the various molded parts became larger due to the repeated usage. With modern technology at the Goebel factory and the use of acrylic resin molds, this problem has been eliminated and today the collector finds very few size differences within a given size designation.

Old style (TM 1)   *New style (TM 6)*

HUM 183
Forest Shrine
First modeled in 1946 by master sculptor Reinhold Unger and can be found with all trademarks except trademark 4. Had been considered rare but was put back into production in 1977 and can be found with 5 and 6 trademarks. Older models have a shiny finish on the deer while newer models have a dull finish. Old name: "Doe at Shrine." This figurine has recently been restyled with a more lifelike finish on the deer.

☐ 183 ..... 9" .... (CE) .. ❶ ... $1300–1800
☐ 183 ..... 9" .... (CE) .. ❷ ... $900–1200
☐ 183 ..... 9" .... (CE) .. ❸ ... $650–900
☐ 183 ..... 9" .... (CE) .. ❺ ... $480–500
☐ 183 ..... 9" .... (CE) .. ❻ ... $460–480
☐ 183 ..... 9" .... (OE) .. ❼ ... $460

```
┌────────────── HUM TERM ──────────────┐
│  DOUBLE CROWN: This term is used to   │
│  describe the Goebel Company trademark│
│  found on some "M.I. Hummel" figurines.│
│  On "double crown" pieces the crown   │
│  trademark is usually found incised and│
│  stamped.                             │
└───────────────────────────────────────┘
```

| Old style (TM 1) | New style (TM 3) | New style (TM 6) |

HUM 184
Latest News

First modeled by master sculptor Arthur Moeller in 1946. Older models were made with square base and boy's eyes open. Restyled in the mid-1960's and changed to round base and boy's eyes looking down at paper. At one time the newspaper was produced without any name so that visitors to the factory could have the name of their choice put on. An endless variety of names can be found. Most common names are: "Das Allerneueste," "Munchener Presse" and "Latest News." Some collectors specialize in collecting the different names on the newspaper and will pay from $500 to $1,000 for some names. Some catalogues list as 184/O.S. which means: Ohne Schrift (without lettering).

☐ 184	5 to 5¼"	(CE)	❶	$700–950
☐ 184	5 to 5¼"	(CE)	❷	$475–600
☐ 184	5 to 5¼"	(CE)	❸	$360–425
☐ 184	5 to 5¼"	(CE)	❹	$300–360
☐ 184	5 to 5¼"	(CE)	❺	$250–260
☐ 184	5 to 5¼"	(CE)	❻	$240–250
☐ 184	5 to 5¼"	(OE)	❼	$240

HUM TERM

MUSTERZIMMER: The German word meaning sample model designating that this piece is to be held at the W. Goebel Porzellanfabrik in the "sample room" to be used for future reference by production artists.

New   **Old**

HUM 185
Accordion Boy

First modeled by master sculptor Reinhold Unger in 1947, this figurine has never had a major restyling although there are many size variations due mainly to "mold growth." In the early years, the molds were made of plaster of paris and had a tendency to "wash out" or erode with use, thereby producing figurines each being slightly larger than the last. Since 1954, the use of acrylic resin for modeling has led to greater uniformity in the figurines themselves. There are some slight color variations on the accordion. Old name: "On the Alpine Pasture." One of several figurines that make up the Hummel orchestra.

☐ 185	5 to 6″	(CE)	❶	$475–650
☐ 185	5 to 6″	(CE)	❷	$325–400
☐ 185	5 to 6″	(CE)	❸	$240–280
☐ 185	5″	(CE)	❹	$200–240
☐ 185	5″	(CE)	❺	$165–175
☐ 185	5″	(CE)	❻	$160–165
☐ 185	5″	(OE)	❼	$160

New   **Old**

HUM 186
Sweet Music

Originally modeled in 1947 by master sculptor Reinhold Unger. Many size variations. Was restyled slightly in the mid-1960's. Some old crown mark pieces have white slippers with blue-green stripes instead of the normal brownish color. This variation will usually sell for $1200 to $1600. Old name: "Playing To The Dance." One of several figurines that make up the Hummel orchestra.

☐ 186	5 to 5½″	(CE)	❶	$1200–1600 (with striped slippers)
☐ 186	5 to 5½″	(CE)	❶	$475–650
☐ 186	5 to 5½″	(CE)	❷	$325–400
☐ 186	5 to 5½″	(CE)	❸	$240–280
☐ 186	5″	(CE)	❹	$200–240
☐ 186	5″	(CE)	❺	$165–175
☐ 186	5″	(CE)	❻	$160–165
☐ 186	5″	(OE)	❼	$160

HUM 187
M.I. Hummel Plaques (In English)

There seems to have been an endless variety of plaques throughout the years, some for dealers and some for collectors. Originally modeled by master sculptor Reinhold Unger in 1947 and later restyled by Gerhard Skrobek in 1962. Two incised copyright dates have been used, 1947 and 1976. Current display plaques for collectors are incised 187 A. At one time in recent years, dealers' names

Australian Dealer

Current model

were printed on the plaques for Australian dealers only. Pictured here is only a small portion of the many variations issued. 187 (with 1947 copyright date) and 187 A (with 1976 copyright date) can both be found with TM 5. Retired from production in 1986 but put back into service in 1990 with new graphics.

☐ 187 ..... 5½ × 4" ..... (CE) .. ❶ ... $1200–1500
☐ 187 ..... 5½ × 4" ..... (CE) .. ❷ ... $600–800
☐ 187 ..... 5½ × 4" ..... (CE) .. ❸ ... $400–600
☐ 187 ..... 5½ × 4" ..... (CE) .. ❹ ... $400–450
☐ 187 ..... 5½ × 4" ..... (CE) .. ❺ ... $150–200
☐ 187A .... 5½ × 4" ..... (CE) .. ❻ ... $150–200
☐ 187A .... 5½ × 4" ..... (CE) .. ❻ ... $125–150
☐ 187A .... 5½ × 4" ..... (CE) .. ❻ ... $75–80
☐ 187A .... 5½ × 4" ..... (OE) .. ❼ ... $75

HUM 187 (SPECIAL)
W.G.P. "Service" Plaque
This service plaque was first introduced in the late 1950's and has become a Goebel tradition. Each employee of W. Goebel Porzellanfabrik, regardless of his position or the department she/he is working in receives such a special paque on the occasion of his/her 25th, 40th or 50th anniversary with Goebel. These special plaques normally sell for $1000–2000 depending on the age, style, and condition of the plaque.

Special personalized plaques were made available to Goebel Collectors' Club *local chapter* members in 1984 for a limited time. It was necessary to belong to an officially authorized "local chapter" of the GCC. The plaque sold for $50.

188/I (TM 6)   *188/0 (TM 6)*

HUM 188
Celestial Musician

Originally molded by master sculptor Reinhold Unger in 1948, this figurine has never had a major restyling. Older models are slightly larger, have a bluish-green gown and an open quartered base. Newer models are slightly smaller, have a green gown and a closed flat base, and some have 1948 incised copyright date. According to factory information, this figurine was also sold in white overglaze finish at one time, but would now be considered extremely rare in that finish. A new smaller size was first released in 1983. Designed by master sculptor Gerhard Skrobek and Maria Mueller in 1982, this new size measures 5½″ and is incised 188/0 on the bottom. Original issue price was $80 in 1983. The older large size has been renumbered 188/1.

☐ 188	7″	(CE)	❶	$1000–1500
☐ 188	7″	(CE)	❷	$650–900
☐ 188	7″	(CE)	❸	$350–400
☐ 188	7″	(CE)	❹	$290–350
☐ 188	7″	(CE)	❺	$250–260
☐ 188	7″	(CE)	❻	$245–250
☐ 188	7″	(CE)	❻	$230–240
☐ 188/I	7″	(OE)	❼	$230
☐ 188/0	5½″	(CE)	❻	$180–$190
☐ 188/0	5½″	(OE)	❼	$180

Incised "M.I. Hummel"

HUM 189
Old Woman Knitting (CN)

This unusual piece was made as a sample only in 1948 by master sculptor Arthur Moeller and was not approved by the Siessen Convent for production. It was not considered typical of Sister M.I. Hummel's work, although it is an exact replica of one of her early sketches. This early sample *does* have the familiar "M.I. Hummel" signature and is part of the Robert L. Miller collection. Listed as a Closed Number on 18 February 1948 and will not be produced again. Often referred to as one of the "Mamas" and the "Papas." Several other examples have been found in recent years.

☐ 189 ..... 6¾" .... (CN) $15,000–20,000

Incised "M.I. Hummel"

HUM 190
Old Woman Walking to Market (CN)

This unusual piece was made as a sample only in 1948 by master sculptor Arthur Moeller and was not approved by the Siessen Convent for production. It was not considered typical of Sister M.I. Hummel's work, although it is an exact replica of one of her early sketches. This early sample *does* have the familiar "M.I. Hummel" signature and is part of the Robert L. Miller collection. Listed as a Closed Number on 18 February 1948 and will not be produced again. Often referred to as one of the "Mamas" and the "Papas." Several other examples have been found in recent years.

☐ 190 ..... 6¾" .... (CN) $15,000–20,000

Old Postcard Drawing

Incised "M.I. Hummel"

HUM 191
Old Man Walking to Market (CN)
This unusual piece was made as a sample only in 1948 by master sculptor Arthur Moeller and was not approved by the Siessen Convent for production. It was not considered typical of Sister M.I. Hummel's work, although it is an exact replica of one of her early sketches. This early sample *does* have the familiar "M.I. Hummel" signature and is part of the Robert L. Miller collection. Listed as a Closed Number on 18 February 1948 and will not be produced again. Often referred to as one of the "Mamas" and the "Papas." Several other examples have been found in recent years. The original drawing appeared on old German post card.

☐ 191 ..... 6¾" .... (CN) $15,000–20,000

HUM TERM

DECIMAL POINT: This incised "period" or dot was used in a somewhat random fashion by the W. Goebel Porzellanfabrik over the years. The decimal point is and was primarily used to reduce confusion in reading the incised numbers on the underside of the figurines. Example: 66. helps one realize that the designation is sixty-six and not ninety-nine.

Old style (TM 2)   *New style (TM 3)*

HUM 192
Candlelight, Candleholder
Originally modeled by master sculptor Reinhold Unger in 1948 with a long red ceramic candle. Later restyled by master sculptor Theo R. Menzenbach in 1958 with a short candleholder ending in angels hands. Both models have a receptical for holding a wax candle. Older models are slightly larger. Old name: "Carrier of Light." The incised copyright date on both models is 1948.

☐ 192	6¾ to 7"	(CE)	❶	$1250–1700
☐ 192	6¾ to 7"	(CE)	❷	$700–900
☐ 192	6¾ to 7"	(CE)	❸	$500–600
☐ 192	6¾ to 7"	(CE)	❹	$240–285
☐ 192	6¾ to 7"	(CE)	❺	$200–210
☐ 192	6¾ to 7"	(CE)	❻	$190–200
☐ 192	6¾ to 7"	(OE)	❼	$190

HUM 193
Angel Duet, Candleholder

First modeled by master sculptor Reinhold Unger in 1948 and later re-styled by master sculptor Theo R. Menzenbach in 1958. Notice the position of angel's arm in rear view—this was changed by Menzenbach because he thought it would be easier for artists to paint—looks better and is a more natural position. Menzenbach began working at the Goebel factory in October 1948, at the age of 18. He left the factory in October 1961 to start his own business as a commercial artist. He is still living and resides in Germany, near Coburg. According to factory information, this figurine was also sold in white overglaze finish at one time—extremely rare. Also produced without holder for candle—see HUM 261.

☐ 193	5″	(CE)	❶	$1250–1700
☐ 193	5″	(CE)	❷	$400–500
☐ 193	5″	(CE)	❸	$275–350
☐ 193	5″	(CE)	❹	$225–275
☐ 193	5″	(CE)	❺	$190–200
☐ 193	5″	(CE)	❻	$180–190
☐ 193	5″	(OE)	❼	$180

New   **Old**

HUM 194
Watchful Angel
Originally modeled by master sculptor Reinhold Unger in 1948 and later restyled by master sculptor Gerhard Skrobek in 1959. Older models are usually larger. Most models have an incised 1948 copyright date. Old name: "Angelic Care" or "Guardian Angel."

☐ 194	6¼ to 6¾″	(CE)	❶	$1250–1700
☐ 194	6¼ to 6¾″	(CE)	❷	$550–675
☐ 194	6¼ to 6¾″	(CE)	❸	$400–475
☐ 194	6¼″	(CE)	❹	$325–400
☐ 194	6¼″	(CE)	❺	$280–295
☐ 194	6¼″	(CE)	❻	$270–280
☐ 194	6¼″	**(OE)**	❼	$270

195/I (TM 2)   *195 2/0 (TM 4)*

HUM 195
Barnyard Hero
First modeled by master sculptor Reinhold Unger in 1948. Originally made in one size only with the incised number 195. A smaller size was produced in the mid-1950's with the incised number 195 2/0. Both sizes have been restyled in recent years. Many size variations as well as variation in position of boy's hands in small size only: old model has one hand on each side of fence; new model, one hand on top of the other one. Most models have an incised 1948 copyright date.

☐ 195 2/0	3¾ to 4"	(CE)	❷	$300–375
☐ 195 2/0	3¾ to 4"	(CE)	❸	$225–250
☐ 195 2/0	3¾ to 4"	(CE)	❹	$175–225
☐ 195 2/0	3¾ to 4"	(CE)	❺	$145–155
☐ 195 2/0	3¾ to 4"	(CE)	❻	$140–145
☐ 195 2/0	3¾ to 4"	(OE)	❼	$140
☐ 195/I	5½"	(CE)	❷	$500–600
☐ 195/I	5½"	(CE)	❸	$400–450
☐ 195/I	5½"	(CE)	❹	$325–400
☐ 195/I	5½"	(CE)	❺	$275–290
☐ 195/I	5½"	(CE)	❻	$265–275
☐ 195/I	5½"	(OE)	❼	$265
☐ 195	5¾ to 6"	(CE)	❶	$800–1000
☐ 195	5¾ to 6"	(CE)	❷	$550–650

196/I (TM 3)　　　　　　*196/0 (TM 2)*

HUM 196
Telling Her Secret

When first modeled in 1948 by master sculptor Reinhold Unger this figurine was produced in one size only with the incised number 196. A smaller size was issued in the mid-1950's with the incised number 196/0. Some older models have "0" size designator directly under the 196 rather than 196/0. At the same time, the large size was changed to 196/I. Slightly restyled in recent years. Most models have an incised 1948 copyright date. Old name: "The Secret." The girl on the right is the same as HUM 258. "Which Hand?" HUM 196/I (large size only) was "temporarily withdrawn" (TW) from production on 31 Deccember 1984, but may be reinstated at some future date.

☐ 196/0	5 to 5½"	(CE)	❷	$500–625
☐ 196/0	5 to 5½"	(CE)	❸	$375–425
☐ 196/0	5 to 5½"	(CE)	❹	$300–375
☐ 196/0	5 to 5½"	(CE)	❺	$260–275
☐ 196/0	5 to 5½"	(CE)	❻	$250–260
☐ 196/0	5 to 5½"	(OE)	❼	$250
☐ 196/I	6½ to 6¾"	(CE)	❷	$650–850
☐ 196/I	6½ to 6¾"	(CE)	❸	$450–500
☐ 196/I	6½ to 6¾"	(CE)	❹	$400–450
☐ 196/I	6½ to 6¾"	(CE)	❺	$375–400
☐ 196/I	6½ to 6¾"	(TW)	❻	$350–375
☐ 196	6¾"	(CE)	❶	$1000–1250
☐ 196	6¾"	(CE)	❷	$700–900

197/I (TM 4)   *197 2/0 (TM 6)*

HUM 197
Be Patient
When first modeled in 1948 by master sculptor Reinhold Unger this figurine was produced in one size only with the incised number 197. A smaller size was issued in the
mid-1950's with the incised number 197 2/0. At the same time, the large size was
changed to 197/I. Both sizes have been restyled with the new textured finish and usually have an incised 1948 copyright date. Old name: "Mother of Ducks."

☐ 197 2/0	4¼ to 4½"	(CE)	❷	$325–400
☐ 197 2/0	4¼ to 4½"	(CE)	❸	$240–280
☐ 197 2/0	4¼ to 4½"	(CE)	❹	$200–240
☐ 197 2/0	4¼ to 4½"	(CE)	❺	$165–175
☐ 197 2/0	4¼ to 4½"	(CE)	❻	$160–165
☐ 197 2/0	4¼ to 4½"	**(OE)**	❼	$160
☐ 197/I	6 to 6¼"	(CE)	❷	$400–550
☐ 197/I	6 to 6¼"	(CE)	❸	$350–400
☐ 197/I	6 to 6¼"	(CE)	❹	$275–350
☐ 197/I	6 to 6¼"	(CE)	❺	$240–250
☐ 197/I	6 to 6¼"	(CE)	❻	$230–240
☐ 197/I	6 to 6¼"	**(OE)**	❼	$230
☐ 197	6¼"	(CE)	❶	$700–900
☐ 197	6¼"	(CE)	❷	$450–600

198/I (TM 3)   198 2/0 (TM 4)

HUM 198
Home From Market
When first modeled in 1948 by master sculptor Arthur Moeller this figurine was produced in one size only with the incised number 198. A smaller size was issued in the
mid-1950's with the incised number 198 2/0. At the same time, the large size was
changed to 198/I. Many size variations with older models slightly larger than new.
Both sizes have been restyled and now have an incised 1948 copyright date.

☐ 198 2/0	4½ to 4¾″	(CE)	❷	$250–300
☐ 198 2/0	4½ to 4¾″	(CE)	❸	$180–210
☐ 198 2/0	4½ to 4¾″	(CE)	❹	$150–180
☐ 198 2/0	4½ to 4¾″	(CE)	❺	$125–130
☐ 198 2/0	4½ to 4¾″	(CE)	❻	$120–125
☐ 198 2/0	4½ to 4¾″	(OE)	❼	$120
☐ 198/I	5½″	(CE)	❷	$350–450
☐ 198/I	5½″	(CE)	❸	$275–315
☐ 198/I	5½″	(CE)	❹	$225–275
☐ 198/I	5½″	(CE)	❺	$190–200
☐ 198/I	5½″	(CE)	❻	$180–190
☐ 198/I	5½″	(OE)	❼	$180
☐ 198	5¾ to 6″	(CE)	❶	$550–700
☐ 198	5¾ to 6″	(CE)	❷	$400–500

Old style   *New style*

HUM 199
Feeding Time

When first modeled in 1948 by master sculptor Arthur Moeller this figurine was produced in one size only with the incised number 199. A smaller size was issued in the mid-1950's with the incised number 199/0. At the same time, the large size was changed to 199/I. Both sizes were restyled in the mid-1960's by master sculptor Gerhard Skrobek. The girl is blonde on older figurines — changed to dark hair and new facial features on newer ones. Note position of girl's hand under bowl in new style figurines. All small size and the new large size figurines have an incised 1948 copyright date. Small size (199/0) sometimes found with old style head and new style hand under bowl.

☐ 199/0	4¼ to 4½"	(CE) ..	❷ ...	$300–400
☐ 199/0	4¼ to 4½"	(CE) ..	❸ ...	$240–280
☐ 199/0	4¼ to 4½"	(CE) ..	❹ ...	$200–240
☐ 199/0	4¼ to 4½"	(CE) ..	❺ ...	$165–175
☐ 199/0	4¼ to 4½"	(CE) ..	❻ ...	$160–165
☐ 199/0	4¼ to 4½"	(OE) ..	❼ ...	$160
☐ 199/I	5½ to 5¾"	(CE) ..	❷ ...	$400–500
☐ 199/I	5½ to 5¾"	(CE) ..	❸ ...	$330–375
☐ 199/I	5½ to 5¾"	(CE) ..	❹ ...	$275–330
☐ 199/I	5½ to 5¾"	(CE) ..	❺ ...	$230–240
☐ 199/I	5½ to 5¾"	(CE) ..	❻ ...	$220–230
☐ 199/I	5½ to 5¾"	(OE) ..	❼ ...	$220
☐ 199	5¾"	(CE) ..	❶ ...	$700–900
☐ 199	5¾"	(CE) ..	❷ ...	$450–550

HUM TERM

FULL BEE: The term "Full Bee" refers to the trademark used by the Goebel Co. from 1950 to 1957. Early usage of this trademark was incised into the material. Later versions of the "full bee" were stamped into the material.

200/I (TM 2)   *200/0 (TM 2)*

HUM 200
Little Goat Herder

When first modeled in 1948 by master sculptor Arthur Moeller this figurine was made in one size only with the incised number 200. A smaller size was issued in the mid-1950's with the incised number 200/0. At the same time, the large size was changed to 200/I. Both sizes have been restyled with only minor changes. Older models have a blade of grass between hind legs of the small goat. Newer models do not. Newer models have an incised 1948 copyright date. Older pieces slightly larger. Old name: "Goat Boy." Some "full bee" (TM 2) trademark examples in the small size (200/0) version have been found with a slight variation in the signature—the initials "M.I." are directly above the "Hummel."

☐ 200/0 .... 4½ to 4¾" .... (CE) .. ❷ ... $300–400
☐ 200/0 .... 4½ to 4¾" .... (CE) .. ❸ ... $240–280
☐ 200/0 .... 4½ to 4¾" .... (CE) .. ❹ ... $200–240
☐ 200/0 .... 4½ to 4¾" .... (CE) .. ❺ ... $165–175
☐ 200/0 .... 4½ to 4¾" .... (CE) .. ❻ ... $160–165
☐ 200/0 .... 4½ to 4¾" .... (OE) .. ❼ ... $160
☐ 200/I .... 5 to 5½" ..... (CE) .. ❷ ... $400–500
☐ 200/I .... 5 to 5½" ..... (CE) .. ❸ ... $300–350
☐ 200/I .... 5 to 5½" ..... (CE) .. ❹ ... $250–300
☐ 200/I .... 5 to 5½" ..... (CE) .. ❺ ... $210–220
☐ 200/I .... 5 to 5½" ..... (CE) .. ❻ ... $200–210
☐ 200/I .... 5 to 5½" ..... (OE) .. ❼ ... $200
☐ 200 ..... 5½ to 5¾" .... (CE) .. ❶ ... $600–800
☐ 200 ..... 5½ to 5¾" .... (CE) .. ❷ ... $450–550

201/I (TM 3)   *201 2/0 (TM 4)*

HUM 201
Retreat To Safety

When first modeled in 1948 by master sculptor Reinhold Unger this figurine was produced in one size only with the incised number 201. A smaller size was issued in the mid-1950's with the incised number 201 2/0. At the same time, the large size was changed to 201/I. Both sizes have been restyled in recent years. Many size variations as well as variation in the position of boy's hands in small size only: old model has one hand on each side of fence; new model, one hand on top of the other one. Most models have an incised 1948 copyright date. Old name: "Afraid."

☐ 201 2/0	3¾ to 4″	..... (CE)	.. ❷	...	$300–375
☐ 201 2/0	3¾ to 4″	..... (CE)	.. ❸	...	$225–250
☐ 201 2/0	3¾ to 4″	..... (CE)	.. ❹	...	$175–225
☐ 201 2/0	3¾ to 4″	..... (CE)	.. ❺	...	$145–155
☐ 201 2/0	3¾ to 4″	..... (CE)	.. ❻	...	$140–145
☐ 201 2/0	3¾ to 4″	..... (OE)	.. ❼	...	$140
☐ 201/I	5½ to 5¾″	.... (CE)	.. ❷	...	$500–600
☐ 201/I	5½ to 5¾″	.... (CE)	.. ❸	...	$375–425
☐ 201/I	5½ to 5¾″	.... (CE)	.. ❹	...	$315–375
☐ 201/I	5½ to 5¾″	.... (CE)	.. ❺	...	$260–275
☐ 201/I	5½ to 5¾″	.... (CE)	.. ❻	...	$250–260
☐ 201/I	5½ to 5¾″	.... (OE)	.. ❼	...	$250
☐ 201	5¾ to 6″	..... (CE)	.. ❶	...	$800–1000
☐ 201	5¾ to 6″	..... (CE)	.. ❷	...	$550–650

Factory sample

Miller collection

HUM 202
Old Man Reading Newspaper,
Table Lamp (CN)

This unusual piece was made as a sample only in 1948 by master sculptor Arthur Moeller and was not approved by the Siessen Convent for production. It was not considered typical of Sister M.I. Hummel's work, although it is an exact replica of one of her early sketches. Same figure as HUM 181 except on lamp base. Listed as a Closed Number on 18 August 1948. The sample model is from Goebel factory archives.

☐ 202 ..... 8¼" .... (CN) .. $15,000–20,000

HUM TERM

DOUGHNUT BASE: A term used to describe the raised circular support on the underside of a figurine. Many figurine bases with a circle inside the regular circular base gave rise to the term, but has now been used to describe many bases with the circular support on the underside.

| 203/I | 203 2/0 (New style) | 203 2/0 (Old style) |

HUM 203
Signs of Spring (CE)
When first modeled in 1948 by master sculptor Arthur Moeller this figurine was produced in one size only with the incised number 203. A smaller size was issued in the mid-1950's with the incised number 203 2/0. At the same time, the large size was changed to 203/I. Many size variations. At one time, small size only, was made with the girl wearing both shoes. Full bee trademark pieces found both with or without shoe. Newer models have an incised 1948 copyright date. Old name: "Scandal." "Two shoe" variety considered rare, usually sells for $750 to $1000. Both sizes of "Signs of Spring" were permanently retired by Goebel in the fall of 1990 and will not be produced again.

☐ 203 2/0	4"	(CE)	❷	$750–1000 (with two shoes)
☐ 203 2/0	4"	(CE)	❷	$375–450
☐ 203 2/0	4"	(CE)	❸	$300–350
☐ 203 2/0	4"	(CE)	❹	$225–300
☐ 203 2/0	4"	(CE)	❺	$200–225
☐ 203 2/0	4"	(CE)	❻	$175–200
☐ 203/I	5 to 5½"	(CE)	❷	$450–550
☐ 203/I	5 to 5½"	(CE)	❸	$350–400
☐ 203/I	5 to 5½"	(CE)	❹	$300–350
☐ 203/I	5 to 5½"	(CE)	❺	$250–275
☐ 203/I	5 to 5½"	(CE)	❻	$225–250
☐ 203	5¼"	(CE)	❶	$700–900
☐ 203	5¼"	(CE)	❷	$500–600

NOTE: See RARE VARIATIONS in the back of book for an unusual variation of this figurine.

Old style (TM 2)   *New style (TM 5)*

HUM 204
Weary Wanderer

Many size variations. Most models have 1949 as the incised copyright date. Old name: "Tired Little Traveler." Has been restyled with the new textured finish. The word "Lauterbach" on the back of figurine is the name of a village used in an old German song. The first model was made by master sculptor Reinhold Unger in 1949. Occasionally found with blue eyes. This variation would command a premium of $1500 to $2000.

☐ 204	5½ to 6"	(CE)	❶	$600–800
☐ 204	5½ to 6"	(CE)	❷	$400–500
☐ 204	5½ to 6"	(CE)	❸	$300–350
☐ 204	5½ to 6"	(CE)	❹	$250–300
☐ 204	5½ to 6"	(CE)	❺	$210–220
☐ 204	5½ to 6"	(CE)	❻	$200–210
☐ 204	5½ to 6"	(OE)	❼	$200

Rear view

190

HUM 205
M.I. Hummel Dealer's Plaque
(in German) (CE)
This German dealer's plaque was first modeled by master sculptor Reinhold Unger in 1949. There are three color variations of lettering: all black lettering, black and red combination, and all black except the capital letters O, H and F in red lettering. Usually has an incised crown mark in addition to other trademarks. The all-black variety usually has a "Made in U.S. Zone, Germany" stamped on bottom. Listed in factory records as a Closed Edition on 18 June 1949 although it is found with the stylized trademark (in addition to the crown), indicating they were painted at a later date.

☐ 205 ..... 5½ × 4¼" ... (CE) .. ❶ ... $1300–1600
☐ 205 ..... 5½ × 4¼" ... (CE) .. ❷ ... $950–1100
☐ 205 ..... 5½ × 4¼" ... (CE) .. ❸ ... $800–950

HUM TERM

DUBLER: A "Dubler" figurine is one produced during the W.W.II time period by the Herbert Dubler Co. Inc. of New York City. These pieces were substitutes for genuine Goebel "M.I. Hummel" figurines when Goebel "Hummels" were not coming into the U.S. The Dubler figurines were made of plaster of paris and were distributed by the Crestwick Co. of New York which later became Hummelwerk and ultimately the present Goebel United States firm.

Crown   Full Bee   Current

HUM 206
Holy Water Font, Angel Cloud

This holy water font was originally modeled by master sculptor Reinhold Unger in 1949 but has been restyled several times. At least three different variations. Early models do not have rim on back side of bowl. Also color variations on lip of water bowl. Has been considered rare in the older trademarks but was put back into current production in 1978 and can now be found with 5 and 6 trademarks at more reasonable prices. Newer models have an incised 1949 copyright date.

☐ 206	3¼ × 4¾"	(CE)	❶	$350–500
☐ 206	3¼ × 4¾"	(CE)	❷	$250–350
☐ 206	3¼ × 4¾"	(CE)	❸	$200–250
☐ 206	3¼ × 4¾"	(CE)	❹	$60–80
☐ 206	3¼ × 4¾"	(CE)	❺	$47–50
☐ 206	3¼ × 4¾"	(CE)	❻	$45–47
☐ 206	3¼ × 4¾"	(OE)	❼	$45

Newer style   Old style

HUM 207
Holy Water Font, Heavenly Angel

This holy water font was originally modeled by master sculptor Reinhold Unger in 1949 and is the highest numbered piece with the crown trademark. Older models have a hole on the back for hanging while the newer models have a visible hole on the front. Early models do not have rim on the back side of bowl. Newer models have an incised 1949 copyright date. The "Heavenly Angel" motif was used on the First Annual Plate HUM 264 in 1971.

☐ 207	3 × 5"	(CE)	❶	$350–500
☐ 207	3 × 5"	(CE)	❷	$125–150
☐ 207	3 × 5"	(CE)	❸	$80–100
☐ 207	3 × 5"	(CE)	❹	$60–80
☐ 207	3 × 5"	(CE)	❺	$47–50
☐ 207	3 × 5"	(CE)	❻	$45–47
☐ 207	3 × 5"	(OE)	❼	$45

Old style   *Newer style*

HUM 208
M.I. Hummel Dealer's Plaque
(In French)(CE)

Originally modeled in 1949 by master sculptor Reinhold Unger. Two known variations. Made with dotted "i" and without quotation marks on Hummel. Newer model has quotation marks: "HUMMEL" + "Reg. trade mark."

☐ 208 ..... 5½ × 4" ..... (CE) .. ❷ ... $6,000–8,000

HUM 209
M.I. Hummel Dealer's Plaque
(In Swedish) (CE)

This extremely rare plaque was first modeled in 1949 by master sculptor Reinhold Unger and was apparently issued in extremely limited quantities. Some have sold for over $7,000.

☐ 209 ..... 5½ × 4" ..... (CE) .. ❷ ... $6,000–8,000

HUM 210
M.I. Hummel Dealer's Plaque
(Schmid Bros.) (CE)

Normal dealers's plaque in English with "SCHMID BROS. INC. BOSTON" embossed on side of satchel of "Merry Wanderer." This extremely rare plaque was first modeled in 1950 by master sculptor Reinhold Unger. Also made with dotted "i" and without quotation marks. Very few are known to exist. Schmid Bros. was one of the early importers of "M.I. Hummel" figurines in 1935, and is now the sole distributor in the United States.

☐ 210 ..... 5½ × 4" ..... (CE) .. ❷ ... $20,000–25,000

Unpainted sample

HUM 211
M.I. Hummel Dealer's Plaque (in English) (CE)

This is probably the most rare of all "M.I. Hummel" dealer's plaques. The only known painted example was located in 1975 by Major Larry Spohn and his wife Anne while they were living in Germany, and is new in the Robert L. Miller collection. All the lettering on this plaque is in lower case and the word "Oeslau" is used as the location of W. Goebel Porzellanfabrik. Modeled in 1950 by master sculptor Reinhold Unger. The exact purpose or reason for designing this plaque still remains a mystery today.

☐ 211 ..... 5½ × 4" ..... (CE) .. ❷ ... $20,000–25,000

HUM TERM

GOEBEL BEE: A name used to describe the trademark used by the Goebel Company from 1972 until 1979. This trademark incorporates the GOEBEL name with the V and bee.

HUM 212
Orchestra (CN)

Most notes from the Goebel factory state: "No information available" on this number. However, one old list indicates "Orchestra A-F" and the date "13 May 51." This is possibly a number assigned to a Hummel orchestra as a set, such as Hummel Nativity Set HUM 214. Another note states: "Modeled by Arthur Moeller in 1951."

☐ 212 . . . . . (CN) . . . .

HUM 213
M.I. Hummel Dealer's Plaque
(in Spanish) (CE)

This Spanish dealer's plaque was first modeled in 1951 by master sculptor Reinhold Unger and apparently only a very limited number were produced. Considered extremely rare.

☐ 213 . . . . . 5¾ × 4¼" . . . . (CE) . . ❷ . . . $10,000–15,000

HUM 214
Nativity Set with Wooden Stable

This set was modeled by master sculptor Reinhold Unger in 1951. First produced and sold in 1952. Normally sold as a set but is also available in individual pieces. At one time this set was produced and sold in white overglaze finish but is no longer sold this way. The white overglaze finish is considered rare and usually brings a premium. Early production of HUM 214 A (Virgin Mary and Infant Jesus) was made in one piece. Because of production problems, it was later produced as two separate pieces, both with the same number (214 A) incised on the bottom of each piece. The one-piece unit was sold in white overglaze finish and are considered rare today. Two different styles of lambs (HUM 214/O) have been used with the Nativity sets—note variations in photo. Some Nativity set pieces have an incised 1951 copyright date. HUM 214/C, 214/D, 214/E and 214/H are not always included in sets and are considered "optional" pieces. The wooden stable is usually sold separately. The sixteenth piece, "Flying Angel" HUM 366, was added to the set in 1963. Goebel also produces three different camels to match this set which do not have the "M.I. Hummel" signature since they were not designed by Sister Hummel. In 1985 the "Infant Jesus" (214/A) was renumbered to *214 A/K* which is now incised on the bottom of this piece only. The "K" refers to the German word "Kinder" which means child in English. New production of the HUM 214 nativity set are now being numbered with (/1) size designator: Example: *214/A* now *214/A/1*.

214 A Virgin Mary and Infant Jesus (one piece-CE)
214/A Virgin Mary
214/A (or 214 A/K) Infant Jesus
214/B Joseph
214/C Angel standing, "Good Night"
214/D Angel kneeling, "Angel Serenade"
214/E We Congratulate
214/F Shepherd standing with sheep
214/G Shepherd kneeling
214/H Shepherd Boy, kneeling with flute "Little Tooter"
214/J Donkey
214/K Ox (cow)
214/L Moorish king, standing
214/M King, kneeling on one knee
214/N King, kneeling with cash-box
214/O Lamb
366 Flying Angel

New   **Old**

Nativity set in color

Discontinued white nativity set

					COLOR	WHITE
☐	214A	1 PIECE 6½"	(CE)	❷	☐ $2000–2500	☐ $2500–3000
☐	214A	6¼ to 6½"	(CE)	❷	☐ $275–375	☐ $375–475
☐	214A	6¼ to 6½"	(CE)	❸	☐ $225–260	☐ $300–375
☐	214A	6¼ to 6½"	(CE)	❹	☐ $185–225	☐ $225–300
☐	214A	6¼ to 6½"	(CE)	❺	☐ $155–165	☐ $175–200
☐	214A	6¼ to 6½"	(CE)	❻	☐ $150–155	☐ $175–200
☐	214A	6¼ to 6½"	(OE)	❼	☐ $150	—
☐	214A	1½ × 3½"	(CE)	❷	☐ $100–125	☐ $200–250
☐	214A	1½ × 3½"	(CE)	❸	☐ $75–85	☐ $150–200
☐	214A	1½ × 3½"	(CE)	❹	☐ $60–75	☐ $75–100
☐	214A	1½ × 3½"	(CE)	❺	☐ $52–55	☐ $50–60
☐	214A/K	1½ × 3½"	(CE)	❻	☐ $50–52	☐ $50–60
☐	214A/K	1½ × 3½"	(OE)	❼	☐ $50	—
☐	214B	7½"	(CE)	❷	☐ $275–375	☐ $325–400
☐	214B	7½"	(CE)	❸	☐ $225–260	☐ $250–325
☐	214B	7½"	(CE)	❹	☐ $185–225	☐ $200–250
☐	214B	7½"	(CE)	❺	☐ $155–165	☐ $150–175
☐	214B	7½"	(CE)	❻	☐ $150–155	☐ $125–150
☐	214B	7½"	(OE)	❼	☐ $150	—
☐	214C	3½"	(CE)	❷	☐ $140–175	☐ $350–400
☐	214C	3½"	(CE)	❸	☐ $105–125	☐ $300–350
☐	214C	3½"	(CE)	❹	☐ $90–105	☐ $250–300
☐	214C	3½"	(CE)	❺	☐ $75–80	– –
☐	214C	3½"	(CE)	❻	☐ $70–75	– –
☐	214C	3½"	(OE)	❼	☐ $70	—
☐	214D	3"	(CE)	❷	☐ $140–175	☐ $225–275
☐	214D	3"	(CE)	❸	☐ $105–125	☐ $200–225
☐	214D	3"	(CE)	❹	☐ $90–105	☐ $150–200
☐	214D	3"	(CE)	❺	☐ $75–80	– –
☐	214D	3"	(CE)	❻	☐ $70–75	– –
☐	214D	3"	(OE)	❼	☐ $70	—
☐	214E	3¾"	(CE)	❷	☐ $280–350	☐ $375–450
☐	214E	3¾"	(CE)	❸	☐ $210–245	☐ $300–375
☐	214E	3¾"	(CE)	❹	☐ $175–210	☐ $250–300
☐	214E	3¾"	(CE)	❺	☐ $145–155	– –
☐	214E	3¾"	(CE)	❻	☐ $140–145	– –
☐	214E	3¾"	(OE)	❼	☐ $140	
☐	214F	7"	(CE)	❷	☐ $300–375	☐ $350–450
☐	214F	7"	(CE)	❸	☐ $230–270	☐ $250–350
☐	214F	7"	(CE)	❹	☐ $190–230	☐ $200–250
☐	214F	7"	(CE)	❺	☐ $160–170	– –
☐	214F	7"	(CE)	❻	☐ $155–160	– –
☐	214F	7"	(OE)	❼	☐ $155	
☐	214G	5"	(CE)	❷	☐ $220–275	☐ $250–300
☐	214G	5"	(CE)	❸	☐ $165–190	☐ $200–250
☐	214G	5"	(CE)	❹	☐ $135–165	☐ $150–200
☐	214G	5"	(CE)	❺	☐ $115–120	– –
☐	214G	5"	(CE)	❻	☐ $110–115	– –
☐	214G	5"	(OE)	❼	☐ $110	—

(Continued on next page)

	Size		Grade	COLOR	WHITE
☐ 214H	3¾ to 4″	(CE)	❷	☐ $200–250	☐ $250–300
☐ 214H	3¾ to 4″	(CE)	❸	☐ $150–175	☐ $200–250
☐ 214H	3¾ to 4″	(CE)	❹	☐ $125–150	☐ $150–200
☐ 214H	3¾ to 4″	(CE)	❺	☐ $105–110	– –
☐ 214H	3¾ to 4″	(CE)	❻	☐ $100–105	– –
☐ 214H	3¾ to 4″	(OE)	❼	☐ $100	–
☐ 214J	5″	(CE)	❷	☐ $120–150	☐ $175–250
☐ 214J	5″	(CE)	❸	☐ $90–105	☐ $150–175
☐ 214J	5″	(CE)	❹	☐ $75–90	☐ $125–150
☐ 214J	5″	(CE)	❺	☐ $62–65	– –
☐ 214J	5″	(CE)	❻	☐ $60–62	– –
☐ 214J	5″	(OE)	❼	☐ $60	–
☐ 214K	3½ to 6¼″	(CE)	❷	☐ $120–150	☐ $175–250
☐ 214K	3½ to 6¼″	(CE)	❸	☐ $90–105	☐ $150–175
☐ 214K	3½ to 6¼″	(CE)	❹	☐ $75–90	☐ $125–150
☐ 214K	3½ to 6¼″	(CE)	❺	☐ $62–65	– –
☐ 214K	3½ to 6¼″	(CE)	❻	☐ $60–62	– –
☐ 214K	3½ to 6¼″	(OE)	❼	☐ $60	–
☐ 214L	8 to 8¼″	(CE)	❷	☐ $300–375	☐ $350–450
☐ 214L	8 to 8¼″	(CE)	❸	☐ $230–270	☐ $250–350
☐ 214L	8 to 8¼″	(CE)	❹	☐ $190–230	☐ $200–250
☐ 214L	8 to 8¼″	(CE)	❺	☐ $160–170	– –
☐ 214L	8 to 8¼″	(CE)	❻	☐ $155–160	– –
☐ 214L	8 to 8¼″	(OE)	❼	☐ $155	–
☐ 214M	5½″	(CE)	❷	☐ $275–375	☐ $350–450
☐ 214M	5½″	(CE)	❸	☐ $225–260	☐ $250–350
☐ 214M	5½″	(CE)	❹	☐ $185–225	☐ $200–250
☐ 214M	5½″	(CE)	❺	☐ $155–165	– –
☐ 214M	5½″	(CE)	❻	☐ $150–155	– –
☐ 214M	5½″	(OE)	❼	☐ $150	–
☐ 214N	5½″	(CE)	❷	☐ $280–350	☐ $350–450
☐ 214N	5½″	(CE)	❸	☐ $210–245	☐ $250–350
☐ 214N	5½″	(CE)	❹	☐ $175–210	☐ $200–250
☐ 214N	5½″	(CE)	❺	☐ $145–155	– –
☐ 214N	5½″	(CE)	❻	☐ $140–145	– –
☐ 214N	5½″	(OE)	❼	☐ $140	–
☐ 214O	1¾ × 2½″	(CE)	❷	☐ $35–45	☐ $100–125
☐ 214O	1¾ × 2½″	(CE)	❸	☐ $27–32	☐ $75–100
☐ 214O	1¾ × 2½″	(CE)	❹	☐ $23–27	☐ $50–65
☐ 214O	1¾ × 2½″	(CE)	❺	☐ $19–20	– –
☐ 214O	1¾ × 2½″	(CE)	❻	☐ $18–19	– –
☐ 214O	1¾ × 2½″	(OE)	❼	☐ $18	–
☐ 366	3½″	(CE)	❹	☐ $175–225	☐ $200–250
☐ 366	3½″	(CE)	❺	☐ $110–115	☐ $125–150
☐ 366	3½″	(CE)	❻	☐ $105–110	☐ $125–150
☐ 366	3½″	(OE)	❼	☐ $105	–

☐ Wooden stable, to fit 12–16 piece sets . . . . Current retail $100
☐ Wooden stable, to fit 3 piece sets . . . . Current retail $45

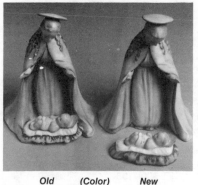

| Old | (Color) | New | | Old | (White) | New |

A new small size Nativity set was first announced in 1988. Three pieces only were released — Mary, Infant Jesus and Joseph — and sold as a set for $185. In 1989 four other pieces were released — the donkey, ox, lamb and Flying Angel. In 1990 the three Kings were released. In 1991 the two Shepherds and Little Tooter were released with the possibility of others to follow in future years.

☐ 214 A/M/0	Mary	5¼″	(CE)	❻	$110–115
☐ 214 A/M/0	Mary	5¼″	(OE)	❼	$110
☐ 214 A/K/0	Infant Jesus	2⅞″	(CE)	❻	$35–37
☐ 214 A/K/0	Infant Jesus	2⅞″	(OE)	❼	$35
☐ 214 B/0	Joseph	6⅛″	(CE)	❻	$110–115
☐ 214 B/0	Joseph	6⅛″	(OE)	❼	$110
☐ 366/0	Flying Angel	2¾″	(CE)	❻	$85–90
☐ 366/0	Flying Angel	2¾″	(OE)	❼	$85
☐ 214 J/0	Donkey	3⅞″	(CE)	❻	$45–47
☐ 214 J/0	Donkey	3⅞″	(OE)	❼	$45
☐ 214 K/0	Ox	2¾″	(CE)	❻	$45–47
☐ 214 K/0	Ox	2¾″	(OE)	❼	$45
☐ 214 O/0	Lamb	1½″	(CE)	❻	$15–16
☐ 214 O/0	Lamb	1½″	(OE)	❼	$15
☐ 214 L/0	King Standing	6¼″	(CE)	❻	$130–135
☐ 214 L/0	King Standing	6¼″	(OE)	❼	$130
☐ 214 M/0	King on one knee	4¼″	(CE)	❻	$120–125
☐ 214 M/0	King on one knee	4¼″	(OE)	❼	$120
☐ 214 N/0	King on two knees	4½″	(CE)	❻	$115–120
☐ 214 N/0	King on two knees	4½″	(OE)	❼	$115
☐ 214 F/0	Shepherd Standing	5¾″	(CE)	❻	$135–140
☐ 214 F/0	Shepherd Standing	5¾″	(OE)	❼	$135
☐ 214 G/0	Shepherd Kneeling	4″	(CE)	❻	$100–105
☐ 214 G/0	Shepherd Kneeling	4″	(OE)	❼	$100
☐ 214 H/0	Little Tooter	3¼″	(CE)	❻	$90–95
☐ 214 H/0	Little Tooter	3¼″	(OE)	❼	$90

HUM 215 (CN)
Factory records indicate: A child Jesus standing with lamb in arms. Listed as a Closed Number on 16 August 1951. No known examples.

☐ 215 . . . . (CN) . . . .

HUM 216 (CN)
Factory records indicate: Joyful, ashtray without rest for cigarette. Listed as a Closed Number on 10 September 1951. No known examples.

☐ 216 . . . . (CN) . . . .

TM 2   *TM 4*

HUM 217
Boy With Toothache
First modeled by master sculptor Arthur Moeller in 1951. Older figurines are slightly larger. Older models have "© WG" after the "M.I Hummel" signature."Old name: "At the Dentist" or "Toothache." Newer models have an incised 1951 copyright date. Some slight variations in color are found, but would not affect value.

☐ 217 . . . . . 5¼ to 5½″ . . . . (CE) . . ❷ . . . $375–450
☐ 217 . . . . . 5¼ to 5½″ . . . . (CE) . . ❸ . . . $275–325
☐ 217 . . . . . 5¼ to 5½″ . . . . (CE) . . ❹ . . . $225–275
☐ 217 . . . . . 5¼ to 5½″ . . . . (CE) . . ❺ . . . $195–200
☐ 217 . . . . . 5¼ to 5½″ . . . . (CE) . . ❻ . . . $185–195
☐ 217 . . . . . 5¼ to 5½″ . . . . **(OE)** . . ❼ . . . $185

New style (OE)   **Old style (CE)**

HUM 218
Birthday Serenade

First modeled by master sculptor Reinhold Unger in 1952. Early models bearing an incised 1952 copyright date have boy playing horn, girl playing accordion. Remodeled in 1964 by master sculptor Gerhard Skrobek. Newer models bearing an incised 1965 copyright date have boy playing accordion, girl playing horn. This change was made at the request of the convent. The large size (HUM 218/0) had been considered rare but is again back in production with current trademark with boy playing accordion and girl playing horn with an incised 1952 copyright date. This was an error as it should have been 1965. Note that a tie has been added to the boy when he plays the accordion. Both styles can be found with TM 3 or TM 4 trademark.

☐ 218 2/0	4¼ to 4½"	(CE)	❷	$550–600	
☐ 218 2/0	4¼ to 4½"	(CE)	❸	$500–550	(Old style)
☐ 218 2/0	4¼ to 4½"	(CE)	❸	$225–250	(New Style)
☐ 218 2/0	4¼ to 4½"	(CE)	❹	$400–500	(Old Style)
☐ 218 2/0	4¼ to 4½"	(CE)	❹	$190–225	(New Style)
☐ 218 2/0	4¼ to 4½"	(CE)	❺	$155–165	
☐ 218 2/0	4¼ to 4½"	(CE)	❻	$150–155	
☐ 218 2/0	4¼ to 4½"	(OE)	❼	$150	
☐ 218/0	5¼"	(CE)	❷	$750–900	
☐ 218/0	5¼"	(CE)	❸	$700–800	(Old Style)
☐ 218/0	5¼"	(CE)	❸	$375–425	(New Style)
☐ 218/0	5¼"	(CE)	❹	$650–750	(Old Style)
☐ 218/0	5¼"	(CE)	❹	$300–375	(New Style)
☐ 218/0	5¼"	(CE)	❺	$260–275	
☐ 218/0	5¼"	(CE)	❻	$250–260	
☐ 218/0	5¼"	(OE)	❼	$250	
☐ 218	5¼"	(CE)	❷	$800–950	

"Little Velma"

HUM 219
Little Velma (CE)
This figurine was designed in 1952 by master sculptor Reinhold Unger. According to factory records this figurine was produced in very limited numbers (possibly less than 100 pieces) because of its similarity to other models. The name "Little Velma" was affectionately assigned to this piece in honor of the lady who first brought it to the attention of, and sold it to, this author. Most of these figurines must have been shipped to Canada as most known examples can be traced to that country.

☐ 219 2/0 .. 4″ .... (CN) .. ❷ ... $5000–6000

——— HUM TERM ———

HOLLOW MOLD: The term used by "M.I. Hummel" collectors to describe a figurine that is open on the underside of the base. With these particular bases the collector can visually see into the cavity of the figurine.

203

220   260F   214E

HUM 220
We Congratulate (with base)

First modeled by master sculptor Arthur Moeller in 1952. Early production pieces have the incised number 220 2/0. Later production dropped the 2/0 size designator and added the 1952 incised copyright date. This figurine is the same as HUM 214/E and HUM 260/F in the Nativity Sets, except with base and no flowers in girl's hair. Also note lederhosen strap added to boy.

☐ 220 ..... 3¾ to 4" ..... (CE) .. ❷ ... $275–350
☐ 220 ..... 3¾ to 4" ..... (CE) .. ❸ ... $200–235
☐ 220 ..... 3¾ to 4" ..... (CE) .. ❹ ... $170–200
☐ 220 ..... 3¾ to 4" ..... (CE) .. ❺ ... $140–150
☐ 220 ..... 3¾ to 4" ..... (CE) .. ❻ ... $135–140
☐ 220 ..... 3¾ to 4" ..... (OE) .. ❼ ... $135
☐ 220 2/0 .. 4" .... (CE) .. ❷ ... $400–500

Incised signature (HUM 214 E)   *Painted signature*

(Factory sample)

HUM 221
Happy Pastime, Candy Jar (CN)
This candy jar was made as a sample only and was never produced for sale. First modeled by master sculptor Arthur Moeller in 1952. To my knowledge, there are no examples in private collections.

☐ 221 .... (CN) $5,000–10,000

Two variations

HUM 222
Madonna Plaque (with metal frame) (CE)
Originally modeled by master sculptor Reinhold Unger in 1952. There are basically two different styles of metal frames — both pictured here. Found without frame with full bee trademark but unconfirmed if actually sold that way. Similar in design to HUM 48 "Madonna Plaque." Usually found with gray felt backing, which would have to be removed to see the incised number.

☐ 222 ..... 4 × 5″ .... (CE) .. ❷ ... $750–1250
☐ 222 ..... 4 × 5″ .... (CE) .. ❸ ... $750–1000

223   101

HUM 223
To Market, Table Lamp

This lamp was originally modeled by master sculptor Arthur Moeller in 1937 as HUM 101 and later restyled by him in 1952. It is similar to the original model with the exception of the size and a flower added to branch of tree trunk. Measures 5¼" across the base. Called "Surprise" in old catalogue and sold for $25 in 1955. "To Market" table lamp was "temporarily withdrawn" from production on 31 December 1989, but may be reinstated at some future date.

☐ 223 ..... 9½" .... (CE) .. ❷ ... $525–700
☐ 223 ..... 9½" .... (CE) .. ❸ ... $450–500
☐ 223 ..... 9½" .... (CE) .. ❹ ... $425–450
☐ 223 ..... 9½" .... (CE) .. ❺ ... $400–425
☐ 223 ..... 9½" .... (TW) .. ❻ ... $375–400

M.I. Hummel Club®

Join up
& Join in

FROM:

Please
Place
Stamp
Here

M.I. HUMMEL CLUB®
GOEBEL PLAZA
P.O. BOX 11
PENNINGTON NJ 08534-0011

Some of our special benefits include:

- The exclusive M.I. Hummel Club figurine, our introductory gift to new Club members. A retail value of $65 US, CDN $85.

- Membership and Redemption Cards, your only way of obtaining Club Exclusives.

- INSIGHTS, the quarterly magazine filled with behind-the-scenes updates, fascinating articles, helpful hints and more.

- A handsome binder to keep your issues of INSIGHTS, complete with divider pages telling the history of *M.I. Hummel* figurines, valued member services, and your own collectors log.

- Exciting Club trips to Europe and the "Members Only" tour of the Goebel factory where *M.I. Hummel* treasures are made.

- Schedule of instore promotions featuring artists and other personalities appearing in your area.

- Local Chapters of the M.I. Hummel Club, to make new friends and to learn even more about *M.I. Hummel.*

- Club services, such as Collectors Market and a Research Department.

J oin up and join in on all the fun and excitement the M.I. Hummel Club has to offer. Make new friends while you learn all about the porcelain children you cherish. *I Brought You A Gift,* the M.I. Hummel Club figurine created for new members, is yours *free* for joining. Don't forget the Club exclusives: Limited edition pieces offered for one year only, never to be issued again and available solely to Club members. Also enjoy an informative, thought-provoking quarterly magazine, Local Chapter get-togethers, and each year the Club offers fabulous trips to Europe with a "members only" tour of the Goebel Factory, where you'll learn all about the intricate production process and meet our master artists busy at their craft.

So whether you're a seasoned collector or a novice, don't hesitate to join up and join in... because there's much to be enjoyed in the M.I. Hummel Club.

224/II   224/I

HUM 224
Wayside Harmony, Table Lamp

This lamp was modeled by master sculptor Reinhold Unger in 1952 and is actually a restyling of HUM II/111 "Wayside Harmony" lamp made in 1938. Large size same as small with the exception of a flower on branch of tree trunk. Small size measures 4¼" across base. Large size measures 6¼" across base. Early examples of the large (9½") size usually found without size designator, incised 224 only and usually have a switch on the base. Both sizes of "Wayside Harmony" table lamps were "temporarily withdrawn" (TW) from production on 31 December 1989, but may be reinstated at some future date.

☐ 224/I	7½"	(CE)	❷	$500–550
☐ 224/I	7½"	(CE)	❸	$380–450
☐ 224/I	7½"	(CE)	❹	$330–380
☐ 224/I	7½"	(CE)	❺	$300–310
☐ 224/I	7½"	(TW)	❻	$290–300
☐ 224/II	9½"	(CE)	❷	$525–700
☐ 224/II	9½"	(CE)	❸	$400–500
☐ 224/II	9½"	(CE)	❹	$375–400
☐ 224/II	9½"	(CE)	❺	$350–375
☐ 224/II	9½"	(TW)	❻	$340–350
☐ 224	9½"	(CE)	❷	$600–800
☐ 224	9½"	(CE)	❸	$475–600

225/II   225/I

HUM 225
Just Resting, Table Lamp
This lamp was modeled by master sculptor Reinhold Unger in 1952 and is actually a restyling of HUM II/112 "Just Resting" lamp made in 1938. Large size same as small with the exception of a flower on branch of tree trunk. Small size measures 4¼" across base. Large size measures 6¼" across base. Early examples of the large (9½") size usually found without size designator, incised 225 only and usually have a switch on the base. Both sizes of "Just Resting" table lamps were "temporarily withdrawn" (TW) from production on 31 December 1989, but may be reinstated at some future date.

☐ 225/I	7½"	(CE)	❷	$500−550
☐ 225/I	7½"	(CE)	❸	$380−450
☐ 225/I	7½"	(CE)	❹	$330−380
☐ 225/I	7½"	(CE)	❺	$300−310
☐ 225/I	7½"	(TW)	❻	$290−300
☐ 225/II	9½"	(CE)	❷	$525−700
☐ 225/II	9½"	(CE)	❸	$400−500
☐ 225/II	9½"	(CE)	❹	$375−400
☐ 225/II	9½"	(CE)	❺	$350−375
☐ 225/II	9½"	(TW)	❻	$340−350
☐ 225	9½"	(CE)	❷	$600−800
☐ 225	9½"	(CE)	❸	$475−600

HUM 226
The Mail Is Here
Originally modeled by master sculptor Arthur Moeller in 1952. Older pieces are slightly larger in size. Also called "Mail Coach." Usually has an incised 1952 copyright date. Some older examples have a very faint "M. I. Hummel" signature while others have the signature painted on because of this light impression.

☐ 226	4½ × 6¼"	(CE)	❷	$950–1150
☐ 226	4¼ × 6"	(CE)	❸	$700–800
☐ 226	4¼ × 6"	(CE)	❹	$575–700
☐ 226	4¼ × 6"	(CE)	❺	$490–515
☐ 226	4¼ × 6"	(CE)	❻	$470–490
☐ 226	4¼ × 6"	(OE)	❼	$470

HUM TERM

MEL: A Goebel-produced figurine with the letters "MEL" incised somewhere on the base of the piece. These pieces were designed from original drawings by Sister M.I. Hummel, but for some undetermined reasons were not approved by the Siessen Convent for inclusion in the "M.I. Hummel" line of figurines.

HUM 227 (TM 4)   *HUM 228 (TM 4)*

HUM 227
She Loves Me, She Loves Me Not Table Lamp
This lamp was first modeled in 1953 by master sculptor Arthur Moeller and has been restyled several times. On the older lamps the figure is much larger and the boy's eyes are open. On the newer models the eyes are looking down. Same motif as HUM 174 of the same name. Measures 4" across the base. Refer to HUM 251 for matching bookends. "She Loves Me, She Loves Me Not" table lamp was "temporarily withdrawn" (TW) from production on 31 December 1989, but may be reinstated at some future date.

☐ 227	7½"	(CE)	❷	$550–750
☐ 227	7½"	(CE)	❸	$375–425
☐ 227	7½"	(CE)	❹	$325–375
☐ 227	7½"	(CE)	❺	$300–325
☐ 227	7½"	(TW)	❻	$275–300

HUM 228
Good Friends, Table Lamp
This lamp was first modeled in 1953 master sculptor Arthur Moeller and had been restyled several times. On the older lamps the figure is much larger and the tree trunk post has a smoother finish. Same motif as HUM 182 of the same name. Measures 4¼" across the base. Refer to HUM 251 for matching bookends. "Good Friends" table lamp was "temporarily withdrawn" (TW) from production on 31 December 1989, but may be reinstated at some future date.

☐ 228	7½"	(CE)	❷	$550–750
☐ 228	7½"	(CE)	❸	$375–425
☐ 228	7½"	(CE)	❹	$325–375
☐ 228	7½"	(CE)	❺	$300–325
☐ 228	7½"	(TW)	❻	$275–300

HUM 229 (TM 5)   *HUM 230 (TM 5)*

HUM 229
Apple Tree Girl, Table Lamp
This lamp was first modeled in 1953 by master sculptor Arthur Moeller and has been restyled several times. On the older lamps the figure is much larger but the post still measures only 7½ inches. Measures 4¼″ across base. Old name: "Spring" or "Springtime." Refer to HUM 252 for matching bookends. "Apple Tree Girl" table lamp was "temporarily withdrawn" (TW) from production on 31 December 1989, but may be reinstated at some future date.

☐ 229	7½″	(CE)	❷	$800–900
☐ 229	7½″	(CE)	❸	$375–425
☐ 229	7½″	(CE)	❹	$325–375
☐ 229	7½″	(CE)	❺	$300–325
☐ 229	7½″	(TW)	❻	$275–300

HUM 230
Apple Tree Boy, Table Lamp
This lamp was first modeled in 1953 by master sculptor Arthur Moeller and has been restyled several times. On the older lamps the figure is much larger but the post still measures only 7½ inches. Measures 4¼″ across base. Old name: "Autumn" or "Fall" table lamp. Refer to HUM 252 for matching bookends. "Apple Tree Boy" table lamp was "temporarily withdrawn" (TW) from production on 31 December 1989, but may be reinstated at some future date.

☐ 230	7½″	(CE)	❷	$800–900
☐ 230	7½″	(CE)	❸	$375–425
☐ 230	7½″	(CE)	❹	$325–375
☐ 230	7½″	(CE)	❺	$300–325
☐ 230	7½″	(TW)	❻	$275–300

| 231 | New style | 234 | 231 | Old style | 234 |

HUM 231
Birthday Serenade, Table Lamp
This lamp was first modeled by master sculptor Reinhold Unger and was restyled in 1976 by master sculptor Rudolf Wittman. The early model measures 6″ across the base and has a hole for electrical switch on top of the base. Had been considered rare but is again in current production with 5 and 6 trademarks. Early models have an incised 1954 copyright date. The musical instruments have been reversed on the current production models. Refer to HUM 218 "Birthday Serenade" figurine for more details. Both sizes of "Birthday Serenade" table lamps were "temporarily withdrawn" (TW) from production on 31 December 1989, but may be reinstated at some future date.

☐ 231 ..... 9¾″ .... (CE) .. ❷ ... $2000–3000
☐ 231 ..... 9¾″ .... (CE) .. ❺ ... $450–500
☐ 231 ..... 9¾″ .... (TW) .. ❻ ... $400–450

HUM 234
Birthday Serenade, Table Lamp
This smaller size lamp was also modeled in 1954 by master sculptor Reinhold Unger and the first sample was painted in October 1954 by artist Georg Mechtold (initials "GM"). Similar to HUM 231 with the exception of having no flower on branch of tree trunk. Older models have an incised 1954 copyright date. Restyled in 1976 by master sculptor Rudolf Wittmann with the musical instruments in the reverse position. Had been considered rare but is again in current production. Trademark 4 examples can be found in either style. Both sizes of "Birthday Serenade" table lamps were "temporarily withdrawn" (TW) from production on 31 December 1989, but may be reinstated at some future date.

☐ 234 ..... 7¾″ .... (CE) .. ❷ ... $1500–2000
☐ 234 ..... 7¾″ .... (CE) .. ❸ ... $1000–1500
☐ 234 ..... 7¾″ .... (CE) .. ❹ ... $400–1000
☐ 234 ..... 7¾″ .... (CE) .. ❺ ... $350–400
☐ 234 ..... 7¾″ .... (TW) .. ❻ ... $325–350

HUM 232 (Old style) *HUM 235 (Old style)*

HUM 232
Happy Days, Table Lamp
This lamp was first modeled in 1954 by master sculptor Reinhold Unger and was restyled in 1976. The early model measures 6″ across the base and has a hole for electrical switch at top of base. Had been considered rare but is again in current production with 5 and 6 trademarks. Early models have an incised 1954 copyright date. Both sizes of "Happy Days" table lamps were "temporarily withdrawn" (TW) from production on 31 December 1989, but may be reinstated at some future date.

☐ 232	9¾″	(CE)	❷	$1000–1500
☐ 232	9¾″	(CE)	❺	$425–450
☐ 232	9¾″	(TW)	❻	$400–425

HUM 233 (CN)
Factory records indicate a sample of a "boy feeding birds." Listed as a Closed Number on 7 September 1954. No known examples. Gerhard Skrobek, current master modeler at the factory, stated that this was the first figure he modeled after starting to work at W. Goebel Porzellanfabrik in 1954. Skrobek later restyled this figurine which now appears as HUM 300 "Bird Watcher," issued in 1979.

HUM 235
Happy Days, Table Lamp
This smaller size lamp was also modeled in 1954 by master sculptor Reinhold Unger and the first sample was painted in October 1954 by artist Georg Mechtold (initials "GM"). Similar to HUM 232 with the exception of having no flower on branch of tree trunk. Older models have an incised 1954 copyright date. Restyled in 1976 and again in current production. Both sizes of "Happy Days" table lamps were "temporarily withdrawn" (TW) from production on 31 December 1989, but may be reinstated at some future date.

☐ 235	7¾″	(CE)	❷	$800–1000
☐ 235	7¾″	(CE)	❸	$525–750
☐ 235	7¾″	(CE)	❹	$450–525
☐ 235	7¾″	(CE)	❺	$375–400
☐ 235	7¾″	(TW)	❻	$350–375

236 A   236 B

HUM 236 A & B (CN)

Original research revealed no information about this number, so it was listed as an open number (ON) in our previous price guide. Sample models were located at the Goebel factory in 1984 and were put on display at the Goebel Collectors' Club in Tarrytown, N.Y. Designed in 1954 by master sculptor Arthur Moeller but for some unknown reason they were not approved by the Siessen Convent for production. Pictured here are the only known examples.

☐ 236 A ... 6½" .... (CN) .. ❷ ... $10,000–15,000
☐ 236 B ... 6½" .... (CN) .. ❷ ... $10,000–15,000

HUM 237
Star Gazer, Wall Plaque (CN)
This plaque was made as a sample only and not produced for sale as an open edition. This white overglaze (unpainted) example was recently located at the Goebel factory and is pictured here for the first time in any book, price guide, or catalogue regarding the subject of "M.I. Hummel" figurines. Was designed in 1954 and apparently rejected by Siessen Convent for production. Note the "M.I. Hummel" signature in the left hand corner. I have not been able to confirm the name of the original modeler of this rare item.

☐ 237 . . . . . 4¾ × 5″ . . . . . (CN) $10,000–15,000

238 A   **238 B**   **238 C**

HUM 238 A
Angel With Lute
One of a set of three small angel figures known as the "Angel Trio." Similar to HUM 38 except without holder for candle. Modeled by master sculptor Gerhard Skrobek in 1967. Has a 1967 incised copyright date and only produced with trademarks 4, 5 and 6.

☐ 238 A . . . 2 to 2½" . . . . . (CE) . . ❹ . . . $60–90
☐ 238 A . . . 2 to 2½" . . . . . (CE) . . ❺ . . . $47–50
☐ 238 A . . . 2 to 2½" . . . . . (CE) . . ❻ . . . $45–47
☐ 238 A . . . 2 to 2½" . . . . . (**OE**) . . ❼ . . . $45

HUM 238 B
Angel With Accordion
One of a set of three small angel figures known as the "Angel Trio." Similar to HUM 39 except without holder for candle. Modeled by master sculptor Gerhard Skrobek in 1967. Has a 1967 incised copyright date and only produced with trademarks 4, 5 and 6.

☐ 238 B . . . 2 to 2½" . . . . . (CE) . . ❹ . . . $60–90
☐ 238 B . . . 2 to 2½" . . . . . (CE) . . ❺ . . . $47–50
☐ 238 B . . . 2 to 2½" . . . . . (CE) . . ❻ . . . $45–47
☐ 238 B . . . 2 to 2½" . . . . . (**OE**) . . ❼ . . . $45

HUM 238 C
Angel With Trumpet
One of a set of three small angel figures known as the "Angel Trio." Similar to HUM 40 except without holder for candle. Modeled by master sculptor Gerhard Skrobek in 1967. Has a 1967 incised copyright date and only produced with trademarks 4, 5 and 6.

☐ 238 C . . . 2 to 2½" . . . . . (CE) . . ❹ . . . $60–90
☐ 238 C . . . 2 to 2½" . . . . . (CE) . . ❺ . . . $47–50
☐ 238 C . . . 2 to 2½" . . . . . (CE) . . ❻ . . . $45–47
☐ 238 C . . . 2 to 2½" . . . . . (**OE**) . . ❼ . . . $45

239 A   239 B   239 C

HUM 239 A
Girl With Nosegay

One of a set of three small children figurines known as the "Children Trio." Similar to HUM 115 except without holder for candle. Modeled by master sculptor Gerhard Skrobek in 1967. Has a 1967 incised copyright date and only produced with trademarks 4, 5 and 6.

☐ 239 A ... 3½" .... (CE) .. ❹ ... $60–90
☐ 239 A ... 3½" .... (CE) .. ❺ ... $47–50
☐ 239 A ... 3½" .... (CE) .. ❻ ... $45–47
☐ 239 A ... 3½" .... (OE) .. ❼ ... $45

HUM 239 B
Girl With Doll

One of a set of three small children figurines known as the "Children Trio." Similar to HUM 116 except without holder for candle. Modeled by master sculptor Gerhard Skrobek in 1967. Has a 1967 incised copyright date and only produced with trademarks 4, 5 and 6.

☐ 239 B ... 3½" .... (CE) .. ❹ ... $60–90
☐ 239 B ... 3½" .... (CE) .. ❺ ... $47–50
☐ 239 B ... 3½" .... (CE) .. ❻ ... $45–47
☐ 239 B ... 3½" .... (OE) .. ❼ ... $45

HUM 239 C
Boy With Horse

One of a set of three small children figurines known as the "Children Trio." Similar to HUM 117 except without holder for candle. Modeled by master sculptor Gerhard Skrobek in 1967. Has a 1967 incised copyright date and only produced with trademarks 4, 5 and 6.

☐ 239 C ... 3½" .... (CE) .. ❹ ... $60–90
☐ 239 C ... 3½" .... (CE) .. ❺ ... $47–50
☐ 239 C ... 3½" .... (CE) .. ❻ ... $45–47
☐ 239 C ... 3½" .... (OE) .. ❼ ... $45

TM 2   *TM 4*

HUM 240
Little Drummer
First modeled by master sculptor Reinhold Unger in 1955. Older pieces are usually slightly larger. Has an incised 1955 copyright date. Sometimes listed as "Drummer" even in recent price lists and catalogues. Similar to boy in HUM 50 "Volunteers."

☐ 240	.....	4 to 4¼"	.....	(CE)	❷ ...	$250–325
☐ 240	.....	4 to 4¼"	.....	(CE)	❸ ...	$190–220
☐ 240	.....	4 to 4¼"	.....	(CE)	❹ ...	$150–190
☐ 240	.....	4 to 4¼"	.....	(CE)	❺ ...	$130–135
☐ 240	.....	4 to 4¼"	.....	(CE)	❻ ...	$125–130
☐ 240	.....	4 to 4¼"	.....	(OE)	❼ ...	$125

HUM 241
Angel Lights, Candleholder
This number was assigned to this newly designed piece in error. Sometimes referred to as "Angel Bridge." Originally modeled by current master sculptor Gerhard Skrobek in 1976, this is an adaptation of HUM 21 "Heavenly Angel." Usually sold with a round plate which this piece is designed to fit. Found with trademarks 5 and 6 only. Sometimes listed as "241 B" but only the number 241 is incised on this item. "Angel Lights" candleholder was "temporarily withdrawn" (TW) from production on 31 December 1989, but may be reinstated at some future date.

☐ 241	.....	10⅓ × 8⅓"	...	(CE)	❺ ...	$250–300
☐ 241	.....	10⅓ × 8⅓"	...	(TW)	❻ ...	$225–250

HUM 241 (CN)

HUM 241
Holy Water Font, Angel Joyous News With Lute (CN)
This font was first modeled by master sculptor Reinhold Unger in 1955. Made as a sample only and not produced for sale as an open edition. Listed as a Closed Number on 6 April 1955.

☐ 241 ..... (Font) .... (CN) $1000–1500

HUM 242 (CN)

HUM 242
Holy Water Font, Angel Joyous News With Trumpet (CN)
This font was first modeled by master sculptor Reinhold Unger in 1955. Made as a sample only and not produced for sale as an open edition. Listed as a Closed Number on 6 April 1955.

☐ 242 ..... (Font) .... (CN) $1000–1500

HUM 243
Holy Water Font, Madonna And Child
This font was first modeled by master sculptor Reinhold Unger in 1955. Has an incised 1955 copyright date. Apparently not put on the market until the mid-1960's. Earliest catalogue listing found is 1967. No known variations have been recorded.

☐ 243	3⅛ × 4″	(CE)	❷	$225–275
☐ 243	3⅛ × 4″	(CE)	❸	$90–125
☐ 243	3⅛ × 4″	(CE)	❹	$60–90
☐ 243	3⅛ × 4″	(CE)	❺	$47–50
☐ 243	3⅛ × 4″	(CE)	❻	$45–47
☐ 243	3⅛ × 4″	(OE)	❼	$45

HUM 244 (ON)
Factory records contain no information at all regarding this number. It has therefore been listed as an Open Number and may be assigned to a future item.

☐ 244 .... (ON) .. ..

HUM 245 (ON)
Factory records contain no information at all regarding this number. It has therefore been listed as an Open Number and may be assigned to a future item.

☐ 245 .... (ON) .. ..

HUM 246
Holy Water Font, Holy Family
Master sculptor Theo R. Menzenbach modeled this font in 1955. Earliest catalogue listing is in 1955 Second Edition Schmid Brothers. Has an incised 1955 copyright date. No known variations have been recorded.

☐ 246	3⅛ × 4½"	(CE)	❷	$225–275
☐ 246	3⅛ × 4½"	(CE)	❸	$90–125
☐ 246	3⅛ × 4½"	(CE)	❹	$60–90
☐ 246	3⅛ × 4½"	(CE)	❺	$47–50
☐ 246	3⅛ × 4½"	(CE)	❻	$45–47
☐ 246	3⅛ × 4½"	(OE)	❼	$45

HUM 247
Standing Madonna With Child (CN)
This beautiful Madonna with Child was made as a sample only and not produced for sale as an open edition. It was modeled by master sculptor Theo R. Menzenbach in 1961 and apparently was rejected by the Siessen Convent for some unknown reason.

☐ 247 ..... 13" .... (CN) $10,000–15,000

248/0   248/I

HUM 248
Holy Water Font, Guardian Angel
This font was first modeled by master sculptor Gerhard Skrobek in 1958. Most models have an incised 1959 copyright date. This is a restyled version of HUM 29 which was discontinued at the time HUM 248 was introduced. This font was originally modeled in two sizes (248/0 and 248/I) but to my knowledge the large size was never put on the market. Factory information reveals that in the future it will be made in only the smaller size and "0" size designator will eventually disappear — so far this has not happened.

☐ 248/0	.... 2⅜ × 5⅜"	... (CE)	.. ❸	... $200–250
☐ 248/0	.... 2⅜ × 5⅜"	... (CE)	.. ❹	... $60–90
☐ 248/0	.... 2⅜ × 5⅜"	... (CE)	.. ❺	... $47–50
☐ 248/0	.... 2¼ × 5½"	... (CE)	.. ❻	... $45–47
☐ 248/0	.... 2¼ × 5½"	... (OE)	.. ❼	... $45
☐ 248/I	..... 2¾ × 6¼"	... (CE)	.. ❽	... $1000–1500

HUM 249
Madonna and Child (in relief)
Wall Plaque (CN)
This wall plaque was made as a sample only and not produced for sale as an open edition. Similar to HUM 48/V except without background or frame. Actually, the piece that I saw and is pictured here was simply a cut-out of HUM 48/V in an unfinished state, with no number or signature on the back — apparently an idea that was rejected or stopped before it was even completed. Possibly the work of master sculptor Reinhold Unger who modeled the first HUM 48 in 1936.

☐ 249 ..... 6¾ × 8¾" ... (CN) $10,000–15,000

250 A & B (priced as set)   *251 A & B (priced as set)*

HUM 250 A
Little Goat Herder, Bookend
HUM 250 B
Feeding Time, Bookend
Factory records indicate these bookends were designed by a team of modelers in 1960. First sold in the U.S in 1964. The bookends are simply normal figurines affixed to a wooden base. Refer to HUM 199 and HUM 200 for more information. Current models have current figurines. This pair of bookends was "temporarily withdrawn" (TW) from production on 31 December 1989, but may be reinstated at some future date.

☐ 250 A&B . 5½" .... (CE) .. ❷ ... $500−700
☐ 250 A&B . 5½" .... (CE) .. ❸ ... $350−400
☐ 250 A&B . 5½" .... (CE) .. ❺ ... $300−325
☐ 250 A&B . 5½" .... (TW) .. ❻ ... $275−300

HUM 251 A
Good Friends, Bookend
HUM 251 B
She Loves Me, She Loves Me Not! Bookend
Factory records indicate these bookends were designed by a team of modelers in 1960. First sold in the U.S. in 1964. The bookends are simply normal figurines affixed to a wooden base. Refer to HUM 174 and HUM 182 for more information. Current models have current figurines. This pair of bookends was "temporarily withdrawn" (TW) from production on 31 December 1989, but may be reinstated at some future date.

☐ 251 A&B . 5" .... (CE) .. ❷ ... $500−700
☐ 251 A&B . 5" .... (CE) .. ❸ ... $350−400
☐ 251 A&B . 5" .... (CE) .. ❺ ... $300−325
☐ 251 A&B . 5" .... (TW) .. ❻ ... $275−300

252 A & B (priced as set)

HUM 252 A
Apple Tree Girl, Bookend
HUM 252 B
Apple Tree Boy, Bookend
Factory records indicate these bookends were designed by a team of modelers in 1962. First sold in the U.S. in 1964. The bookends are simply normal figurines affixed to a wooden base. Refer to HUM 141 and HUM 142 for more information. Current models have current figurine. "Apple Tree Girl and Boy" bookends were "temporarily withdrawn" (TW) from production on 31 December 1989, but may be reinstated at some future date.

☐ 252 A&B . 5″ . . . . (CE) . . ❸ . . . $350–400
☐ 252 A&B . 5″ . . . . (CE) . . ❺ . . . $300–325
☐ 252 A&B . 5″ . . . . (TW) . . ❻ . . . $275–300

HUM 253 (CN)
Factory records indicate a girl with basket similar to the one in HUM 52 "Going to Grandma's." No known examples.

☐ 253 . . . . . 4½″ . . . . (CN) . .

HUM 254 (CN)
Factory records indicate a girl playing a mandolin similar to the one in HUM 150 "Happy Days." No known examples.

☐ 254 . . . . . 4¼″ . . . . (CN) . .

HUM 255
Stitch in Time

First modeled by a combination of sculptors in 1962. Has an incised 1963 copyright date. First sold in the U.S. in 1964. Similar to one of the girls used in HUM 256 "Knitting Lesson" and HUM 177 "School Girls." No unusual variations have been recorded. A new miniature size figurine was issued in 1990 with a suggested retail price of $65 to match a new miniature plate series called the "Little Homemakers" — one each year for four years. This is the third in the series. The normal size will be renumbered 255/0 and the old number 255 is now classified as a closed edition because of this change.

☐ 255 4/0	3"	(CE)	❻	$80–85
☐ 255 4/0	3"	(OE)	❼	$80
☐ 255	6½ to 6¾"	(CE)	❸	$350–600
☐ 255	6½ to 6¾"	(CE)	❹	$275–350
☐ 255	6½ to 6¾"	(CE)	❺	$240–250
☐ 255	6½ to 6¾"	(CE)	❻	$235–240
☐ 255/0	6½ to 6¾"	(CE)	❻	$230–235
☐ 255/0	6½ to 6¾"	(OE)	❼	$230

HUM 256
Knitting Lesson

First modeled by a combination of sculptors in 1962. Has an incised 1963 copyright date. First sold in the U.S. in 1964. Similar to two girls used in HUM 177 "School Girls." No unusual variations have been recorded.

☐ 256	7½"	(CE)	❸	$650–900
☐ 256	7½"	(CE)	❹	$550–650
☐ 256	7½"	(CE)	❺	$460–480
☐ 256	7½"	(CE)	❻	$440–460
☐ 256	7½"	(OE)	❼	$440

257 (TM 5)   257 2/0 (TM 6)

HUM 257
For Mother

First modeled by a combination of sculptors in 1962. Has an incised 1963 copyright date. First sold in the U.S. in 1964. No unusual variations have been recorded. A new small size HUM 257 2/0 was issued in 1985 at a suggested retail price of $50. This new small size figurine has an incised 1984 copyright date. The large size has now been renumbered 257/0.

☐ 257 2/0 .. 4" .... (CE) .. ❻ ... $105–110
☐ 257 2/0 .. 4" .... (OE) .. ❼ ... $105
☐ 257 ..... 5 to 5¼" ..... (CE) .. ❸ ... $325–600
☐ 257 ..... 5 to 5¼" ..... (CE) .. ❹ ... $200–250
☐ 257 ..... 5 to 5¼" ..... (CE) .. ❺ ... $185–190
☐ 257 ..... 5 to 5¼" ..... (CE) .. ❻ ... $175–185
☐ 257/0 .... 5 to 5¼" ..... (CE) .. ❻ ... $170–175
☐ 257/0 .... 5 to 5¼" ..... (OE) .. ❼ ... $170

```
───────── HUM TERM ─────────

OESLAU: Name for the village where the
W. Goebel Porzellanfabrik is located. Oes-
lau is now a part of the City of Roedental,
W. Germany. The name "Oeslau" appears
on HUM 348 "Ring Around The Rosie."
```

HUM 258
Which Hand?

First modeled by a combination of sculptors in 1962. Has an incised 1963 copyright date. First sold in the U.S. in 1964. Similar to girl used in HUM 196 "Telling Her Secret." No unusual variations have been recorded.

☐ 258	5¼ to 5½"	(CE)	❸	$350–650
☐ 258	5¼ to 5½"	(CE)	❹	$200–250
☐ 258	5¼ to 5½"	(CE)	❺	$170–180
☐ 258	5¼ to 5½"	(CE)	❻	$165–170
☐ 258	5¼ to 5½"	(OE)	❼	$165

(Factory sample)

HUM 259
Girl With Accordion (CN)

Modeled by a combination of sculptors in 1962, this figurine depicts a girl playing an accordion as in HUM 218 "Birthday Serenade." This piece was made as a sample only and not produced for sale as an open edition. Listed as a Closed Number on factory records of 8 November 1962.

☐ 259 ..... 4" .... (CN) .. ❸ ... $5,000–10,000

Large size nativity set

HUM 260
Large Nativity Set (with wooden stable)
This large size Nativity Set was first modeled in 1968 by current master sculptor Gerhard Skrobek. First sold in the U.S. in the early 1970's. Various styles of wooden stables have been produced through the years. The stable is priced at $350 currently, although it is usually included in the price of the set. This set consists of sixteen pieces, larger and more detailed than the small Nativity set HUM 214. Individual pieces can be purchased separately but are normally sold as a set. This large size Nativity Set was "temporarily withdrawn" (TW) from production on 31 December 1989, but may be reinstated at some future date.

260 A Madonna
260 B Saint Joseph
260 C Infant Jesus
260 D Good Night
260 E Angel Serenade
260 F We Congratulate
260 G Shepherd, standing
260 H Sheep, standing with lamb
260 J Shepherd Boy, kneeling
260 K Little Tooter
260 L Donkey, standing
260 M Cow, lying
260 N Moorish King, standing
260 O King, standing
260 P King, kneeling
260 R One Sheep, lying

☐ 260	. . . . . SET 16 PIECES .	(CE)	. . ❹ . . .	$5100–5400	(includes stable)
☐ 260	. . . . . SET 16 PIECES .	(CE)	. . ❺ . . .	$5000–5100	(includes stable)
☐ 260	. . . . . SET 16 PIECES .	(TW)	. . ❻ . . .	$4900–5000	(includes stable)
☐ 260A	. . . . 9¾″	(CE)	. . ❹ . .	$540–550	
☐ 260A	. . . . 9¾″	(CE)	. . ❺ . .	$530–540	
☐ 260A	. . . . 9¾″	(TW)	. . ❻ . .	$520–530	
☐ 260B	. . . . 11¾″	(CE)	. . ❹ . .	$540–550	
☐ 260B	. . . . 11¾″	(CE)	. . ❺ . .	$530–540	
☐ 260B	. . . . 11¾″	(TW)	. . ❻ . .	$520–530	
☐ 260C	. . . . 5¾″	(CE)	. . ❹ . .	$115–120	
☐ 260C	. . . . 5¾″	(CE)	. . ❺ . .	$110–115	
☐ 260C	. . . . 5¾″	(TW)	. . ❻ . .	$105–110	
☐ 260D	. . . . 5¼″	(CE)	. . ❹ . .	$140–150	
☐ 260D	. . . . 5¼″	(CE)	. . ❺ . .	$135–140	
☐ 260D	. . . . 5¼″	(TW)	. . ❻ . .	$130–135	
☐ 260E	. . . . 4¼″	(CE)	. . ❹ . .	$135–140	
☐ 260E	. . . . 4¼″	(CE)	. . ❺ . .	$130–135	
☐ 260E	. . . . 4¼″	(TW)	. . ❻ . .	$125–130	
☐ 260F	. . . . 6¼″	(CE)	. . ❹ . .	$380–405	
☐ 260F	. . . . 6¼″	(CE)	. . ❺ . .	$370–380	
☐ 260F	. . . . 6¼″	(TW)	. . ❻ . .	$360–370	
☐ 260G	. . . . 11¾″	(CE)	. . ❹ . .	$550–575	
☐ 260G	. . . . 11¾″	(CE)	. . ❺ . .	$530–550	
☐ 260G	. . . . 11¾″	(TW)	. . ❻ . .	$525–530	
☐ 260H	. . . . 3¾″	(CE)	. . ❹ . .	$100–105	
☐ 260H	. . . . 3¾″	(CE)	. . ❺ . .	$95–100	
☐ 260H	. . . . 3¾″	(TW)	. . ❻ . .	$90–95	
☐ 260J	. . . . 7″	(CE)	. . ❹ . .	$310–325	
☐ 260J	. . . . 7″	(CE)	. . ❺ . .	$300–310	
☐ 260J	. . . . 7″	(TW)	. . ❻ . .	$295–300	
☐ 260K	. . . . 5⅛″	(CE)	. . ❹ . .	$165–170	
☐ 260K	. . . . 5⅛″	(CE)	. . ❺ . .	$160–165	
☐ 260K	. . . . 5⅛″	(TW)	. . ❻ . .	$155–160	
☐ 260L	. . . . 7½″	(CE)	. . ❹ . .	$135–140	
☐ 260L	. . . . 7½″	(CE)	. . ❺ . .	$130–135	
☐ 260L	. . . . 7½″	(TW)	. . ❻ . .	$125–130	
☐ 260M	. . . . 6 × 11″	(CE)	. . ❹ . .	$150–160	
☐ 260M	. . . . 6 × 11″	(CE)	. . ❺ . .	$145–150	
☐ 260M	. . . . 6 × 11″	(TW)	. . ❻ . .	$140–145	
☐ 260N	. . . . 12¾″	(CE)	. . ❹ . .	$510–540	
☐ 260N	. . . . 12¾″	(CE)	. . ❺ . .	$500–510	
☐ 260N	. . . . 12¾″	(TW)	. . ❻ . .	$490–500	
☐ 260O	. . . . 12″	(CE)	. . ❹ . .	$510–540	
☐ 260O	. . . . 12″	(CE)	. . ❺ . .	$500–510	
☐ 260O	. . . . 12″	(TW)	. . ❻ . .	$490–500	
☐ 260P	. . . . 9″	(CE)	. . ❹ . .	$490–500	
☐ 260P	. . . . 9″	(CE)	. . ❺ . .	$480–490	
☐ 260P	. . . . 9″	(TW)	. . ❻ . .	$470–480	
☐ 260R	. . . . 3¼ × 4″	(CE)	. . ❹ . .	$55–60	
☐ 260R	. . . . 3¼ × 4″	(CE)	. . ❺ . .	$50–55	
☐ 260R	. . . . 3¼ × 4″	(TW)	. . ❻ . .	$45–50	
☐ 260S	. . . . . STABLE	**(OE)**	. . – . . .	$400	

HUM 261
Angel Duet
Same name and same design as HUM 193 but without holder for candle. Modeled by master sculptor Gerhard Skrobek in 1968. Has an incised copyright date of 1968 on the bottom of each piece. Notice position of angel's arm in rear view. HUM 193 candle-holder can be found with arms in either position while HUM 261 is found with arm in lower position only. Difficult to find with 4 trademark.

☐ 261 ..... 5″ .... (CE) .. ❹ ... $500–750
☐ 261 ..... 5″ .... (CE) .. ❺ ... $190–200
☐ 261 ..... 5″ .... (CE) .. ❻ ... $180–190
☐ 261 ..... 5″ .... (**OE**) .. ❼ ... $180

    261   *193*

HUM 262
Heavenly Lullaby
This is the same design as HUM 24/I "Lullaby" without the hole for candle. Modeled by master sculptor Gerhard Skrobek in 1968. Has an incised copyright date of 1968 on the bottom of each piece. Difficult to find with 4 trademark.

☐ 262 ..... 3½ × 5" ..... (CE) .. ❹ ... $500–750
☐ 262 ..... 3½ × 5" ..... (CE) .. ❺ ... $160–170
☐ 262 ..... 3½ × 5" ..... (CE) .. ❻ ... $155–160
☐ 262 ..... 3½ × 5" ..... (OE) .. ❼ ... $155

HUM 263 (CN)
Merry Wanderer, Wall Plaque (in relief)
This unique wall plaque, modeled by master sculptor Gerhard Skrobek in 1968, was made as a sample model only and not produced for sale as an open edition. It is simply a "Merry Wanderer" figurine made without a base, slightly flattened on the back side with a hole provided for hanging. The example in our collection has the incised number 263 and the "three line" (TM4) trademark as well as the incised "M.I. Hummel" signature. The front view photo does not give the appearance of depth that can be shown in the rear view. It looks like it would be possible for a collector to make such a plaque by taking HUM 7/0, "Merry Wanderer," removing the base and grinding the back so that it would hang flat against the wall. But then, of course, you would *not* have the incised number or signature, nor the "three line" trademark!

☐ 263 ..... 4 × 5⅜" ..... (CN) .. ❹ ... $10,000–15,000

Special Worker's Plate Inscription

HUM 264
Annual Plate, 1971
Heavenly Angel (CE)

1971 was the 100th anniversary of W. Goebel Porzellanfabrik. The annual plate was issued in commemoration of that occasion. Each employee of the company was presented with a 1971 Annual Plate bearing a special inscription on the back. These plates with the special inscription have become a highly sought-after collector's item because of the very limited production. Produced with the 4 trademark only. The original issue price was $25.

☐ 264 ..... 7½" .... (CE) .. ❹ ... $700–900
☐ 264 ..... 7½" .... (CE) .. ❹ ... $1000–1200 (Worker's Plate)

Rare factory sample of 1948 Christmas plate.
Never issued or sold on the market.

Note: There were some 1971 Hummel plates made without the two holes on the back, which were normally placed there so that cord or wire could be put through them for hanging purposes. These plates were purposely made without the holes and were shipped to the British Isles in order to qualify for a lower rate of duty. With the hanging holes made in the plates, British Customs Department would charge a higher rate of duty since the plate would be classified as a decorative or luxury item rather than the more practical dinner plate classification. In my opinion, the missing holes will not affect the value of your plate one way or the other. In fact, some collectors may prefer the more rare one without the holes!

HUM 265
Annual Plate, 1972
Hear Ye, Hear Ye (CE)
Produced with TM 4 and TM 5 trademarks. Change was made in mid-production year. The original issue price was $30.

☐ 265 . . . . . 7½″ . . . . (CE) . . ❹ . . . $80–125
☐ 265 . . . . . 7½″ . . . . (CE) . . ❺ . . . $80–125

HUM 266
Annual Plate,1973
Globe Trotter(CE)
The original issue price was $32.50.

☐ 266 . . . . . 7½″ . . . . (CE) . . ❺ . . . $175–250

HUM 267
Annual Plate, 1974
Goose Girl (CE)
The original issue price was $40.

☐ 267 . . . . . 7½" . . . . (CE) . . ❺ . . . $80–125

"Winner"

"Loser"

HUM 268
Annual Plate, 1975
Ride Into Christmas (CE)
Two different samples were produced for the 1975 plate. The winning design was "Ride Into Christmas." The losing design was the "Little Fiddler" plate pictured here. There were only two or three of these samples produced—so actually it is a "winner" as far as value is concerned! Value: $5,000 +. The original issue price was $50.

☐ 268 . . . . . 7½" . . . . (CE) . . ❺ . . . $80–125

HUM 269
Annual Plate, 1976
Apple Tree Girl (CE)
The original issue price was $50.

☐ 269 ..... 7½" .... (CE) .. ❺ ... $80–125

Early sample   *Restyled version*

HUM 270
Annual Plate, 1977 Apple Tree Boy (CE)
Note the picture on the 1977 plate. The one shown here on the left is an early sample piece. Before production commenced, the boy's shoes were changed to a slightly different angle and the boy's stockings were reversed (his right one is higher than the left in most known examples). If your plate is exactly like this picture, you have a rare plate! The original issue price was $52.50.

☐ 270 ..... 7½" .... (CE) .. ❺ ... $80–125

HUM 271
Annual Plate, 1978
Happy Pastime (CE)
The original issue price was $65

☐ 271 ..... 7½″ .... (CE) .. ❺ ... $80–125

HUM 272
Annual Plate, 1979
Singing Lesson (CE)
The original issue price was $90.

☐ 272 ..... 7½″ .... (CE) .. ❺ ... $80–125

HUM 273
Annual Plate, 1980
School Girl (CE)
The original issue price was $100.

☐ 273 ..... 7½″ .... (CE) .. ❻ ... $75–100

HUM 274
Annual Plate, 1981
Umbrella Boy (CE)
The original issue price was $100.

☐ 274 ..... 7½" .... (CE) .. ❻ ... $80–125

HUM 275
Annual Plate, 1982
Umbrella Girl (CE)
The original issue price was $100.

☐ 275 ..... 7½" .... (CE) .. ❻ ... $150–175

HUM 276
Annual Plate, 1983
Postman (CE)
The original issue price was $108.

☐ 276 ..... 7½" .... (CE) .. ❻ ... $225–250

HUM 277
Annual Plate, 1984
Little Helper (CE)
The original issue price was $108

☐ 277 ..... 7½" .... (CE) .. ❻ ... $80−125

HUM 278
Annual Plate, 1985
Chick Girl (CE)
The original issue price was $110.

☐ 278 ..... 7½" .... (CE) .. ❻ ... $80−125

HUM 279
Annual Plate, 1986
Playmates (CE)
The original issue price was $125.

☐ 279 ..... 7½" .... (CE) .. ❻ ... $150−200

HUM 280
Anniversary Plate, 1975
Stormy Weather (CE)
First edition of a series of plates issued at five year intervals. The inscription on the back applied by blue decal reads: "First edition M.I. Hummel Anniversary Plate 'Stormy Weather' 1975 hand painted." The original issue price was $100.

☐ 280 ..... 10″ .... (CE) .. ❺ ... $125–175

HUM 281
Anniversary Plate, 1980
Ring Around The Rosie (two girls only) (CE)
Second edition of a series of plates issued at five year intervals. The inscription on the back reads: "Second edition M.I. Hummel Anniversary Plate 1980 'Spring Dance' hand painted." Trademark: (TM 6) 1978. Labeled "Spring Dance" in error. See HUM 353 "Spring Dance" and HUM 348 "Ring Around the Rosie." The original issue price was $225.

☐ 281 ..... 10″ .... (CE) .. ❻ ... $100–125

HUM 282
Anniversary Plate, 1985
Auf Wiedersehen (CE)
Third and last of a series of plates issued at five year intervals. The inscription on the back reads: "Third and final edition M.I. Hummel Anniversary Plate 1985 hand painted." A small round decal reads: "50 Jahre 1935–1985 M.I. Hummel Figuren." Trademark (TM 6) 1980. The original issue price was $225.

☐ 282 ..... 10″ .... (CE) .. ❻ ... $200–250

HUM 283
Annual Plate, 1987
Feeding Time (CE)
Designed by master sculptor Gerhard Skrobek in 1983. The original issue price was $135.

☐ 283 ..... 7½" .... (CE) .. ❻ ... $275–350

HUM 284
Annual Plate, 1988
Little Goat Herder (CE)
Designed by master sculptor Gerhard Skrobek in 1983. The original issue price was $145.

☐ 284 ..... 7½" .... (CE) .. ❻ ... $150–175

HUM 285
Annual Plate, 1989
Farm Boy (CE)
Designed by master sculptor Gerhard Skrobek in 1983. The original issue price was $160.

☐ 285 ..... 7½" .... (CE) .. ❻ ... $175–200

HUM 286
Annual Plate, 1990
Shepherd's Boy (CE)
Designed by master sculptor Gerhard Skrobek in 1983. The original issue price was $170.

□ 286 . . . . . 7½" . . . . (CE) . . ❻ . . . $200–225

HUM 287
Annual Plate, 1991
Just Resting (CE)
Designed by master sculptor Gerhard Skrobek in 1983. The original issue price was $196.

□ 287 . . . . . 7½" . . . . (CE) . . ❻ . . . $200–225
□ 287 . . . . . 7½" . . . . (CE) . . ❼ . . . $200–225

HUM 288
Annual Plate, 1992
Wayside Harmony
Designed by master sculptor Gerhard Skrobek in 1983. 22nd in a series of 25. The original issue price was $196.

□ 288 . . . . . 7½" . . . . (**OE**) . . ❼ . . . $210

HUM 289–1993 Annual Plate (PFE)
HUM 290–1994 Annual Plate (PFE)
HUM 291–1995 Annual Plate (PFE)

Hum 292
Meditation Plate
First released in the U.S. market in 1992, the first in the Annual Series of four plates called "Friends Forever". The original issue price was $180.

☐ 292 ..... 7⅛" .... (**OE**) .. ❼ ... $180

Hum 293 For Father Plate 1993 Release (PFE)
Hum 294 Sweet Greetings Plate 1994 Release (PFE)
Hum 295 Surprise Plate 1995 Release (PFE)
Hum 296–299 Open Numbers
Open Number (ON): An identification number, which in W. Goebel's numerical identification system has not yet been used, but which may be used to identify new "M.I. Hummel" figurines as they are released in the future.

Hum 300
Bird Watcher
First sold in the U.S. in 1979. The original issue price was $80. At one time called "Tenderness." Has an incised 1956 copyright date. An early sample of this figure was modeled in 1954 by Gerhard Skrobek and was assigned the number HUM 233 (CN). Skrobek stated that this was the first figure he modeled after starting to work at the Goebel factory in 1954. An early sample model with the full bee trademark, incised 1954 date, is in the Robert L. Miller collection.

☐ 300 ...... 5" .... (CE) .. ❷ ... $4000–5000
☐ 300 ...... 5" .... (CE) .. ❸ ... $2000–2500
☐ 300 ...... 5" .... (CE) .. ❹ ... $1500–2000
☐ 300 ...... 5" .... (CE) .. ❺ ... $200–210
☐ 300 ...... 5" .... (CE) .. ❻ ... $190–200
☐ 300 ...... 5" .... (**OE**) .. ❼ ... $190

Old   *New*

HUM 301
Christmas Angel

First released in the U.S. market in 1989. Originally called: "Delivery Angel." An early sample model of this figure was modeled by Theo R. Menzenbach in 1957. Menzenbach stated that it was not approved by the Siessen Convent for production. The sample model in our collection has an early stylized trademark 3 and 1957 incised copyright date. Original issue price was $160 in 1989. Was restyled by master sculptor Gerhard Skrobek in the late 1980's but still has the 1957 copyright date.

☐ 301 ..... 6¼" .... (CE) .. ❸ ... $4000–5000
☐ 301 ..... 6" .... (CE) .. ❻ ... $210–220
☐ 301 ..... 6" .... **(OE)** .. ❼ ... $210

HUM 302
Concentration (PFE)

First modeled by master sculptor Arthur Moeller in 1955. Originally called "Knit One, Purl Two." Girl is similar to HUM 255 "Stitch in Time." Listed on factory records as a Possible Future Edition (PFE) and may be released at some future date, subject to possible minor changes.

☐ 302 ..... 5" .... (PFE) . .....

243

HUM 303
Arithmetic Lesson (PFE)

Originally called "School Lesson." Modeled by master sculptor Arthur Moeller in 1955. Notice similarity to middle boy in HUM 170 "School Boys" and girl from HUM 177 "School Girls." Listed on factory records as a Possible Future Edition (PFE) and may be released at some future date, subject to possible minor changes.

☐ 303 ..... 5¼" .... (PFE) . .....

HUM 304
Artist

Originally modeled by master sculptor Karl Wagner in 1955 and later restyled by master sculptor Gerhard Skrobek in 1970. First introduced in the U.S. market in 1971. Has an incised 1955 copyright date. Could possibly be found in trademarks 2 and 3, but would be considered extremely rare. Would have trademark 4 when first issued in quantity in 1971. Note: artist Karl Wagner is no longer living. The original issue price in 1971 was $18.

☐ 304	.....	5½"	.... (CE)	.. ❷ ...	$4000–5000
☐ 304	.....	5½"	.... (CE)	.. ❸ ...	$2000–3000
☐ 304	.....	5½"	.... (CE)	.. ❹ ...	$500–750
☐ 304	.....	5½"	.... (CE)	.. ❺ ...	$210–220
☐ 304	.....	5½"	.... (CE)	.. ❻ ...	$200–210
☐ 304	.....	5½"	.... (OE)	.. ❼ ...	$200

HUM 305
Builder
First introduced in the U.S. market in 1963, this figurine was originally modeled in 1955 by master sculptor Gerhard Skrobek. Has an incised 1955 copyright date. An example with trademark 2 would be considered rare.

☐ 305	5½"	(CE)	❷	...	$4000–5000
☐ 305	5½"	(CE)	❸	...	$550–800
☐ 305	5½"	(CE)	❹	...	$250–350
☐ 305	5½"	(CE)	❺	...	$210–220
☐ 305	5½"	(CE)	❻	...	$200–210
☐ 305	5½"	(OE)	❼	...	$200

HUM 306
Little Bookkeeper
First introduced in the U.S. market in 1962, this figurine was originally modeled in 1955 by master sculptor Arthur Moeller. Has an incised 1955 copyright date. A "Little Bookkeeper" with a full bee, trademark 2, was recently purchased at auction in New York at a fraction of the true value. An example with trademark 2 would be considered rare.

☐ 306	4¾"	(CE)	❷	...	$4000–5000
☐ 306	4¾"	(CE)	❸	...	$550–800
☐ 306	4¾"	(CE)	❹	...	$300–375
☐ 306	4¾"	(CE)	❺	...	$250–260
☐ 306	4¾"	(CE)	❻	...	$240–250
☐ 306	4¾"	(OE)	❼	...	$240

New style (TM 4)   *Old style (TM 4)*

HUM 307
Good Hunting

First introduced in the U.S. market in 1962, this figurine was originally modeled by master sculptor Reinhold Unger and sculptor Helmut Wehlte in 1955. Has an incised 1955 copyright date. Hat, brush, collar, hair and position of binoculars have some variations. An example with trademark 2 would be considered rare. The word "muster-zimmer" means "painter's sample" and should not have been removed from factory. Possibly shipped out by accident.

☐ 307 ..... 5″ .... (CE) .. ❷ ... $4000–5000
☐ 307 ..... 5″ .... (CE) .. ❸ ... $550–800
☐ 307 ..... 5″ .... (CE) .. ❹ ... $300–375
☐ 307 ..... 5″ .... (CE) .. ❺ ... $210–220
☐ 307 ..... 5″ .... (CE) .. ❻ ... $200–210
☐ 307 ..... 5″ .... (OE) .. ❼ ... $200

New   Old

HUM 308
Little Tailor
First introduced in the U.S. market in 1972. Originally modeled by master sculptor Horst Ashermann in 1955. Later restyled by current master sculptor Gerhard Skrobek in 1972. Early model on the right has an incised 1955 copyright date while the restyled version on the left has an incised 1972 copyright date. Both styles can be found in trademark 5. The original issue price was $24 in 1972.

☐ 308 . . . . . 5¼ to 5¾" . . . . (CE) . . ❷ . . . $4000–5000
☐ 308 . . . . . 5¼ to 5¾" . . . . (CE) . . ❸ . . . $2000–3000
☐ 308 . . . . . 5¼ to 5¾" . . . . (CE) . . ❹ . . . $750–1000
☐ 308 . . . . . 5¼ to 5¾" . . . . (CE) . . ❺ . . . $600–750 (Old Style)
☐ 308 . . . . . 5¼ to 5¾" . . . . (CE) . . ❺ . . . $210–220 (New Style)
☐ 308 . . . . . 5¼ to 5¾" . . . . (CE) . . ❻ . . . $200–210
☐ 308 . . . . . 5¼ to 5¾" . . . . (OE) . . ❼ . . . $200

Early sample   *Current production*

HUM 309
With Loving Greetings

First released in the U.S. market in 1983. Modeled in 1955 by master sculptor Karl Wagner. Originally called "Greetings From" on old factory records, but later changed to "With Loving Greetings." The original issue price was $80 in 1983. Notice the ink stopper beside the ink bottle and an extra paint brush under the boy's left arm. This is an early sample model and these two items were eliminated for production reasons. When originally introduced in 1983, the ink bottle was blue and the message was a deep turquoise. In 1987 this was changed to a brown ink bottle and the message to a periwinkle blue.

☐ 309	3½"	(CE)	❷	$4000–5000
☐ 309	3¼ to 3½"	(CE)	❸	$3000–4000
☐ 309	3¼ to 3½"	(CE)	❹	$2000–3000
☐ 309	3¼ to 3½"	(CE)	❺	$1000–2000
☐ 309	3¼ to 3½"	(CE)	❻	$200–250 (Blue)
☐ 309	3¼ to 3½"	(CE)	❻	$160–165 (Brown)
☐ 309	3¼ to 3½"	(OE)	❼	$160

HUM 310
Searching Angel, Wall Plaque

First introduced in the U.S. market in 1979 along with two other "M.I. Hummel" items. This plaque was originally called "Angelic Concern" on factory records, but later changed to above name. Has an incised 1955 copyright date and was modeled by master sculptor Gerhard Skrobek in 1955. Some catalogues list this piece as number 310 A in error; the incised number is 310 only. The original issue price was $55 in 1979.

☐ 310	4¼ to 3¼"	(CE)	❷	$2000–3000
☐ 310	4¼ to 3¼"	(CE)	❸	$1000–1500
☐ 310	4¼ to 3¼"	(CE)	❹	$1000–1500
☐ 310	4¼ to 3¼"	(CE)	❺	$110–115
☐ 310	4¼ to 3¼"	(CE)	❻	$105–110
☐ 310	4¼ to 3¼"	(OE)	❼	$105

New   *Old*

HUM 311
Kiss Me
First introduced in the U.S. market in 1961. Originally modeled by master sculptor Reinhold Unger in 1955. Later restyled in 1963 by master sculptor Gerhard Skrobek at the request of the Convent. The doll was redesigned to look more like a doll instead of a child. Has an incised 1955 copyright date. Both styles can be found with 3 and 4 trademarks. An example with trademark 2 would be considered rare.

☐ 311 ..... 6 to 6¼″ ..... (CE) .. ❷ ... $4000–5000
☐ 311 ..... 6 to 6¼″ ..... (CE) .. ❸ ... $350–1000
☐ 311 ..... 6 to 6¼″ ..... (CE) .. ❹ ... $275–850
☐ 311 ..... 6 to 6¼″ ..... (CE) .. ❺ ... $240–250
☐ 311 ..... 6 to 6¼″ ..... (CE) .. ❻ ... $230–240
☐ 311 ..... 6 to 6¼″ ..... (OE) .. ❼ ... $230

HUM 312
Honey Lover (EE)
First modeled by master sculptor Helmut Wehlte in 1955. This figurine was originally called "In the Jam Pot" on factory records, but later changed to the above name. This early sample model pictured here has a "full bee" (TM 2) trademark and is part of the Robert L. Miller collection. Announced in 1991, "Honey Lover" will be an EXCLUSIVE EDITION available to "M.I. Hummel Club" members only, who have belonged to the Club continuously for 15 years. Issued by means of a redemption card to those who are eligible. The original issue price was $190.

☐ 312 ..... 3¾" .... (CE) .. ❷ ... $4000–5000
☐ 312/1 .... 3¾" .... (EE) .. ❻ ... $225–250
☐ 312/1 .... 3¾" .... (EE) .. ❼ ... $190
(M.I.H. Club Members only)

HUM 313
Sunny Morning (PFE)
This figurine was originally called "Slumber Serenade" on factory records, but later changed to "Sunny Morning." Modeled in 1955 by master sculptor Arthur Moeller. Listed on factory records as a Possible Future Edition (PFE) and may be released at some future date, subject to possible minor changes.

☐ 313 ..... 3¾" .... (PFE) ....

Old   New

HUM 314
Confidentially
First introduced in the U.S. market in 1972. Originally modeled by master sculptor Horst Ashermann in 1955. Later restyled by master sculptor Gerhard Skrobek in 1972. Skrobek completely restyled it by changing the stand, adding a tie to the boy and giving it the new textured finish. The early models have an incised 1955 copyright date while the restyled version has an incised 1972 copyright date. When first put on the market in 1972 it was in the old style and had the 4 trademark. Older trademarks such as 2 and 3 would be considered rare. The original issue price in 1972 was $22.50.

☐ 314	..... 5¼ to 5¾"	.... (CE)	.. ❷	...	$4000–5000
☐ 314	..... 5¼ to 5¾"	.... (CE)	.. ❸	...	$2000–3000
☐ 314	..... 5¼ to 5¾"	.... (CE)	.. ❹	...	$750–1000
☐ 314	..... 5¼ to 5¾"	.... (CE)	.. ❺	...	$600–750 (Old Style)
☐ 314	..... 5¼ to 5¾"	.... (CE)	.. ❺	...	$240–250 (New Style)
☐ 314	..... 5¼ to 5¾"	.... (CE)	.. ❻	...	$230–240
☐ 314	..... 5¼ to 5¾"	.... (OE)	.. ❼	...	$230

Early sample model

HUM 315
Mountaineer
First introduced in the U.S. market at the N.Y. World's Fair in 1964. Has an incised 1955 copyright date. Originally modeled by master sculptor Gerhard Skrobek in 1955. Older models are slightly smaller and have a green stick rather than the dark gray stick found on the newer models. If found with trademark 2 would be considered rare.

☐ 315 ..... 5" .... (CE) .. ❷ ... $4000–5000
☐ 315 ..... 5" .... (CE) .. ❸ ... $750–1000
☐ 315 ..... 5" .... (CE) .. ❹ ... $250–350
☐ 315 ..... 5" .... (CE) .. ❺ ... $190–200
☐ 315 ..... 5" .... (CE) .. ❻ ... $180–190
☐ 315 ..... 5" .... (OE) .. ❼ ... $180

HUM 316
Relaxation (PFE)
This figurine was originally called "Nightly Ritual" on factory records, but later changed to "Relaxation." Modeled by master sculptor Karl Wagner in 1955. Listed on factory records as a Possible Future Edition (PFE) and may be released at some future date, subject to possible minor changes.

☐ 316 ..... 4" .... (PFE) ....

HUM 317
Not For You!

First introduced in the U.S. market in 1961. Has an incised 1955 copyright date. Originally modeled by master sculptor Arthur Moeller in 1955. Some catalogues and price lists incorrectly show size as 6″. The collector should not rely on the measurements in price lists and catalogues as being absolutely accurate, as there have been many typographical errors in them throughout the years. In this book, we used the "bracket" system and show the smallest to the largest size known, verified by actual measurement. If found with trademark 2 would be considered rare.

☐ 317	5½″	(CE)	❷	$4000−5000
☐ 317	5½″	(CE)	❸	$750−1000
☐ 317	5½″	(CE)	❹	$250−350
☐ 317	5½″	(CE)	❺	$210−220
☐ 317	5½″	(CE)	❻	$200−210
☐ 317	5½″	(OE)	❼	$200

HUM 318
Art Critic

First modeled by master sculptor Horst Ashermann in 1955. First released in the U.S. Market in 1991. The original issue price was $230.

☐ 318	5½″	(CE)	❷	$4000−5000
☐ 318	5¾″	(CE)	❻	$240−250
☐ 318	5¾″	(OE)	❼	$240

HUM 319
Doll Bath
First introduced in the U.S. market in 1962. Has an incised 1956 copyright date. Originally modeled by master sculptor Gerhard Skrobek in 1956 and was restyled with the new textured finish in the early 1970's. If found with trademark 2 would be considered rare.

☐ 319 ..... 5″ .... (CE) .. ❷ ... $4000–5000
☐ 319 ..... 5″ .... (CE) .. ❸ ... $750–1000
☐ 319 ..... 5″ .... (CE) .. ❹ ... $300–350
☐ 319 ..... 5″ .... (CE) .. ❺ ... $240–250
☐ 319 ..... 5″ .... (CE) .. ❻ ... $230–240
☐ 319 ..... 5″ .... (OE) .. ❼ ... $230

Front view

Back view

HUM 320
The Professor
Originally modeled in 1955 by master sculptor Gerhard Skrobek. First released in the U.S. market in the fall of 1991. 320/0 has an incised 1989 copyright date.

☐ 320 ..... 5¾″ .... (CE) .. ❷ ... $4000–5000
☐ 320/0 .... 4⅞″ .... (OE) .. ❼ ... $180

254

Early sample model   *Current style*

HUM 321
Wash Day

First introduced in the U.S. market in 1963. Has an incised 1957 copyright date. Originally modeled in 1955 by master sculptor Reinhold Unger and Helmut Wehlte. Notice early sample model pictured here. Older pieces are usually slightly larger in size. If found with trademark 2 would be considered rare. A new miniature size figurine was issued in 1989 with a suggested retail price of $60 to match a new miniature plate series called the "Little Homemakers"—one each year for four years. This is the second in the series. The miniature size figurine has an incised 1987 copyright date. The original size will be renumbered 321/0 and the old number 321 is now classified as a closed edition (CE) because of this change.

☐ 321 4/0 .. 3" .... (CE) .. ❻ ... $80–85
☐ 321 4/0 .. 3" .... (**OE**) .. ❼ ... $80
☐ 321 ..... 5½ to 6" ..... (CE) .. ❷ ... $4000–5000
☐ 321 ..... 5½ to 6" ..... (CE) .. ❸ ... $500–750
☐ 321 ..... 5½ to 6" ..... (CE) .. ❹ ... $275–350
☐ 321 ..... 5½ to 6" ..... (CE) .. ❺ ... $240–255
☐ 321 ..... 5½ to 6" ..... (CE) .. ❻ ... $230–240
☐ 321/0 .... 5½ to 6" ..... (CE) .. ❻ ... $230–240
☐ 321/0 .... 5½ to 6" ..... (**OE**) .. ❼ ... $230

321 4/0

German   Spanish   English

HUM 322
Little Pharmacist

First introduced in the U.S. market in 1962. Originally modeled by master sculptor Karl Wagner in 1955. Most examples have an incised 1955 copyright date. Older models are slightly larger in size. Several variations on label of bottle; "Rizinusol" (German for Castor Oil) and "Vitamins" are most common. Also found with "Castor bil" (Spanish for Castor Oil). If found with trademark 2 would be considered rare. On 31 December 1984 the German language variation was temporarily withdrawn (TW) from production but may be reinstated at some future date. This variation now commands a premium of $100–200 more than "Vitamins" when found. "Little Pharmacist" was restyled in the fall of 1987. The figurine has a new base with a smoother surface and rounded corners and edges. It is slightly smaller in size, the eyeglass stems disappear into the hair and his bowtie has been straightened. On his coat the button tape now runs along a curve rather than straight up and down, and a breast pocket has been added. Also, on the back there is a wider coat strap with two buttons instead of one.

☐ 322	5¾ to 6″	(CE)	❷	$4000–5000
☐ 322	5¾ to 6″	(CE)	❸	$500–750
☐ 322	5¾ to 6″	(CE)	❹	$250–350
☐ 322	5¾ to 6″	(CE)	❺	$210–220
☐ 322	5¾ to 6″	(CE)	❻	$200–210
☐ 322	5¾ to 6″	(OE)	❼	$200
☐ 322	5¾ to 6″	(CE)	❹	$2000–3000 (Castor Bil)

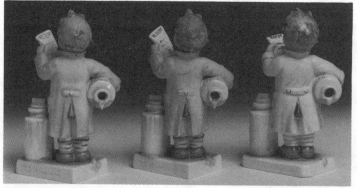

Back view   Old   Old   New

HUM 323
Merry Christmas, Wall Plaque
First introduced in the U.S. market in 1979 along with two other "M.I. Hummel" items, HUM 310 "Searching Angel" plaque and HUM 300 "Bird Watcher." Has an incised 1955 copyright date. Originally modeled by master sculptor Gerhard Skrobek in 1955. The original issue price in 1979 was $55.

☐ 323	..... 5¼ × 3½"	... (CE)	.. ❷	...	$2000–3000
☐ 323	..... 5¼ × 3½"	... (CE)	.. ❸	...	$1000–1500
☐ 323	..... 5¼ × 3½"	... (CE)	.. ❹	...	$1000–1500
☐ 323	..... 5¼ × 3½"	... (CE)	.. ❺	...	$115–150
☐ 323	..... 5¼ × 3½"	... (CE)	.. ❻	...	$110–115
☐ 323	..... 5¼ × 3½"	... (OE)	.. ❼	...	$110

HUM 324
At The Fence (PFE)
Originally called "The Other Side of the Fence" on factory records, but later changed to "At The Fence." Modeled in 1955 by master sculptor Arthur Moeller. Listed on factory records as a Possible Future Edition (PFE) and may be released at some future date, subject to possible minor changes.

☐ 324 ..... 4¾" .... (PFE) ....

HUM 325
Helping Mother (PFE)

This figurine was originally modeled by master sculptor Arthur Moeller in August 1955 and the first sample was painted in July 1956 by artist "F/K"—the initials used by Franz Kirchner. Originally called "Mother's Aid" on old factory records but later changed to "Helping Mother." Similar in design to HUM 133 "Mother's Helper" and when released will only be the second "M.I. Hummel" figurine designed with a cat. This early sample model pictured here has the full bee trademark and is in the Robert L. Miller collection.

☐ 325 ..... 5" .... (CE) .. ❷ ... $4000–5000
☐ 325 ..... 5" .... (PFE) ....

HUM 326
Being Punished, Wall Plaque (PFE)

This figurine was originally modeled by master sculptor Gerhard Skrobek in July 1957 and the first sample was painted by artist Franz Kirchner in August 1957. Originally called "Naughty Boy" on old factory records but later changed to "Being Punished." This piece has a hole on the back for hanging as a plaque or will sit upright on base. Has an incised 1955 copyright date on back. This early sample model pictured here has the full bee trademark and is part of the Robert L. Miller collection.

☐ 326 ..... 4 × 5" .... (CE) .. ❷ ... $4000–5000
☐ 326 ..... 4 × 5" .... (PFE) ....

New style (TM 5)   *Old style (TM 5)*

HUM 327
(The) Run-A-Way

First introduced in the U.S. market in 1972. Originally modeled by master sculptor Helmut Wehlte in 1955 and later restyled by current master sculptor Gerhard Skrobek in 1972. Skrobek completely restyled this figure with the new textured finish and variations in the location of basket, hat and shoes. Slight color variations also. The early models have an incised 1955 copyright date while the restyled version has an incised 1972 copyright date. When first put on the market in 1972 it was in the old style and had the 4 trademark. Older trademarks such as 2 and 3 would be considered rare. The original issue price in 1972 was $28.50.

☐ 327 ..... 5¼" .... (CE) .. ❷ ... $4000–5000
☐ 327 ..... 5¼" .... (CE) .. ❸ ... $2000–3000
☐ 327 ..... 5¼" .... (CE) .. ❹ ... $1000–1200
☐ 327 ..... 5¼" .... (CE) .. ❺ ... $750–850 (Old Style)
☐ 327 ..... 5¼" .... (CE) .. ❻ ... $220–230 (New Style)
☐ 327 ..... 5¼" .... (CE) .. ❻ ... $210–220
☐ 327 ..... 5¼" .... (OE) .. ❼ ... $210

HUM TERM

FULL BEE: The term "Full Bee" refers to the trademark used by the Goebel Co. from 1950 to 1957. Early usage of this trademark was incised into the material. Later versions of the "full bee" were stamped into the material.

Old postcard drawing

HUM 328
Carnival
First introduced in the U.S. market in 1963. Originally modeled by master sculptors Reinhold Unger and Helmut Wehlte in 1955. Early sample model with full bee trademark has a 1955 incised copyright date. Later models have a 1957 incised copyright date. Older examples are slightly larger with only minor variations. The object under the child's arm is a noise maker or "slapstick," a device generally made of wood and paper or cloth — popular with stage comedians.

☐ 328	5¾ to 6″	(CE)	❷	$4000–5000
☐ 328	5¾ to 6″	(CE)	❸	$750–1000
☐ 328	5¾ to 6″	(CE)	❹	$235–285
☐ 328	5¾ to 6″	(CE)	❺	$200–210
☐ 328	5¾ to 6″	(CE)	❻	$190–200
☐ 328	5¾ to 6″	(OE)	❼	$190

HUM 329
Off To School (PFE)
Originally called "Kindergarten Romance" on factory records, but later changed to "Off To School." Modeled by master sculptor Arthur Moeller in 1955. The boy is quite similar to HUM 82 "School Boy" while the girl is completely new. Listed on factory records as a Possible Future Edition (PFE) and may be released at some future date, subject to possible minor changes.

☐ 329 . . . . . 5" . . . . (PFE) . . . .

HUM 330
Baking Day
First introduced to the U.S. market in 1985. Originally called "Kneading Dough" on old factory records, but later changed to "Baking Day." Modeled by master sculptor Gerhard Skrobek in 1955. It has an incised 1955 copyright date. The original issue price in 1985 was $95.

☐ 330	5¼"	(CE)	❷	$4000–5000
☐ 330	5¼"	(CE)	❸	$2500–3000
☐ 330	5¼"	(CE)	❹	$2000–2500
☐ 330	5¼"	(CE)	❺	$1500–2000
☐ 330	5¼"	(CE)	❻	$220–230
☐ 330	5¼"	(OE)	❼	$220

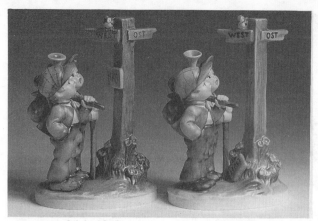

Original Style   *Commemorative Issue*

HUM 331
Crossroads

First introduced in the U.S. market in 1972. Has an incised 1955 copyright date. Modeled by master sculptor Arthur Moeller in 1955. This early sample model has the trombone reversed. Research at the factory indicated this was probably an accident in assembling the separate clay molds and possibly this is the only one made that way. We are unaware of any others having been found. The full bee example in our collection has the trombone in the normal position. The original issue price in 1972 was $45.00. In the summer of 1990, Goebel announced a worldwide limited edition of 20,000 pieces in a uniquely altered form, to commemorate the first anniversary of the opening of the Berlin Wall. The difference between the original 1972 version and the new limited-edition version is significant and symbolic. Originally, midway up the signpost was a small sign which read "HALT." Now, like so many similar signs along the East/West border, the sign lies on the ground. Original issue price of commemorative issue was $360.

☐ 331 ..... 6¾" .... (CE) .. ❷ ... $4000–5000
☐ 331 ..... 6¾" .... (CE) .. ❸ ... $2000–3000
☐ 331 ..... 6¾" .... (CE) .. ❹ ... $750–1000
☐ 331 ..... 6¾" .... (CE) .. ❺ ... $365–400
☐ 331 ..... 6¾" .... (CE) .. ❻ ... $350–365 (Original Style)
☐ 331 ..... 6¾" .... (CE) .. ❻ ... $750–900 (Commemorative)
☐ 331 ..... 6¾" .... (CE) .. ❼ ... $950–1200 (Commemorative)
☐ 331 ..... 6¾" .... (OE) .. ❼ ... $350 (Original Style)

Rare old style   **New style**

HUM 332
Soldier Boy
First introduced in the U.S. market in 1963. Modeled by master sculptor Gerhard Skrobek in 1955. The early prototype model in our collection has a full bee trademark and a 1955 incised copyright date. Later models have a 1957 incised copyright date. Older pieces are slightly larger and usually have a red ornament on hat while the newer pieces have a blue one. Trademark 4 can be found with either red or blue. On older models the "M.I. Hummel" signature is located on the side of the base while newer models have signature on top of the base.

☐ 332	5¾ to 6″	(CE)	❷	$4000–5000
☐ 332	5¾ to 6″	(CE)	❸	$500–1000
☐ 332	5¾ to 6″	(CE)	❹	$225–600
☐ 332	5¾ to 6″	(CE)	❺	$190–200
☐ 332	5¾ to 6″	(CE)	❻	$180–190
☐ 332	5¾ to 6″	(OE)	❼	$180

HUM 333
Blessed Event
First introduced in the U.S. market at the N.Y. World's Fair in 1964. Originally modeled by master sculptor Arthur Moeller in 1955. Found with either 1955, 1956 or 1957 incised copyright dates.

☐ 333	5¼ to 5½″	(CE)	❷	$4000–5000
☐ 333	5¼ to 5½″	(CE)	❸	$750–1000
☐ 333	5¼ to 5½″	(CE)	❹	$400–550
☐ 333	5¼ to 5½″	(CE)	❺	$290–310
☐ 333	5¼ to 5½″	(CE)	❻	$280–290
☐ 333	5¼ to 5½″	(OE)	❼	$280

Old style   *New style*

HUM 334
Homeward Bound

First introduced in the U.S. market in 1971 along with three other new releases: HUM 304 "Artist," HUM 340 "Letter to Santa Claus" and HUM 347 "Adventure Bound." "Homeward Bound" was originally modeled by master sculptor Arthur Moeller in 1956 and later restyled by master sculptor Gerhard Skrobek in1974. Found with either 1955 or 1956 incised copyright dates in early models. The restyled version has the new textured finish and no support pedestal under the goat. Current model has an incised 1975 copyright date. The original issue price in 1971 was $35.

☐ 334	5¼"	(CE)	❷	$4000–5000	
☐ 334	5¼"	(CE)	❸	$1000–1500	
☐ 334	5¼"	(CE)	❹	$600–750	
☐ 334	5¼"	(CE)	❺	$350–500	(Old style)
☐ 334	5¼"	(CE)	❺	$310–325	(New style)
☐ 334	5¼"	(CE)	❻	$295–310	
☐ 334	5¼"	**(OE)**	❼	$295	

─────── **HUM TERM** ───────

SIESSEN CONVENT: Located in Wuerttemberg region of West Germany near Saulgau. This facility is where Sister M.I. Hummel resided after taking her vows. She continued to sketch in a studio inside the convent until her untimely death at the age of 37 in 1946. The Siessen Convent houses the Sisters of the Third Order of St. Francis. Sister Hummel is buried in the cemetery located on the Convent grounds.

HUM 335
Lucky Boy (PFE)
Originally called "Fair Prizes" on old factory records, but later changed to "Lucky Boy." Modeled by master sculptor Arthur Moeller in 1956. Now listed on factory records as a Possible Future Edition (PFE) and may be released at some future date, subject to possible minor changes.

☐ 335 ..... 5¾ to 6″ ..... (PFE) ....

New   *Old*

HUM 336
Close Harmony
First introduced in the U.S. market in 1963. Found with either 1955, 1956 or 1957 copyright dates. Originally modeled in 1956 by master modeler Gerhard Skrobek and in 1962 he also restyled it. The current production has been restyled but bears the 1955 incised copyright date. Older models have variations in girl's hairstyle and position of stockings.

☐ 336 ..... 5¼ to 5½″ .... (CE) .. ❷ ... $4000–5000
☐ 336 ..... 5¼ to 5½″ .... (CE) .. ❸ ... $600–700
☐ 336 ..... 5¼ to 5½″ .... (CE) .. ❹ ... $300–500
☐ 336 ..... 5¼ to 5½″ .... (CE) .. ❺ ... $250–265
☐ 336 ..... 5¼ to 5½″ .... (CE) .. ❻ ... $240–250
☐ 336 ..... 5¼ to 5½″ .... (OE) .. ❼ ... $240

New   Old

HUM 337
Cinderella

First introduced in the U.S. market in 1972. First modeled by master sculptor Arthur Moeller in March 1956. First sample painted by artist Franz Kirchner in July 1956. Later restyled by master sculptor Gerhard Skrobek in 1972. Early models have a 1958 or 1960 incised copyright date while the restyled version has a 1972 copyright date. Completely restyled with Skrobek's new textured finish and girl's eyes looking down. The older models have eyes open. When first put on the market in 1972 it was in the old style and had the 4 trademark. Older trademarks such as 2 and 3 would be considered rare. The original issue price in 1972 was $26.50.

☐ 337 ..... 4½" .... (CE) .. ❷ ... $4000–5000
☐ 337 ..... 4½" .... (CE) .. ❸ ... $2000–3000
☐ 337 ..... 4½" .... (CE) .. ❹ ... $1200–1500
☐ 337 ..... 4½" .... (CE) .. ❺ ... $800–1000 (Old style)
☐ 337 ..... 4½" .... (CE) .. ❺ ... $250–265 (New style)
☐ 337 ..... 4½" .... (CE) .. ❻ ... $240–250
☐ 337 ..... 4½" .... (OE) .. ❼ ... $240

HUM 338
Birthday Cake, Candleholder

First released in the U.S. market in 1989. Has an incised 1956 copyright date. The original issue price was $95 in 1989. Originally called "A Birthday Wish" on old factory records, but later changed to "Birthday Cake." Modeled by master sculptor Gerhard Skrobek in March 1956. First sample painted by Harald Sommer in July 1956. This early prototype model pictured here has the full bee trademark and is part of the Robert L. Miller collection.

☐ 338 ..... 3¾" .... (CE) .. ❷ ... $4000–5000
☐ 338 ..... 3½" .... (CE) .. ❻ ... $120–125
☐ 338 ..... 3½" .... (OE) .. ❼ ... $120

HUM 339
Behave! (PFE)

Originally called "Walking Her Dog" on old factory records, but later changed to "Behave!" Modeled by master sculptor Helmut Wehlte in 1956. Now listed on factory records as a Possible Future Edition (PFE) and may be released at some future date, subject to possible minor changes. An early stylized trademark (TM 3) sample model of this figurine was recently found in a home in New York City. It had originally been on display at the New York World's Fair in 1964. Has an incised 1956 copyright date and a painting date of 5/60 with O.S. artist initials. It is now part of the Robert L. Miller collection.

☐ 339 ..... 5¾" .... (CE) .. ❸ ... $5000–10,000
☐ 339 ..... 5¾" .... (PFE) ....

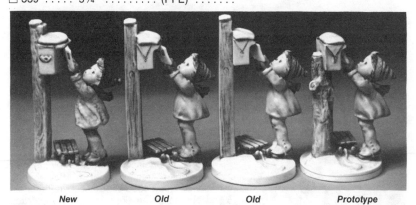

New   **Old**   **Old**   **Prototype**

HUM 340
Letter to Santa Claus

First introduced in the U.S. market in 1971. Originally modeled by master sculptor Helmut Wehlte in April 1956. Early sample was painted in September 1957 by artist Guenther Neubauer (now Chief Sample Painter at Goebel). Completely restyled by current master sculptor Gerhard Skrobek in 1970. The prototype mailbox on a tree trunk apparently was rejected in favor of the wooden post style. This piece has a full bee trademark, stamped 1956 copyright date and artist initials "HS" (probably Harald Sommer) along with a June 1956 date. The current production has new textured finish and color variations on girl's hats and leggings. Trademark 4, 5, and 6 models have an incised 1957 copyright date. The original issue price in 1971 was $30.

☐ 340 ..... Prototype ..... (CE) .. ❷ ... $15,000–20,000
☐ 340 ..... 7¼" .... (CE) .. ❷ ... $4000–5000
☐ 340 ..... 7¼" .... (CE) .. ❸ ... $3000–4000
☐ 340 ..... 7¼" .... (CE) .. ❹ ... $500–650
☐ 340 ..... 7¼" .... (CE) .. ❺ ... $300–315
☐ 340 ..... 7¼" .... (CE) .. ❻ ... $285–300
☐ 340 ..... 7¼" .... (OE) .. ❼ ... $285

HUM 341
Birthday Present (PFE)
Originally called "The Birthday Present" on old factory records, but later changed to just "Birthday Present." First modeled by master sculptor Gerhard Skrobek in 1956. Now listed on factory records as a Possible Future Edition (PFE) and may be released at some future date, subject to possible minor changes.

☐ 341 ..... 5 to 5⅓" ..... (PFE) ....

HUM 342
Mischief Maker
First introduced in the U. S. market in 1972. Originally modeled by master sculptor Arthur Moeller in 1956. Found with either 1958 or 1960 copyright dates. No major variations have been recorded in size or design. Older models have a dark green hat on boy while newer models have a blue hat. The original issue price in 1972 was $26.50.

☐ 342	5"	(CE)	❷	$4000–5000
☐ 342	5"	(CE)	❸	$2000–3000
☐ 342	5"	(CE)	❹	$500–750
☐ 342	5"	(CE)	❺	$230–240
☐ 342	5"	(CE)	❻	$220–230
☐ 342	5"	(OE)	❼	$220

HUM 343
Christmas Song
First introduced in the U.S. market in 1981. Originally called "Singing Angel" on old factory records, but later changed to "Christmas Song." Modeled by master sculptor Gerhard Skrobek in 1956. The original issue price in 1981 was $85. An early stylized (TM 3) sample model was recently located in the Philadelphia area. It has a 1957 incised copyright date and a painting date of 6/60 with O.S. artist initials. It is now part of the Robert L. Miller collection.

☐ 343	..... 6½"	.... (CE)	.. ❷	... $4000–5000
☐ 343	..... 6½"	.... (CE)	.. ❸	... $2000–3000
☐ 343	..... 6½"	.... (CE)	.. ❹	... $1000–2000
☐ 343	..... 6½"	.... (CE)	.. ❺	... $500–1000
☐ 343	..... 6½"	.... (CE)	.. ❻	... $180–190
☐ 343	..... 6½"	.... (OE)	.. ❼	... $180

HUM 344
Feathered Friends
First introduced in the U.S. market in 1972. Modeled by master sculptor Gerhard Skrobek in 1956. Has an incised 1956 copyright date on the base. Full bee and early stylized examples have appeared on the market. The original issue price in 1972 was $27.50.

☐ 344	..... 4¾"	.... (CE)	.. ❷	... $4000–5000
☐ 344	..... 4¾"	.... (CE)	.. ❸	... $2000–3000
☐ 344	..... 4¾"	.... (CE)	.. ❹	... $500–750
☐ 344	..... 4¾"	.... (CE)	.. ❺	... $230–240
☐ 344	..... 4¾"	.... (CE)	.. ❻	... $220–230
☐ 344	..... 4¾"	.... (OE)	.. ❼	... $220

New   Old

HUM 345
A Fair Measure

First introduced in the U.S. market in 1972. Originally modeled by master sculptor Helmut Wehlte in August 1956. First sample was painted by artist "W/Ha" Werner Hausschild in August 1957. Later restyled by master sculptor Gerhard Skrobek in 1972. Early full bee prototype has a stamped 1957 copyright date. Early production models have 1956 incised copyright date. Completely restyled with new textured finish, boy's eyes looking down and weights on scale reversed. Current model has a 1972 incised copyright date. Original issue price in 1972 was $27.50.

☐ 345 ..... 5½ to 5¾" .... (CE) .. ❷ ... $4000–5000
☐ 345 ..... 5½ to 5¾" .... (CE) .. ❸ ... $2000–3000
☐ 345 ..... 5½ to 5¾" .... (CE) .. ❹ ... $800–1000
☐ 345 ..... 5½ to 5¾" .... (CE) .. ❺ ... $650–800 (Old Style)
☐ 345 ..... 5½ to 5¾" .... (CE) .. ❺ ... $240–250 (New Style)
☐ 345 ..... 5½ to 5¾" .... (CE) .. ❻ ... $230–240
☐ 345 ..... 5½ to 5¾" .... (OE) .. ❼ ... $230

Hum 346
Smart Little Sister

First introduced in the U. S. market in 1962. Originally modeled by master sculptor Gerhard Skrobek in 1956. Has an incised 1956 copyright date on the bottom. No unusual variations have been recorded. Girl is similar to HUM 367, "Busy Student."

☐ 346 ..... 4¾" .... (CE) .. ❷ ... $4000–5000
☐ 346 ..... 4¾" .... (CE) .. ❸ ... $1000–1500
☐ 346 ..... 4¾" .... (CE) .. ❹ ... $250–325
☐ 346 ..... 4¾" .... (CE) .. ❺ ... $220–230
☐ 346 ..... 4¾" .... (CE) .. ❻ ... $210–220
☐ 346 ..... 4¾" .... (OE) .. ❼ ... $210

HUM 347
Adventure Bound
First introduced in the U.S. market in 1971. The original issue price in 1971 was $400. Sometimes known as the "Seven Swabians." Has an incised 1957 copyright date. The original clay model was sculpted by Theo R. Menzenbach. Menzenbach began working at the Goebel factory in October 1948, at the age of 18. He left the factory in October 1961 to start his own business as a commercial artist. He is still living and resides in Germany, near Coburg. An early prototype with full bee trademark was painted in October 1957 and is now part of the Robert L. Miller collection.

☐ 347	7½ × 8¼"	(CE)	❷	$10,000–15,000
☐ 347	7½ × 8¼"	(CE)	❸	$5000–6000
☐ 347	7½ × 8¼"	(CE)	❹	$4000–5000
☐ 347	7½ × 8¼"	(CE)	❺	$3400–3500
☐ 347	7½ × 8¼"	(CE)	❻	$3300–3400
☐ 347	7½ × 8¼"	(**OE**)	❼	$3300

> **NOTE:** Sister Hummel's original drawing was based upon an old Swabian fairy tale about seven children out in the woods, thought they saw a *big* lion but only turned out to be a *little* bunny rabbit!

HUM 348
Ring Around The Rosie

The original clay model was sculpted by Gerhard Skrobek, current master modeler at the factory, in 1957. First introduced in the U.S. market in 1960 for the 25th anniversary of the introduction of "M.I. Hummel" figurines. Incised on the bottom: " © by W. Goebel, Oeslau 1957." Older models are usually slightly larger. Originally sold for less than $100 when first introduced for sale.

☐ 348 ..... 6¾ to 7" ..... (CE) .. ❷ ... $10,000–15,000
☐ 348 ..... 6¾ to 7" ..... (CE) .. ❸ ... $3500–4000
☐ 348 ..... 6¾" .... (CE) .. ❹ ... $2700–3500
☐ 348 ..... 6¾" .... (CE) .. ❺ ... $2400–2500
☐ 348 ..... 6¾" .... (CE) .. ❻ ... $2300–2400
☐ 348 ..... 6¾" .... (OE) .. ❼ ... $2300

HUM TERM

OESLAU: Name for the village where the W. Goebel Porzellanfabrik is located. Oeslau is now a part of the City of Roedental, West Germany.

HUM 349
Florist (PFE)

Originally called "Flower Lover" on old factory records, but later changed to "The Florist" and finally just "Florist." First modeled by master sculptor Gerhard Skrobek in 1957. Now listed on factory records as a Possible Future Edition (PFE) and may be released at some future date, subject to possible minor changes.

☐ 349 ..... 7 to 7½" ..... (PFE) ....

HUM 350
On Holiday

First introduced in the U.S. market in 1981. Originally called "Holiday Shopper" on old factory records, but later changed to "On Holiday." Modeled by master sculptor Gerhard Skrobek in 1964. Original issue price was $85 in 1981. Has an incised 1965 copyright date. This figurine was recently found with TM 4, a painting date of 12/80, and artist's initials "Bo." Apparently this piece was made in the late 1960's but *not* painted until just before its release in 1981.

☐ 350 ..... 4¼" .... (CE) .. ❸ ... $2000–2500
☐ 350 ..... 4¼" .... (CE) .. ❹ ... $1500–2000
☐ 350 ..... 4¼" .... (CE) .. ❺ ... $1000–1500
☐ 350 ..... 4¼" .... (CE) .. ❻ ... $145–150
☐ 350 ..... 4¼" .... (**OE**) .. ❼ ... $145

HUM 351
Botanist

First introduced in the U.S. market in the fall of 1982. Originally called "Remembering" on old factory records, but later changed to "The Botanist" and finally just "Botanist." First modeled by master sculptor Gerhard Skrobek in 1965. Has an incised 1972 copyright date on the bottom. The original issue price was $84 in 1982. At date of publication, no examples with older trademarks have been located in private collections.

☐ 351	4 to 4¼"	(CE)	❹	$1500–2000
☐ 351	4 to 4¼"	(CE)	❺	$1000–1500
☐ 351	4 to 4¼"	(CE)	❻	$185–195
☐ 351	4 to 4¼"	**(OE)**	❼	$185

HUM 352
Sweet Greetings

First released in the U.S. market in 1981. Originally called "Musical Morning" on old factory records, but later changed to "Sweet Greetings." Modeled by master sculptor Gerhard Skrobek in 1964. Has an incised 1964 copyright date on the bottom of the base. The original issue price was $85 in 1981. At date of publication, no examples with older trademarks have been located in private collections.

☐ 352	4¼"	(CE)	❹	$1500–2000
☐ 352	4¼"	(CE)	❺	$1000–1500
☐ 352	4¼"	(CE)	❻	$185–195
☐ 352	4¼"	**(OE)**	❼	$185

353/I   *353/0*

HUM 353
Spring Dance

First introduced in the U.S. market in 1964. According to factory records, this was first modeled in 1962 by a combination of modelers. Until recently, "Spring Dance" was the highest numbered figurine made in two sizes; HUM 396 "Ride Into Christmas" now has that distinction. Note: HUM 408/0 "Smiling Through" (CE) — the /0 indicates that more than one size was produced, but so far a larger size has not been put on the market. (See HUM 408). The small size 353/0 has been considered rare, having been produced in very limited quantities in 1964 and then not produced again until 1978. Some of the early pieces have sold for as high as $3,000. It is again in current production with the 5 and 6 trademarks. Both sizes have an incised 1963 copyright date. In 1982 the large size 353/I was listed as "temporarily withdrawn" on company records, to be possibly reinstated at a future date. The "Spring Dance" design consists of two of the four girls from HUM 348 "Ring Around The Rosie."

☐ 353/0	5¼"	(CE)	❹	$2000–3000
☐ 353/0	5¼"	(CE)	❺	$265–280
☐ 353/0	5¼"	(CE)	❻	$255–265
☐ 353/0	5¼"	(OE)	❼	$255
☐ 353/I	6¾"	(CE)	❸	$750–1000
☐ 353/I	6¾"	(CE)	❹	$550–650
☐ 353/I	6¾"	(CE)	❺	$500–550
☐ 353/I	6¾"	(TW)	❻	$475–500

354 A   *354 B*   *354 C*

HUM 354 A
Holy Water Font, Angel With Lantern (CN)
This early prototype font has the incised number 354 only, on the back. According to factory information, this design was not approved by the Siessen Convent as a font. It was then restyled into a figurine and approved as HUM 357 "Guiding Angel." Now listed on factory records as a Closed Number.

☐ 354 A . . . . 3¼ x 5″ . . . . . . (CN) . . . .

HUM 354 B
Holy Water Font, Angel With Trumpet (CN)
This early prototype font has the incised number 355 only, on the back. According to factory information, this design was not approved by the Siessen Convent as a font. It was then restyled into a figurine and approved as HUM 359 "Tuneful Angel." Now listed on factory records as a Closed Number.

☐ 354 B . . . . 3¼ x 5″ . . . . . . (CN) . . . .

HUM 354 C
Holy Water Font, Angel With Bird (CN)
This early prototype font has the incised number 356 only, on the back. According to factory information, this design was not approved by the Siessen Convent as a font. It was then restyled into a figurine and approved as HUM 358 "Shining Light." Now listed on factory records as a Closed Number.

☐ 354 C . . . 3¼ x 5″ . . . . . . (CN) . . . .

HUM 355
Autumn Harvest
First introduced in the U.S. market in 1972. Originally modeled by master sculptor Gerhard Skrobek in 1963. Has an incised 1964 copyright date on the bottom. No major variations have been recorded in size, color or design. The original issue price in 1972 was $22.50.

☐ 355	5″	(CE)	❸	$2000–2500
☐ 355	5″	(CE)	❹	$750–1000
☐ 355	5″	(CE)	❺	$190–210
☐ 355	5″	(CE)	❻	$180–190
☐ 355	5″	**(OE)**	❼	$180

HUM 356
Gay Adventure
Was originally called "Joyful Adventure" when first released in the U.S. market in 1972. Originally modeled by master sculptor Gerhard Skrobek in 1963. It has an incised 1971 copyright date on the bottom. Slightly restyled with the new textured finish on current models. Early models have slightly different construction on the underside of base. The original issue price in 1972 was $22.50.

☐ 356	4¾″	(CE)	❸	$2000–2500
☐ 356	4¾″	(CE)	❹	$750–1000
☐ 356	4¾″	(CE)	❺	$170–180
☐ 356	4¾″	(CE)	❻	$160–170
☐ 356	4¾″	**(OE)**	❼	$160

357   358   359

HUM 357
Guiding Angel
First released in the U.S. market in 1972. Originally modeled by master sculptor Reinhold Unger in 1958. Has an incised 1960 copyright date. The original issue price in 1972 was $11. Usually offered, along with HUM 358 and HUM 359, as a set of three angels, although priced separately.

☐ 357 ..... 2¾" .... (CE) .. ❹ ... $125–150
☐ 357 ..... 2¾" .... (CE) .. ❺ ... $75–80
☐ 357 ..... 2¾" .... (CE) .. ❻ ... $70–75
☐ 357 ..... 2¾" .... (OE) .. ❼ ... $70

HUM 358
Shining Light
First released in the U.S. market in 1972. Originally modeled by master sculptor Reinhold Unger in 1958. Has an incised 1960 copyright date. The original issue price in 1972 was $11. Usually offered, along with HUM 357 and HUM 359, as a set of three angels, although priced separately.

☐ 358 ..... 2¾" .... (CE) .. ❹ ... $125–150
☐ 358 ..... 2¾" .... (CE) .. ❺ ... $75–80
☐ 358 ..... 2¾" .... (CE) .. ❻ ... $70–75
☐ 358 ..... 2¾" .... (OE) .. ❼ ... $70

HUM 359
Tuneful Angel
First released in the U.S. market in 1972. Originally modeled by master sculptor Reinhold Unger in 1958. Has an incised 1960 copyright date. Usually offered, along with HUM 357 and HUM 358, as a set of three angels, although priced separately. The original issue price in 1972 was $11.

☐ 359 ..... 2¾" .... (CE) .. ❹ ... $125–150
☐ 359 ..... 2¾" .... (CE) .. ❺ ... $75–80
☐ 359 ..... 2¾" .... (CE) .. ❻ ... $70–75
☐ 359 ..... 2¾" .... (OE) .. ❼ ... $70

360 B   360 A   360 C

HUM 360/A
Wall Vase, Boy and Girl
One of a set of three wall vases that had been considered rare but is again in current production with the 5 and 6 trademarks. According to factory records, this vase was modeled by master sculptor Gerhard Skrobek in 1959. Early models incised on back: "© by W. Goebel 1958." The new model reissued in 1979 has been slightly restyled and has copyright date 1958 only incised on back. "Temporarily withdrawn" (TW) from production on 31 December 1989, but may be reinstated at some future date.

☐ 360A .... 4½ × 6″ ..... (CE) .. ❸ ... $400–600
☐ 360A .... 4½ × 6″ ..... (CE) .. ❺ ... $140–150
☐ 360A .... 4½ × 6″ ..... **(TW)** .. ❻ ... $130–140

HUM 360/B
Wall Vase, Boy
One of a set of three wall vases that had been considered rare but is again in current production with the 5 and 6 trademarks. According to factory records, this vase was modeled by master sculptor Gerhard Skrobek in 1959. Early models incised on back: "© by W. Goebel 1958." The new model reissued in 1979 has been slightly restyled and has copyright date 1958 only incised on back. "Temporarily withdrawn" (TW) from production on 31 December 1989, but may be reinstated at some future date.

☐ 360B .... 4½ × 6″ ..... (CE) .. ❸ ... $400–600
☐ 360B .... 4½ × 6″ ..... (CE) .. ❺ ... $120–130
☐ 360B .... 4½ × 6″ ..... **(TW)** .. ❻ ... $110–120

HUM 360/C
Wall Vase, Girl
One of a set of three wall vases that had been considered rare but is again in current production with the 5 and 6 trademarks. According to factory records, this vase was modeled by master sculptor Gerhard Skrobek in 1959. Early models incised on back: "© by W. Goebel 1958." The new model reissued in 1979 has the trunk of the tree slightly restyled and has copyright date 1958 only incised on back. "Temporarily withdrawn" (TW) from production on 31 December 1989, but may be reinstated at some future date.

☐ 360C .... 4½ × 6″ ..... (CE) .. ❸ ... $400–600
☐ 360C .... 4½ × 6″ ..... (CE) .. ❺ ... $120–130
☐ 360C .... 4½ × 6″ ..... **(TW)** .. ❻ ... $110–120

HUM 361
Favorite Pet

First released in the U.S. market at the N.Y. World's Fair in 1964. Originally modeled by master sculptor Theo R. Menzenbach in 1959. Has an incised 1960 copyright date. No unusual variations have been recorded.

☐ 361 ..... 4½" .... (CE) .. ❸ ... $750–1000
☐ 361 ..... 4½" .... (CE) .. ❹ ... $275–350
☐ 361 ..... 4½" .... (CE) .. ❺ ... $240–255
☐ 361 ..... 4½" .... (CE) .. ❻ ... $230–240
☐ 361 ..... 4½" .... (OE) .. ❼ ... $230

HUM 362
I Forgot (PFE)

Originally called "Thoughtful" on old factory records, but later changed to "I Forgot." First modeled by master sculptor Theo R. Menzenbach in 1959. Now listed on factory records as a Possible Future Edition (PFE) and may be released at some future date, subject to possible minor changes.

☐ 362 ..... 5½" .... (PFE) ....

HUM 363
Big Housecleaning

First introduced in the U.S. market in 1972. Originally modeled by master sculptor Gerhard Skrobek in 1959. Has as incised 1960 copyright date on the bottom. No major variations have been recorded in size, color or design. The original issue price in 1972 was $28.50.

☐ 363	.....	4″	....	(CE)	.. ❸ ...	$2000–2500
☐ 363	.....	4″	....	(CE)	.. ❹ ...	$750–1000
☐ 363	.....	4″	....	(CE)	.. ❺ ...	$240–255
☐ 363	.....	4″	....	(CE)	.. ❻ ...	$230–240
☐ 363	.....	4″	....	(OE)	.. ❼ ...	$230

─── HUM TERM ───

CURRENT TRADEMARK: Designates the symbol presently being used by the W. Goebel Porzellanfabrik to represent the company's trademark.

HUM 364
Supreme Protection (CE)
Modeled by master sculptor Gerhard Skrobek in 1963. Originally called "Blessed Madonna and Child" on old factory records but later changed to "Supreme Protection." First put on the market in 1984 and was limited to the total of that year's production and will not be produced in future years. It has an incised 1964 copyright date. The inscription on the bottom of the figurine applied by blue decal reads: "1909–1984 IN CELEBRATION OF THE 75th ANNIVERSARY OF THE BIRTH OF SISTER M.I. HUMMEL" plus the current TM 6 Goebel trademark. Early production of this figurine had an error in the decal that read "M.*J.* Hummel" rather that "M.*I.* Hummel." This was first corrected by cutting off the hook of the "J" on the decal, but still did not completely look like an "I." Ultimately corrected to read "M.I. Hummel." Of the three versions, the most difficult variation to find is the "altered J" variety. The original issue price in 1984 was $150. Originally came in a dark brown, specially designed, padded presentation case with brass fasteners. The box was inscribed: "M.I. Hummel-IN CELEBRATION OF THE 75th ANNIVERSARY OF THE BIRTH OF SISTER MARIA INNOCENTIA HUMMEL" in gold lettering. "Supreme Protection" is now listed as a Closed Edition (CE) and will *not* be produced again.

☐ 364 . . . . . 9 to 9¼" . . . . . (CE) . . ❻ . . . $250–300
☐ 364 . . . . . 9 to 9¼" . . . . . (CE) . . ❻ . . . $400–600 ("M.J." variation)
☐ 364 . . . . . . 9 to 9¼" . . . . . (CE) . . ❻ . . . $600–850 (Altered "J" variation)

HUM 365
Littlest Angel (PFE)
Originally called "The Wee Angel" on old factory records, but later changed to "Littlest Angel." Modeled by master sculptor Gerhard Skrobek in 1963. Now listed on factory records as Possible Future Edition (PFE) and may be released at some future date, subject to possible minor changes.

☐ 365 . . . . . 2¼ to 2¾" . . . . (PFE) . . . .

HUM 366
Flying Angel
First modeled by master sculptor Gerhard Skrobek in 1963, this piece was designed as an addition to the small Nativity Set, HUM 214. Makes an excellent decoration or ornament for hanging on the Christmas tree. See photo of HUM 214 Nativity Set for application. At one time was produced and sold in white overglaze finish. It is presently limited to full color finish only. In 1989 a new smaller size "Flying Angel" was released in the U.S. market. It has an incised 366/0 model number and a 1987 copyright date. The issue price was $65 in 1989. The large size 366 will possibly be renumbered 366/I but unconfirmed at date of publication.

☐ 366/0 . . . . 3" . . . . (CE) . . ❻ . . . $85–90
☐ 366/0 . . . . 3" . . . . (OE) . . ❼ . . . $85
☐ 366 . . . . . 3½" . . . . (CE) . . ❹ . . . $175–225
☐ 366 . . . . . 3½" . . . . (CE) . . ❺ . . . $110–115
☐ 366 . . . . . 3½" . . . . (CE) . . ❻ . . . $105–110
☐ 366 . . . . . 3½" . . . . (OE) . . ❼ . . . $105

HUM 367
Busy Student
First released in the U.S. market in 1964. Originally modeled in 1962 by a combination of modelers. Has an incised 1963 copyright date. Similar to the little girl in HUM 346 "Smart Little Sister." No major variations have been reported in size, color or design.

☐ 367	4¼"	(CE)	❸	$550–750
☐ 367	4¼"	(CE)	❹	$175–225
☐ 367	4¼"	(CE)	❺	$145–155
☐ 367	4¼"	(CE)	❻	$140–145
☐ 367	4¼"	(OE)	❼	$140

HUM 368
Lute Song (PFE)
Originally called "Lute Player" on old factory records, but later changed to "Lute Song." First modeled by master sculptor Gerhard Skrobek in July 1964. Notice the similarity between this figure and the girl in HUM 336 "Close Harmony." Now listed on factory records as a Possible Future Edition (PFE) and may be released at some future date, subject to possible minor changes.

☐ 368 * . . . . . 5" . . . . (PFE) . . . .

HUM 369
Follow The Leader
First introduced in the U.S. market in 1972. This figurine was first modeled by master
sculptor Gerhard Skrobek in February 1964. It has an incised 1964 copyright date on
the bottom. The original issue price in 1972 was $110. No major variations have been
recorded in size, color or design.

☐ 369 ..... 7" .... (CE) .. ❸ ... $2500–3000
☐ 369 ..... 7" .... (CE) .. ❹ ... $1250–1500
☐ 369 ..... 7" .... (CE) .. ❺ ... $1050–1100
☐ 369 ..... 7" .... (CE) .. ❻ ... $1000–1050
☐ 369 ..... 7" .... (**OE**) .. ❼ ... $1000

HUM TERM

MODEL: This term most often refers to a
particular "M.I. Hummel" figurine, plate,
bell, or other item in the line. When not
used in reference to a specific motif, the
word model also can refer to the sculptor's
working model from which the figurines are
made.

HUM 370
Companions (PFE)

Originally called "Brotherly Love" on old factory records, but later changed to "Companions." Originally modeled by master sculptor Gerhard Skrobek in May 1964. Now listed on factory records as a Possible Future Edition (PFE) and may be released at some future date, subject to possible minor changes.

☐ 370 ..... 4¼ to 4¾" .... (PFE) ....

HUM 371
Daddy's Girls

First introduced in the U.S. market in 1989. Originally called "Sisterly Love" on old factory records, but later changed to "Daddy's Girls". Modeled by master sculptor Gerhard Skrobek in May 1964. The original issue price was $130 in 1989. It has an incised 1964 copyright date.

☐ 371 ..... 4¾" .... (CE) .. ❻ ... $200–210
☐ 371 ..... 4¾" .... (OE) .. ❼ ... $200

HUM 372
Blessed Mother (PFE)

Originally called "Virgin Mother and Child" on old factory records, but later changed to "Blessed Mother." Modeled by master sculptor Gerhard Skrobek in May 1964. Now listed on factory records as a Possible Future Edition (PFE) and may be released at some future date, subject to possible minor changes.

☐ 372 ..... 10¼" .... (PFE) ....

HUM 373
Just Fishing

This figurine was first released in the U.S. market in 1985. Originally called "The Fisherman" on old factory records, but later changed to "Just Fishing." Modeled by master sculptor Gerhard Skrobek in 1964. It has an incised 1965 copyright date on the bottom. The original issue price was $85 in 1985. Was first listed as an ashtray on Goebel price lists but later changed to a figurine listing.

☐ 373 ..... 4¼ to 4½" .... (CE) .. ❻ ... $190–200
☐ 373 ..... 4¼ to 4½" .... (OE) .. ❼ ... $190

HUM 374
Lost Stocking
This figurine was one of twenty-four new motifs first released in the U.S. market in 1972. Originally modeled by master sculptor Gerhard Skrobek in 1965. It has an incised 1965 copyright date. No major variations have been recorded in size, color or design. The original issue price in 1972 was $17.50.

☐ 374 ..... 4½" .... (CE) .. ❸ ... $2000–2500
☐ 374 ..... 4½" .... (CE) .. ❹ ... $750–1000
☐ 374 ..... 4½" .... (CE) .. ❺ ... $125–135
☐ 374 ..... 4½" .... (CE) .. ❻ ... $120–125
☐ 374 ..... 4½" .... (OE) .. ❼ ... $120

HUM 375
Morning Stroll (PFE)
Originally called "Walking the Baby" on old factory records, but later changed to "Morning Stroll." This figurine was first modeled by master sculptor Gerhard Skrobek in November 1964. It is now listed on factory records as a Possible Future Edition (PFE) and may be released at some future date, subject to possible minor changes.

☐ 375 ..... 4¼" .... (PFE) ....

HUM 376
Little Nurse
This figurine was first released in the U.S. market in the fall of 1982. Originally called "First Aid" on old factory records, but later changed to "Little Nurse." Modeled by master sculptor Gerhard Skrobek in April 1965. It has an incised 1972 copyright date on the bottom. The original issue price was $95 in 1982.

☐ 376 ..... 4" .... (CE) .. ❻ ... $210–220
☐ 376 ..... 4" .... (OE) .. ❼ ... $210

HUM 377
Bashful!
First released in the U.S. market in 1972. Originally modeled by master sculptor Gerhard Skrobek in January 1966. It usually was found with an incised 1966 copyright date, but occasionally found with a 1971 incised date. Models in current production have no incised date at all. No major variations have been recorded in size, color or design. The original issue price was $17.50 in 1972.

☐ 377 ..... 4¾" .... (CE) .. ❹ ... $750–1000
☐ 377 ..... 4¾" .... (CE) .. ❺ ... $175–190
☐ 377 ..... 4¾" .... (CE) .. ❻ ... $170–175
☐ 377 ..... 4¾" .... (OE) .. ❼ ... $170

HUM 378
Easter Greetings!
First released in the U.S. market in 1972 as one of twenty-four new motifs released that year. Originally modeled by master sculptor Gerhard Skrobek in January 1966. It has an incised 1971 copyright date on the bottom. No major variations have been found in size, color or design. The original issue price was $24 in 1972.

☐ 378	5"	(CE)	❹	$750–1000
☐ 378	5"	(CE)	❺	$195–205
☐ 378	5"	(CE)	❻	$185–195
☐ 378	5"	(OE)	❼	$185

HUM 379
Don't Be Shy (PFE)
Originally called "One For You — One For Me" on old factory records, but later changed to "Don't Be Shy." This figurine was first modeled by master sculptor Gerhard Skrobek in February 1966. It is now listed on factory records as a Possible Future Edition (PFE) and may be released at some future date, subject to possible minor changes.

☐ 379 ..... 4¼ to 4½" .... (PFE) ....

HUM 380
Daisies Don't Tell (CE)
First introduced in 1981 for members of the Goebel Collector's Club only as "Special Edition No. 5." Was not sold as an open edition but can be purchased on the secondary market at premium prices. The original issue price was $80 in the U.S. and $95 in Canada. It has an incised 1972 copyright date and the 6 trademark. The original name was "Does He?" on old factory records. Modeled by master sculptor Gerhard Skrobek in February 1966.

□ 380 ..... 4½ to 5" ..... (CE) .. ❻ ... $250–300

HUM 381
Flower Vendor
First introduced in the U.S. market in 1972. Originally modeled by master sculptor Gerhard Skrobek in October 1966. It has an incised 1971 copyright date on the underside of the base. No major variations have been found in size, color or design. The original issue price was $24 in 1972.

□ 381 ..... 5¼" .... (CE) .. ❹ ... $750–1000
□ 381 ..... 5¼" .... (CE) .. ❺ ... $210–220
□ 381 ..... 5¼" .... (CE) .. ❻ ... $200–210
□ 381 ..... 5¼" .... (OE) .. ❼ ... $200

HUM 382
Visiting An Invalid
First released in the U.S. market in 1972. Originally modeled by master sculptor Gerhard Skrobek in October 1966. It has an incised 1971 copyright date on the underside of the base. No major variations have been noticed in size, color or design. The original issue price was $26.50 in 1972.

☐ 382	5"	(CE)	❹	$750–1000
☐ 382	5"	(CE)	❺	$195–205
☐ 382	5"	(CE)	❻	$185–195
☐ 382	5"	(OE)	❼	$185

HUM 383
Going Home
This figurine was first released in the U.S. market in the spring of 1985. Originally called "Fancy Free" on old factory records, but later changed to "Going Home." Modeled by master sculptor Gerhard Skrobek in November 1966. It has an incised 1972 copyright date on the bottom. The original issue price in 1985 was $125. "Going Home" has now been made into two separate figurines. See HUM 561 "Grandma's Girl" and HUM 562 "Grandpa's Boy".

☐ 383	4¼ to 4¾"	(CE)	❻	$260–275
☐ 383	4¼ to 4¾"	(OE)	❼	$260

HUM 384
Easter Time
First introduced in the U.S. market in 1972. Originally modeled by master sculptor Gerhard Skrobek in January 1967. It has an incised 1971 copyright date on the underside of the base. No major variations have been recorded in size, color or design. The original issue price was $27.50 in 1972. Also called "Easter Playmates" in some catalogues.

☐ 384	4″	(CE)	❹	$750–1000
☐ 384	4″	(CE)	❺	$235–250
☐ 384	4″	(CE)	❻	$225–235
☐ 384	4″	(OE)	❼	$225

HUM 385
Chicken-Licken
First introduced in the U.S. market in 1972 as one of twenty-four new motifs released that year. Originally modeled by master sculptor Gerhard Skrobek in June 1967. It has an incised 1971 copyright date on the bottom of the base. No major variations have been recorded in size, color or design. The original issue price was $28.50 in 1972. A new miniature size figurine was issued in 1991 with a suggested retail price of $80 to match a new miniature plate series called the "Little Homemakers"—one each year for four years. This is the fourth and last in this series. It has an incised 1987 copyright date.

☐ 385 4/0	3¼″	(CE)	❻	$85–90
☐ 385 4/0	3¼″	(OE)	❼	$85
☐ 385	4¾″	(CE)	❹	$750–1000
☐ 385	4¾″	(CE)	❺	$250–265
☐ 385	4¾″	(CE)	❻	$240–250
☐ 385	4¾″	(OE)	❼	$240

HUM 386
On Secret Path
First introduced in the U.S. market 1972. Originally modeled by master sculptor Gerhard Skrobek in July 1967. It has an incised 1971 copyright date on the bottom of the base. No major variations have been found in size, color or design. The original issue price was $26.50 in 1972.

☐ 386	..... 5¼"	....	(CE)	.. ❹ ...	$750–1000
☐ 386	..... 5¼"	....	(CE)	.. ❺ ...	$220–235
☐ 386	..... 5¼"	....	(CE)	.. ❻ ...	$210–220
☐ 386	..... 5¼"	....	(OE)	.. ❼ ...	$210

HUM 387
Valentine Gift (CE)
This figurine was first introduced in 1977 for members of the Goebel Collectors' Club only and not sold in Open Edition. Originally modeled by master sculptor Gerhard Skrobek in July 1967. It has an incised 1972 copyright date along with the 5 trademark. Also bears the inscription "EXCLUSIVE SPECIAL EDITION No. 1 FOR MEMBERS OF THE GOEBEL COLLECTORS' CLUB" applied by blue decal. The original issue price was $45 in addition to the member's redemption card. Translation of message on heart: "I Love You Very Much" or "I Like You." Several examples without the special inscription but with trademark 4 only have appeared on the market. Some have 1968 copyright date and usually sell for $1500–2000.

☐ 387	..... 5¾"	....	(CE)	.. ❹ ...	$1500–2000
☐ 387	..... 5¾"	....	(CE)	.. ❺ ...	$600–800

388

HUM 388
Little Band, Candleholder

This piece is a candleholder with three figurines, HUM 389, HUM 390 and HUM 391, attached to a round ceramic base. Modeled by master sculptor Gerhard Skrobek in December 1967. It has an incised 1968 copyright date. Little Band, Candleholder was "Temporarily Withdrawn" (TW) from production on 31 December 1990, but may be reinstated at some future date.

☐ 388 ..... 3 × 4¾" ..... (CE) .. ❹ ... $250–350
☐ 388 ..... 3 × 4¾" ..... (CE) .. ❺ ... $225–240
☐ 388 ..... 3 × 4¾" ..... (TW) .. ❻ ... $220–225

388 M

HUM 388 M
Little Band, Candleholder on Music Box

Same as HUM 388 but fastened on a music box. There are variations in type of music box as well as tunes played. The music box is usually Swiss-made and not produced by Goebel. This Music Box was "Temporarily Withdrawn" (TW) from production on 31 December 1990, but may be reinstated at some future date.

☐ 388M .... 3 × 4¾" ..... (CE) .. ❹ ... $375–400
☐ 388M .... 3 × 4¾" ..... (CE) .. ❺ ... $350–375
☐ 388M .... 3 × 4¾" ..... (TW) .. ❻ ... $330–340

389 390 391

HUM 389
Girl With Sheet of Music
One of a set of three sometimes referred to as the "Little Band." Originally modeled by master sculptor Gerhard Skrobek in May 1968. It has an incised 1968 copyright date and only found in trademarks 4, 5 and 6.

☐ 389 ..... 2½" .... (CE) .. ❹ ... $100–125
☐ 389 ..... 2½" .... (CE) .. ❺ ... $75–80
☐ 389 ..... 2½" .... (CE) .. ❻ ... $70–75
☐ 389 ..... 2½" .... (OE) .. ❼ ... $70

HUM 390
Boy With Accordion
One of a set of three sometimes referred to as the "Little Band." Originally modeled by master sculptor Gerhard Skrobek in May 1968. It has an incised 1968 copyright date and only found in trademarks 4, 5 and 6.

☐ 390 ..... 2½" .... (CE) .. ❹ ... $100–125
☐ 390 ..... 2½" .... (CE) .. ❺ ... $75–80
☐ 390 ..... 2½" .... (CE) .. ❻ ... $70–75
☐ 390 ..... 2½" .... (OE) .. ❼ ... $70

HUM 391
Girl With Trumpet
One of a set of three sometimes referred to as the "Little Band." Originally modeled by master sculptor Gerhard Skrobek in May 1968. It has an incised 1968 copyright date and only found in trademarks 4, 5 and 6.

☐ 391 ..... 2½" .... (CE) .. ❹ ... $100–125
☐ 391 ..... 2½" .... (CE) .. ❺ ... $75–80
☐ 391 ..... 2½" .... (CE) .. ❻ ... $70–75
☐ 391 ..... 2½" .... (OE) .. ❼ ... $70

392

HUM 392
Little Band (on base)
Same as HUM 388 but without socket for candle. Modeled by master sculptor Gerhard Skrobek in May 1968. It has an incised 1968 copyright date. On 31 December 1984 this figurine was listed as "temporarily withdrawn" (TW) from production by Goebel but could possibly be reinstated at some future date.

☐ 392 . . . . . 3 × 4¾" . . . . . (CE) . . ❹ . . $250–350
☐ 392 . . . . . 3 × 4¾" . . . . . (CE) . . ❺ . . $225–240
☐ 392 . . . . . 3 × 4¾" . . . . . **(TW)** . . ❻ . . $220–225

392 M

HUM 392 M
Little Band on Music Box
Same as HUM 392 but fastened on a music box. There are variations in type of music box as well as in tunes played. The music box is usually Swiss-made and not produced by Goebel. This Music Box was "Temporarily Withdrawn" (TW) from production on 31 December 1990, but may be reinstated at some future date.

☐ 392 M . . . 3 × 4¾" . . . . . (CE) . . ❹ . . $375–400
☐ 392 M . . . 3 × 4¾" . . . . . (CE) . . ❺ . . $350–375
☐ 392 M . . . 3 × 4¾" . . . . . (TW) . . ❻ . . $330–340

HUM 393
Holy Water Font, Dove (PFE)
This holy water font was modeled by master sculptor Gerhard Skrobek in June 1968. The inscription reads: "Come Holy Spirit." Now listed on factory records as a Possible Future Edition (PFE) and may be released at some future date, subject to possible minor changes.

☐ 393 ..... 2¾ × 4¼" ... (PFE) ....

HUM 394
Timid Little Sister
First released in the U.S. market in 1981 along with five other figurines. Originally modeled by master sculptor Gerhard Skrobek in February 1972. It has an incised 1972 copyright date on the underside of the base. The original issue price was $190 in 1981. The girl normally does *not* have eyelashes.

☐ 394 ..... 7" .... (CE) .. ❻ ... $360–380
☐ 394 ..... 7" .... (OE) .. ❼ ... $360

HUM 395
Shepherd Boy (PFE)

Originally named "Young Shepherd" on old factory records, but later changed to "Shepherd Boy." This figurine was modeled by master sculptor Gerhard Skrobek in February 1971. It is now listed as a Possible Future Edition (PFE) on factory records and may be released at some future date, subject to possible minor changes.

☐ 395 . . . . . 6 to 6½" . . . . . (PFE) . . . .

HUM 396
Ride Into Christmas

This design was first introduced in the U.S. market in 1972. First modeled by master sculptor Gerhard Skrobek in December 1970. It has an incised 1971 copyright date. The original issue price was $48.50 on the 1972 price list. A smaller model was released in 1982 with the incised number 396 2/0 and incised 1981 copyright date. The small version was also modeled by Gerhard Skrobek but in 1980. The original issue price was $95 in 1982. The large size has been renumbered 396/I and the old number 396 is now classified as a closed edition because of this change. This same motif is used on the 1975 Annual Plate, HUM 268.

☐ 396 2/0	4¼"	(CE)	❻	$200–210
☐ 396 2/0	4¼"	(OE)	❼	$200
☐ 396	5¾"	(CE)	❹	$1500–2000
☐ 396	5¾"	(CE)	❺	$400–425
☐ 396	5¾"	(CE)	❻	$375–400
☐ 396/I	5¾"	(CE)	❻	$360–375
☐ 396/I	5¾"	(OE)	❼	$360

HUM 397
Poet (PFE)
This figurine was first modeled by master sculptor Gerhard Skrobek in 1973. Presently listed on factory records as a Possible Future Edition (PFE) and may be released at some future date, subject to possible minor changes.

☐ 397 ..... 6″ .... (PFE) ....

HUM 398
Spring Bouquet (PFE)
This figurine was first modeled by master sculptor Gerhard Skrobek in 1973. Presently listed on factory records as a Possible Future Edition (PFE) and may be released at some future date, subject to possible minor changes.

☐ 398 ..... 6¼″ .... (PFE) ....

HUM 399
Valentine Joy (CE)

This figurine was first introduced in 1980 for members of the Goebel Collectors' Club only and not sold as an Open Edition. Originally modeled by master sculptor Gerhard Skrobek from an original drawing by Sister M.I. Hummel. It has an incised 1979 copyright date along with the 6 trademark. Also bears the inscription "EXCLUSIVE SPECIAL EDITION No. 4 FOR MEMBERS OF THE GOEBEL COLLECTORS' CLUB" applied by blue decal. The original issue price was $95 in the U.S. and $105 in Canada, in addition to the member's redemption card. Translation of message on heart: "I Like You." This figurine can be purchased on the secondary market at premium prices.

☐ 399 . . . . . 5¾" . . . . (CE) . . ❻ . . . $200–250

HUM 400
Well Done! (PFE)

This figurine was first modeled by master sculptor Gerhard Skrobek in 1973. Presently listed on factory records as a Possible Future Edition (PFE) and may be released at some future date, subject to possible minor changes.

☐ 400 . . . . . 6¼" . . . . (PFE) . . . . . .

HUM 401
Forty Winks (PFE)
This figurine was first modeled by master sculptor Gerhard Skrobek in 1973. Presently listed on factory records as a Possible Future Edition (PFE) and may be released at some future date, subject to possible minor changes.

☐ 401 ..... 5¼" .... (PFE) . .....

HUM 402
True Friendship (PFE)
This figurine was first modeled by master sculptor Gerhard Skrobek in 1973. Presently listed on factory records as a Possible Future Edition (PFE) and may be released at some future date, subject to possible minor changes.

☐ 402 ..... 4¾" .... (PFE) . .....

HUM 403
An Apple A Day
This figurine was first modeled by master sculptor Gerhard Skrobek in 1973. First released in the U.S. Market in 1989. It has an incised 1974 copyright date. The original issue price was $195 in 1989.

☐ 403 . . . . . 6½" . . . . (CE) . . ❻ . . . $240–250
☐ 403 . . . . . 6½" . . . . (OE) . . ❼ . . . $240

HUM 404
Sad Song (PFE)
This figurine was first modeled by master sculptor Gerhard Skrobek in 1973. Presently listed on factory records as a Possible Future Edition (PFE) and may be released at some future date, subject to possible minor changes.

☐ 404 . . . . . 6¼" . . . . (PFE) . . . .

HUM 405
Sing With Me

This figurine was first released in the U.S. market in 1985 along with three other new models formerly listed as Possible Future Editions (PFE). Modeled by master sculptor Gerhard Skrobek in 1973. It has an incised 1974 copyright date on the bottom. The original issue price was $125 in the U.S. and $158 in Canada.

☐ 405 ..... 5" .... (CE) .. ❻ ... $260–270
☐ 405 ..... 5" .... (**OE**) .. ❼ ... $260

HUM 406
Pleasant Journey (CE)

This figurine was first released in the U.S. market in 1987 along with four other new figurines. This is the second figurine in the Century Collection and was produced for this one year only in the twentieth century. It was modeled by master sculptor Gerhard Skrobek in 1974 but has an incised 1976 copyright date. A circular inscription applied by blue decal reads: "M.I. HUMMEL CENTURY COLLECTION 1987 XX" and the name "PLEASANT JOURNEY" along with the (TM 6) trademark. The issue price was $500 in the U.S. and $695 in Canada.

☐ 406 ..... 7⅛ × 6½" ... (CE) .. ❻ ... $1600–1800

HUM 407
Flute Song (PFE)
This figurine was first modeled by master sculptor Gerhard Skrobek in 1974. Presently listed on factory records as a Possible Future Edition (PFE) and may be released at some future date, subject to possible minor changes.

☐ 407 ..... 6" .... (PFE) . .....

HUM 408
Smiling Through (CE)
This figurine was first introduced in 1985 for members of the Goebel Collector's Club only and not sold as an Open Edition. Originally modeled by master sculptor Gerhard Skrobek from an original drawing by sister M.I. Hummel. It has an incised 1983 copyright date along with the (TM 6) trademark. Also bears the inscription "EXCLUSIVE SPECIAL EDITION No. 9 FOR MEMBERS OF THE GOEBEL COLLECTORS' CLUB" applied by blue decal. The original issue price was $125 in the U.S. and $165 in Canada, in addition to the member's redemption card. It is interesting to note the incised model number of 408/0, which indicates that more than one size was produced. The piece photographed here was the larger sample model. The club piece was designed to be smaller, more uniform in size to the other club figurines. "Smiling Through" can now be purchased on the secondary market at premium prices. See HUM 690 for more information.

☐ 408/0 .... 4¾" .... (CE) .. ❻ ... $275–325

HUM 409
Coffee Break (CE)

This figurine was first introduced in 1984 for members of the Goebel Collector's Club only and not sold as an Open Edition. Originally modeled by master sculptor Gerhard Skrobek from an original drawing by Sister M.I. Hummel. It has an incised 1976 copyright date along with the (TM 6) trademark. Also bears the inscription "EXCLUSIVE SPECIAL EDITION No. 8 FOR MEMBERS OF THE GOEBEL COLLECTORS' CLUB" applied by blue decal. The original issue price was $90 in the U.S. and $110 in Canada, in addition to the member's redemption card. "Coffee Break" can now be purchased on the secondary market at premium prices.

☐ 409 ..... 4" .... (CE) .. ❻ ... $200–250

HUM 410
Truant (PFE)

This figurine was first modeled by master sculptor Gerhard Skrobek in 1978. Presently listed on factory records as a Possible Future Edition (PFE) and may be released at some future date, subject to possible minor changes.

☐ 410 ..... 6" .... (PFE) . .....

HUM 411
Do I Dare? (PFE)
This figurine was first modeled by master sculptor Gerhard Skrobek in 1978. Presently listed on factory records as a Possible Future Edition (PFE) and may be released at some future date, subject to possible minor changes.

☐ 411 ..... 6″ .... (PFE) . ...

HUM 412
Bath Time
This figurine was first modeled by master sculptor Gerhard Skrobek in 1978. First introduced in the U.S. market in 1990. It has an incised 1978 copyright date. Original issue price was $300 in 1990.

☐ 412 ..... 6¼″ .... (CE) .. ❻ ... $350–370
☐ 412 ..... 6¼″ .... (OE) .. ❼ ... $350

HUM 413
Whistler's Duet
This figurine was first modeled by master sculptor Gerhard Skrobek in 1979. First released in the U.S. market in the fall of 1991, the original issue price was $235.

☐ 413 ..... 4¼" .... **(OE)** .. ❼ ... $235

HUM 414
In Tune
First released in the U.S. market in 1981. Modeled by Gerhard Skrobek in 1979. This figurine was designed to match the fourth edition of the annual bell series, HUM 703 "In Tune" 1981 Annual. The figurine has an incised 1979 copyright date on the bottom of the base and is found only in 6 trademark. The original issue price was $115 in 1981.

☐ 414 ..... 4" .... **(CE)** .. ❻ ... $230–240
☐ 414 ..... 4" .... **(OE)** .. ❼ ... $230

HUM 415
Thoughtful
First released in the U.S. market in 1981. Modeled by Gerhard Skrobek in 1979. This figurine was designed to match the third edition of the annual bell series, HUM 702 "Thoughtful" 1980 Annual. The figurine has an incised 1980 copyright date on the bottom of the base and is found only in 6 trademark. The original issue price was $105 in 1981.

☐ 415 ..... 4½" .... (CE) .. ❻ ... $190–200
☐ 415 ..... 4½" .... **(OE)** .. ❼ ... $190

HUM 416
Jubilee (CE)
This special limited edition figurine was issued in 1985 in celebration of the Golden Anniversary of the introduction of the first "M.I. Hummel" figurines in 1935. It was modeled by master sculptor Gerhard Skrobek in 1979 and has an incised 1980 copyright date. This figurine was limited to the total of the 1985 production and will not be produced in future years. On the bottom is the special inscription which reads: "50 YEARS M.I. HUMMEL FIGURINES 1935–1985" in a circular design. Directly below is "THE LOVE LIVES ON" in addition to the current (TM 6) trademark, all applied by blue decal. Originally sold in a special white padded presentation case. The original issue price was $200 in the U.S. and $270 in Canada.

☐ 416 ..... 6¼" .... (CE) .. ❻ ... $200–300

HUM 417
Where Did You Get That? (PFE)
This figurine was first modeled by master sculptor Gerhard Skrobek in 1982 and has an incised 1982 copyright date. Presently listed on factory records as a Possible Future Edition (PFE) and may be released at some future date, subject to possible minor changes. This figurine has now been made into two separate figurines. See HUM 485 "Gift From A Friend" and HUM 486 "I Wonder."

☐ 417 ..... 5¼" .... (PFE) . .....

HUM 418
What's New?
First introduced in the U.S. market in 1990. This figurine was modeled by master sculptor Gerhard Skrobek in 1980. It has an incised 1980 copyright date. Original issue price was $200 in 1990.

☐ 418 ..... 5¼" .... (CE) .. ❻ ... $240–250
☐ 418 ..... 5¼" .... (OE) .. ❼ ... $240

HUM 419
Good Luck! (PFE)
This figurine was first modeled by master sculptor Gerhard Skrobek in 1981. Presently listed on factory records as a Possible Future Edition (PFE) and may be released at some future date, subject to possible minor changes.

☐ 419 ..... 6¼" .... (PFE) . .....

HUM 420
Is It Raining?
First introduced in the U.S. market in 1989. This figurine was modeled by master sculptor Gerhard Skrobek in 1981. It has an incised 1981 copyright date. Original issue price was $175 in 1989.

☐ 420 ..... 6" .... (CE) .. ❻ ... $225–235
☐ 420 ..... 6" .... (**OE**) .. ❼ ... $225

HUM 421
It's Cold (CE)
This figurine was first introduced in 1982 for members of the Goebel Collectors' Club only and not sold as an Open Edition. Originally modeled by master sculptor Gerhard Skrobek from an original drawing by Sister M.I. Hummel. It has an incised 1981 copyright date along with the 6 trademark. Also bears the inscription "EXCLUSIVE SPECIAL EDITION No. 6 FOR MEMBERS OF THE GOEBEL COLLECTORS' CLUB" applied by blue decal. The official issue price was $80 in the U.S. and $95 in Canada, in addition to the member's redemption card. This figurine can be purchased on the secondary market at premium prices.

☐ 421 ..... 5 to 5¼" ..... (CE) .. ❻ ... $250–300

HUM 422
What Now? (CE)
This figurine was first introduced in 1983 for members of the Goebel Collectors' Club only and not sold as an Open Edition. Originally modeled by master sculptor Gerhard Skrobek from an original drawing by Sister M.I. Hummel. It has an incised 1981 copyright date along with the (TM 6) trademark. Also bears the inscription "EXCLUSIVE SPECIAL EDITION No. 7 FOR MEMBERS OF THE GOEBEL COLLECTORS' CLUB" applied by blue decal. The official issue price was $80 in the U.S. and $95 in Canada, in addition to the member's redemption card. This figurine can be purchased on the secondary market at premium prices.

☐ 422 ..... 5¼" .... (CE) .. ❻ ... $250–300

HUM 423
Horse Trainer
First introduced in the U.S. market in 1990. This figurine was modeled by master sculptor Gerhard Skrobek in 1980. It has an incised 1981 copyright date. The original issue price was $155 in 1990.

☐ 423 ..... 4½" .... (CE) .. ❻ ... $185–195
☐ 423 ..... 4½" .... (OE) .. ❼ ... $185

HUM 424
Sleep Tight
First released in the U.S. market in 1990. This figurine was modeled by master sculptor Gerhard Skrobek in 1980. It has an incised 1981 copyright date. The original issue price was $155 in 1990.

☐ 424 ..... 4½" .... (CE) .. ❻ ... $185–195
☐ 424 ..... 4½" .... (OE) .. ❼ ... $185

HUM 425
Pleasant Moment (PFE)
This figurine was first modeled by master sculptor Gerhard Skrobek in 1980. It has an incised 1981 copyright date. Presently listed on factory records as a Possible Future Edition (PFE) and may be released at some future date, subject to possible minor changes.

☐ 425 ..... 4½" .... (PFE) . .....

HUM 426
Pay Attention (PFE)
This figurine was first modeled by master sculptor Gerhard Skrobek in 1980. It has an incised 1981 copyright date. Presently listed on factory records as a Possible Future Edition (PFE) and may be released at some future date, subject to possible minor changes.

☐ 426 ..... 5¾" .... (PFE) . .....

HUM 427
Where Are You? (PFE)
This figurine was first modeled by master sculptor Gerhard Skrobek in 1980. It has an incised 1981 copyright date. Presently listed on factory records as a Possible Future Edition (PFE) and may be released at some future date, subject to possible minor changes.

☐ 427 . . . . . 5¾″ . . . . (PFE) . . . . . .

HUM 428
I Won't Hurt You (PFE)
This figurine was first modeled by master sculptor Gerhard Skrobek in 1980. It has an incised 1981 copyright date. Presently listed on factory records as a Possible Future Edition (PFE) and may be released at some future date, subject to possible minor changes.

☐ 428 . . . . . 5¾″ . . . . (PFE) . . . . . .

HUM 429
Hello World (CE)

This figurine was first introduced in 1989 for members of the M.I. Hummel Club only and not sold as an Open Edition. Originally modeled by master sculptor Gerhard Skrobek in 1980. It has an incised 1983 copyright date along with either the (TM6) or (TM7) trademark. Also bears the inscription: "EXCLUSIVE EDITION 1989/90 M.I. HUMMEL CLUB" applied by blue decal. A large black flying bumble bee is located on the bottom. The official price was $130 in the U.S., in addition to the member's redemption card. This figurine can now be purchased on the secondary market at premium prices. Early production pieces are labeled "Goebel Collectors' Club" while later pieces have "M.I. Hummel Club" decal.

☐ 429 ..... 5½" .... (CE) .. ❻ ... $200–250
☐ 429 ..... 5½" .... (CE) .. ❼ ... $200–250

HUM 430
In "D" Major

First released in the U.S. market in 1989. This figurine was modeled by master sculptor Gerhard Skrobek in 1980. It has an incised 1981 copyright date. The original issue price was $135 in 1989.

☐ 430 ..... 4¼" .... (CE) .. ❻ ... $170–180
☐ 430 ..... 4¼" .... (OE) .. ❼ ... $170

HUM 431
The Surprise (CE)

This figurine was first introduced in 1988 for members of the Goebel Collectors' Club only and not sold as an Open Edition. Originally modeled by master sculptor Gerhard Skrobek in 1980. It has an incised 1981 copyright date along with the current (TM6) trademark. Also bears the inscription: "EXCLUSIVE SPECIAL EDITION No. 12 FOR MEMBERS OF THE GOEBEL COLLECTORS' CLUB" applied by blue decal. A large black flying bumble bee is located on the bottom of the base. The original price was $125 in the U.S., in addition to the member's redemption card. "The Surprise" can now be purchased on the secondary market at premium prices.

☐ 431 ..... 4¼" .... (CE) .. ❻ ... $225–275

HUM 432
Knit One, Purl One

First released in the U.S. market in 1983. Modeled by master sculptor Gerhard Skrobek in 1982. This figurine was designed especially to match the sixth edition of the annual bell series, HUM 705 "Knit One" 1983 annual. The figurine has an incised 1982 copyright date on the bottom of the base and is found only in the current (TM 6) trademark. The original issue price was $52 in the U.S. and $74 in Canada.

☐ 432 ..... 3" .... (CE) .. ❻ ... $105–110
☐ 432 ..... 3" .... (OE) .. ❼ ... $105

HUM 433
Sing Along
First released in the U.S. market in 1987. Modeled by master sculptor Gerhard Skrobek in 1981. This figurine was designed especially to match the ninth edition of the annual bell series, HUM 708 "Sing Along" 1986 annual. The figurine has an incised 1982 copyright date on the bottom of the base. The original issue price was $145 in the U.S. and $200 in Canada.

☐ 433 . . . . . 4½" . . . . (CE) . . ❻ . . . $240–250
☐ 433 . . . . . 4½" . . . . (OE) . . ❼ . . . $240

HUM 434
Friend or Foe
First released in the U.S. market in 1991. Modeled by master sculptor Gerhard Skrobek in 1981. It has an incised 1982 copyright date. The original issue price was $190.

☐ 434 . . . . . 4" . . . . (CE) . . ❻ . . . $195–225
☐ 434 . . . . . 4" . . . . (OE) . . ❼ . . . $195

HUM 435
Delicious (PFE)

This figurine was first modeled by master sculptor Gerhard Skrobek in 1981. It has an incised 1982 copyright date. Presently listed on factory records as a Possible Future Edition (PFE) and may be released at some future date, subject to possible minor changes.

☐ 435 ..... 6″ .... (PFE) . .....

HUM 436
An Emergency (PFE)

This figurine was first modeled by master sculptor Gerhard Skrobek in 1981. It has an incised 1983 copyright date. Presently listed on factory records as a Possible Future Edition (PFE) and may be released at some future date, subject to possible minor changes.

☐ 436 ..... 5½″ .... (PFE) . .....

HUM 437
Tuba Player
First released in the U.S. market in 1989. This figurine was modeled by master sculptor Gerhard Skrobek in 1982. It has an incised 1983 copyright date. The original issue price was $160 in 1989.

☐ 437 ..... 6¼" .... (CE) .. ❻ ... $225–235
☐ 437 ..... 6¼" .... **(OE)** .. ❼ ... $225

HUM 438
Sounds of the Mandolin
First released in the U.S. market in 1988. This figurine was modeled by master sculptor Gerhard Skrobek in 1982. It has an incised 1984 copyright date. It was originally called "Mandolin Serenade" but later changed to "Sounds of the Mandolin" at time of release. The original issue price was $65 in 1988.

☐ 438 ..... 3¾" .... (CE) .. ❻ ... $100–105
☐ 438 ..... 3¾" .... **(OE)** .. ❼ ... $100

HUM 439
A Gentle Glow, Candleholder

First released in the U.S. market in 1987. Modeled by master sculptor Gerhard Skrobek in 1982. The figurine has an incised 1983 copyright date on the bottom of the base and is found only in the current (TM6) trademark. The original issue price was $110 in the U.S. and $160 in Canada.

☐ 439 ..... 5¼ to 5½" .... (CE) .. ❻ ... $175–180
☐ 439 ..... 5¼ to 5½" .... (OE) .. ❼ ... $175

HUM 440
Birthday Candle, Candleholder (CE)

This figurine was first introduced in 1986 for members of the Goebel Collectors' Club only and not sold as an Open Edition. Originally modeled by master sculptor Gerhard Skrobek from an original drawing by Sister M.I. Hummel. It has an incised 1983 copyright date along with the current (TM6) trademark. Also bears the inscription "EXCLUSIVE SPECIAL EDITION No. 10 FOR MEMBERS OF THE GOEBEL COLLECTORS' CLUB" applied by blue decal. Also a circular "CELEBRATING 10 YEARS OF THE GOEBEL COLLECTORS' CLUB." The original issue price was $95 in the U.S. and $140 in Canada, in addition to the member's redemption card. "Birthday Candle" can now be purchased on the secondary market at premium prices.

☐ 440 ..... 5½" .... (CE) .. ❻ ... $250–300

HUM 441
Call To Worship, Clock (CE)
First released in the U.S. market in 1988. This figurine, an actual working clock, was
modeled by master sculptor Gerhard Skrobek in 1982. This is the third figurine in the
Century Collection and was produced for only this one year in the twentieth century. It
has an incised 1983 copyright date. A circular inscription applied by blue decal reads:
"M.I. HUMMEL CENTURY COLLECTION 1988 XX" and the (TM6) trademark. The
issue price was $600 in 1988.

☐ 441 ..... 13″ .... (CE) .. ❻ ... $650–800

HUM 442 (TM 6)   *Rear view*

Painted windows variation   *Open windows/open hole*   *Open windows/closed hole*

HUM 442
Chapel Time, Clock (CE)

This figurine, an actual working clock, was first modeled by master sculptor Gerhard Skrobek in 1982. It has an incised 1983 copyright date. Released in 1986, it was produced for one year only as a limited edition and will be not produced again in the twentieth century. Hand lettered XX to signify the twentieth century. The suggested retail price was $500 in the U.S. and $650 in Canada. Several variations are noted: Early production of "Chapel Time" had a closed bell tower with only painted windows. In later production, the bell tower windows were opened to allow air to escape more easily during the firing process. A third variation is in the small round window directly beneath the bell tower but above the clock. Slight variations have been noted in the base construction and color variations on the face of the clock. The clock is battery operated, using one "C" cell battery and keeps accurate time.

☐ 442 .. 11½" ..... (CE) ... ❻ ... $1000–1250 (Open windows/closed hole)
☐ 442 .. 11½" ..... (CE) ... ❻ ... $2000–2500 (Painted windows variation)
☐ 442 .. 11½" ..... (CE) ... ❻ ... $2500–3000 (Open windows/open hole)

Rear view

HUM 443
Country Song, Clock (PFE)

This figurine, an actual working clock, was first modeled by master sculptor Gerhard Skrobek in 1982. It has an incised 1983 copyright date. Presently listed on factory records as a Possible Future Edition (PFE) and may be released at some future date, subject to possible minor changes.

☐ 443 ..... 8″ .... (PFE) . .....

HUM 444 — Still under development (PFE)
HUM 445 — Still under development (PFE)

HUM 446
A Personal Message (PFE)

This figurine was first modeled by master sculptor Gerhard Skrobek in 1983. Presently listed on factory records as a Possible Future Edition (PFE) and may be released at some future date, subject to possible minor changes.

☐ 446 ..... 3¾″ .... (PFE) . .....

HUM 447
Morning Concert (CE)

This figurine was first introduced in 1987 for members of the Goebel Collectors' Club only and not sold as an Open Edition. Originally modeled by master sculptor Gerhard Skrobek from an original drawing by Sister M. I. Hummel. It has an incised 1984 copyright date along with the current (TM6) trademark. Also bears the inscription: "EXCLUSIVE SPECIAL EDITION No. 11 FOR MEMBERS OF THE GOEBEL COLLECTORS' CLUB" applied by blue decal. The original issue price was $98 in the U. S., in addition to the member's redemption card. "Morning Concert" can now be purchased on the secondary market at premium prices.

☐ 447 ..... 5¼" .... (CE) .. ❻ ... $200–250

HUM 448 Rear view

HUM 448 Side view

325

HUM 448
Children's Prayer (PFE)
This beautiful figurine was modeled by master sculptor Gerhard Skrobek in 1983. It has an incised 1984 copyright date. Presently listed on factory records as a Possible Future Edition (PFE) and may be released at some future date, subject to possible minor changes.

☐ 448 . . . . . 8¼" . . . . (PFE) . . . . . .

HUM 449
The Little Pair (EE)

This figurine was first modeled by master sculptor Gerhard Skrobek in 1984. It has an incised 1985 copyright date. Announced in 1990, "The Little Pair" will be an EXCLUSIVE EDITION available to "M.I. Hummel Club" members only, who have belonged to the Club continuously for 10 years. Issued by means of a redemption card to those who are eligible. The original issue price was $170.

☐ 449 . . . . . 5 to 5¼" . . . . . (EE) . . ❻ . . . $225–250
☐ 449 . . . . . 5 to 5¼" . . . . . (EE) . . ❼ . . . $185
(M.I.H. Club Members Only)

HUM 450
Will It Sting? (PFE)

This figurine was first modeled by master sculptor Gerhard Skrobek in 1984. Presently listed on factory records as a Possible Future Edition (PFE) and may be released at some future date, subject to possible minor changes.

☐ 450 . . . . . 5¾" . . . . (PFE) . . . . . .

HUM 451
Just Dozing (PFE)

This figurine was first modeled by master sculptor Gerhard Skrobek in 1984. Presently listed on factory records as a Possible Future Edition (PFE) and may be released at some future dated, subject to possible minor changes.

☐ 451 ..... 4¼" .... (PFE) . .....

HUM 452
Flying High (CE)

First released in the U. S. market in 1988 as a hanging ornament. Modeled by master sculptor Gerhard Skrobek in 1984. It has an incised 1984 copyright date. The original issue price was $75 in 1988. Early releases were not dated. Later pieces dated 1988 with "First Edition" decal. Third variation were dated but without "First Edition" decal. Undated pieces bring a premium.

☐ 452 ..... 4½" × 2¾" ... (CE) .. ❻ ... $125–150
☐ 452 ..... 4½" × 2¾" ... (CE) .. ❻ ... $150–200 (undated)

HUM 453
The Accompanist
First released in the U. S. market in 1988. Modeled by master sculptor Gerhard Skrobek in 1984. It has an incised 1984 copyright date. The original issue price was $39 in 1988.

☐ 453 ..... 3¼" .... (CE) .. ❻ ... $80–85
☐ 453 ..... 3¼" .... (OE) .. ❼ ... $80

HUM 454
Song Of Praise
First released in the U. S. market in 1988. Modeled by master sculptor Gerhard Skrobek in 1984. It has an incised 1984 copyright date. The original issue price was $39 in 1988.

☐ 454 ..... 3" .... (CE) .. ❻ ... $80–85
☐ 454 ..... 3" .... (OE) .. ❼ ... $80

HUM 455
The Guardians
First released in the U.S. market in 1991. Modeled by master sculptor Gerhard Skrobek in 1984. It has an incised 1985 copyright date. The original issue price was $140.

□ 455 ..... 2¾" × 3½" ... (CE) .. ❻ ... $145–175
□ 455 ..... 2¾" × 3½" ... **(OE)** .. ❼ ... $145

HUM 456
Sleep, Little One, Sleep (PFE)
This figurine was first modeled by master sculptor Gerhard Skrobek in 1984. Presently listed on factory records as a Possible Future Edition (PFE) and may be released at some future date, subject to possible minor changes.

□ 456 ..... 4¼" .... (PFE) . .....

HUM 457
Sound The Trumpet
First released in the U. S. market in 1988. Modeled by master sculptor Gerhard Skrobek in 1984. It has an incised 1984 copyright date. The original issue price was $45 in 1988.

☐ 457 ..... 3" .... (CE) .. ❻ ... $80–85
☐ 457 ..... 3" .... (OE) .. ❼ ... $80

HUM 458
Storybook Time
First released in the U.S. market in the fall of 1991. Modeled by master sculptor Gerhard Skrobek in 1984. It has an incised 1985 copyright date. The original issue price was $330.

☐ 458 ..... 5¼" .... (OE) .. ❼ ... $330

HUM 459
In The Meadow
First released in the U. S. market in 1987. Modeled by master sculptor Gerhard Skrobek in 1984. The figurine has an incised 1985 copyright date. The original issue price was $110 in the U. S. and $160 in Canada.

☐ 459 ..... 4" .... (CE) .. ❻ ... $170–180
☐ 459 ..... 4" .... (OE) .. ❼ ... $170

HUM 460
Goebel Authorized Retailer Plaque (CE)
This authorized retailer plaque was issued to all authorized "M. I. Hummel" retailers in 1986 and became the official identification for distributors of Hummel figurines. It replaced the older HUM 187 dealers plaque with "Merry Wanderer" that has been in use, with many variations, since the late 1940's. You will notice the boy is similar to the middle boy on HUM 170 "School Boys." The new plaque has an incised "M. I. Hummel" signature on the back as well as the decal signature on the front. It has an incised 1984 copyright date along with the current (TM 6) trademark on the bottom. It is also known as "The Tally." This plaque was issued in eight decal variations for use in other countries (languages). Discontinued in December 1989, to be replaced by HUM 187A with new graphics. (See HUM 187)

☐ 460 ..... 5" × 6" U.S. VERSION . (CE) ... ❻ $150–200
☐ 460 ..... 5" × 6" BRITISH ..... (CE) ... ❻ $750–1000
☐ 460 ..... 5" × 6" GERMAN .... (CE) ... ❻ $1200–1500
☐ 460 ..... 5" × 6" DUTCH ...... (CE) ... ❻ $1500–2000
☐ 460 ..... 5" × 6" ITALIAN ..... (CE) ... ❻ $1500–2000
☐ 460 ..... 5" × 6" FRENCH .... (CE) ... ❻ $1200–1500
☐ 460 ..... 5" × 6" SWEDISH .... (CE) ... ❻ $1200–1500
☐ 460 ..... 5" × 6" SPANISH .... (CE) ... ❻ $1500–2000

☐ UNITED STATES

☐ BRITISH

☐ GERMAN

☐ DUTCH

☐ ITALIAN

☐ FRENCH

☐ SWEDISH

☐ SPANISH

HUM 461
In The Orchard (PFE)
This figurine was first modeled by master
sculptor Gerhard Skrobek in 1984. Presently listed on factory records as a Possible Future Edition (PFE) and may be
released at some future date, subject to
possible minor changes.

☐ 461 ..... 5½" .... (PFE) . .....

HUM 462
Tit For Tat (PFE)
This figurine was first modeled by master
sculptor Gerhard Skrobek in 1984. Presently listed on factory records as a Possible Future Edition (PFE) and may be
released at some future date, subject to
possible minor changes.

☐ 462 ..... 3¾" .... (PFE) . .....

HUM 463
My Wish Is Small (EE)
This is the 1992/93 Exclusive Edition for members of the M. I. Hummel Club. It is for members only and will not be sold as an open edition to the general public. First modeled by master sculptor Gerhard Skrobek in 1985. The original issue price is $170 in the U.S., in addition to the member's redemption card.

☐ 463 . . . . . 5½" . . . . (EE) . . ❼ . . . $170
(MIH Club Members Only)

HUM 464
Young Scholar (PFE)
This figurine was first modeled by master sculptor Gerhard Skrobek in 1985. Presently listed on factory records as a Possible Future Edition (PFE) and may be released at some future date, subject to possible minor changes.

☐ 464 . . . . . 5⅛" . . . . (PFE) . . . . . .

HUM 465
Where Shall I Go? (PFE)
This figurine was first modeled by master sculptor Gerhard Skrobek in 1985. It is based on a portrait sketched by Sister Hummel in 1938. The boy, now a grown man, still resides in Germany at the present time. This figurine is presently listed on factory records as a Possible Future Edition (PFE) and may be released at some future date, subject to possible changes. The original drawing is owned by Mr. & Mrs. Robert L. Miller.

☐ 465 . . . . . 4¼" . . . . (PFE) . . . . . .

HUM 466
DoReMi (PFE)
This figurine was first modeled by master sculptor Gerhard Shrobek in 1985. Presently listed on factory records as a Possible Future Edition (PFE) and may be released at some future date, subject to possible minor changes.

☐ 466 . . . . . 5½" . . . . (PFE) . . . . . .

HUM 467
Kindergartner
First released in the U. S. market in 1987. Modeled by master sculptor Gerhard Skrobek in 1985. The figurine has an incised 1985 copyright date. The original issue price was $100 in 1987.

☐ 467 ..... 5¼" .... (CE) .. ❻ ... $170–180
☐ 467 ..... 5¼" .... (OE) .. ❼ ... $170

HUM 468
Come On (PFE)
This figurine was first modeled by master sculptor Gerhard Skrobek in 1986. Presently listed on factory records as a Possible Future Edition (PFE) and may be released at some future date, subject to possible minor changes.

☐ 468 ..... 5¼" .... (PFE) . .....

HUM 469
Starting Young (PFE)
This figurine was first modeled by master sculptor Gerhard Skrobek in 1986. Presently listed on factory records as a Possible Future Edition (PFE) and may be released at some future date, subject to possible minor changes.

☐ 469 ..... 4¾" .... (PFE) ....

HUM 470
Time Out (PFE)
This figurine was first modeled by master sculptor Gerhard Skrobek in 1986. Presently listed on factory records as a Possible Future Edition (PFE) and may be released at some future date, subject to possible minor changes.

☐ 470 ..... 4½" .... (PFE) ....

338

HUM 471
Harmony In Four Parts (CE)
This figurine was first released in the U.S. market in 1989 along with seven other new figurines. This is the fourth figurine in the Century Collection and was produced for only this one year in the twentieth century. It was modeled by master sculptor Gerhard Skrobek in 1986. It has an incised 1987 copyright date. A circular inscription applied by blue decal reads: "M.I. HUMMEL CENTURY COLLECTION 1989 XX" and the name "HARMONY IN FOUR PARTS" along with the (TM6) trademark. The issue price was $850 in 1989.

☐ 471 . . . . . 9¾" . . . . (CE) . . ❻ . . . $1500–1750

HUM 472
On Our Way

This figurine was first released in the U.S. market in 1992 along with five other new figurines. This is the seventh figurine in the Century Collection and will be produced for this one year only in the twentieth century. It was modeled by master sculptor Gerhard Skrobek in 1986 but has an incised 1987 copyright date. A circular inscription applied by blue decal reads: "M.I. HUMMEL CENTURY COLLECTION 1992 XX" and the name "ON OUR WAY" along with the current (TM7) trademark. The issue price was $950 in the U.S.

☐ 472 ..... 8 to 8¼" ..... (OE) .. ❼ ... $950

HUM 473
Father Christmas (PFE)

This figurine was first modeled by master sculptor Gerhard Skrobek in 1986. Presently listed on factory records as a Possible Future Edition (PFE) and may be released at some future date, subject to possible minor changes.

☐ 473 ..... 6" .... (PFE) ....

HUM 474
Gentle Care (PFE)
This figurine was first modeled by master sculptor Gerhard Skrobek in 1986. Presently listed on factory records as a Possible Future Edition (PFE) and may be released at some future date, subject to possible minor changes.

☐ 474 ..... 6″ .... (PFE) ....

HUM 475
Make A Wish
First released in the U.S. market in 1989. This figurine was modeled by master sculptor Gerhard Skrobek in 1986. It has an incised 1987 copyright date. Original issue price was $135 in 1989.

☐ 475 ..... 4½″ .... (CE) .. ❻ ... $160–170
☐ 475 ..... 4½″ .... (OE) .. ❼ ... $160

HUM 476
Winter Song
First released in the U.S. market in 1988. Modeled by master sculptor Gerhard Skrobek in 1987. It has an incised 1987 copyright date. The original issue price was $45 in 1988.

☐ 476 ..... 4" .... (CE) .. ❻ ... $95–100
☐ 476 ..... 4" .... (**OE**) .. ❼ ... $95

HUM 477
A Budding Maestro
First released in the U.S. market in 1988. Modeled by master sculptor Gerhard Skrobek in 1987. It has an incised 1987 copyright date. The original issue price was $45 in 1988.

☐ 477 ..... 4" .... (CE) .. ❻ ... $90–95
☐ 477 ..... 4" .... (**OE**) .. ❼ ... $90

HUM 478
I'm Here
First released in the U.S. market in 1989. Modeled by master sculptor Gerhard Skrobek in 1987. It has an incised 1987 copyright date. The original issue price was $50 in 1989.

☐ 478 ..... 3" .... (CE) .. ❻ ... $85–90
☐ 478 ..... 3" .... (OE) .. ❼ ... $85

HUM 479
I Brought You A Gift
First released in the U.S. market in 1989 as a *free* gift for joining the M.I. HUMMEL CLUB (formerly Goebel Collectors' Club). Modeled by master sculptor Gerhard Skrobek in 1987. It has an incised 1987 copyright date. Early models have a special blue decal: "Goebel Collectors' Club" in addition to a black flying bumble bee, in a half circle. Later models have: "M.I. Hummel Club". Some examples have eye lashes, some do not.

☐ 479 ..... 4" .... (EE) .. ❻ ... $75–100
☐ 479 ..... 4" .... (EE) .. ❼ ... $75–100
(MIH Club Members Only)

343

HUM 480
Hosanna
First released in the U.S. market in 1989. Modeled by master sculptor Gerhard Skrobek in 1987. It has an incised 1987 copyright date. The original issue price was $68 in 1989.

☐ 480 ..... 4″ .... (CE) .. ❻ ... $80–85
☐ 480 ..... 4″ .... (**OE**) .. ❼ ... $80

HUM 481
Love From Above (CE)
First released in the U.S. market in 1989, the second in the annual series of ornaments. Modeled by master sculptor Gerhard Skrobek in 1987. It has an incised 1987 copyright date. The original issue price was $75 in 1989.

☐ 481 ..... 3¼″ .... (CE) .. ❻ ... $100–125

HUM 482
One For You, One For Me
First released in the U.S. market in 1989. Modeled by master sculptor Gerhard Skrobek in 1987. It has an incised 1987 copyright date. The original issue price was $50 in 1989.

☐ 482 ..... 3″ .... (CE) .. ❻ ... $85–90
☐ 482 ..... 3″ .... (OE) .. ❼ ... $85

HUM 483
I'll Protect Him
First released in the U.S. market in 1989. Modeled by master sculptor Gerhard Skrobek in 1987. It has an incised 1987 copyright date. The original issue price was $55 in 1989.

☐ 483 ..... 3¾″ .... (CE) .. ❻ ... $70–75
☐ 483 ..... 3¾″ .... (OE) .. ❼ ... $70

HUM 484
Peace On Earth (CE)
First released in the U.S. market in 1990, the third in the Annual Series of Ornaments. Modeled by master sculptor Gerhard Skrobek in 1987. It has an incised 1987 copyright date. The original issue price was $80.

☐ 484 ..... 3¼" .... (CE) .. ❻ ... $100–125

HUM 485
Gift From A Friend (EE)
This is the latest Exclusive Edition produced for members of the M.I. Hummel Club. It is for members only and will not be sold as an open edition to the general public. Modeled by master sculptor Gerhard Skrobek in 1988. It has an incised 1988 copyright date along with the current (TM 7) trademark. Also bears the inscription: "EXCLUSIVE EDITION 1991/ 92 M.I. HUMMEL CLUB" applied by blue decal. A large black flying bumble bee is located on the bottom. The official issue price is $160 in the U.S., in addition to the member's redemption card.

☐ 485 ..... 5" .... (EE) .. ❼ ... $160
(M.I.H. club members only)

HUM 486
I Wonder (CE)
This figurine was first introduced in 1990 for members of the M.I. Hummel Club only and not sold as an open edition. Modeled by master sculptor Helmut Fischer in 1988. It has an incised 1988 copyright date along with the (TM 6) trademark. Also bears the inscription: "EXCLUSIVE EDITION 1990/91 M.I. HUMMEL CLUB" applied by blue decal. A large black flying bumble bee is located on the bottom. The official issue price was $140 in the U.S., in addition to the member's redemption card.

☐ 486 ..... 5¼" .... (CE) .. ❻ ... $175–185
☐ 486 ..... 5¼" .... (CE) .. ❼ ... $160–175

HUM 487
Let's Tell The World (CE)
This figurine was first released in the U.S. market in 1990. This is the fifth figurine in the Century Collection and was produced for only this one year in the twentieth century. It was modeled by master sculptor Gerhard Skrobek in 1987. The original issue price was $875 in 1990.

☐ 487 ..... 10½ × 7" .... (CE) .. ❻ ... $1000–1200

HUM 493
Two Hands, One Treat (EE)
First released in the U.S. market in 1991 as a *free* gift for renewing membership in the M.I. HUMMEL CLUB for the 1991/92 Club year. Modeled by master sculptor Helmut Fischer in 1988. It has an incised 1988 copyright date, in addition to a special blue decal: "M.I. HUMMEL CLUB" along with a black flying bumble bee, in a half circle.

☐ 493 ..... 4″ .... (EE) .. ❼ ... $75–100
(M.I.H. club members only)

HUM 494   STILL UNDER DEVELOPMENT (ON)

HUM 495
Evening Prayer
First released in the U.S. market in the fall of 1991. Modeled by master sculptor Helmut Fischer in 1988. It has an incised 1988 copyright date. The original issue price was $95 in 1991.

☐ 495 ..... 3¾″ .... (OE) .. ❼ ... $95

HUM 496–499   STILL UNDER DEVELOPMENT (ON)

HUM 500
This number was assigned to a Mother's Day plate that was never issued.

HUM 501–508   DOLL HEADS

HUM 509–511   DOLL PARTS (ARMS & LEGS)

HUM 512–519   DANBURY MINT DOLL PARTS

HUM 520–529   STILL UNDER DEVELOPMENT (ON)
Listed as Open Numbers (ON) — an identification number, which in W. Goebel's numerical identification system, has not yet been used, but which may be used to identify new "M.I. Hummel" figurines as they are released in the future.

HUM 530
Land in Sight
First released in the U.S. market in the fall of 1991. Modeled by master sculptor Gerhard Skrobek in 1988. Issued as a limited production of 30,000 pieces, individually numbered, to commemorate the 500th anniversary of Columbus's discovery of America. The inscription reads: "1492-1992 – The Quincentennial of America's Discovery" applied by blue decal. It has an incised 1988 copyright date. The "M.I. Hummel" signature is located on the back side of the boat. The original issue price was $1600.

☐ 530 . . . . . 9″ × 9½″ . . . . . **(OE)** . . ❼ . . . $1600

HUM 531–533 STILL UNDER DEVELOPMENT (ON)

HUM 534
A Nap
First released in the U.S. market in 1991. Modeled by master sculptor Gerhard Skrobek in 1988. It has an incised 1988 copyright date. The original issue price was $95 in 1991.

☐ 534 ..... 2¼" .... (OE) .. ❼ ... $100

HUM 535–547 STILL UNDER DEVELOPMENT (ON)

HUM 548
Flower Girl (EE)
Announced in 1990, "Flower Girl" will be an EXCLUSIVE EDITION available to "M.I. Hummel Club" members only, who have belonged to the Club continuously for 5 years. Issued by means of a redemption card to those who are eligible. Modeled by master sculptor Helmut Fischer in 1989. It has an incised 1989 copyright date. The original issue price was $105.

☐ 548 ..... 4½" .... (EE) .. ❻ ... $125–150
☐ 548 ..... 4½" .... (EE) .. ❼ ... $115
(M.I.H. club members only)

HUM 553
Scamp
First released in the U.S. market in the fall of 1991. Modeled by master sculptor Helmut Fischer in 1989. It has an incised 1989 copyright date. The boy is the same as "Max" on HUM 123 "Max and Moritz". The original issue price was $95 in 1991.

☐ 553 . . . . . 3½" . . . . (OE) . . ❼ . . . $95

HUM 554   Cheeky Fellow – M.I.H. Club Exclusive Edition
HUM 555–560   STILL UNDER DEVELOPMENT (ON)

HUM 561
Grandma's Girl
First released in the U.S. market in the summer of 1990. Modeled by master sculptor Helmut Fischer in 1989. It has an incised 1989 copyright date. The girl is a smaller version of the same girl on HUM 383 "Going Home". The original issue price was $100 in 1990.

☐ 561 . . . . . 4" . . . . (CE) . . ❻ . . . $125–135
☐ 561 . . . . . 4" . . . . (OE) . . ❼ . . . $125

HUM 562
Grandpa's Boy
First released in the U.S. market in the summer of 1990. Modeled by master sculptor Helmut Fischer in 1989. It has an incised 1989 copyright date. The boy is a smaller version of the same boy on HUM 383 "Going Home". The original issue price was $100 in 1990.

☐ 562 ..... 4¼" .... (CE) .. ❻ ... $125–135
☐ 562 ..... 4¼" .... **(OE)** .. ❼ ... $125

HUM 563–570 STILL UNDER DEVELOPMENT (ON)

HUM 571
Angelic Guide (CE)
First released in the U.S. market in 1991, the fourth in the Annual Series of ornaments. Modeled by master sculptor Gerhard Skrobek in 1989. It has an incised 1989 copyright date. The original issue price was $95 in 1991.

☐ 571 ..... 4" .... (CE) .. ❻ ... $125–150
☐ 571 ..... 4" .... (CE) .. ❼ ... $100–125

HUM 572–574 STILL UNDER DEVELOPMENT (ON)

M.I. Hummel
ANGELS OF CHRISTMAS
ORNAMENT SERIES

First released in the U.S. market in 1990 and were sold exclusively by mail order through the Danbury Mint of Norwalk, Connecticut, at the rate of one every other month. Modeled by master sculptor Helmut Fischer in 1988. They have an incised "M.I. Hummel" signature and the Goebel (TM 6) trademark, but do *NOT* have an incised model number. The original issue price was $39.50 each (plus sales tax and $2.50 shipping and handling).

HUM 575

HUM 576

HUM 577

HUM 578

HUM 581

HUM 582

HUM 579

HUM 580

HUM 585

HUM 586

☐ 575 ..... 3″ .... **(OE)** .. **⑥** ... $42 (Plus tax)
☐ 576 ..... 3″ .... **(OE)** .. **⑥** ... $42 (Plus tax)
☐ 577 ..... 3″ .... **(OE)** .. **⑥** ... $42 (Plus tax)
☐ 578 ..... 3″ .... **(OE)** .. **⑥** ... $42 (Plus tax)
☐ 579 ..... 2½″ .... **(OE)** .. **⑥** ... $42 (Plus tax)
☐ 580 ..... 2½″ .... **(OE)** .. **⑥** ... $42 (Plus tax)
☐ 581 ..... 3″ .... **(OE)** .. **⑥** ... $42 (Plus tax)
☐ 582 ..... 3″ .... **(OE)** .. **⑥** ... $42 (Plus tax)
☐ 583 ..... OPEN NUMBER **(ON)**
☐ 584 ..... OPEN NUMBER **(ON)**
☐ 585 ..... 2½″ .... **(OE)** .. **⑥** ... $42 (Plus tax)
☐ 586 ..... 2½″ .... **(OE)** .. **⑥** ... $42 (Plus tax)

HUM 587–599 OPEN NUMBERS (ON)

HUM 600
We Wish You The Best (CE)
This figurine was first released in the U.S. market in 1991. This is sixth figurine in the Century Collection and was produced for only this one year in the twentieth century. Modeled by master sculptor Helmut Fischer in 1989. It has an incised 1989 copyright date. A circular inscription applied by blue decal reads: "M.I. HUMMEL CENTURY COLLECTION 1991 XX" and the name "We Wish You The Best" along the (TM 7) trademark. The original issue price was $1300 in 1991.

☐ 600 ..... 8¼″ × 9½″ ... (CE) .. ❻ ... $1400–1500
☐ 600 ..... 8¼″ × 9½″ ... (CE) .. ❼ ... $1300–1400

HUM 601–621   OPEN NUMBERS (ON)

HUM 622
Light Up The Night
First released in the U.S. market in 1992, the fifth in the Annual Series of Ornaments. Modeled by master sculptor Gerhard Skrobek in 1990. It has an incised 1990 copyright date. The original issue price was $95.

☐ 622 ..... 3¼″ × 9½″ ... (OE) .. ❼ ... $100

HUM 623–668   OPEN NUMBERS (ON)

M.I. Hummel
KITCHEN MOULD COLLECTION
First released in the U.S. market in 1991 and were sold exclusively by mail order through The Danbury Mint of Norwalk, Connecticut, at the rate of one every three months. They have an incised "M.I. Hummel" signature and the Goebel (TM 6 or TM 7) trademark, but do *NOT* have an incised model number. Modeled by master sculptor Helmut Fischer in 1989. The original issue price was $99 each (plus sales tax and $4.50 shipping and handling).

HUM 669

HUM 670

HUM 671

HUM 672

HUM 673

HUM 674

☐ 669 ..... 7½" .... **(OE)** .. ❼ ... $103.50 (Plus tax)
☐ 670 ..... 7½" .... **(OE)** .. ❻ ... $103.50 (Plus tax)
☐ 671 ..... 7½" .... **(OE)** .. ❻ ... $103.50 (Plus tax)
☐ 672 ..... 8" .... **(OE)** .. ❻ ... $103.50 (Plus tax)
☐ 673 ..... 8" .... **(OE)** .. ❼ ... $103.50 (Plus tax)
☐ 674 ..... 8" .... **(OE)** .. ❼ ... $103.50 (Plus tax)

HUM 675   OPEN NUMBER (ON)

HUM 676

HUM 677

HUM 676–677
Apple Tree Girl/Apple Tree Boy, Candle Stick Holders

First released in the U.S. market in 1989 and were sold exclusively by mail order through The Danbury Mint of Norwalk, Connecticut, at the rate of one every three months. Modeled by master sculptor Helmut Fischer in 1989. They have an incised 1988 copyright date. The original issue price was $142.50 each (plus sales tax and $3.00 shipping and handling).

☐ 676 ..... 6½" .... **(OE)** .. Ⓖ ... $145.50 (plus tax)
☐ 677 ..... 6½" .... **(OE)** .. Ⓖ ... $145.50 (plus tax)

HUM 678

HUM 679

HUM 678–679
She Loves Me, She Loves Me Not/Good Friends Candle Stick Holders

First released in the U.S. market in 1990 and were sold exclusively by mail order through The Danbury Mint of Norwalk, Connecticut, at the rate of one every three months. Modeled by master sculptor Helmut Fischer in 1989. They have an incised 1989 copyright date. The original issue price was $142.50 each (plus sales tax and $3.00 shipping and handling).

☐ 678 ..... 6½" .... **(OE)** .. Ⓖ ... $145.50 (plus tax)
☐ 679 ..... 6½" .... **(OE)** .. Ⓖ ... $145.50 (plus tax)

HUM 690
Smiling Through, Plaque (CE)
This round plaque was first issued in 1978 for members of the Goebel Collector's Club only and not sold as an Open Edition. Originally modeled by master sculptor Gerhard Skrobek from an original drawing by Sister M.I. Hummel. There is nothing incised on the back but the inscription "EXCLUSIVE SPECIAL EDITION No. 2 HUM 690 FOR MEMBERS OF THE GOEBEL COLLECTORS' CLUB" is applied by blue decal. Also has (TM 5) trademark and W. Germany 1978. No holes are provided for hanging. The original issue price was $50 in the U.S. and $55 in Canada, in addition to the member's redemption card. This plaque can be purchased on the secondary market at premium prices. This same motif of "Smiling Through" was made into a figurine and released in 1985 as "EXCLUSIVE SPECIAL EDITION No. 9" for members of the Goebel Collectors' Club. See HUM 408.

☐ 690 . . . . . 5¾" . . . . (CE) . . ❺ . . . $200–250

HUM 691–699   OPEN NUMBERS (ON)

HUM 700
Annual Bell 1978, Let's Sing (CE)
First edition in a series of annual bells. The motif of HUM 110 "Let's Sing" is in bas-relief on the front, and 1978 is embossed in red on the reverse side along with the "M.I. Hummel" signature. "HUM 700" is affixed by blue decal along with the (TM 5) trademark on the inside of the bell. The original issue price was $50 in 1978.

☐ 700 . . . . . 6" . . . . (CE) . . ❺ . . . $75–100

HUM 701
Annual Bell 1979, Farewell (CE)
Second edition in a series of annual bells. The motif of HUM 65 "Farewell" is in bas-relief on the front, and 1979 is embossed in red on the reverse side along with the "M.I. Hummel" signature. "HUM 701" is affixed by blue decal along with the (TM 5) trademark on the inside of bell. The original issue price was $70 in 1979.

☐ 701 ..... 6" .... (CE) .. ❺ ... $50–75

HUM 702
Annual Bell 1980, Thoughtful (CE)
Third edition in a series of annual bells. The motif of HUM 415 "Thoughtful" is in bas-relief on the front, and 1980 is embossed in red on the reverse side along with the "M.I. Hummel" signature. "HUM 702" is affixed by blue decal along with the (TM 6) trademark on the inside of bell. The original issue price was $85 in 1980.

☐ 702 ..... 6" .... (CE) .. ❻ ... $50–75

HUM 703
Annual Bell 1981, In Tune (CE)
Fourth edition of the annual bell series. The motif of HUM 414 "In Tune" is in bas-relief on the front, and 1981 is embossed in red on the reverse side along with the "M.I. Hummel" signature. "HUM 703" is affixed by blue decal along with the (TM 6) trademark on the inside of bell. The original issue price was $85 in 1981.

☐ 703 ..... 6" .... (CE) .. ❻ ... $75–100

HUM 704
Annual Bell 1982, She Loves Me (CE)
Fifth edition of the annual bell series. The motif of HUM 174 "She Loves Me, She Loves Me Not!" is in bas-relief on the front, and 1982 is embossed in red on the reverse side along with the "M.I. Hummel" signature. "HUM 704" is affixed by blue decal along with the (TM 6) trademark on the inside of bell. The original issue price was $85 in 1982.

☐ 704 ..... 6" .... (CE) .. ⊙ ... $100–125

HUM 705
Annual Bell 1983, Knit One (CE)
Sixth edition of the annual bell series. The motif of HUM 432 "Knit One, Purl Two" is in bas-relief on the front, and 1983 is embossed in red on the reverse side along with the "M.I. Hummel" signature. "HUM 705" is affixed by blue decal along with the (TM 6) trademark on the inside of bell. The original issue price was $90 in 1983.

☐ 705 ..... 6" .... (CE) .. ⊙ ... $100–125

HUM 706
Annual Bell 1984, Mountaineer (CE)
Seventh edition of the annual bell series. The motif of HUM 315 "Mountaineer" is in bas-relief on the front, and 1984 is embossed in red on the reverse side along with the "M.I. Hummel" signature. "HUM 706" is affixed by blue decal along with the (TM 6) trademark on the inside of bell. The original issue price was $90 in 1984.

☐ 706 ..... 6" .... (CE) .. ⊙ ... $100–125

HUM 707
Annual Bell 1985, Sweet Song (CE)
Eighth edition of the annual bell series.
The motif of HUM 389 "Girl with Sheet of
Music" is in bas-relief on the front, and
1985 is embossed in red on the reverse
side along with the "M.I. Hummel" signature. "HUM 707" is affixed by blue decal
along with the (TM 6) trademark on the
inside of bell. The original issue price
was $90 in 1985.

□ 707 ..... 6″ .... (CE) .. ❻ ... $100–125

HUM 708
Annual Bell 1986, Sing Along (CE)
Ninth edition of the annual bell series.
The motif of HUM 433 "Sing Along" was
released in 1987, is in bas-relief on the
front, and 1986 is embossed in red on the
reverse side along with the "M.I. Hummel" signature. "HUM 708" is affixed by
blue decal along with the (TM 6) trademark on the inside of bell. The original
issue price was $100 in 1986.

□ 708 ..... 6″ .... (CE) .. ❻ ... $150–200

HUM 709
**Annual Bell 1987, With Loving Greet-
ings (CE)**
Tenth edition of the annual bell series.
The motif of HUM 309 "With Loving
Greetings" is in bas-relief on the front,
and 1987 is embossed in red on the reverse side along with the "M.I. Hummel"
signature. "HUM 709" is affixed by blue
decal along with the (TM 6) trademark on
the inside of bell. The original issue price
was $110 in 1987.

□ 709 ..... 6″ .... (CE) .. ❻ ... $175–225

HUM 710
Annual Bell 1988, Busy Student (CE)
Eleventh edition of the annual bell series. The motif of HUM 367 "Busy Student" is in bas-relief on the front, and 1988 in red on the reverse side along with the "M.I. Hummel" signature. "HUM 710" is affixed by blue decal along with the (TM 6) trademark on the inside of bell. The original issue price was $120 in 1988.

☐ 710 ..... 6" .... (CE) .. ❻ ... $150–200

HUM 711
Annual Bell 1989, Latest News (CE)
Twelfth edition of the annual bell series. The motif of HUM 184 "Latest News" is in bas-relief on the front, and 1989 in red on the reverse side along with the "M.I. Hummel" signature. "HUM 711" is affixed by blue decal along with the (TM 6) trademark on the inside of bell. The original issue price was $135 in 1989.

☐ 711 ..... 6" .... (CE) .. ❻ ... $150–200

HUM 712
Annual Bell 1990, What's New? (CE)
Thirteenth edition of the annual bell series. The motif of HUM 418 "What's New?" is in bas-relief on the front, and 1990 in red on the reverse side along with the "M.I. Hummel" signature. "HUM 712" is affixed by blue decal along with the (TM 6) trademark on the inside of bell. The original issue price was $140 in 1990.

☐ 712 ..... 6" .... (CE) .. ❻ ... $150–200

HUM 713
Annual Bell 1991, Favorite Pet (CE)
Fourteenth edition of the annual bell series. The motif of HUM 361 "Favorite Pet" is in bas-relief on the front, and 1991 in red on the reverse side along with the "M.I. Hummel" signature. "HUM 713" is affixed by blue decal along with the (TM 7) trademark on the inside of the bell. The original issue price was $150 in 1991.

☐ 713 ..... 6" .... (CE) .. ❼ ... $150–200

HUM 714
Annual Bell 1992, Whistler's Duet
Fifteenth and *final* edition of the annual bell series. The motif of HUM 413 "Whistler's Duet" is in bas-relief on the front, and 1992 in red on the reverse side along with the "M.I. Hummel" signature. "HUM 714" is affixed by blue decal along with the (TM 7) trademark on the inside of the bell. The original issue price was $160 in 1992.

☐ 714 ..... 6" .... (OE) .. ❼ ... $165

HUM 730
Anniversary Bell 1985, Just Resting (CN)
This bell was designed by master sculptor Gerhard Skrobek in 1978 for release in 1985 but was NEVER ISSUED.

☐ 730 ..... 7⅛ × 4″ ..... (CN) .. ❻ ... $500–1000

HUM 731–734   OPEN NUMBERS

HUM 735 (1989)

HUM 736 (1988)

HUM 737 (1987)

HUM 738 (1986)

HUM 735–738
Celebration Plate Series (CE)

To celebrate the tenth anniversary of The Goebel Collectors' Club, a special series of four plates was issued for members of the Goebel Collectors' Club only. Each plate features a former club figurine in bas-relief. Issued one per year starting in 1986. Not sold as an Open Edition, but available with a redemption card only. The first edition in the series is "Valentine Gift" HUM 738. In the subsequent three years, the motif was "Valentine Joy" HUM 737, "Daisies Don't Tell" HUM 736 and "It's Cold" HUM 735. This series was designed by master sculptor Gerhard Skrobek in 1985. Each plate measures 6¼ inches in diameter, has the incised "M.I. Hummel" signature, and has the special inscription on the back: "EXCLUSIVELY FOR MEMBERS OF THE GOEBEL COLLECTORS' CLUB" affixed by blue decal.

☐ 735 ..... 6¼" .... (CE) .. ⑥ ... $120–130
☐ 736 ..... 6¼" .... (CE) .. ⑥ ... $120–130
☐ 737 ..... 6¼" .... (CE) .. ⑥ ... $120–130
☐ 738 ..... 6¼" .... (CE) .. ⑥ ... $120–130

HUM 739–740   OPEN NUMBERS

HUM 741 (1985)

HUM 742 (1987)

HUM 743 (1986)

HUM 744 (1984)

HUM 741–744
Little Music Maker Series (CE)

This series was first issued in 1984 as a four part bisque-porcelain "M.I. Hummel" miniature plate series called the "Little Music Makers." Each was a limited production plate which was produced for one year only. Modeled by master sculptor Gerhard Skrobek in 1982. A matching miniature figurine was released each year as an open edition to coincide with each plate. The original plate issue price was $30 in 1984, $30 in 1985, $35 in 1986 and $40 in 1987.

☐ 741 ..... 4" .... (CE) .. ❻ ... $75–100
☐ 742 ..... 4" .... (CE) .. ❻ ... $75–100
☐ 743 ..... 4" .... (CE) .. ❻ ... $75–100
☐ 744 ..... 4" .... (CE) .. ❻ ... $75–100

HUM 745 (1988)

HUM 746 (1989)

HUM 747 (1990)

HUM 748 (1991)

HUM 745–748
Little Homemakers (CE)

This series was first issued in 1988 as a four part bisque-porcelain "M.I. Hummel" miniature plate series called the "Little Homemakers." Each is a limited production plate being produced for one year only. Modeled by master sculptor Gerhard Skrobek in 1986. A matching figurine is released each year as an open edition to coincide with each plate. The original issue price was $45 in 1988, $50 in 1989, $50 in 1990, $70 in 1991.

☐ 745 ..... 4″ .... (CE) .. ❻ ... $80–90
☐ 746 ..... 4″ .... (CE) .. ❻ ... $80–90
☐ 747 ..... 4″ .... (CE) .. ❻ ... $80–90
☐ 748 ..... 4″ .... (CE) .. ❼ ... $80–90

HUM 749–774   OPEN NUMBERS

HUM 775

HUM 776

HUM 777

HUM 778

HUM 775–778
Christmas Bells

This series was first issued in 1989 as a four part bisque-porcelain bell series. Each is a limited production item being produced for one year only. Modeled by master sculptor Helmut Fischer in 1987–88. The original issue price was $35 in 1989, $37.50 in 1990, $39.50 in 1991 and $45 in 1992.

☐ 775 ..... 3¼″ .... (CE) .. ❻ ... $50–60
☐ 776 ..... 3¼″ .... (CE) .. ❻ ... $50–60
☐ 777 ..... 3¼″ .... (CE) .. ❼ ... $50–60
☐ 778 ..... 3¼″ .... (**OE**) .. ❼ ... $50

HUM 779–799   OPEN NUMBERS

369

International "M.I. Hummel" Figurines

The following eight "M.I. Hummel" figurines are the original "Hungarian" figurines discovered in 1976 by a man in Vienna, Austria. He had acquired them from a lady in Budapest, who had purchased them at the weekly flea market — one at a time, over a six-month period. He in turn sold them to (this author) collector Robert L. Miller, a supermarket owner in Eaton, Ohio, as a gift for his wife, Ruth.

"M.I. Hummel" figurines have always been typically German, with German-style dress or costumes, in 1940 the W. Goebel company decided to produced a line of "M.I. Hummel" figurines in the national dress of other countries. Sister M.I. Hummel made many sketches of children in their native costumes. Master modelers Rienhold Unger and Arthur Moeller then turned the sketches into the adorable figurines you see on the following pages. Due to the events of World War II,

production of the International Figurines series was not started. After the discovery in 1976 of the "Hungarian" figurines, a thorough search of the factory was conducted, including the checking and re-checking of old records. Twenty-four prototypes were found and are pictured here. Most of the people involved in the original project are no longer living; therefore the information contained here may not be absolutely accurate or complete. Since 1976, several duplicates of some models and new variations of others have been found, usually selling in the $10,000 to 15,000 price range, depending on condition. Several models have also been found *without* the "M.I. Hummel" signature; these would have much less value to most collectors. Author/collector Miller says, "I feel certain that there are still more rare finds to be made in the future, maybe even some Russian models! Happy Hunting!"

HUM 809   HUM 807   HUM 832   HUM 854

| HUM 904 | HUM 806 | HUM 841 | HUM 851 |

The following thirty International "M.I. Hummel" figurines are a combination of the Robert L. Miller Collection as well as the Goebel Archives Collection.

HUM 806 Bulgarian A. Moeller, 1940   *HUM 807 Bulgarian A. Moeller, 1940*   *HUM 808 Bulgarian A. Moeller, 1940*

HUM 809 Bulgarian A. Moeller, 1940   *HUM 810 Bulgarian R. Unger, 1940*   *HUM 810 Bulgarian R. Unger, 1940*

HUM 811 Bulgarian R. Unger 1940   *HUM 812 Serbian R. Unger, 1940*   *HUM 812 Serbian R. Unger, 1940*

HUM 813 Serbian R. Unger, 1940   *HUM 824 Swedish A. Moeller, 1940*   *HUM 824 Swedish A. Moeller, 1940*

HUM 825 Swedish A. Moeller, 1940   *HUM 825 Swedish A. Moeller, 1940*   *HUM 831 Slovak R. Unger, 1940*

HUM 832 Slovak R. Unger, 1940   *HUM 833 Slovak R. Unger, 1940*   *HUM 841 Czech R. Unger, 1940*

HUM 842 Czech R. Unger, 1940   *HUM 842 Czech R. Unger, 1940*   *HUM 851 Hungarian A. Moeller, 1940*

HUM 852 Hungarian A. Moeller, 1940

HUM 852 Hungarian A. Moeller, 1940

HUM 853 Hungarian A. Moeller, 1940

HUM 853 Hungarian A. Moeller, 1940

HUM 854 Hungarian A. Moeller, 1940

HUM 904   Serbian   R. Unger, 1940

HUM 913   Serbian   R. Unger, 1940

HUM 947 Serbian A. Moeller, 1940

HUM 968   Serbian   R. Unger, 1940

374

Other Hummel Related Items

Unnumbered
"M.I. Hummel" Figurine
"Madonna With Wings"

This very rare, unusual, signed "M.I. Hummel" figurine is truly a collector's item. Found several years ago in Munich, Germany, this beautiful "Madonna with Wings" figurine had been in the possession of a German family for many years, but they could not remember its background or from where it came. The figurine is not numbered nor does it have a trademark — only an incised "X" on the bottom, in addition to the "M.I. Hummel" signature on the back. Research reveals that this piece was in all probability modeled by master sculptor Reinhold Unger in the late 1930's or early 1940's. For some unknown reason it was not approved for production by the Siessen Convent or possibly by Sister Hummel herself. This piece, however, is found pictured in an old 1950 Goebel catalogue listed has "Mel 08" and priced at 11 DM. It is not known whether it was actually produced and marketed at that time. If they were produced, they would not have the "M.I. Hummel" signature. It is the signature that makes this figurine unique, rare and fascinating.

Bust of Sister M.I. Hummel

HU 1

This white bisque bust in the likeness of Sister Maria Innocentia Hummel was created by master sculptor Gerhard Skrobek in 1965. It was originally used as a display piece for showrooms or dealer displays featuring Hummel items. It has the signature of "Skrobek 1965" in addition to "HU1" incised on the back. In recent years it has become a collector's item and is sought after by many avid "M.I. Hummel" lovers. They were originally given to dealers at no cost; but we did, however, purchase two of these large busts in the early 1970's from a store in New York at a cost of $30 each. A smaller version of the same bust with the "M.I. Hummel" signature incised on the front of the base was put on the market in 1967 with the in-

cised number "HU2" and the 4 trademark. These originally sold for $6 each. This same small-size bust was again put on the market in 1977 for a brief time, retailing for $15 to $17 each, but has once again been discontinued from current production. A third variation of the Sister Hummel bust was issued in 1979 as: "EXCLUSIVE SPECIAL EDITION No. 3 FOR MEMBERS OF THE GOEBEL COLLECTORS' CLUB" only. This piece has an incised "HU 3" as well as 1978 incised copyright date on the bottom. It is in full color with the "M.I. Hummel" signature painted in white on the front. While these busts are not officially classified as true Hummel figurines, they do make a nice addition to any Hummel collection.

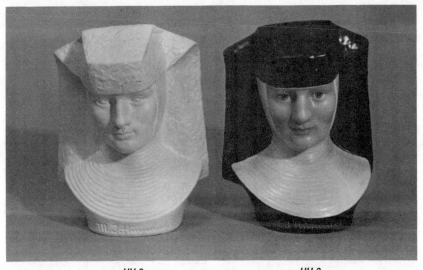

	HU 2		HU 3

☐ HU1 .... 13" .... (CE) .. ❹ ... $2000–2500
☐ HU2 .... 5½" .... (CE) .. ❹ ... $125–150
☐ HU2 .... 5½" .... (CE) .. ❺ ... $100–125
☐ HU3 .... 5½" .... (CE) .. ❺ ... $250–300

Factory Workers Plate

This anniversary plate was produced by the W. Goebel Company, by and for the workers at the factory where the Goebel annual plates are manufactured. Probably as few as 100 were produced and were not made available to the general public. The "M.I. Hummel" signature is on each of the ten individual plates.

☐ Factory Workers Plate .... $1500–2000 (uncolored)
☐ Factory Workers Plate .... $2000–2500 (colored variation)

Goebel Camels:
Traditionally Used With "M.I. Hummel" Nativity Sets

These three Goebel camels were designed to be used with the "M.I. Hummel" Nativity Sets, either HUM 214 or HUM 260. The standing camel HX306/0 has an incised 1960 copyright date and has been on the market since the early 1960's. The kneeling camel (Dromedary) and the lying camel (Bactrian) were both released in 1980 for the first time. All three have been produced both in full color and white overglaze (unpainted) finishes. All models are in current production and are usually found wherever the "M.I. Hummel" figurines are sold. Currently being produced in color only. In 1991 three smaller versions of the same camels were added to the line to go with the new smaller size nativity sets, HUM 214/0.

☐ HX 306/0	. . . . . 8½"	. . . . . **(OE)**	. . . . Standing	. . . . . (color)	. . . .	$190
☐ HX 306/0	. . . . . 8½"	. . . . . **(TW)**	. . . . Standing	. . . . . (white)	. . .	$200–250
☐ 46 820–12	. . . . 5½"	. . . . . **(OE)**	. . . . Kneeling	. . . . . (color)	. . . .	$190
☐ 46 820–12	. . . . 5½"	. . . . . **(TW)**	. . . . Kneeling	. . . . . (white)	. . .	$200–250
☐ 46 821–11	. . . . 4½"	. . . . . **(OE)**	. . . . Lying	. . . . (color)	. . . .	$190
☐ 46 821–11	. . . . 4½"	. . . . . **(TW)**	. . . . Lying	. . . . (white)	. . .	$200–250
☐ 46 837	. . . . . . 6½"	. . . . . **(OE)**	. . . . Standing	. . . . . (color)	. . . .	$145
☐ 46 838	. . . . 4"	. . . . . **(OE)**	. . . . Kneeling	. . . . . (color)	. . . .	$145
☐ 46 839–09	. . . . 3¼"	. . . . . **(OE)**	. . . . Lying	. . . . (color)	. . . .	$145

WOODEN DEALER PLAQUE

☐ Wooden Dealer Plaque . . . . . 33″ × 22½″ × 2½″ $5,000–10,000

These large wooden dealer plaques were made by a woodworking shop in the Goebel factory area of Rödental, West Germany in the mid 1950's. According to factory records, about 100 plaques were made and given to good customers for display purposes. They were hand decorated with artist's oil paints by Messrs. Gunther Neubauer and Harald Sommer. The plaques weigh approximately twenty pounds and measure 33 inches long by 22½ inches high. They vary in thickness from ⅞ inch to 2½ inches at the thickest part. Most of plaques have been found in Germany, but many years ago we purchased one in the Boston area. There is no Goebel trademark, only a large "A" within a circle and a bolt of lightning running through the "A" incised on the back.

International "M.I. Hummel" Festival Commemorative Bisque Plaques

These white bisque plaques are produced by W. Goebel Porzellanfabrik, Roedental, West Germany, and have been designed by master modeler Gerhard Skrobek. Each plaque is designed in bas-relief and includes the familiar "M.I. Hummel" signature. The back commemorates the date and location of each Festival. Not only is Eaton, Ohio, the site for an annual gathering of "M.I. Hummel" enthusiasts, but the community serves as the official Sister City to Roedental, West Germany. The community of Eaton, Ohio, feels highly honored to serve as a Sister City with the home of the W. Goebel Porzellanfabrik and has enjoyed hosting visitors from Roedental and Goebel on several occasions. Many "M.I. Hummel" collectors have enjoyed collecting sets of these special commemorative bisque plaques. The W. Goebel Porzellanfabrik has stated that they will no longer be able to produce these commemorative bisque plaques. Therefore, these items should become highly collectible due to their unavailability.

☐ 1979 .... 3″ ... (CE) ... $25–30
☐ 1980 .... 3″ ... (CE) ... $20–25
☐ 1981 .... 3″ ... (CE) ... $15–20
☐ 1982 .... 3″ ... (CE) ... $15–20
☐ 1986 .... 3½″ .. (CE) ... $15–20

The "Mel" Signature Hum"mel"

A collector will occasionally happen on to a "Hummel"-like figurine that does not have the usual "M.I. Hummel" signature on it. The figurine will have all of the general appearances of an older genuine "M.I. Hummel" figurine, including the Goebel factory trademark, in addition to the letters "Mel" (the last part of "Hummel") incised on it.

To the best of my knowledge, these items have been designed from original drawings by Sister M.I. Hummel, but for some undetermined reasons were not approved by the Siessen Convent for inclusion in the "M.I. Hummel" line of figurines.

Notice the photo of the "Child in Bed" candy dish. Goebel master sculptor Arthur Moeller modeled this piece in 1945. Since it did not win convent approval, it was later marketed with "Mel 6" incised on the bottom of it. Several other "Mel" items have appeared through the years. The most common of these are the Mel 1, Mel 2 and Mel 3 candlestick holders, modeled by former master sculptor Reinhold Unger in 1939. In the mid-1950's, these items were remodeled by master sculptor Gerhard Skrobek and assigned the model numbers Hum 115 "Girl with Nosegay," Hum 116 "Girl with Fir Tree" and Hum 117 "Boy with Horse" candlesticks with the "M.I. Hummel" signature.

Also modeled by master sculptor Arthur Moeller were Mel 4 "Box with Boy on Top" in 1942, Mel 5 "Box with Girl on Top" in 1942, Mel 6 "Box with Child in Bed on Top" in 1945 and Mel 7 "Box with Sitting Child on Top" in 1946. All "Mel" items were discontinued in 1962, according to Goebel factory information.

Apparently, the "Mel" designation must have been a "catch-all" label intended as a way of marketing these rejected items. I am of the opinion, however, that it was also used to designate *experimental* items. In our years of research, we have accidentally "stumbled" on two other figurine models with the "Mel" label. Both of them were "International" designs. How many more "Mel" designs will show up in the future is anyone's guess.

Mel 6

Mel 7

Copies from Around the World

I
t has been said that one of the most sincere compliments that can be given to an artist is to have his work copied. I think this holds true when it comes to the "M.I. Hummel" figurines. W. Goebel Porzellanfabrik of Roedental, West Germany, has had the exclusive right to produce Hummel figurines, based upon the artwork of Sister Maria Innocentia Hummel, since 1935. The figurines have become so popular over the years that many countries around the world have tried to copy these designs. Korea, Taiwan, Japan, Germany, England and even the United States have all made copies. Most of these are quite inferior in quality when compared to the originals made by Goebel. But a few of the copies are better than others—namely, the Japanese and the English—and we've chosen to show you some of these better copies.

The Japanese have probably succeeded in making the best copies, with the English running a close second. The Japanese finish and colors are more like the originals and sometimes, at first glance, they may fool even an experienced collector. The Japanese have copied the designs but, to my knowledge, have never gone so far as to copy the familiar "M.I. Hummel" signature. On the other hand the English finish is quite shiny and they did copy the signature on their early production models. The English figurines were made by "Beswick" during the war years of 1940 and 1941.

It is, of course, most unethical, if not always illegal, to make copies of Hummel figurines. The question of copies, look-alikes, fakes and their legality is a lengthy and complicated subject and it is not our intention here to delve into that issue. We want only to show readers a few of the better examples of copies that have been done, so as to show how closely they may resemble the originals.

Top photo: HUM 97 (far left) beside English copy #903; HUM 5 (far right) beside English copy #906. Middle photo at left, HUM 71 (far left) with English copy #908; photo at right, HUM 184 (far right) with Japanese copy. HUM 201 with Japanese copy at left.

Copies from Around the World

M.I. Hummel" figurines have been around for over 50 years now. Copies of these world-famous collectibles have been on the market almost as long. To many collectors the copies have nearly as much appeal as the originals.

An interesting item we recently acquired for our collection was this metal figurine mounted on a marble base. The figurine pictured here was made in the early 1940's by the Herbert Dubler Co. of New York City. The Dubler figurines were normally made of plaster of Paris and carried the "B. Hummel" signature rather than the "M.I. Hummel" signature used by the German Firm of W. Goebel Porzellanfabrik. (The Goebel firm has been granted the exclusive rights to produce "M.I. Hummel" figurines by the Siessen Convent.) These Dubler figurines were rather crudely made and being of plaster of Paris, did not hold up well over the years.

Some collectors refer to the Dubler

figurines as fake Hummels, but I prefer to call them war-time Hummel figurines and feel that they should be considered part of the history of Hummel art. It is my feeling that all Hummel collections should include an example of this type of figurine if only for the sake of conversation.

This figurine being made of metal (silver) has survived the years in excellent condition. As you can see, it is a copy of Hum 171 "Little Sweeper." We continue to call this piece by the name of "Little Genevieve" in honor of the lady, now residing Florida, from whom we purchased it.

Just how many of the Dubler figurines were cast in metal is unknown, however, we do also have a pair of metal bookends with the same "Little Sweeper" design. There has been increasing interest in the Dubler figurines and prices recently have ranged from about $10 to as much as $500. Remember, prices for this type item still depend upon a "willing buyer-willing seller" arrangement.

"M.I. Hummel"
FOUR SEASONS MUSIC BOX SERIES

1987 Winter

1988 Spring

1989 Summer

1990 Fall

This series of four limited edition music boxes was first released in 1987, then one each succeeding year. Called the "Four Season Music Box" series with a world wide limited production of 10,000 pieces individually numbered. Originally sculpted by master sculptor Gerhard Skrobek and chief master sample painter Gunther Neubauer, who created the model, which was then carried out in the wood-carving by Anri of Italy. Inside the box is a goldplated 36-note Swiss movement by Reuge. Each piece carries the M.I. Hummel signature carved in wood on the top.

		Issue Price		
☐ 1987	Ride into Christmas	$390	(CE)	$600–750
☐ 1988	Chick Girl	$400	(CE)	$500–600
☐ 1989	In Tune	$425	(CE)	$550–650
☐ 1990	Umbrella Girl	$450	(CE)	$500–600

ARS AG — CHRISTMAS PLATES
1987–1990

Celestial Musician

Angel Duet

Guiding Light

Tender Watch

This series was first issued in 1987 as a four part, decal produced, Christmas plate. Each plate was limited to 20,000 consecutively numbered pieces. Produced in the Goebel factory depicting original drawings of Sister M.I. Hummel under license of ARS AG, Switzerland, owner of the copyrights of the original paintings.

☐ 1987 .... 7½" .... (CE) .. ⑥ ... $60–75
☐ 1988 .... 7½" .... (CE) .. ⑥ ... $50–60
☐ 1989 .... 7½" .... (CE) .. ⑥ ... $50–60
☐ 1990 .... 7½" .... (CE) .. ⑥ ... $50–60

"M.I. Hummel" Calendars/Kalenders

M.I. Hummel Kalenders (German) were first published by Goebel in 1951 in the German version only. Each kalender contained thirteen color photographs of M.I. Hummel figurines with varying backgrounds. The first English version calendar was published for the 1954 year using the same photographs that were used in the 1953 German version. This continued on with few exceptions, (note 1964 German/1965 English and 1975 German/1976 English) until the 1988/1989 years when the size, style and format were drastically changed. These older Calendar/Kalenders are now highly collectible and bring from $50 to $2,000 on the secondary market.

HUMMEL-KALENDER 1951

HUMMEL-KALENDER 1952

1953 German

1954 English

1954 German

1955 English

1955 German

1956 English

1956 German

1957 English

1957 German

1958 English

1958 German

1959 English

1959 German

1960 English

1960 German

1961 English

1961 German

1962 English

1962 German

1963 English

1963 German

1964 English

1964 German

1965 English

1965 German

1966 English

1966 German

1967 English

1967 German

1968 English

1968 German

1969 English

1969 German

1970 English

1970 German

1971 English

1971 German

1972 English

1972 German

1973 English

1973 German

1974 English

1974 German

1975 English

1975 German

1976 English

1976 German

1977 English

1977 German

1978 English

1978 German

1979 English

1979 German

1980 English

393

1980 German

1981 English

1981 German

1982 English

1982 German

1983 English

1983 German

1984 English

1984 German

1985 English

1985 German

1986 English

1986 German

1987 English

1988 English

1989 English

GOEBEL
CRYSTAL "M.I. HUMMEL" FIGURINES

First released in Europe as a test market item early in 1991 and then in the U.S. market in the summer of 1991. These twelve models, rendered in 24% lead crystal with a silky matte finish, are replicas of the original ceramic "M.I. Hummel" figurines. They have an incised "M.I. Hummel" signature and the Goebel (TM 6) trademark with a 1990 date. They do not have an incised model number. The motifs currently available in this new three-dimensional form are:

Apple Tree Girl	3¾"	(OE)	❻	$59
Botanist	3⅛"	(OE)	❻	$59
Visiting An Invalid	3¾"	(OE)	❻	$59
Meditation	3½"	(OE)	❻	$59
Merry Wanderer	3½"	(OE)	❻	$59
Postman	3⅞"	(OE)	❻	$59
Soloist	3"	(OE)	❻	$39
Little Sweeper	2⅞"	(OE)	❻	$39
Village Boy	3"	(OE)	❻	$39
For Mother	2⅞"	(OE)	❻	$39
Sister	2⅞"	(OE)	❻	$39
March Winds	2⅞"	(OE)	❻	$39

M.I. HUMMEL POSTCARDS

I n recent years, M.I. Hummel Postcards have been rediscovered by Hummel collectors. The M.I. Hummel postcards are authentic reproductions of the original artwork of Sister M.I. Hummel. The first M.I. Hummel postcards were printed in October, 1933 in Munich, Germany by the ARS SACRA firm. In fact, it was these printed cards that Franz Goebel noticed in a German store that prompted the eventual production of the three dimensional M.I. Hummel figurines by the Goebel Porzellanfabrik.

Today most of the printed M.I. Hummel postcards are produced by Ars Edition of Munich and are licensed by ARS AG of Zug, Switzerland. In July of 1990, Miller's Gift Gallery of Eaton, Ohio entered into a contract with Ars Edition, Gmbh of Munich for sole, exclusive distribution of M.I. Hummel postcards in the United States. These collectible M.I. Hummel postcards are sold by Schmid and can be found at your authorized M.I. Hummel retail locations throughout the United States.

The current retail price for the Hummel postcards is $1.25. Many of the older cards have been selling at collector events for prices ranging from $2.00 to $25.00.

Collectors of M.I. Hummel postcards owe a debt of gratitude to Marion J. Sansalone of Dearborn, Michigan for compiling an informative and thorough reference manual on M.I. Hummel postcards. Mrs. Sansalone has spoken to many collector groups about the joy of collecting the M.I. Hummel art in the form of postcards.

A RARE VARIATION
YOU BE THE JUDGE!
UNSIGNED "M.I. HUMMEL" FIGURINE

Signed "Ugr"

Old Postcard Drawing

This figurine was recently located in the City of Coburg, Germany, approximately five miles from Rödental where the Goebel factory is located. It does *not* have the usual "M.I. Hummel" signature nor the Goebel trademark. The only markings is the incised "Ugr." on the bottom, which undoubtedly stands for Reinhold Unger, one of the first Goebel master sculptors to translate Sister M.I. Hummel's artwork into three dimentional form. Unger also created "Stormy Weather" based upon another Hummel drawing. This figurine, based upon the drawing of "Sunny Days", apparently was rejected by the sisters at Siessen Convent. It is now part of the Robert L. Miller collection.

A RARE VARIATION

Rare Variation HUM 203

Old Postcard Drawing

As I have always said, you can never tell when or where a *rare* "M.I. Hummel" figurine will turn up. This is a good example. This rare prototype (four post version) of HUM 203 "Signs of Spring" was recently found in Arizona. Sold by a retired military man who had served in Europe during WW II. He was stationed close to the area of Germany where the Goebel factory was located — that a young German girl would visit the Army quarters each week and would sell "M.I. Hummel" figurines as souvenirs. He had purchased a number of figurines and had kept them all through the years until recently, when he decided to dispose of some of his old items. He sold 39 figurines to a local antique shop. An alert "Hummel" dealer spotted them and purchased all 39 items. Noticing the difference between this old "Signs of Spring" and the current model, he gave me a call for my opinion. I stated that I had never seen or heard of a major variation of this figurine and requested a photograph for comparison. After receiving the photos and several phone calls later, this rare prototype "Signs of Spring" is now part of the Robert L. Miller collection. I would be remiss if I did not commend the alert dealer, Ron Brixey for his professional, business-like and ethical handling of the sale of this figurine.

RARE/UNIQUE SAMPLE VERSION OF HUM 13/0 "MEDITATION" IS FOUND

HUM 13/0 with attached pot

HUM 17/0 with attached pot

Pictured here for the first time is a rare early sample piece recently found in Germany. This version of HUM 13/0 "Meditation" with attached pot previously was neither known to exist nor had it been recorded on any known records.

Webster's definitions—RARE: marked by unusual quality, merit, or appeal. Distinctive, superlative or extreme of its kind, seldom occuring or found, uncommon. UNIQUE: being the only one, sole, being without a like or equal. I truly believe this example fits Webster's definitions of both rare and unique at this point in time.

The only *similar* piece known to exist is a rare early sample piece of HUM 17/0 "Congratulations" with the same exact pot attached. At this point in time, this piece also fits Webster's definitions of both rare and unique.

For some unknown reason, the sisters at Siessen Convent, who must approve for production all figurines based upon Sister M.I. Hummel's artwork, did not approve these two versions. Possibly they felt it would lessen the value of the original artwork when using it in a utilitarian item. This is only speculation on my part because they did approve useful items such as ashtrays, candy bowls, lamp bases, book ends, candleholders and wall vases. Possibly only a whim, impulse, or passing fancy prevented these unique pieces from being produced and sold on the open market.

Whatever the reason, I, for one, am extremely pleased that these two pieces are in our collection!

Rare? Or Not So Rare?

HUM 77
Holy Water Font, Cross With Doves

HUM 77 "Cross With Doves" Holy Water Font was modeled by the late master sculptor Reinhold Unger (1880-1974) in 1937, but was made as samples only and never put into production. It is listed on factory records as a closed edition (CE) on 21 October 1937.

The photograph accompanying this story was taken in 1978 at the Goebel factory archives. It was the only piece then known to be in existence.

In 1979 we were informed by a lady in California that she had purchased the second known example of this font at an estate sale for a very nominal price. Since the original owner is now deceased, we were unable to confirm when, where, or under what conditions she had acquired it.

The new owner would be willing to sell her font for $20,000! A situation such as this presents a dilemma for the avid collector. Do you pay the price or wait and see if more examples turn up? I offered her $10,000 for it at that time — I am now happy to say that she turned me down!

Several years ago two more examples of HUM 77 turned up in the Chicago area. One was unpainted in white overglaze, and the other was fully painted. They were both purchased by an avid collector in the Kansas City area.

This past summer I received a phone call from a young lady in California. She, too, possessed an example of this rare HUM 77 Holy Water Font! She had received hers as a gift from a relative living in Minnesota who had purchased it at a garage sale for a few dollars. This young lady was a collector of M.I. Hummel figurines, but did not want to keep such a rare item in her collection and decided to sell it to us. We greatly appreciated her feelings and thanked her for allowing us to add it to our collection!

A few weeks ago we had another phone call from "Grace" (no last name), who lives on the East Coast. She informed us that she had recently inherited a small collection of M.I. Hummel figurines from a now deceased relative. She has two HUM 77 Holy Water Fonts! According to her account, the relative had been a priest in the U.S. Army stationed in the Goebel factory area. He had become acquainted with Mr. Franz Goebel, owner of the Goebel factory at that time. Apparently they became good friends, and Mr. Goebel would give him boxes of figurines as gifts! Franz Goebel was a very generous man, as I have heard many such stories about his giving away figurines (then of very nominal value, but now very valuable collector's items).

I have also been told of a former Goebel factory figurine painter living in the Munich, Germany, area who also claims to have an example of the HUM 77 Holy Water Font. As of this date that totals eight which are known to exist! Where, when, or how many more will turn up is anybody's guess! Personally I believe that more will surface as time goes on.

Now my dilemma is: When does RARE cease to be rare, and when should an item be classified as SCARCE? (Webster: SCARCE–infrequently seen or found, not plentiful or abundant; RARE–marked by unusual quality, merit, or appeal; distinctive–superlative, seldom occurring or found.) These definitions are for my wife's benefit, as she often takes issue with my use of these terms!

The Final Word: Ruth says regardless of what anyone else thinks, the HUM 77 Holy Water Font is still RARE!!!!

ERROR IN ASSEMBLY
CREATES NEW VARIATION

Left: A correctly assembled HUM 65 "Farewell." **Right:** An example of an error in the assembly of an HUM 65. Note the position of the basket and the arm.

Q. I recently purchased the Hummel figurine called "Farewell" from my local dealer. After I took it home and looked at it more closely, I discovered that part of the basket was missing. When I returned it to the dealer, the other two he had were the same way. Is this something new? If so, why? Or is it a mistake? I would appreciate your opinion.

Thank you for your comments.

—F. L., Dayton, Ohio.

A. After receiving your letter, I examined many different examples of HUM 65 "Farewell" in our personal collection, as well as several currently produced pieces here in the shop. We have three pieces just like the one you described in your letter. This is definitely an error and was not intended to be that way!

An authentic "M.I. Hummel" figurine is constructed of several different moldings of various parts. "Farewell" probably has at least six or seven different parts that are assembled while the clay is still soft.

It is obvious to me that in this assembly process, the edge of the basket was placed too low and the girl's arm was raised too high. Her arm should be touching the edge of the basket (note the accompanying photo).

This error has been reported to the factory in Germany and the necesary steps have been taken to correct this error. Personally, I intend to keep the one example we have in our collection; I consider it to be a new variation of "Farewell." This missing handle variation is quite interesting and now commands a premium price among avid "Hummel" figurine collectors!

You are to be commended for your keen observation, and I do thank you for your question.

Readers who would like their questions on Hummels answered may write to:

> Robert L. Miller
> 112 Woodland Drive
> Eaton, Ohio 45320

"FOREST SHRINE": HUM 183 AUTHENTIC OR FAKE?

"Forest Shrine" HUM 183 Japanese imitation marked
SH477

A number of years ago I was approached by a person who believed he owned the "M.I. Hummel" figurine of "Forest Shrine" HUM 183 with the reclining deer facing in the opposite direction from the normal version. He also claimed that it had an incised "crown" trademark and "M.I. Hummel" signature.

I informed him that this might be possible since the figurines were made in several separate moldings and then assembled while the clay was still soft. However, I also felt that it was very unlikely.

Eventually I had the opportunity to see this unusual figurine and was able to conclude that it actually was a Japanese copy of "Forest Shrine." Someone had taken a sharp instrument and crudely scratched the signature and "crown" trademark on this figurine. It was a fake!

Recently I located one of these Japanese copies for our collection. Of course, it did not have the "M.I. Hummel" signature; only the number SH477 was on the bottom. Also pictured is Sister Maria's original drawing upon which both of these pieces were based. Note the position of the reclining deer.

This information is shared with readers to point out how unscrupulous some individuals can be. The old adage of "let the buyer beware" should be kept in mind. When purchasing a figurine that seems too good to be true — it probably isn't!

"HUMMEL-HUMMEL"

"HUMMEL-HUMMEL"

"MORS-MORS"

We regularly receive many letters and phone calls regarding HUMMEL-HUMMEL. This figurine actually has no connection at all with the "M.I. Hummel" figurines made by W. Goebel Porzellanfabrik of Roedental, Germany. A very good German friend of ours, who now lives in Kansas City, Missouri, gave us a copy of this story many years ago when we had asked him about HUMMEL-HUMMEL.

THE HUMMEL-HUMMEL
STORY

"About 100 years ago, there lived in the German city of Hamburg a man by the name of Hummel. Since Hamburg, like a lot of cities along the German coast, did not have good drinking water and very few wells with pure water, Mr. Hummel made a living by catering water to the well-to-do citizens of that town.

"He was a gruff, gaunt looking character, dressed in a soot-black suit and wearing a stove-pipe hat. With the two wooden buckets hanging from the yoke across his shoulders, he was one of the most familiar sights in Hamburg at that time. People, especially children, used to taunt him by hollering 'Hummel-Hummel' when they passed him; his short retort always was 'Mors-Mors' (kiss my fanny).

"Over the years this has become a sort of greeting for Hambug citizens wherever they meet in the world. It is their good-natured way of saying 'Hello' and striking up new friendships. The man with the water buckets and the 'HUMMEL-HUMMEL' has become the symbol of the city of Hamburg, and the likeness of this man can be found in various shapes and materials in the shops of Hamburg."

The city of Hamburg has even erected a large granite statue as a monument of "Old Mister Hummel" to help perpetuate this legend.

The photographs illustrating this page are of a figurine that was actually produced by the Goebel company and is sold in the shops of Hamburg.

RARE FIGURINE
FOUND IN NEW YORK

HUM 339 Behave! (PFE)

The original drawing by Sister Maria Innocentia for the figurine "Behave!"

A recent addition to our personal collection is this "M.I. Hummel" figurine "Behave!" (HUM 339). A very astute collector happened to be visiting in a home and saw this figurine, along with a few others, sitting on a shelf.

The collector was familiar enough to know that it was unusual and purchased the group of figurines from the owner. She then contacted a friend who in turn contacted me for information as to the rarity, value, etc. My wife and I eventually purchased this particular piece for our collection.

It is believed that this group of "M. I. Hummel" figurines was on display at the New York World's Fair in 1964. After the fair was over, apparently they were given, sold or otherwise taken home by someone as a souvenir of the fair.

The figurine is a PFE, Possible Future Edition. This means that so far it has never been sold as an open edition nor has it been officially put on the market or made available for collectors.

The figurine was modeled by Goebel master sculptor Helmut Wehlte in 1956 and was originally called "Walking Her Dog." It is based on Sister Maria Innocentia's drawing which is owned by Ars Ag, Zug, Switzerland, who published the drawing in the form of a postcard, No. 14303.

We are very grateful to the collector who informed us of this rare find and handled the transaction for us. One never knows when or where an unusual piece such as this will be found! The thrill of collecting is exemplified by this example.

BACKS ARE INTERESTING, TOO!

HUM 214E: incised signature on the left and painted signature on the right.

HUM 193: new style with arm at waist (left) and old style with arm on shoulder.

It is always interesting, and informative as well as rewarding to look at the back side of your M.I. Hummel figurines. You never know what you might learn through careful examination.

Several years ago, while we were unpacking a shipment of figurines, I happened to look at the figurine called "We Congratulate" (HUM 214E). I noticed that it has a clear, incised Hummel signature—but only HUMMEL, not M.I. HUMMEL. I immediately looked at another "We Congratulate" and to my surprise, instead of an incised signature, it was painted or stamped on with green paint! Both figurines have the TM 6 trademark and "81" date along with the incised signature on the left and the painted signature on the right.

Another fascinating rear view is "Angel Duet" candleholder (HUM 193). The older models have one angel's hand on the other angel's shoulder, while the newer version has the arm around the waist. This figurine was originally modeled by former master sculptor Reinhold Unger in 1948 and later restyled by sculptor Theo R. Mensenbach in 1958. Menzenbach stated that it was restyled because the new position looks more natural and is easier for the artist to paint. I am sure that you will enjoy your Hummel collection even more if you learn to watch for these interesing details!

WHEN <u>ONE</u> SHALL BECOME <u>THREE</u>!

HUM 383
"Going Home"

HUM 562
"Grandpa's Boy"

HUM 561
"Grandma's Girl"

"**G**oing Home" HUM 383 was first released in the U.S. market in the spring of 1985, having been modeled by master sculptor Gerhard Skrobek in November 1966. The two little companions: "Grandpa's Boy" HUM 562 and "Grandma's Girl" HUM 561 were both released in the summer of 1990.

The photo appears that this group could be: Father, Mother, Son and Daughter!

We often hear the question: when will they run out of original drawings of Sister M.I. Hummel on which to base future figurines? I always state that it will be many, many years before that will ever happen. Example: This one drawing has produced three different figurines. I can visualize *several* more from this same drawing! How about: Father and Son, Mother and Daughter, Father and Daughter, Mother and Son — that's four more!

I, for one, look forward with great *expectations*, that they will *never* run out! Keep up the good work, Goebel!

GOEBEL M.I. HUMMEL DOLLS

Goebel dollmaking has seen two periods, the first lasting from about 1900 until the early 1930's and the second beginning after World War II and continuing through the present time. W. Goebel, already a well-known procelain factory with early Thuringian tradition, recognized the potential for dolls and began producing their own porcelain dolls around 1900. W. Goebel also at that time produced doll's heads and limbs for big toy wholesale firms like Max Handwerk and others. These antique dolls from that early period now command high prices on the secondary market.

It was around 1900 that W. Goebel also started producing the porcelain half-dolls which are also called tea cozies and pin-cushions.

In the mid-thirties, Goebel's line of products had grown tremendously and production of the doll line was temporarily suspended. With the onset of the war, government-enforced production left no room for dollmaking.

After World War II doll production was then resumed. Records from Goebel's model books for 1949 and the early 1950's show 6,000 numbers reserved for licensed dolls like M.I. Hummel, Nasha, Charlot Byj, Disney and other artists.

Although M.I. Hummel figurines were first produced in 1935, no M.I. Hummel dolls were produced before 1949/50. The very first M.I. Hummel dolls were sculpted by Karl Wagner and were made of a special rubber-ceramic body which was developed by former technical director Max Pechtold. This material did not hold up well and was replaced with the all vinyl bodies that were used from 1952 until 1982. It was in 1982 that Goebel once again returned to the tradition of producing dolls with porcelain head and limbs. The porcelain heads for the 1983/1984 introduction of M.I. Hummel dolls were sculpted by Helmut Fischer, former pupil of the Goebel doll expert, Karl Wagner. Eight porcelain dolls were introduced by Goebel in 1983/84: Lost Sheep, Postman, Signs of Spring, Birthday Serenade (Boy & Girl), Carnival, On Holiday, and Easter Greetings.

Master Sculptor Gerhard Skrobek was consulted and gave his approval to the porcelain dolls before they were taken to the Siessen Convent for approval. At present Gerhard Skrobek is working on an M.I. Hummel doll series to be exclusively distributed by the Danbury Mint.

NOTE: The Goebel company has stated that their doll records are rather incomplete and that there may be inaccuracies hidden in the following listings of the M.I. Hummel doll series. We offer our sincere thanks to Manfred Arras of the W. Goebel Porzellan-fabrik for his excellent research efforts to obtain this interesting M.I. Hummel doll production history. We invite doll collectors worldwide to share any additional information that may add to this existing body of information.

M.I. HUMMEL DOLLS
W. GOEBEL PRODUCTION RECORDS

M.I. Hummel Dolls

1101 Series

☐ 1101 A–H Baby (with dress variations) .... 13″ .... (CE) ... $100–200

Description: Handpainted face, modelled hair, moveable head, arms and legs. Two
variations produced: 1) with glass eyes, 2) with "sleeping" eyes.
Hair sewn in. Sold with cradle

1102 Series

☐ 1102 A–H Baby (with dress variations) .... 10″ .... (CE) ... $100–200

Description: Handpainted face, modelled hair, moveable head, arms and legs. Two
variations produced: 1) with glass eyes, 2) with "sleeping" eyes.
Sold with cradle

1500 Series

- [ ] 1501 — Gretl (Sister) .... 17" .... (CE) ... $150–250
- [ ] 1502 — Seppl (Brother) .... 17" .... (CE) ... $150–250
- [ ] 1503 — Bertl (Little Shopper) .... 17" .... (CE) ... $150–250
- [ ] 1504 — Hansl (Little Hiker) .... 17" .... (CE) ... $150–250
- [ ] 1505 — Strickliesl (Happy Pastime) .... 17" .... (CE) ... $150–250
- [ ] 1506 — Max (Brother) .... 17" .... (CE) ... $150–250
- [ ] 1507 — Wanderbub (Merry Wanderer) .... 17" .... (CE) ... $150–250

Description: Hand painted faces, modelled hair, moveable legs.

1600 Series

- [ ] 1601 — Gretl (Sister) .... 11" .... (CE) ... $150–200
- [ ] 1602 — Seppl (Brother) .... 11" .... (CE) ... $150–200
- [ ] 1603 — Bertl (Little Shopper) .... 11" .... (CE) ... $150–200
- [ ] 1604 — Hansl (Little Hiker) .... 11" .... (CE) ... $150–200
- [ ] 1605 — Strickliesl (Happy Pastime) .... 11" .... (CE) ... $150–200
- [ ] 1606 — Max (Brother) .... 11" .... (CE) ... $150–200
- [ ] 1607 — Wanderbub (Merry Wanderer) .... 11" .... (CE) ... $150–200
- [ ] 1608 — Felix (Chimney Sweep) .... 11" .... (CE) ... $150–200

Description: Handpainted faces, modelled hair, immoveable legs.

1700 Series

- [ ] 1701 — Gretl (Sister) .... 11" .... (CE) ... $150–200
- [ ] 1702 — Seppl (Brother) .... 11" .... (CE) ... $150–200
- [ ] 1703 — Bertl (Little Shopper) .... 11" .... (CE) ... $150–200
- [ ] 1704 — Hansl (Little Hiker) .... 11" .... (CE) ... $150–200
- [ ] 1705 — Strickliesl (Happy Pastime) .... 11" .... (CE) ... $150–200
- [ ] 1706 — Max (Brother) .... 11" .... (CE) ... $150–200
- [ ] 1707 — Wanderbub (Merry Wanderer) .... 11" .... (CE) ... $150–200
- [ ] 1708 — Felix (Chimney Sweep) .... 11" .... (CE) ... $150–200
- [ ] 1709 — Rosl .... 11" .... (CE) ... $100–200
- [ ] 1710 — Peterle .... 11" .... (CE) ... $100–200
- [ ] 1711 — (No information available)
- [ ] 1712 — (No information available)
- [ ] 1713 — Mariandl .... 11" .... (CE) ... $100–200
- [ ] 1714 — Jackl .... 11" .... (CE) ... $100–200
- [ ] 1715 — Christl .... 11" .... (CE) ... $100–200
- [ ] 1716 — Schorschl .... 11" .... (CE) ... $100–200
- [ ] 1717 — Ganseliesl (Goose Girl) .... 11" .... (CE) ... $150–200
- [ ] 1718 — Anderl .... 11" .... (CE) ... $100–200
- [ ] 1719 — Nachwachter (Hear Ye, Hear Ye) .... 11" .... (CE) ... $150–200
- [ ] 1720 — Brieftrager (Postman) .... 11" .... (CE) ... $150–200
- [ ] 1721 — Schusterbub (Baker) .... 11" .... (CE) ... $150–200
- [ ] 1722 — Skihaserl (Skier) .... 11" .... (CE) ... $150–200
- [ ] 1723 — Konditor (Baker) .... 11" .... (CE) ... $150–200
- [ ] 1724 — Radi-Bub (For Father) .... 11" .... (CE) ... $150–200
- [ ] 1725 — Puppenmetterchen (Doll Mother) .... 11" .... (CE) ... $150–200

Description: Handpainted faces, modelled hair, moveable head, arms, and legs.

1800 Series

- ☐ 1801 — Rosl .... 7⅘″ ... (CE) ... $100–200
- ☐ 1801 — Rosl .... 14″ .... (CE) ... $125–250
- ☐ 1802 — Rudi .... 7⅘″ ... (CE) ... $100–200
- ☐ 1802 — Rudi .... 14″ .... (CE) ... $125–250
- ☐ 1803 — Vroni .... 7⅘″ ... (CE) ... $100–200
- ☐ 1803 — Vroni .... 14″ .... (CE) ... $125–250
- ☐ 1804 — Seppl .... 7⅘″ ... (CE) ... $100–200
- ☐ 1804 — Seppl .... 14″ .... (CE) ... $125–250
- ☐ 1805 — Mariandl .... 7⅘″ ... (CE) ... $100–200
- ☐ 1805 — Mariandl .... 14″ .... (CE) ... $125–250
- ☐ 1806 — Jackl .... 7⅘″ ... (CE) ... $100–200
- ☐ 1806 — Jackl .... 14″ .... (CE) ... $125–250
- ☐ 1807 — (No information available)
- ☐ 1808 — (No information available)
- ☐ 1809 — Rosl* .... ? ...... (CE) ... $100–200
- ☐ 1810 — Peterle* .... ? ...... (CE) ... $100–200
- ☐ 1811 — Mirzl* .... ? ...... (CE) ... $100–200
- ☐ 1812 — Franzl* .... ? ...... (CE) ... $100–200

*Produced later than 1801–1808 models; Numbers 1809–1812 were a different size, but W. GOEBEL records cannot be located to accurately list the size.

Description: Handpainted faces, modelled hair, moveable head, arms and legs. Two variations produced: 1) with glass eyes and hair sewn in, 2) with "sleeping" eyes and hair sewn in.

1900 Series

- ☐ 1901 — Gretel .... 11½″ .. (CE) ... $100–150
- ☐ 1902 — Hansel .... 11½″ .. (CE) ... $100–150
- ☐ 1904/B — Rosa-Blue Baby .... 11″ .... (CE) ... $75–100
- ☐ 1904/P — Rosa-Pink Baby .... 11″ .... (CE) ... $75–100
- ☐ 1905 — Little Knitter .... 11½″ .. (CE) ... $100–150
- ☐ 1906 — Merry Wanderer .... 11½″ .. (CE) ... $100–150
- ☐ 1908 — Chimney Sweep .... 11½″ .. (CE) ... $100–150
- ☐ 1909 — School Girl .... 11½″ .. (CE) ... $100–150
- ☐ 1910 — School Boy .... 11½″ .. (CE) ... $100–150
- ☐ 1914 — Goose Girl .... 11½″ .. (CE) ... $100–150
- ☐ 1917 — For Father .... 11½″ .. (CE) ... $100–150
- ☐ 1925 — Merry Wanderer .... 11½″ .. (CE) ... $100–150
- ☐ 1926 — Lost Stocking .... 11½″ .. (CE) ... $100–150
- ☐ 1927 — Visiting An Invalid .... 11½″ .. (CE) ... $100–150
- ☐ 1928 — On Secret Path .... 11½″ .. (CE) ... $100–150

Description: Handpainted faces, vinyl heads and bodies. Moveable head, arms, and legs.

PORCELAIN DOLLS

- ☐ Lost Sheep .... 15¾" ...... (CE) ...... ❻ $250–300
- ☐ Postman .... 15¾" ...... (CE) ...... ❻ $250–300
- ☐ Signs of Spring .... 15¾" ...... (CE) ...... ❻ $250–300
- ☐ Birthday Serenade/Boy ..... 15¾" ...... (CE) ...... ❻ $250–300
- ☐ Birthday Serenade/Girl ..... 15¾" ...... (CE) ...... ❻ $250–300
- ☐ Carnival .... 15¾" ...... (CE) ...... ❻ $250–300
- ☐ On Holiday .... 15¾" ...... (CE) ...... ❻ $250–300
- ☐ Easter Greetings .... 15¾" ...... (CE) ...... ❻ $250–300

GOEBEL MINIATURE STUDIO, CAMARILLO, CALIFORNIA

Formed in 1978, Goebel Miniatures produces fine collectible miniature figurines and jewelry by using the centuries old "lost wax" process developed by Egyptian and Chinese artists more than 5,000 years ago.

After first embarking on a line of miniature furniture known as the Butterfly Collection for the dollhouse market, the company soon discovered that the tiny handcrafted figurines produced by Master Artist Robert Olszewski would be the company's future. The furniture line was discontinued in early years.

In 1980 the company moved to larger offices in order to accommodate its growing staff and by 1984 was doubling its size every year.

One of the goals of Goebel Miniatures is to reproduce in miniature some of the finest examples of antique and contemporary masterpieces. Goebel Miniatures takes great pride in honoring the companies and artists who produced the full-scale originals.

Although some designs are released as limited editions (usually due to the amount of difficulty involved in reproduction) it is rare for the company to do so. Goebel Miniatures believes that limiting an edition is no guarantee of artistic worth. The real value of a work of art comes from its artistic quality. Goebel Miniatures' first limited edition "Alice in the Garden" (based on the Lewis Carroll works and commissioned in 1981 by Miniature Collector Magazine) was released at $60.00 per figurine and now commands as much as $1,000 per figurine on the secondary market.

Goebel Miniatures figurines range in themes from children, women, wildlife, and history to the art of Ted DeGrazia, Walt Disney and M.I. Hummel. Each piece is cast in bronze, is no more than one-and-a-half inches tall and has a display environment to accompany the series.

Owned by W. Goebel Porzellanfabrik, the West German firm that produces M.I. Hummel figurines, Goebel Miniatures has grown to a staff of over 100 and is today the largest studio producing miniature figurines, objects of art and collectible jewelry in the United States.

Bavarian Country School (left), and *Wayside Shrine* (right), two additions created by artisans from Goebel Miniatures studios, Camarillo CA, frame a cozy wooded glen for KinderWay.

Available separately, Bavarian Country School measures 4¾" and has suggested retailed price of $100 while Wayside Shrine measures 4 inches and retails at $60.

"PRE-GOEBEL" M.I. HUMMEL MINIATURES
by OLSZEWSKI

In 1977, master artist Robert Olszewski began production of miniature M.I. Hummel figurines. These pieces were not authorized at that time by the W. Goebel Porzellan-fabrik in Roedental, W. Germany. Mr. Olszewski had naively begun production of these pieces without giving any thought to any infringement of the Goebel copyright. When this matter was brought to Mr. Olszewski's attention in July of 1978, he immediately sent a letter to Mr. Goebel explaining what had happened. Word soon came from the Goebel company that Mr. Dieter Schneider from Goebel would visit and tour the Olszewski miniature studio. Soon after Mr. Schneider's visit, Mr. Olszewski accepted a contract to begin work for the W. GOEBEL PORZELLANFABRIK. In order to observe the provisions of this contract, Mr. Olszewski could not produce any of the 14 miniatures he had previously made. Of those fourteen miniatures, five were miniature M.I. Hummel figurines. These Olszewski pre-Goebel M.I. Hummel Miniatures have become quite valuable to both Hummel collectors and miniature collectors. Original Olszewski handcrafted boxes for the "pre-Goebels" are valued at $100 each.

☐ Kiss Me . . . . (CE) $1600–2000
☐ Stormy Weather . . . . . . (CE) $1600–1900
☐ Barnyard Hero . . . . (CE) $1500–1800
☐ Ring Around the Rosie . . (CE) $3000–3500
☐ Ride Into Christmas . . . . (CE) $1600–2000

© 1989 Goebel

250-P

251-P

252-P

253-P

Actual size ⅞"

□ GMS No. 250-P .... ⅞" ..... Little Fiddler ....(OE) $110–155

This miniature M.I. Hummel figurine was sculpted by Master Artist Robert Olszewski and was first released to collectors in 1988. 10,000 pieces were issued in 1988 with each box marked "First Edition."

□ GMS No. 251-P .... ⅞" ..... Stormy Weather .....(OE) $130–175

This miniature M.I. Hummel figurine was sculpted by Master Artist Robert Olszewski and was first released to collectors in 1988. 10,000 pieces were issued in 1988 with each box marked "First Edition."

□ GMS No. 252-P .... ⅞" ..... Doll Bath ....(OE) $105–150

This miniature M.I. Hummel figurine was sculpted by Master Artist Robert Olszewski and was first released to collectors in 1988. 10,000 pieces were issued in 1988 with each box marked "First Edition."

□ GMS No. 253-P .... ⅞" ..... Little Sweeper ......(OE) $105–150

This miniature M.I. Hummel figurine was sculpted by Master Artist Robert Olszewski and was first released to collectors in 1988. 10,000 pieces were issued in 1988 with each box marked "First Edition."

© 1989 Goebel **255-P**

254-P

Actual size ⁷⁄₈″ **256-P**

257-P

☐ GMS No. 254-P .... ⁷⁄₈″ ..... Merry Wanderer .....(OE) $105–195

This miniature M.I. Hummel figurine was sculpted by Master Artist Robert Olszewski and was first released to collectors in 1988. 10,000 pieces were issued in 1988 with each box marked "First Edition."

☐ GMS No. 255-P .... ⁷⁄₈″ ..... Postman ....(OE) $105–115

This miniature M.I. Hummel figurine was sculpted by Master Artist Robert Olszewski and was first released to collectors in 1989. 10,000 pieces were issued in 1989 with the bases marked with the wording "USA 1989" and "1st EDITION."

☐ GMS No. 256-P .... ⁷⁄₈″ ..... Visiting An Invalid ...(OE) $115–125

This miniature M.I. Hummel figurine was sculpted by Master Artist Robert Olszewski and was first released to collectors in 1989. 10,000 pieces were issued in 1989 with the bases marked with the wording "USA 1989" and "1st EDITION."

☐ GMS No. 257-P .... ⁷⁄₈″ ..... Apple Tree Boy .....(OE) $130–155

This miniature M.I. Hummel figurine was sculpted by Master Artist Robert Olszewski and was first released to collectors in 1989. 10,000 pieces were issued in 1989 with the bases marked with the wording "USA 1989" and "1st EDITION."

GOEBEL M.I. HUMMEL MINIATURES — Jewelry

Valentine Gift — Pendant
GMS 248–P

☐ GMS No. 248-P .... ⅞" ..... Valentine Gift .... (CE) \$275–325
This Closed Edition Goebel M.I. Hummel Miniature was available for sale by redemption card only to members of the Goebel Collectors' Club. Only members who joined or renewed their club membership between June 1, 1983 and May 31, 1984 were allowed to purchase this figurine. This M.I. Hummel Miniature is Robert Olszewski's reduction from the original HUM 387 first sculpted by Gerhard Skrobek. Valentine Gift was the first M.I. Hummel figurine approved for miniaturization by the Siessen Convent. Issue price was \$85.00.

What Now — Pendant
GMS 249–P

☐ GMS No. 249-P .... ⅞" ..... What Now .... (CE) \$225–250
This Closed Edition Goebel M.I. Hummel Miniature was available for sale by redemption card only to Goebel Collectors' Club members. Only members who joined or renewed their club membership between June 1, 1986 and May 31, 1987 were allowed to purchase this figurine. This M.I. Hummel Miniature is Robert Olszewski's reduction from the original HUM 422 originally sculpted by Gerhard Skrobek. This M.I. Hummel Miniature was the second to be offered to Members of the Goebel Collectors' Club (The first being Valentine Gift Pendant offered in 1983.) Isse price was \$125.

262-P   263-P   264-P   265-P

☐ GMS No. 262-P .... 1" ..... Baker .... (OE) \$105–115
This miniature M.I. Hummel figurine was sculpted by Master Artist Robert Olszewski and was first released in 1990 with each figurine marked "First Edition". 1990 was the first year that the Goebel Miniatures Studio marked the figurines themselves with the "First Edition" wording.

☐ GMS No. 263-P .... 1" ..... Waiter .... (OE) \$115–125
This miniature M.I. Hummel figurine was sculpted by Master Artist Robert Olszewski and was first released to collectors in 1990 with each figurine marked "First Edition".

☐ GMS No. 264-P .... ¾" ..... Cinderella .... (OE) \$115–125
This miniature M.I. Hummel figurine was sculpted by Master Artist Robert Olszewski and was first released in 1990 with each figurine marked "First Edition".

☐ GMS No. 265-P .... ⅞" ..... Serenade .... (OE) \$105–115
This M.I. Hummel figurine was sculpted by Master Artist Robert Olszewski and was first released to collectors in 1991 with each figurine marked "First Edition".

266-P   **267-P**   **268-P**

☐ GMS No. 266-P .... ⅞" ..... Accordian Boy ......(OE) $105–115
This miniature M.I. Hummel figurine was sculpted by Master Artist Robert Olszewski
and was first released in 1991 with each figurine marked "First Edition".

☐ GMS No. 267-P .... ⅞" ..... We Congratulate ....(OE) $130–140
This miniature M.I. Hummel figurine was sculpted by Master Artist Robert Olszewski
and was first released in 1991 with each figurine marked "First Edition".

☐ GMS No. 268-P .... ¾" ..... Busy Student ....(OE) $105–115
This miniature M.I. Hummel figurine was sculpted by Master Artist Robert Olszewski
and was first released in 1991 with each figurine marked "First Edition".

☐ GMS No. 269-P .... ⅞" ..... Morning Concert ....(EE) $175
This miniature M.I. Hummel figurine was sculpted by Master Artist Robert Olszewski
and was only issued to members of the M.I. Hummel Club by Redemption Card. Redemption expiration on this figurine is *31 May 1993*.

☐ GMS No. 279-P .... ¹³/₁₆" ... Ride Into Christmas ..(OE) $195
This miniature M.I. Hummel figurine was sculpted by Master Artist Robert Olszewski
and was first released in 1991 in conjunction with the display called "Winterfest". The
figurine issued in 1991 was marked "First Edition".

☐ GMS No. 280-P .... 1" × ¾" . Merry Wanderer Plaque . (OE) $130
This miniature display plaque was sculpted by Master Artist Robert Olszewski and
was first released in 1991 with each plaque marked "First Edition". Also was produced
in a German language version.

☐ GMS No. 281-P .... ⅞" ..... School Boy ....(OE) $120
This miniature M.I. Hummel figurine was sculpted by Master Artist Robert Olszewski
and was first released in 1992 with each figurine marked "First Edition".

☐ GMS No. 282-P .... ⅞" ..... Wayside Harmony ...(OE) $140
This miniature M.I. Hummel figurine was sculpted by Master Artist Robert Olszewski
and was first released in 1992 with each figurine marked "First Edition".

☐ GMS No. 283-P .... ⅞" ..... Goose Girl ....(OE) $130
This miniature M.I. Hummel figurine was sculpted by Master Artist Robert Olszewski
and was first released in 1992 with each figurine marked "First Edition".

The M.I. Hummel Club
(Formerly: Goebel Collectors' Club)

M.I. HUMMEL CLUB
Division of Goebel Art GmbH

(The Club's logo, enlarged)

Founded in 1977 as the Goebel Collectors' Club, the first of its kind, this important organization continues its early established tradition as a collector's information service.

The services it imparts are many. By having constant access to its members through its quarterly magazine, *INSIGHTS*, personal correspondence between members and Club staff, and one-on-one discussions at various collectors' shows and in-store promotions, the Club is constantly aware of the needs of its members and seeks to respond in as much depth as possible.

There is a variety of aspects to Club membership, enough to satisfy collectors at all levels. Whether one owns one *M.I. Hummel* figurine, or 100, or any number in-between, the pages of *INSIGHTS* can open doors of knowledge.

With special articles focusing on the history of the figurines, life of M.I. Hummel, the intricacies of production, and the helpful hints on how to display either individual pieces or groupings, its pages are filled with pleasurable reading and full-color photographs.

For the intermediate and advanced collector there is the knowledge that any question, no matter how obscure, will be thoroughly researched by the Club, calling on the available records at the factory as well as its own files developed over the years.

M.I. HUMMEL CLUB

Special backstamp for exclusive M.I. Hummel figurines created for Club members only. Featuring the all-important bumble bee, it is shown larger than actual size.

All members can share in the Club's expanded opportunities by joining a Local Chapter, comprised of members in any given regional area who meet on a regular basis for the purpose of sharing and imparting knowledge, and having a great deal of fun while doing it.

There are exclusive purchase opportunities for Club members as well. In each year of membership, *M.I. Hummel* treasures are produced *for members only*, with the Club's own backstamp attesting to that exclusivity. Through a redemption card issued for each, these handcrafted motifs are available for purchase by members at select stores throughout North America.

A winsome *M.I. Hummel* gift is presented from the Club to each new member; through this unique welcome gift, members can already feel the specialness of the organization they have just joined.

A custom designed fact-filled binder, each member's introduction to knowledge, is another exciting benefit.

In 1985 the Club instituted a travel program which keeps getting better each year. Hundreds have traveled on these trips designed for lovers of *M.I. Hummel* figurines, and their guests. Each trip to Europe includes a behind-the-scenes tour of the Goebel factory in Bavaria, West Germany (the home of the figurines), available *only* to members on these trips. (Members who travel on their own know to carry their membership cards with them; the card, their "passport" to many pleasures, is their free ticket to lunch when visiting the factory.)

In 1989 a major event took place: with the introduction of the M.I. Hummel Club in Europe, the International M.I. Hummel Club was launched. As this develops it will give members worldwide an unprecedented opportunity to make fascinating contacts beyond their borders.

The M.I. Hummel Club — your open door to enjoyment, fascination and a fulfilling experience.

For more information, write the M.I. Hummel Club, Goebel Plaza, P.O. Box 11, Pennington NJ 08534.

Figurines Issued Exclusively for Members of The Goebel Collectors' Club
(Now: "M.I. Hummel Club")

				Issue Price
☐ Valentine Gift	HUM 387	No. 1	1977	$45
☐ Smiling Through, Plaque	HUM 690	No. 2	1978	$50
☐ Sister M.I. Hummel Bust	HU 3	No. 3	1979	$75
☐ Valentine Joy	HUM 399	No. 4	1980	$95
☐ Daisies Don't Tell	HUM 380	No. 5	1981	$80
☐ It's Cold	HUM 421	No. 6	1982	$80
☐ What Now?	HUM 422	No. 7	1983	$90
☐ Coffee Break	HUM 409	No. 8	1984	$90
☐ Smiling Through	HUM 408	No. 9	1985	$125
☐ Birthday Candle	HUM 440	No. 10	1986	$95
☐ Morning Concert	HUM 447	No. 11	1987	$98
☐ The Surprise	HUM 431	No. 12	1988	$125
☐ Hello World	HUM 429	No. 13	1989	$130
☐ I Wonder	HUM 486	No. 14	1990	$140
☐ Gift from a Friend	HUM 485	No. 15	1991	$160
☐ My Wish Is Small	HUM 463	No. 16	1992	$170
☐ Miniature Valentine Gift Necklace			1983	$85
☐ Miniature What Now? Necklace			1986	$125
☐ I Brought You a Gift	HUM 479		1989–90	FREE GIFT
☐ Merry Wanderer Pendant	Stering Silver		1990–91	FREE GIFT
☐ Two Hands, One Treat	HUM 493		1991–92	FREE GIFT

CELEBRATION PLATE SERIES

☐ Valentine Gift	HUM 738	1986	$90
☐ Valentine Joy	HUM 737	1987	$98
☐ Daisies Don't Tell	HUM 736	1988	$115
☐ It's Cold	HUM 735	1989	$120

ANNIVERSARY FIGURINES

☐ Flower Girl (5 years)	HUM 548	$105
☐ Little Pair (10 years)	HUM 449	$170
☐ Honey Lover (15 years)	HUM 312	$190

Glossary of Terms

AIR HOLES: Air holes are tiny holes intentionally made in the figurines during production to prevent the pieces from exploding during the firing process. These air holes are usually placed so carefully in the figurines that often times they go unnoticed by the casual observer.

ARS: The shortened form of ARS EDITION GmbH of Munich, West Germany. Ars Edition was formerly known as Ars Sacra Josef Müeller Verlag, a German publishing house, selling postcards, postcard-calendars and prints of M.I. Hummel, which first published the Hummel Art. Today Ars Edition GmbH is an exclusive licensee for Hummel books, calendars, cards and stationary. Owner: Mr. Marcel Nauer (grandson of Dr. Herbert Dubler).

ARS AG: A corporation based in Zug, Switzerland holding the two-dimensional rights of original M.I. Hummel drawings as well as the two-dimensional rights for reproductions of M.I. Hummel products made by Goebel. "Ars" is the Latin word for art. Owner: 50% Mr. Jacques Nauer (grandson of Dr. Herbert Dubler), 50% Goebel Art GmbH, President Board of Directors: J. Nauer.

ARTIST'S MARK: The artist's mark is the signature of the artist who has completed the painting of the figurine. This signature is usually in the form of initials accompanied by the date. These artist's marks almost always appear in black on the underside of the figurine's base.

BAS RELIEF: Sculptural relief in which the projection from the surrounding surface is slight. This type of raised work is found on the annual and anniversary "M.I. Hummel" plates.

BESWICK: The Beswick Company of England produced some copies of "M.I. Hummel" figurines around the W.W. II time period. There are approximately eleven known models of "Beswick Hummels." The Beswick pieces usually have a very shiny appearance and are marked on the underside with a model number incised into the base and the Beswick trademark which reads "Beswick England" set in a circle. A facsimile of the "M.I. Hummel" signature was used along with the term "Original Hummel Studios." The Beswick Company was acquired by the Royal Doulton Company of England. No records are known to exist of any agreement or contracts which might have given the Beswick Company the right to produce "M.I. Hummel" figurines.

BISQUE: This is a term used to describe ceramic pieces which have not been glazed, but are hard-fired and vitreous.

CHIP: The term used to describe a flaw in a ceramic figurine which reaches beyond the painted surface and the glazing. A chip in a ceramic figurine is usually rough to the touch and greatly affects the value of the item.

CLOSED EDITION: Pieces formerly in W. Goebel production program but no longer produced.

CLOSED NUMBER: An identification number in W. Goebel's numerical identification system that was used to identify a design or sample models for possible production, but then for various reasons never authorized for release.

COPYRIGHT DATE: This is the date that is often times incised into the bottom of an M.I. Hummel figurine. This date represents the year in which the figurine design was registered with the United States copyright office. Many M.I. Hummel figurines are registered and then do not go into general production for several years after the initial copyright is registered. The incised date is *NOT* the date that the figurine was necessarily produced or painted.

CRAZING: This is the term used to describe the existence of several minute cracks in the glaze of a figurine. This is a natural condition that develops as the ceramic material ages. Some pieces will become "crazed" at a faster rate than others. Many factors of production as well as the humidity of the environment where the figurine is displayed can play a part in this process.

CURRENT PRODUCTION: The term used to describe those items currently being produced by the W. Goebel Porzellanfabrik Roedental, West Germany.

CURRENT TRADEMARK: Designates the symbol presently being used by the W. Goebel Porzellanfabrik to represent the company's trademark.

DECIMAL POINT: This incised "period" or dot was used in a somewhat random fashion by the W. Goebel Porzellanfabrik over the years. The decimal point is and was primarily used to reduce confusion in reading the incised numbers on the underside of the figurines. Example: 66. helps one realize that the designation is sixty-six and not ninety-nine.

DOUBLE CROWN: This term is used to describe the Goebel Company trademark found on some "M.I. Hummel" figurines. On "double crown" pieces the crown trademark is usually found incised and stamped.

DOUGHNUT BASE: A term used to describe the raised circular support on the underside of a figurine. Many figurine bases with a circle inside the regular circular base gave rise to the term, but has now been used to describe many bases with the circular support on the underside.

DUBLER: A "Dubler" figurine is one produced during the W.W. II time period by the Herbert Dubler Co. Inc. of New York City. These pieces were substitutes for genuine Goebel "M.I. Hummel" figurines when Goebel "Hummels" were not coming into the U.S. The Dubler figurines were made of plaster of paris and were distributed by the Crestwick Co. of New York which later became Hummelwerk and ultimately the present Goebel United States firm.

FULL BEE: The term "Full Bee" refers to the trademark used by the Goebel Co. from 1950 to 1957. Early usage of this trademark was incised into the material. Later versions of the "full bee" were stamped into the material.

GOEBEL BEE: A name used to describe the trademark used by the Goebel Company from 1972 until 1979. This trademark incorporates the GOEBEL name with the V and bee.

GOEBEL COLLECTORS' CLUB: The name given to the organization formerly located in Tarrytown, New York for collectors of items produced by the W. Goebel Porzellanfabrik of West Germany. In 1989 the name was officially changed to the "M.I. Hummel Club."

HERBERT DUBLER, INC: Founded in 1934 in New York, importing products from the publishing house "Ars Sacra Joseph Mueller Munich", named after Dr. Herbert Dubler, son in law of Mr. Joseph Mueller. During WW II and thereafter this company distributed Hummel products such as cards, calendars and books. During that time the "Dubler Figurines" were put on the market. Herbert Dubler, Inc. was renamed "CHRESTWICK, INC." honoring the president, Mr. Alfred E. Wick. In 1956 the company was sold to W. Goebel Porzellanfabrik and became known as "Hummelwerk, Inc." and later changed to "Goebel United States".

HOLLOW MOLD: The term used by "M.I. Hummel" collectors to describe a figurine that is open on the underside of the base. With these particular bases the collector can visually see into the cavity of the figurine.

"INTERNATIONAL": This name is given to the group of M.I. Hummel figurines that were produced in 1940 with the national dress of other countries. Master sculptors Reinhold Unger and Arthur Moeller translated Sister Hummel's sketches into Goebel M.I. Hummel figurines. The "Internationals" are highly sought-after by collectors.

MEL: A Goebel-produced figurine with the letters "MEL" incised somewhere on the base of the piece. These pieces were designed from original drawings by Sister M.I. Hummel, but for some undetermined reasons were not approved by the Siessen Convent for inclusion in the "M.I. Hummel" line of figurines.

MODEL: This term most often refers to a particular "M.I. Hummel" figurine, plate, bell, or other item in the line. When not used in reference to a specific motif, the word model also can refer to the sculptor's working model from which the figurines are made.

MOLD GROWTH: In the earlier days of figurine production the working molds were made of plaster of paris. As these molds were used, the various molded parts became larger due to the repeated usage. With modern technology at the Goebel factory and the use of acrylic resin molds, this problem has been eliminated and today the collector finds very few size differences within a given size designation.

MUSTERZIMMER: The German word meaning sample model designating that this piece is to be held at the W. Goebel Prozellanfabrik in the "sample room" to be used for future reference by production artists.

OESLAU: Name for the village where the W. Goebel Porzellanfabrik is located. Oeslau is now a part of the City of Roedental, W. Germany. The name Oeslau appears on Hum 348 "Ring Around The Rosie".

OPEN EDITION: Pieces currently in W. Goebel's production program.

OUT OF PRODUCTION: A term used by the Goebel Company to designate items that are not currently in production, yet have not been given an official classification as to their eventual fate. Some items listed as out of production may become closed editions, remain temporarily withdrawn, or ultimately return to current production status.

OVERSIZE: This description refers to a piece that has experienced "mold growth" size expansion. A figurine that measures larger than the standard size is said to be "oversized."

PAINT FLAKE: The term used to designate a flaw in a ceramic figurine whereby the paint has been chipped. This type flaw does not go beyond the glazed surface.

PAINT RUB: A general wearing away of the paint surface of a figurine in a particular spot. This condition is usually caused by excessive handling of a figurine, thin paint in a given area of the figurine, or the excessive use of abrasive cleaners.

PAINTER'S SAMPLE: A figurine used by the painters at the Goebel factory which serves as a reference figurine for the painting of subsequent pieces. The painters of "M.I. Hummel" figurines attempt to paint their individual pieces to match the painter's sample as precisely as possible. Painter's Samples are sometimes marked with a red line around the side of the base.

RATTLE: All "M.I. Hummel" figurines are hollow on the inside. Occasionally, when the figurine is fired, a small piece of clay will drop off on the inside. This little bit of clay when dry will cause a slight rattle. Actually, it does not hurt the figurine or affect the value one way or the other. I would not even call it a flaw, as it does not detract from the appearance. Actually, it is one means of identification that might come in handy sometime!

REINSTATED: The term used to indicate that a figurine has been placed back into production by the W. Goebel Porzellanfabrik after some prior classification of non-production.

ROEDENTAL: The town in West Germany where the W. Goebel Porzellanfabrik is situated. Roedental is located near

Coburg and lies only a few miles from the East German border. In 1981 Roedental became the official Sister City of Eaton, Ohio due to the longtime "Hummel" relationship with Robert L. Miller and the International "Hummel" Festival held annually at Eaton, Ohio.

SAMPLE MODEL: Generally a figurine that was made as a sample only and not approved by the Siessen Convent for production. Sample models (in the true sense of the term) are extremely rare items and command a premium price on the secondary market.

SECONDARY MARKET: The buying and selling of items after the initial retail purchase has been transacted. Often times this post-retail trading is also referred to as the "after market." This very publication is intended to serve as a guide for the secondary market values of "M.I. Hummel" items.

SIESSEN CONVENT: Located in Wuerttemberg region of West Germany near Saulgau. This facility is where Sister M.I. Hummel resided after taking her vows. She continued to sketch in a studio inside the convent until her untimely death at the age of 37 in 1946. The Siessen Convent houses the Sisters of the Third Order of St. Francis. Sister Hummel is buried in the cemetery located on the Convent grounds.

"SLASH" MARK: At one time, an imperfect or flawed figurine produced by Goebel and found during final inspection was marked by grinding a small groove or "slash" through the trademark. These pieces were then sold to factory employees as "seconds." Some of these "slash" marked pieces eventually found their way on to the secondary market and sold to uninformed collectors. Goebel abandoned this practice many years ago.

STYLIZED TRADEMARK: The symbol used by the Goebel Company from 1957 until 1964. It is recognized by the V with a bumblebee that has triangular or "stylized" wings.

TEMPORARILY WITHDRAWN: A designation assigned by the W. Goebel Porzellanfabrik to indicate that a particular item is being withdrawn from production for some time, but may be reinstated at a future date.

TERRA COTTA: A reddish clay used in an experimental fashion by artisans at the W. Goebel Porzellanfabrik. There are a few sample pieces of "M.I. Hummel" figurines that were produced with the terra cotta material. These terra cotta pieces have the look of the reddish-brown clay and were not painted.

THREE LINE TRADEMARK: The symbol used by the W. Goebel Porzellanfabrik from 1964 until 1972 as their factory trademark. The name for this trademark was adopted to recognize that the V and bee was accompanied by three lines of print to the right of the V. also known as TM 4.

TM: Abbreviation for trademark.

TW: Abbreviation for temporarily withdrawn.

UNDERGLAZE: The term used to describe especially the number 5 trademark that appears actually underneath the glaze as opposed to the later version of the number 5 trademark that appears on the top of the glaze.

U.S. ZONE: The words "U.S. ZONE—GERMANY" were used on figurines produced by the W. Goebel Porzellanfabrik after W.W. II when the country of Germany was yet undivided and the Goebel factory was part of the U.S. Zone. The U.S. ZONE marking was used either alone or with the Crown trademark from 1946 until 1948. Once the country was divided into East and West, the W. Goebel Porzellanfabrik used the Western or West designation.

WAFFLE BASE: Another term to describe the quartered or divided bases.

WHITE OVERGLAZE: The term used to designate an item that has not been painted, but has been glazed and fired. These pieces are completely white. All "M.I. Hummel" items are produced in this finish before being individually hand painted.

About the Artists

Handmade in the W. Goebel Porzellanfabrik studios in Roedental, West Germany, "M.I. Hummel" figurines enjoy a unique advantage. This art form has been developed in close cooperation with and through the personal assistance and advice of the artist herself, **Sister Maria Innocentia Hummel,** both at the factory and at the Convent of Siessen. Though gentle and gifted with a fine sense of humor, she was very demanding when it came to her art. Master sculptors Arthur Moeller and Reinhold Unger had many discussions with her, and she commented in detail in her bold, clear handwriting when she looked at samples. She did not hesitate to take up the modeler's stick or the painter's fine brush to make her intentions understood. Millions of collectors and friends all over the world have loved and revered the outcome of this artistic collaboration which continues today, long after the death of Sister Maria Innocentia, through the art authorities at the convent.

The sculptors, known for so masterfully transforming two-dimensional art into this new dimension, brought varied experience and training to their work. **Arthur Moeller** was born in 1885 at Rudolstadt in Thuringia. After completing basic studies of modeling at a fine arts studio, he left home to work with a number of porcelain factories. He developed his talents at the Arts and Crafts Academy in Dresden and afterwards at the Academy for Applied Arts in Munich, the same school where Sister M.I. Hummel was to enroll one generation later. From his artistic hands and imagination came works that were shown in Paris and Munich. In 1911, Max Louis Goebel, third-generation head of the company, became aware of this talented young artist and invited him to work with the company. When Moeller died in 1972 in the

Arthur Moeller

86th year of his life, he had been with the company for nearly 50 years. Besides his demanding tasks at the Goebel atelier, Moeller found time to exhibit at fine art shows in Munich, Coburg and Kulmbach. He was a master of the small form. This very special gift enabled him to contribute an immense wealth to the Goebel range. When the time came to create charming figurines from Sister M.I. Hummel's artwork, he and his equally gifted colleague, Reinhold Unger, were the right men for the task.

Reinhold Unger also came from Thuringia where he was born in 1880, near where the Goebel factory owned its ancestral porcelain factory. Unger studied at the Fine Art School of Professor Hutschenreuther in Lichte and worked afterwards with the Kunstanstalt Gaigl in Munich.

His works were shown at fine art exhibitions in Munich and he came to work in the Goebel atelier upon the invitation of Max Louis Goebel in 1915. After a fine and

Reinhold Unger

Gerhard Skrobek

fruitful collaboration of 50 years, Unger died in 1974 in the 94th year of his life. His work was highly praised by the press and fine art authorities. On special trips into Upper Bavaria he had absorbed impressions of both the folk art and the deep religious feelings of the area, all of which were incorporated into his artwork. This ability enabled him to develop, through close collaboration with Arthur Moeller and Sister M.I. Hummel, those lovely figurines which were to conquer the hearts of millions. In general, it can be said that most of the religious items incised "M.I. Hummel" and made before 1958 were sculpted by Unger.

Third in this prestigious line of "M.I. Hummel" sculptors is **Gerhard Skrobek,** who joined Goebel in 1951. After his birth in Silesia in 1922, his parents, who thrived in an environment of music and painting, soon moved to Berlin where young Gerhard was exposed to a wealth of museums. He would go to the zoological gardens and sit for hours observing and sketching the animals. His decision to turn to sculpture led him to the renowned Reimannschule where he studied under the prestigious Melzer. In 1946, Skrobek went to Coburg to continue his art studies with the well-known sculptor Poertzel, who created many porcelain pieces for W. Goebel Porzellanfabrik. Skrobek travelled extensively at this time and exhibited in Coburg and Munich. In 1951 he joined Goebel and soon became one of its leading sculptors. He was entrusted to continue the tradition of sculpting the "M.I. Hummel" figurines, and under his talented and guiding hands much of the original artwork was turned into figurines. He also contributed the "M.I. Hummel" plates and bells to the line and created the eight-foot "Merry Wanderer," the famous landmark in front of the Goebel Collectors' Club Gallery and Museum in Tarrytown, New York. "Today's Children" and "Co-Boy" figurines are his creations, and many Goebel series such as Charlot Byj and the Wildlife Collection attest to his talents.

Traditions of quality continue, and the closeness between the Convent of Siessen and the sculptor's atelier at Goebel is strongly maintained.

Karl Wagner

Gunther Neubauer

Karl Wagner was born on March 30, 1900 in Holenbrunn/Oberfranken. At the age of 16, he entered the Nuernberg School of Arts where his work won one award and six commendations. From 1920 to 1922 he studied at the Art Academy of Stuttgart. After completing his studies, he entered the ceramics industry as an artist and sculptor. In 1936 he joined W. Goebel Porzellanfabrik.

From 1936 until 1972, when the sculptor retired, he created many figurines for Goebel including several in the **M.I. Hummel** and **Disney** lines. In 1949, Wagner was named master sculptor for Goebel's new toy division, **Hummelwerk-Spielwaren KG.** He was responsible for the modelling and technical preparations of all of the products, including animals and the **M.I. Hummel** dolls.

Two years after his retirement, Karl Wagner died on December 4, 1974.

Guenthur Neubauer was born on February 3, 1932 in Noerdbohmen, in what is today Czechoslovakia. When he was a schoolboy the war brought him to Coburg, Bavaria, where he began his apprenticeship with W. Goebel Porzellanfabrik in March 1948.

Mr. Neubauer's tremendous creative talent, especially evident in his drawings, was recognized and encouraged by his teacher, master sculptor Arthur Moeller. After three years of schooling in the factory, Neubauer passed the arduous ceramic and porcelain tests. The most artistically talented graduate of his class, he was im-mediately brought into production to decorate the more difficult figurines. During this time, he accomplished the rare feat of becoming an expert in both under and overglaze decorating.

The following years were marked by Neubauer's rapid advancement through the artistic ranks at Goebel. In 1953 he became the sample painter for a group of approximately 30 artists. Two years later he assumed the responsibility for the design development of new products and of new production methods. After passing the state exams in 1961, he was certified as a master of ceramics.

Since 1960 Neubauer has participated in both the teaching of apprentices and the development of production methods. As department manager and chief master sample painter, he is responsible for the decoration of all underglazed and overglazed collectibles. As a teacher, he instructed all of the apprentices in the fine ceramic division from 1966 through 1974, and today he is the prime instructor for the underglaze painting education of all apprentices.

In 1956 Neubauer married another talented sample painter with Goebel, who died after a long illness in 1985. Their only daughter, Heike, has inherited her parents' artistic aptitude, and is an interior decorator.

In addition to being an active sportsman, participating in swimming, walking and skiing, Mr. Neubauer enjoys painting in both watercolors and oils, and he is an accomplished photographer.

Franz Kirchner

Robert Olszewski

Franz Kirchner was born on September 12, 1935 in Neersof, a town not far from W. Goebel Porzellanfabrik in Roedental, Bavaria. Upon graduation from junior high school, he decided to pursue a career as an artist and, on August 8, 1949, entered the three-year apprentice program at Goebel.

After the successful completion of the program in 1952, he began work in Goebel's decorating department. Through continued schooling and expanded artistic experience, he became a qualified master of under and overglaze painting.

Due to his artistic talent and conscientiousness, Mr. Kirchner was made a master sample painter in 1955. Today as assistant manager of the decorating department, he is responsible for the sample decoration of new pieces.

Mr. Kirchner has travelled throughout W. Germany and in the U.S. demonstrating his craft. On a recent trip to the U.S. he appeared at the Hunter Mt., NY German Alps Festival and at the International Plate and Collectibles Exposition in South Bend, IN.

In his spare time, he develops his talents as a fine artist, specializing in landscapes. He is also a musician, and is an active member of a band focusing on traditional German music, in which he plays both the clarinet and saxophone. He also enjoys walking and working in his garden.

Robert Olszewski As strange as it may seem, Robert Olszewski (Ol-shes-ski) credits an art theft for introducing him to the world of miniature art. Some years ago, a painting by this renowned American artist was stolen from a Las Vegas gallery. Because a photograph was not available for the police, he painted a miniature reproduction of the work. "I realized," he said reflecting on the incident, "that the small replica contained all the elements of the original painting. In addition, it was just as much a work of art as the first one." Olszewski has found that through the reduction of a piece of art he could create great artistic works in a size that would make them appealing to a great number of people. This incident turned out to be the first in a series of events that would eventually lead him to a career in the field of miniatures.

Olszewski originally studied art at Indiana University in Pennsylvania and then became an established painter with work well received in numerous art galleries. After moving to California, he spent the next 11 years teaching art by day and continuing with his painting by night.

After the theft incident, he began to develop his interest in miniatures, first with miniature furniture reproduction and then with figurines. Working full time, he re-discovered the ancient "lost wax" process wherein the subject is carved in wax and later cast in bronze. In order to create a single figurine, he spends up to 200 hours carving a tiny cube of wax with the aid of a jeweler's glass. Attention is given to every little detail, down to and including the tiny petals and stem of a flower in the hand of a figurine. The wax original is then encased in plaster which is allowed to harden in a carefully controlled oven heated at 1200°F so that the wax melts and runs out. Left behind is a plaster reverse image replica of the wax carving, and if all goes well, each detail is perfectly intact. The process is so delicate that it is considered an art. It is in this initial stage that the slightest mishap could cause the original sculpture to be lost forever.

The next step includes the careful pouring of molten sterling into the hollow mold. This results in a metal replica of the wax carving which is the model used to create a master mold from which all subsequent wax models will be produced. The creation of every single figurine requires a new wax model which is ultimately melted and lost in the mold-to-bronze process. Worthy of the painstaking time and effort, the resulting miniatures are perfect in every detail and yet tiny enough to fit comfortably within a walnut shell!

The renaissance of miniature art owes much to the genius of Olszewski. He has helped re-educate collectors to this age-old tradition of artistic expression. And through the Goebel Miniatures Company, his work is now able to reach more and more of this vast audience. Goebel Miniatures breathe fresh, new life into an artistic tradition as significant in today's world as it has ever been.

Helmut Fischer A mind soaring with imagination and a careful attention to detail are two qualities that Helmut Fischer blends together in every piece of sculpture. Since entering the W. Goebel Porzel-lanfabrik apprentice program over twenty years ago, Fischer has demonstrated this skilled creativity in the more than six hundred varied models he has created for Goebel!

As a schoolboy he showed a marked creative aptitude. His father, who was a craftsman in Bavaria, recognized his son's talent while Helmut was still quite young, and encouraged his development.

In 1964, at the age of 14, Fischer followed his father's suggestion and enrolled in the Goebel apprentice program. Since that time, he has created models for a fascinating variety of popular series including *Serengheti, Donald and His Friends* (from the *Walt Disney* series), *Glanimals*, glass miniatures, and butterflies from the *Wild Life Collection*.

A striking example of Fisher's artistic expertise and creative versatility is the DeGrazia figurine collection. Though he has not yet been to the American Southwest, he captures the essence of the area with an amazing feel. Using Ted De-Grazia's colorful and vibrant paintings, Fischer creates in each figurine the same love DeGrazia put on canvas. It is this artistry that makes Fischer a leading sculptor.

Since the late 80's, when Gerhard Skrobek retired from full-time employment at Goebel, Helmut Fischer has assumed the reins of the Master M. I. Hummel sculptor at W. Goebel Porzellanfabrik. Through Goebel M. I. Hummel figurines, Helmut Fischer shares with the world his special talent for capturing a moment in time and immortalizing it for all eternity.